ASKING THE RIGHT QUESTIONS WITH READINGS

A GUIDE TO CRITICAL THINKING

M. Neil Browne

Stuart M. Keeley

Bowling Green State University

Prentice Hall

Boston Columbus Indianapolis New York San Francisco Upper Saddle River Amsterdam
Cape Town Dubai London Madrid Milan Munich Paris Montreal Toronto Delhi Mexico City
São Paulo Sydney Hong Kong Seoul Singapore Taipei Tokyo

Editorial Director: Joe Opiela
Senior Acquisitions Editor: Brad Potthoff
Senior Marketing Manager: Sandra McGuire
Editorial Assistant: Nancy Lee
Managing Editor: Linda Mihatov Behrens
Associate Managing Editor: Bayani Mendoza de Leon
Production Manager: Kathleen Sleys
Permissions Specialist: Kathleen Karcher
Design Director: Jayne Conte
Cover Designer: Suzanne Behnke
Cover Illustration/Photo: (c) Clark Dunbar / CORBIS
Full Service Project Management/Composition: Aparna Yellai/PreMediaGlobal

Library of Congress Cataloging-in-Publication Data
Browne, M. Neil
  Asking the right questions with readings / M. Neil Browne, Stuart M. Keeley. — 1st ed.
    p. cm.
  Includes bibliographical references and index.
  ISBN-13: 978-0-205-64928-0 (alk. paper)
  ISBN-10: 0-205-64928-9 (alk. paper)
  1. Criticism.   2. Critical thinking.   3. Criticism—Problems, exercises, etc.   4. Critical thinking—
Problems, exercises, etc.   5. College readers.   I. Keeley, Stuart M., 1941-   II. Title.
  PN83.B7853 2011
  808—dc22

                                                                        2010025245

1 2 3 4 5 6 7 8 9 10—CRS—13 12 11 10

Prentice Hall
is an imprint of

www.pearsonhighered.com

ISBN 13: 978-0-205-64928-0
ISBN 10:   0-205-64928-9

CONTENTS

PREFACE

Critical thinking is a set of skills and attitudes that permit us to evaluate beliefs and claims. But like almost everything else that we learn, these skills and attitudes take life only when they are applied to questions and events that are real to the learner.

Asking the Right Questions with Readings is derived from a highly successful critical thinking text in its ninth edition, *Asking the Right Questions: A Guide to Critical Thinking* (ARQ). Like other critical thinking texts, ARQ has many examples and practice passages to provide concrete stimuli and reinforcement to the critical thinking instruction that is the focus of that text.

However, a number of those who taught and learned from ARQ felt as we do that they needed to supplement ARQ with a readings book that would provide longer, more complex arguments. *Asking the Right Questions with Readings* is an attempt to combine the need for a text and the desire for a readings book in a single volume. To accomplish this objective, we have added five sets of readings as the second part of the new book.

In addition, we have long thought that teaching is more effective when learners can hear others voice the trial and error associated with mastering an argument and then assessing its quality. Hence, this new book has multiple opportunities for learners to see the blind alleys and insightful moments associated with the use of critical thinking. As writers, we parted the curtain to share the thoughts we might have as we struggled with an evaluation of an argument. This approach seems so much more helpful than their watching a seeming wizard nail the evaluation.

DISTINGUISHING FEATURES

A. FOCUS

The central goal throughout *Asking the Right Questions with Readings* is to instill confidence in its readers so that they have the skills to ask critical thinking questions whenever the situation calls for such questioning. These situations have in common the communication of information meant to persuade or convince others of an idea or set of ideas. Thus, we want learners to become adept at asking effective questions of professors, textbooks and other kinds of books, politicians, advertisements, media pundits, local and national speakers, Web sites, blogs, and peers and parents.

To be an effective critical thinking questioner, individuals need to know WHAT questions to ask and HOW to ask such questions; and they also need to WANT to ask such questions. Combining *Asking the Right Questions* with a set of lengthy contemporary readings to which students can easily relate and prompting them to critically engage such readings greatly facilitates achieving these needs.

B. ORGANIZATION

The first part of *Asking the Right Questions with Readings* is the 9th Edition of *Asking the Right Questions*. Most of these chapters now include individual articles as well as focusing on a general issue in more depth. The second part of the book consists of five chapters featuring lengthy readings each related to a common controversy.

Each reading is followed by a set of critical thinking questions especially relevant to the article, which prompt readers to more closely ponder particular questions from *Asking the Right Questions with Readings*. In addition, several essay questions that require in depth integrative critical thought are provided following each of the five sets of readings in the second part of this book.

Readings are quite diverse and taken from many sources. All address contemporary issues and address topics that most students should be able to relate to.

ADDITIONAL STUDENT LEARNING AIDS

A student companion Web site for *Asking the Right Questions,* 9th Edition, can be found at **http://www.prenhall.com/browne**. It provides students with several kinds of learning assistance for each chapter. These include additional practice exercises accompanied by author feedback, as well as multiple choice and true/false questions.

The Web site also includes examples of putting all the critical thinking questions together in response to lengthy articles. It can be useful for students to observe this section early in the course to see how all the questions that they are and will be learning fit into a meaningful whole or gestalt. Readers can locate these lengthy examples at the Companion Web site under Chapter 14. In addition, each chapter includes answers by the authors to frequently asked student questions stimulated by the chapter reading.

The newly added "think aloud" passages at the end of most chapter provide the students with a unique exposure to the ongoing thinking process involved in critical evaluation. They get to "see how it's done."

Readers and reviewers have consistently praised the effectiveness, systematic nature and user friendliness of this organization. My heartfelt thanks to the following reviewers: Majid Amini, Virginia State University; Stacey Curdie, Plymouth State University; Alan I. Goldman, Massachusetts Bay Community College; Ramona Goth, Scottsdale Community College; Jenny Grosvenor, University of Vermont; Jefferson Hancock, Cabrillo College; Victoria F. Sarkisian, Marist College; Andrew Scott, Ball State University; Alex Sterling, Los Medanos College; Robert Trempy, Diablo Valley College.

We deeply appreciate the thousands of readers in schools, government agencies and business organizations who have found our approach to critical thinking useful in their lives. Their testimony provides more than the glimmer of meaning that most of us so earnestly pursue.

This particular book gained both insight and dedication from the efforts of Bethany Nanamaker and Lauren Biksacky. In addition, there would have been no such book without the encouragement from our editor, Brad Potthoff.

CHAPTER 1

The Benefit of Asking the Right Questions

INTRODUCTION

Any of us who enjoy movies are curious about the quality of the latest films. Should we go see them now, wait for them to show up at our preferred rental location, or avoid them altogether? Lots of film experts are available to advise us. But which of their opinions should we follow? Opinions are cheap; anyone can have one of those. But which film expert possesses the kind of knowledge that gives us an opinion on which we can rely? Which film authority provides convincing reasons on a regular basis to support his conclusion?

The authors of this book are film fanatics, but, like you, we do not want to see every film. Deciding which to see is hard work. To make the task easier, we often use one of our favorite Web sites, http://www.rottentomatoes.com.

However, as soon as you arrive at that site, you quickly notice that film experts almost never agree among themselves. Pick any movie you wish; check the reviews. Regardless of how many reviewers hated the movie, some reviewer somewhere will string together a positive review. Similarly, pick the most popular movie in history; go to the reviews. What do you find? Some expert thought it was a loser.

This experience is a metaphor for much of life. Doctors, legislators, architects, plumbers, and detectives all disagree among themselves about the proper course of action in particular circumstances. How are we consumers of opinions to respond? The book you are about to read contains the best answer we know. You need to build skills and attitudes that will enable you to decide for yourself which opinions to make your own.

As a thoughtful person you must make a choice about how you will react to what you see and hear. One alternative is to just accept whatever you encounter; doing so automatically results in your making someone else's opinion your own. No one wants to be another person's mental slave.

A more active alternative, something about which you can be justifiably proud, consists of asking questions in an effort to reach a personal decision about the worth of what you have experienced. This book is written for those who prefer the second alternative. While we will give you a lot of guidance about what questions to ask and when to ask them, for now all we want to say is that the path to reasonable conclusions begins with questions.

CRITICAL THINKING TO THE RESCUE

Listening and reading critically—that is, reacting with systematic evaluation to what you have heard and read—requires a set of skills and attitudes. These skills and attitudes are built around a series of related critical questions. While we will learn them one by one, our goal is to be able to use them together to identify the best decision available. Ideally, the questions will become part of who you are, not just something you read in a book.

We could have expressed them as a list of things you should do, but a system of questions is more consistent with the spirit of curiosity, wonder, and intellectual adventure essential to critical thinking. Thinking carefully is always an unfinished project, a story looking for an ending that will never arrive. Critical questions provide a stimulus and direction for critical thinking; they move us forward toward a continual, ongoing search for better opinions, decisions, or judgments.

Consequently, *critical thinking*, as we will use the term, refers to the following:

1. awareness of a set of interrelated critical questions;
2. ability to ask and answer critical questions at appropriate times; and the
3. desire to actively use the critical questions.

The goal of this book is to encourage you in all three of these dimensions.

Questions require the person being asked the question to act in response. By our questions, we are saying to the person: I am curious; I want to know more; help me. This request shows respect for the other person. The critical questions exist to inform and provide direction for all who hear them. In that respect, critical thinking begins with the desire to improve what we think. We all want *improved* beliefs and conclusions. The point of your questions is to help construct better directions and plans for yourself.

The critical questions are also useful in improving your own writing and speaking because they will assist you when you:

1. react critically to an essay or to evidence presented in a textbook, a periodical, or on a Web site;
2. judge the quality of a lecture or speech;
3. form an argument;
4. write an essay based on a reading assignment; or
5. participate in class.

Attention: Critical thinking consists of an awareness of a set of interrelated critical questions, plus the ability and willingness to ask and answer them at appropriate times.

As a citizen and consumer, you should find them especially helpful in shaping your voting behavior and your purchasing decisions, as well as in improving your self-confidence by increasing your sense of intellectual independence.

THE SPONGE AND PANNING FOR GOLD: ALTERNATIVE THINKING STYLES

One common approach to thinking is similar to the way in which a sponge reacts to water: by absorbing. This popular approach has some clear advantages.

First, the more information you absorb about the world, the more capable you are of understanding its complexities. Knowledge you have acquired provides a foundation for more complicated thinking later.

A second advantage of the sponge approach is that it is relatively passive. Rather than requiring strenuous mental effort, it tends to be rather quick and easy, especially when the material is presented in a clear and interesting fashion. The primary mental effort for acting like a sponge involves concentration and memory.

While absorbing information provides a productive start toward becoming a thoughtful person, the sponge approach has a serious and devastating disadvantage: It provides no method for deciding which information and opinions to believe and which to reject. If a reader relied on the sponge approach all the time, he would believe whatever he read last. The idea of being the mental puppet of whomever one happens to encounter is horrible imagery for a person and a community. Decisions become accidents of association, instead of reflective judgments.

We think you would rather choose for yourself what to absorb and what to ignore. To make this choice, you must read with a special attitude—a question-asking attitude. Such a thinking style requires active participation. The writer is trying to speak to you, and you should try to talk back to him, even though he is not present.

We call this interactive approach the panning-for-gold style of thinking. The process of panning for gold provides a model for active readers and listeners as they try to determine the worth of what they read and hear. The task is challenging and sometimes tedious, but the reward can be tremendous. To distinguish the gold from the gravel in a conversation requires you to ask frequent questions and to reflect on the answers.

The sponge approach emphasizes knowledge acquisition; the panning-for-gold approach stresses active interaction with knowledge as it is being

---

EXHIBIT 1.1   Mental Check: *Am I Panning for Gold?*

✓ Did I ask "why" someone wants me to believe something?

✓ Did I take notes as I thought about potential problems with what was being said?

✓ Did I evaluate what was being said?

✓ Did I form my own conclusion about the topic based on the reasonableness of what was said?

---

acquired. Thus, the two approaches complement each other. To pan for intellectual gold, there must be something in your pan to evaluate. In addition, to evaluate arguments, we must possess knowledge, dependable opinions.

Let us examine more closely how the two approaches lead to different behavior. What does the individual who takes the sponge approach do when he reads material? He reads sentences carefully, trying to remember as much as he can. He may underline or highlight key words and sentences. He may take notes summarizing the major topics and major points. He checks his underlining or notes to be sure that he is not forgetting anything important. His mission is to find and understand what the author has to say. He memorizes the reasoning, but he doesn't evaluate it.

What does the reader who takes the panning-for-gold approach do? Like the person using the sponge approach, she approaches her reading with the hope that she will acquire new knowledge. There the similarity ends. The panning-for-gold approach requires that the reader asks herself a number of questions designed to uncover the best available decisions or beliefs.

The reader who uses the panning-for-gold approach frequently questions why the author makes various claims. He writes notes to himself in the margins indicating problems with the reasoning. He continually interacts with the material. His intent is to critically evaluate the material and formulate personal conclusions based on the evaluation.

AN EXAMPLE OF THE PANNING-FOR-GOLD APPROACH

A major enduring issue in American society concerns what kind of gun control laws we need. Let's look at one position on this issue. Try to decide whether the argument is convincing.

> Arguments for banning guns are mostly myths, and what we need now is not more laws, but more law enforcement. One myth is that most murderers are ordinary, law-abiding citizens who kill a relative or acquaintance in a moment of anger only because a gun is available. In fact, every study of homicide shows the overwhelming majority of murderers are career criminals, people with

lifelong histories of violence. The typical murderer has a prior criminal history averaging at least six years, with four major felony arrests.

Another myth is that gun owners are ignorant rednecks given to senseless violence. However, studies consistently show that, on the average, gun owners are better educated and have more prestigious jobs than non-owners. To judge by their applications for permits to carry guns, the following are (or were) gun owners: Eleanor Roosevelt, Joan Rivers, Donald Trump, and David Rockefeller.

Even if gun laws do potentially reduce gun-related crime, the present laws are all that are needed if they are enforced. What good would stronger laws do when the courts have demonstrated that they will not enforce them?

If you apply the sponge approach to the passage, you probably will try to remember the reasons that we don't need further controls on guns. If so, you will have absorbed some knowledge. However, how convinced should you be by the above reasons? You can't evaluate them until you have applied the panning-for-gold approach to the passage—that is, until you have asked the right questions.

By asking the right questions, you would discover a number of possible weaknesses in the communicator's arguments. For instance, you might be concerned about all of the following:

1. What does the author mean by "overwhelming majority" or by "typical murderer"? Is the minority still a substantial number of murderers who kill relatives in a moment of anger?
2. What does "gun owners" mean? Are they the ones who buy the kind of guns that gun control advocates are trying to ban?
3. How adequate were the cited research studies? Were the samples sufficiently large, random, and diverse?
4. What possible benefits of gun control are not mentioned? Have important studies that disagree with the author's position been omitted?
5. Is it legitimate to assume that because some famous people own guns, then owning guns is desirable? Do these people have special expertise concerning the pros and cons of gun ownership?
6. How many people killed each year by handguns would not have been killed were such guns not available?
7. Why did the person writing the essay fail to explain how we could encourage better enforcement of existing gun control laws to demonstrate his sensitivity to the harm that guns sometimes facilitate?

If you would enjoy asking these kinds of questions, this book is especially for you. Its primary purpose is to help you know when and how to ask questions that will enable you to decide what to believe.

The most important characteristic of the panning-for-gold approach is interactive involvement—a dialogue between the writer and the reader, or the speaker and the listener. You are willing to agree, but first you need some convincing answers to your questions.

Clearly, there are times when the sponge approach is appropriate. Most of you have used it regularly and have acquired some level of success with it. It is much less likely that you are in the habit of employing the panning-for-gold approach—in part, simply because you have not had the appropriate training and practice. This book will not only help you ask the right questions, but will also provide frequent opportunities for practicing their use.

PANNING FOR GOLD: ASKING CRITICAL QUESTIONS

It would be relaxing if what other people were really saying were always obvious, if all their essential thoughts were clearly labeled for us, if the writer or speaker never made an error in her reasoning, and if all knowledgeable people agreed about answers to important questions. If this were the case, we could read and listen passively and let others do our thinking for us.

However, the true state of affairs is quite the opposite. A person's reasoning is often not obvious. Important elements are often missing. Many of the elements that are present are unclear. Consequently, you need critical reading and listening skills to help you determine what makes sense and distinguish this clear thinking from the sloppy thinking that characterizes much of what you will encounter.

The inadequacies in what someone says will not always leap out at you. You must be an *active* reader and listener. You can do this by *asking questions.* The best search strategy is a critical-questioning strategy. A powerful advantage of these questions is that they permit you to ask searching questions even when you know very little about the topic being discussed. For example, you do not need to be an expert on childcare to ask critical questions about the adequacy of day-care centers.

THE MYTH OF THE "RIGHT ANSWER"

Our ability to find definite answers to questions often depends on the type of question that puzzles us. Scientific questions about the physical world are the most likely to have answers that almost all reasonable people will accept, because the physical world is in certain ways more dependable or predictable than the social world. While the precise distance to the moon or the age of a newly discovered bone from an ancient civilization may not be absolutely certain, agreement about the dimensions of our physical environment is widespread. Thus, in the physical sciences, we frequently can arrive at "the right answer."

Questions about human behavior and about the meaning of our behavior are different. The causes of human behavior are so complex that we frequently cannot do much more than form intelligent guesses about why or when certain behavior will occur. In addition, because many of us care a great deal about explanations and descriptions of human behavior, we prefer that explanations or descriptions of the rate of abortion, the effects of obesity, or the causes of child abuse be consistent with what we want to believe. Hence, we bring our preferences to any discussion of those issues and resist arguments that are inconsistent with them.

Because human behavior is so controversial and complex, the best answers that we can find for many questions about our behavior will be probabilistic in nature. Even if we were aware of every bit of evidence about the effects of exercise on our mental health, we could still not expect certainty about those effects. We still need to commit to a particular course of action to prevent our becoming a "hollow man" or a "nowhere woman." But once we acknowledge that our commitments are based on probability and not certainty, we will be much more open to the reasoning of those who are trying to persuade us to change our minds. After all, we may well be wrong about some of our beliefs. We have to listen respectfully to those with whom we disagree. They just may be right.

Regardless of the type of questions being asked, the issues that require your closest scrutiny are usually those about which "reasonable people" disagree. In fact, many issues are interesting exactly because there is strong disagreement about how to resolve them. Any controversy involves more than one position. Several positions may be supported with good reasons. There will seldom be a position on a social controversy about which you will be able to say, "This is clearly the right position on the issue." If such certainty were possible, reasonable people would not be debating the issue. Our focus in this book will be on such social controversies.

Even though you will not necessarily arrive at the "right answer" to social controversies, this book is designed to give you the skills to develop your best and most reasonable answer, given the nature of the problem and the available information. Decisions usually must be made in the face of uncertainty. Often we will not have the time or the ability to discover many of the important facts about a decision we must make. For example, it is simply unwise to ask all the right questions when someone you love is complaining of sharp chest pains and wants you to transport him to the emergency room.

THE USEFULNESS OF ASKING THE QUESTION, "WHO CARES?"

Asking good questions is difficult but rewarding work. Some controversies will be much more important to you than others. When the consequences of a controversy for you and your community are minimal, you will want to spend less time and energy thinking critically about it than about more important controversies. For example, it makes sense to critically evaluate arguments for and against the protection of endangered species, because different positions on this issue lead to important consequences for society. It makes less sense to devote energy to evaluating whether blue is the favorite color of most corporate executives.

Your time is valuable. Before taking the time to critically evaluate an issue, ask the question, "Who cares?"

WEAK-SENSE AND STRONG-SENSE CRITICAL THINKING

Previous sections mentioned that you already have opinions about many personal and social issues. You are willing right now to take a position on such questions as: Should prostitution be legalized? Is alcoholism a disease or willful misconduct? Was George Bush a successful president? You bring these initial opinions to what you hear and read.

Critical thinking can be used to either (1) defend *or* (2) evaluate and revise your initial beliefs. Professor Richard Paul's distinction between weak-sense and strong-sense critical thinking helps us appreciate these two antagonistic uses of critical thinking.

> **Attention:** *Weak-sense critical thinking is the use of critical thinking to defend your current beliefs. Strong-sense critical thinking is the use of the same skills to evaluate all claims and beliefs, especially your own.*

If you approach critical thinking as a method for defending your initial beliefs or those you are paid to have, you are engaged in *weak-sense critical thinking.* Why is it weak? To use critical-thinking skills in this manner is to be unconcerned with moving toward truth or virtue. The purpose of weak-sense critical thinking is to resist and annihilate opinions and reasoning different from yours. To see domination and victory over those who disagree with you as the objective of critical thinking is to ruin the potentially humane and progressive aspects of critical thinking.

In contrast, *strong-sense critical thinking* requires us to apply the critical questions to all claims, including our own. By forcing ourselves to look critically at our initial beliefs, we help protect against self-deception and conformity. It is easy to just stick with current beliefs, particularly when many people share them. But when we take this easy road, we run the strong risk of making mistakes we could otherwise avoid.

Strong-sense critical thinking does not necessarily force us to give up our initial beliefs. It can provide a basis for strengthening them because critical examination of those beliefs will sometimes reinforce our original commitment to them. A long time ago, John Stuart Mill warned us of the emptiness of a set of opinions accumulated without the help of strong-sense critical thinking:

> He who knows only his side of the case knows little of that. His reasons may have been good, and no one may have been able to refute them. But if he is equally unable to refute the reasons on the opposite side he has no ground for preferring either opinion.

To feel proud of a particular opinion, it should be one we have selected—selected from alternative opinions that we have understood and evaluated.

THE SATISFACTION OF PANNING FOR GOLD

Doing is usually more fun than watching; doing well is more fun than simply doing. If you start using the interactive process taught in this book, you can feel the same sense of pride in your reading and listening that you normally get from successful participation in physical activities.

Critical thinkers find it satisfying to know when to say "no" to an idea or opinion and to know why that response is appropriate. If you regularly use the panning-for-gold approach, then anything that gets into your head will have been systematically examined first. When an idea or belief *does* pass the criteria developed here, it will make sense to agree with it—at least until new evidence appears.

Imagine how good you will feel if you know *why* you should ignore or accept a particular bit of advice. Frequently, those faced with an opinion different from their own respond by saying, "Oh, that's just your opinion." But the issue should not be whose opinion it is, but rather whether it is a good opinion. Armed with the critical questions discussed in this book, you can experience the satisfaction of knowing why certain advice is nonsense.

The sponge approach is often satisfying because it permits you to accumulate information on which you can depend. Reading and listening become much richer as you begin to see things that others may have missed. As you learn to select information and opinions systematically, you will probably desire to read more and more in a lifelong effort to decide which advice makes sense and to talk to people who differ from you in their viewpoints.

EFFECTIVE COMMUNICATION AND CRITICAL THINKING

Many of the skills you will learn, as you become a more critical thinker, will improve the quality of your writing and speaking. As you write and speak, it helps to be aware of the expectations careful thinkers will have. Because your objective is communication, many of the questions the thoughtful person will ask in evaluating your writing or speech should serve as guides for your own attempts to communicate well. Several of the critical questions that we urge you to ask highlight problems you will want to avoid as you write or speak.

While the emphasis in this book is on effective thinking, the link to competent communication is so direct that it will be a theme throughout. Wherever appropriate, we will mention how the skill being encouraged is an aid to improved communication.

THE IMPORTANCE OF PRACTICE

Learning new critical-thinking skills is a lot like learning new physical skills. You cannot learn simply by being told what to do or by watching others. You have to practice, and frequently the practice will be both rewarding and hard work. Our goal is to make your learning as simple as possible. However, acquiring the habit of critical thinking will initially take a lot of practice.

The practice exercises and sample responses at the end of each chapter, starting with Chapter 3, are an important part of this text. Try to do the exercises and, only then, compare your answers with ours. Our answers are not necessarily the only correct ones, but they provide illustrations of how to apply the question-asking skills. We intentionally failed to provide sample answers for the third passage at the end of each chapter. Our objective is to give you the opportunity to struggle with the answer using your knowledge of the chapter you have just studied. We want you to feel the accomplishment of no longer necessarily needing us to guide you.

THE RIGHT QUESTIONS

To give you an initial sense of the skills that *Asking the Right Questions* will help you acquire, we will list the critical questions for you here. By the end of the book, you should know when and how to ask these questions effectively:

1. What are the issues and the conclusions?
2. What are the reasons?
3. Which words or phrases are ambiguous?
4. What are the value and descriptive assumptions?
5. Are there any fallacies in the reasoning?
6. How good is the evidence?
7. Are there rival causes?
8. Are the statistics deceptive?
9. What significant information is omitted?
10. What reasonable conclusions are possible?

CHAPTER 2

Critical Thinking as a Social Activity

Much of our thinking is not a solo activity; it involves other people. We move forward by listening to other people; without them we are lost as learners. Critical thinking leans heavily on being able to listen with respect to what others have to say. The conclusions we hold at any time are the fruit of our interactions with family, friends, teachers, and a wide assortment of influential members of our larger community. We can handle these interactions in a manner that stimulates our continued growth as a thinking person. However, if we are not careful, we can work, live, and play with others in a manner that will shut off the many insights possessed by our associates. By assisting us to work more effectively with other people this chapter can be seen as a booster chair, raising us to a higher level of skill as a thinker.

But we would be oversimplifying the social dimension of critical thinking if we did not think carefully about the negative effects that other people can have on our reasoning. Part of being an effective critical thinker is *thinking for yourself*. Yes, you learn from and with other people, BUT your interactions with other people can prevent you from thinking critically. Out of respect for this problem, this chapter concludes by increasing your awareness of the dangers of social interaction for those of us wishing to think for ourselves.

VALUES AND OTHER PEOPLE

Think of other people as your most valuable resource, the basis for the facts, opinions, and conclusions that you will eventually have. In an important and ongoing manner, other people are part of your extended family, those who nurture your conclusions. The theme here is connectedness.

How these interactions work is shaped by your values and the values you perceive in those with whom you interact. Before you can discover the importance of values in shaping conclusions, you must have some understanding of what a value is. *Values*, as we will use the term, are ideas that someone thinks are worthwhile. You will find that it is the importance one assigns to *abstract ideas* that has the major influence on one's choices and behavior.

Usually objects, experiences, and actions are desired because of some idea we value. For example, we may choose to do things that provide us with contacts with important people. We value "important people" (concrete idea) because we value "status" (abstract idea). When we use the word *value* in this chapter, we will be referring to an (abstract) idea representing what someone thinks is important and good.

Attention: *Values are the unstated ideas that people see as worthwhile. They provide standards of conduct by which we measure the quality of human behavior.*

To better familiarize yourself with values, write down some of your own values. Try to avoid writing down the names of people, tangible objects, or actions. Pizza and playing tennis may be important to you, but it is the importance you assign to abstract ideas that most influences your choices and behavior concerning controversial public issues. Your willingness to argue for or against capital punishment, for instance, is strongly related to the importance you assign to the sanctity of human life—an abstract idea. The sanctity of human life is a value that affects our opinions about war, abortion, drug usage, and mercy killing. As you create your list of values, focus on those that are so significant that they affect your opinions and behavior in many ways.

Did you have problems making your list? We can suggest two further aids that may help. First, another definition! Values are *standards of conduct* that we endorse and expect people to meet. When we expect our political representatives to "tell the truth," we are indicating to them and to ourselves that honesty is one of our most cherished values. Ask yourself what you expect your friends to be like. What standards of conduct would you want your children to develop? Answers to these questions should help you enlarge your understanding of values.

Now let us give you an aid for identifying values—a list of a few commonly held values. Every value on our list may be an attractive candidate for your list. Thus, after you look at our list, pause for a moment and choose those values that are most important to you. They will be those values that most often play a role in shaping your opinions and behavior.

Common Values

adventure	courage	justice
ambition	excellence	rationality
autonomy	flexibility	security
collective responsibility	freedom of speech	spontaneity
comfort	generosity	tolerance
competition	harmony	tradition
cooperation	honesty	wisdom

Let's remind ourselves how knowledge about values relates to the social nature of critical thinking. While we must require ourselves to listen deeply to those who have value priorities different from our own, the most obvious social link established by values is similarity. Those of us who see individual responsibility as an extremely important value tend to be comfortable with and to seek out those who similarly believe that *improved personal choices* are the solution to most human problems. Hence, many of our most valuable social interactions or learning experiences start with communications among those with similar value priorities. Our huge challenge in this regard is to require ourselves to work hard to understand the reasoning of those whose value priorities *differ* from ours.

THE PRIMARY VALUES OF A CRITICAL THINKER

Our normal tendency to listen to only those with similar value priorities needs our active resistance. We have to fight against the tendency.

Let us give you some ammunition. This book is dedicated to help you become a critical thinker. As a critical thinker, you will be pursuing *better* conclusions, *better* beliefs, and *better* decisions. Certain values advance your effort to do so; others do not. By knowing and appreciating the primary values of a critical thinker, you have some mental muscle that you can use to remind yourself of the necessity of your paying close attention to those who do not share your value priorities.

What are the primary values of a critical thinker?

- *Autonomy.* At first this value may have little to do with encouraging people to pay attention to those with different perspectives. How does a drive to form one's own conclusions encourage us in any fashion to seek and listen to views that are not our own? Aha! And what raw material should you use in pursuing this autonomy? Surely, we all want to pick and choose from the widest possible array of possibilities; otherwise, we may miss the one decision or option that we *would have chosen* if only we had not paid attention solely to those who shared our value priorities. Supercharged autonomy requires us to listen to those with value priorities different from our own. For example, Democrats make a huge mistake when they listen only to other Democrats.

- *Curiosity.* To take advantage of the panning-for-gold method of living your life, you need to listen and read, **really** listen and read. Other people have the power to move you forward, to liberate you from your current condition of partial knowledge. To be a critical thinker requires you to then ask questions about what you have encountered. Part of what you gain from other people is their insights and understanding, **when what they have to offer meets the standards of good reasoning** that you will learn in *Asking the Right Questions.*
- *Humility.* Recognizing that even the smartest person in the world makes many mistakes each week provides the ideal platform for engaging actively with other people. Certainly some of us have insights that others do not have, but each of us is very limited in what we can do, and at honest moments we echo Socrates when he said that he knew that he did not know. Once we accept this reality, we can better recognize that our experiences with other people can fill in at least a few of the gaps in our present understanding.
- *Respect for good reasoning wherever you find it.* While we want to respect and listen to other voices, all conclusions or all opinions are not equally worthwhile. The critical questions you will learn as you study this book provide a framework to assist you in picking and choosing from among all the ideas trying to influence you. When you find strong reasoning, regardless of the race, age, wealth, or citizenship of the speaker or writer, rely on it until a better set of reasoning comes along.

Live by these value priorities, and you can have justifiable satisfaction about the beliefs you possess. Live by these value priorities, and you will keep searching for additional evidence that strengthens these beliefs, as well as for new reasons and evidence that might alter your beliefs. By all means act with confidence based on your beliefs, but hold your conclusions with only that degree of firmness that permits you to still wonder to yourself, "Might I be wrong?"

THINKING AND FEELINGS

Making a list of the primary values of a critical thinker and describing them is relatively easy. But living those values is extraordinarily difficult. When you first encounter a conclusion, you do so with a history. You have learned to care about certain things, to support particular interests, and to discount claims of a particular type. So you always start to think critically in the midst of existing opinions. You have emotional commitments to these existing opinions.

They are *your* opinions, and you quite understandably feel protective of them. It almost seems as if you are admitting you have been a gigantic failure when you change your mind. Having the courage to change your mind in the face of stronger reasoning that points you in a new direction requires superior dedication to creating the very best version of yourself that can be created. There is certainly no wisdom in changing your mind all the time just to show you are flexible. But when you encounter new evidence and fresh reasons that you can see are better than what you had been relying on, you owe it to yourself to move forward. You want to embrace this modified picture of your world, confident that it is more reliable.

Keep in mind that when we are thinking, we have a purpose. In other words, we think to achieve something. When our thinking is motivated by a desire to keep heading in the same direction as our previous thinking, we are not reflecting the values of a critical thinker. Instead, we are an advocate, searching for better ways to protect the views we currently hold. From this perspective, to think is to defend. The brighter alternative is to think so that we can achieve more depth and better accuracy. To achieve that purpose, we have to train ourselves to listen to the arguments of those with whom we disagree. We are already familiar with our own arguments; we stand to learn the most by familiarizing with those other arguments, the ones we really have not explored very thoroughly.

This point deserves special emphasis. We bring lots of personal baggage to every decision we make—experiences, dreams, values, training, and cultural habits.

However, if you are to grow, you need to recognize these feelings, and, as much as you are able, put them on a shelf for a bit. Only that effort will enable you to listen carefully when others offer arguments that threaten or violate your current beliefs. This openness is important because many of our own positions on issues are not especially reasonable ones; they are opinions given to us by others, and over many years we develop emotional attachments to them. Indeed, we frequently believe that we are being personally attacked when someone presents a conclusion contrary to our own. The danger of being emotionally involved in an issue is that you may fail to consider potential good reasons for other positions—reasons that might be sufficient to change your mind on the issue if only you would listen to them.

Remember: Emotional involvement should not be the primary basis for accepting or rejecting a position. Ideally, emotional involvement should be most intense *after* reasoning has occurred. Thus, when you read, try to avoid letting emotional involvement cut you off from the reasoning of those with whom you initially disagree. A successful active learner is one who is willing to change his mind. If you are ever to change your mind, you must be as open as possible to ideas that strike you as weird or dangerous when you first encounter them.

Critical thinkers, however, are not machines. They care greatly about many issues. The depth of that concern can be seen in their willingness to do all the hard mental work associated with critical thinking. But any passion felt by critical thinkers is moderated by the recognition that their current beliefs are open to revision.

KEEPING THE CONVERSATION GOING

Because critical thinking is a social activity, we need to consider how other people are likely to react to us when we ask them questions about their beliefs and conclusions. As long as we are interacting with others who share the primary values of critical thinking, our questions will be received as evidence that we are a partner in the search for better answers to the questions we share. But that terrific opportunity to grow together is not going to be the only kind of social interaction you will have.

Many people are not eager to have their thinking questioned; often they experience questioning as annoying and unfriendly. Some may wonder, "Why is she asking me all these challenging questions? Why does she not just agree with me?" Don't be surprised if someone reacts to your quest to learn more by asking you why you are being so mean. Many people are unaccustomed to situations where someone is so excited to know more about why a particular viewpoint is held.

The new critical thinker may be confused by this reaction. Later in Chapter 4 we will introduce in a formal sense the concept of "an argument." What do you think about when you see that word? In ordinary conversation, an argument refers to a disagreement, a time when blood pressure soars. In this sense to argue is to try to win, to somehow dominate the other person.

For example, in a bestselling book a decade ago, Gerry Spence taught readers *How to Argue and Win Every Time.* He claimed in the subtitle of the book that he would teach the reader how to win *At Home, At Work, In Court, Everywhere, Everyday.* He urged readers to be winners and not losers.

That kind of attitude would put a dramatic end, in many instances, to critical thinking, as we understand it. The conversation would be over prematurely. Who wants to participate for long in a situation where winning, not learning, is the focus? What kind of arrogance would make any of us think that we should win all arguments? Such an approach sounds more like war than like curious thinkers at work.

For purposes of critical thinking, an argument is altogether something very different from a battle. Because we see argument as the mechanism whereby we fertilize and prune our current conclusions, we will use the concept in a very different manner. An *argument* is a combination of two forms of statements: a conclusion and the reasons allegedly supporting it. The partnership between reasons and conclusion establishes a person's argument. It is something we provide because we care about how people live their lives and what they believe. Our continual improvement depends on someone's caring enough about us to offer us arguments and to evaluate the ones we make. Only then will we be able to develop as thoughtful people.

Ending the conversation before it starts

What can we do to assure those we are interacting with that we are gen-uine seekers who care about truth and who respect reason wherever we find it, even in the mouths or pages of those who almost never agree with us? How can you relate to other people such that they will join you in productive interchange?

As with so much behavior that affects other people, we can establish some basic ground rules for using critical thinking with others by asking how we want them to interact with us. First, we want an assurance that they respect us in the sense that they will try to hear us. They are speaking with us, not at us. In addition, we want them to be able to distinguish between a conclusion we hold and the many components that make us who we are. We want them to recognize that there is no need to engage in some kind of personal attack simply because we disagree; there are no doubt many other things about which we do agree. A person is so much more than a single conclusion.

Above all else, when you use your critical thinking, make it clear to other people that you want to learn. Furthermore, give them assurances that you wish them well, and that any disagreement you have with them, as seri-ous and important as that disagreement might be, need not result in a verbal bloodbath. What follows are a few verbal strategies that you can use to keep the conversation going:

1. Try to clarify your understanding of what the other person said by asking: "Did I hear you say _____?"
2. Ask the other person whether there is any evidence that would cause him to change his mind.
3. Suggest a time-out period in which each of you will try to find the very best evidence for the conclusion you hold.

4. Ask why the person thinks the evidence on which you are relying is so weak.
5. Try to come together. If you take that person's best reasons and put them together with your best reasons, is there some conclusion that both of you could embrace?
6. Search for common values or other shared conclusions to serve as a basis for determining where the disagreement first appeared in your conversation.
7. Try to present a model of caring and calm curiosity; as soon as the verbal heat turns up, try to remind yourselves that you are learners, not warriors.
8. Make certain that your face and body suggest humility, rather than the demeanor of a know-it-all.

AVOIDING THE DANGERS OF GROUPTHINK

We conclude this chapter with a warning. Social interactions have the potential to harm your thinking when you are not careful. As social beings, we understandably wish others to think well of us. When the people with whom we interact are collectively engaged in sloppy reasoning, the pressures to go along with them can test the character of even the best critical thinkers. A person with a minority point of view cannot help but wonder when faced with a large number of people who believe something else, "Did I miss something?"

In 1972 Irving Janis coined the term *groupthink* to capture the negative effects of group pressure on our thinking. Especially dangerous are closely knit groups who are thinking sloppily because independent thinking in such a setting seems disloyal and rude. Good illustrations are available from many of the wars we have fought. Leaders who are quite capable of critical thinking in certain settings surround themselves with people who tell them what they want to hear, and each time another member of the group announces support for the decision to go to war, the group feels more and more hostility toward anyone who might question the evidence justifying war. When we see people who should know better fail to ask critical questions, it should give us all pause. Being a critical thinker takes constant vigilance.

As with the story of the young child who was the only one willing to say out loud that the emperor was wearing no clothes at all, being willing to ask critical questions in the midst of groupthink can provide the greatest possible service to the long-run interests of the group, whether it is a society, a family, or a bunch of friends. The approval of other people can be a huge obstacle to critical thinking, but only if we let it be. The best medicine for curing the tendency to go along with a group when it is relying on sloppy thinking is your confidence in the wisdom of being a critical thinker—looking for the best reasoning, regardless of what other people are doing.

CHAPTER 3

What Are the Issue and the Conclusion?

Before we evaluate someone's reasoning, we must first find it. Doing so sounds simple; it isn't. To get started as a critical thinker, you must practice the identification of the issue and the conclusion. Start by considering how you might begin questioning the following brief essay.

> Cell phones are becoming a large part of today's society bringing with them benefits and drawbacks. They are beneficial for those with tight schedules and in case of emergencies. Cell phones can also come in handy for parents to check up on their children. Even though cell phones do carry benefits, the drawbacks are in their inappropriate use. When a cell phone rings or owners talk on them during a lecture or a concert, a major disruption in the concentration of others is inevitable. Even though there are suggestions in polite society to leave them off, perhaps we need stronger penalties associated with abuse of the growing population of cell phones.

The person who wrote this assessment of cell phones very much wants you to believe something. But what is that something and why are we supposed to believe any such thing?

In general, those who create Web pages, editorials, books, magazine articles, or speeches are trying to change your perceptions or beliefs. For you to form a reasonable reaction to their persuasive effort, you must first identify the controversy or *issue* as well as the thesis or conclusion being pushed onto you. (Someone's *conclusion* is her intended message to you. Its purpose is to shape your beliefs and/or behavior.) Fail to identify the author's conclusion, and you will be reacting to a distorted version of the attempted communication.

When we read or listen, it is so easy to ignore what was said in the previous paragraph. We often react to the images, dramatic illustrations, or tone of what was said instead of the conclusion that was intended by the person communicating with us. Each time we fail to react to the intended conclusion, human conversation has experienced a defeat. We are not connecting as the person who wrote or spoke to us intended. So, getting straight about the person's conclusion and issue is an essential first step in effective human interaction.

When you have completed this chapter, you should be able to answer the first of our critical questions successfully:

 Critical Question: **What are the issue and the conclusion?**

Attention: An issue is a question or controversy responsible for the conversation or discussion. It is the stimulus for what is being said.

KINDS OF ISSUES

It will be helpful at this point to identify two kinds of issues you will typically encounter. The following questions illustrate one of these:

Do families who own pets have fewer arguments with one another?

What causes high blood pressure?

Who made the decision to increase our tuition?

How much will college cost in the year 2012?

All these questions have one thing in common. They require answers attempting to describe the way the world is, was, or is going to be. For example, answers to the first two questions might be, "In general, families with pets have fewer arguments with one another," and "Poor dietary habits cause high blood pressure."

Such issues are *descriptive issues*. They are commonly found in textbooks, magazines, the Internet, and television. Such issues reflect our curiosity about patterns or order in the world. Note the boldfaced words that begin each question above; when questions begin with these words, they will probably be descriptive questions.

Attention: Descriptive issues are those that raise questions about the accuracy of descriptions of the past, present, or future.

Now let's look at examples of a second kind of question:

Should capital punishment be abolished?

What ought to be done about social security?

Must we outlaw SUVs or face increasing rates of asthma?

All of these questions require answers suggesting the way the world *ought to be.* For example, answers to the first two questions might be, "Capital punishment *should be* abolished," and "We *ought* to increase social security benefits."

These issues are ethical, or moral, issues; they raise questions about what is right or wrong, desirable or undesirable, good or bad. They demand prescriptive answers. Thus, we will refer to these issues as *prescriptive issues.* Social controversies are often prescriptive issues.

We have somewhat oversimplified. Sometimes it will be difficult to decide what kind of issue is being discussed. It will be useful to keep these distinctions in mind, however, because the kinds of critical evaluations you eventually make will differ depending on the kind of issue to which you are responding.

Attention: Prescriptive issues are those that raise questions about what we should do or what is right or wrong, good, or bad.

SEARCHING FOR THE ISSUE

How does one go about determining the basic question or issue? Sometimes it is very simple: The writer or speaker will tell you what it is. Alternatively, the issue may be identified in the body of the text, usually right at the beginning, or it may even be found in the title. When the issue is explicitly stated, it will be indicated by phrases such as the following:

The question I am raising is: Why must we have laws requiring seat belts in cars?

Lowering the legal drinking age: *Is it the right thing to do?*

Should sex education be taught in the schools?

Unfortunately, the question is not always explicitly stated and instead must be inferred from other clues in the communication. For example, many writers or speakers are reacting to some current event that concerns them, such as a series of violent acts in schools. Asking "What is the author reacting to?" will often suggest the central issue of a communication. Another good clue is knowledge of the author's background, such as organizations to which she belongs. So check for background information about the author as you try to determine the issue.

When you are identifying the issue, try to resist the idea that there is one and only one correct way to state the issue. Once you have found a question that the entire essay or speech is addressing, and you can show the link between that question and the essay or speech, *you have found the issue.* Just make certain that what you are calling an issue meets the definitional criteria that define an "issue."

The surest way to detect an issue when it is not explicitly stated, however, is to locate the *conclusion*. In many cases, the conclusion must be found before you can identify the issue. Thus, in such cases, the first step in critical evaluation is to find the conclusion—a frequently difficult step.

WE CANNOT CRITICALLY EVALUATE UNTIL WE FIND THE CONCLUSION!

Let's see how we go about looking for that very important structural element.

> **Attention:** *A conclusion is the message that the speaker or writer wishes you to accept.*

SEARCHING FOR THE AUTHOR'S OR SPEAKER'S CONCLUSION

To identify the conclusion, the critical thinker must ask, "What is the writer or speaker trying to prove?" or "What is the communicator's main point?" The answer to either of these questions will be the conclusion. Any answer to the question provided by the speaker or writer will be the conclusion.

In searching for a conclusion, you will be looking for a statement or set of statements that the writer or speaker wants you to believe. She wants you to believe the conclusion on the basis of her other statements. In short, the basic structure of persuasive communication or argument is: *This* because of *that*. *This* refers to the conclusion; *that* refers to the support for the conclusion. This structure represents the process of *inference*.

Conclusions are *inferred*; they are derived from reasoning. Conclusions are ideas that require other ideas to support them. Thus, whenever someone claims something is true or ought to be done and provides no statements to support her claim, that claim is not a conclusion because no one has offered any basis for belief. In contrast, unsupported claims are what we refer to as *mere* opinions.

The last paragraph says a lot. It would be a good idea for you to read it again. Understanding the nature of a conclusion is an essential step toward critical reading and listening. Let's look closely at a conclusion and at the inference process. Here is a brief paragraph; see whether you can identify the conclusion, then the statements that support it.

Factory farming should not be legal. There are other more natural ways to produce needed food supply.

"Factory farming should not be legal" is the author's answer to the question: should factory farming be legalized? It is her conclusion. The author supports this belief with another: "There are other more natural ways to produce needed food supply."

Do you see why the supporting belief is not a conclusion? It is not the conclusion because it is used to prove something else. *Remember.* To believe one statement (the conclusion) because you think it is well supported by *other* beliefs is to make an inference. When people engage in this process, they are reasoning; the conclusion is the outcome of this reasoning.

Sometimes, communicators will not make their conclusions explicit; in such cases you will have to infer the conclusion from what you believe the author is trying to prove by the set of ideas she has presented.

USING THIS CRITICAL QUESTION

Once you have found the conclusion, use it as the focus of your evaluation. It is the destination that the writer or speaker wants you to choose. Your ongoing concern is: Should I accept that conclusion on the basis of what is supporting the claim?

CLUES TO DISCOVERY: HOW TO FIND
THE CONCLUSION

There are a number of clues to help you identify the conclusion.

Clue No. 1: **Ask what the issue is**. Because a conclusion is always a response to an issue, it will help you find the conclusion if you know the issue. We discussed earlier how to identify the issue. First, look at the title. Next, look at the opening paragraphs. If this technique does not help, skimming several pages may be necessary.

Clue No. 2: **Look for indicator words.** The conclusion will frequently be preceded by indicator words that announce a conclusion is coming. When you see these indicator words, take note of them. They tell you that a conclusion may follow. A list of such indicator words follows:

consequently	suggests that
therefore	thus
it follows that	the point I'm trying to make is
shows that	proves that
indicates that	the truth of the matter is

Read the following passage; then identify and highlight the indicator words. By doing so, you will have identified the statements containing the conclusion.

Because of the wording of the Constitution, it follows that prayer should not be allowed in public schools. When the schools favor any particular religion, they are hampering the freedom of those who embrace a different religion. The idea of freedom of religion is what the country was founded on.

You should have highlighted the following phrase: *it follows.* The conclusion follows these words.

Unfortunately, many written and spoken communications do not introduce the conclusion with indicator words. However, when *you* write, you should draw attention to your thesis with indicator words. Those words act as a neon sign, drawing attention to the point you want the reader to accept.

Clue No. 3:   **Look in likely locations.** Conclusions tend to occupy certain locations. The first two places to look are at the beginning and at the end. Many writers begin with a statement of purpose, containing what they are trying to prove. Others summarize their conclusions at the end. If you are reading a long, complex passage and are having difficulty seeing where it is going, skip ahead to the end.

Clue No. 4:   **Remember what a conclusion is not.** Conclusions will not be any of the following:

- examples
- statistics
- definitions
- background information
- evidence

Clue No. 5:   **Check the context of the communication and the author's background.** Often writers, speakers, or Internet sites take predictable positions on issues. Knowing probable biases of the source and the background of authors can be especially valuable clues when the conclusion is not explicit. Be especially alert to information about organizations with which writers or speakers may be associated.

Clue No. 6:   **Ask the question, "and therefore?"** Because conclusions are often implied, ask for the identity of the "and therefore" element. Ask, "Does the author want us to draw an implied conclusion from the information communicated?" Conclusions like "candidate X will be soft on crime" are often left for the reader or viewer to infer from the limited information presented in a political ad.

CRITICAL THINKING AND YOUR OWN WRITING AND SPEAKING

Because readers of your writing will be looking for *your* thesis or conclusion, help them by giving it the clarity it deserves. It is the central message you want to deliver. Emphasize it; leave no doubt about what it actually is. Making your conclusion easily identifiable not only makes a reader's task easier, it also may improve the logic of your writing. An effective way to emphasize the conclusion is to insert it at the beginning or end of your essay and precede it with an indicator word.

In addition, take a close look at your conclusion to make certain that it is a direct response to the issue you intended to address. For example, suppose the issue you are attempting to address is: Will owning a pet increase how long we live? If your conclusion is: "yes, it will increase our life span by an average of 15 years," there is a match between issue and conclusion. But were your conclusion, instead, that pets bring joy to the lives of everyone who owns them, your reasoning is confused. The latter conclusion is responding to a different issue, namely, do pets bring joy to our lives?

Practice Exercises

 *Critical Question: **What are the issue and the conclusion?***

In the following passages, locate the issue and conclusion. As you search, be sure to look for indicator words. Notice that a model of this critical thinking process follows the first practice passage. By thinking aloud about how we would approach this passage, we hope to make it easier for you to ask and answer the critical question in the future. We provide a more condensed version of a sample response for Passage 2 and leave you on your own to find the issue and conclusion for the third practice passage. Passage 4 then gives you the opportunity to practice what you have learned from this chapter to a lengthy passage of a published article. Again, for comparison purposes, we include a think aloud, step-by-step example of thinking through the chapter's critical thinking question.

Passage 1

Home schooling is a valid concept if the parent makes teaching a full time job, and has the insight, knowledge and patience to do so. However, the truth of the matter is that few parents who home school their child are capable of doing so.

Parents may choose to pull their student out of public schools for the wrong reasons. Sometimes, when children are a discipline problem, the parents will pull them out of school rather than tolerating the rules associated with the punishment. Such a motivation does not speak well for the probable results of the home schooling that follows. In addition, when there are no other adults to monitor what is going on at home, it is likely that if there is a case of abuse in the home it will go unnoticed. Society needs to know whether these children are getting the education and treatment they deserve.

Passage 2

Television advertising agencies are very clever in the way that they construct ads. Often the ads are similar to the cartoons that the children enjoy. Children see these characters interacting with a certain product and associate their affection for the character with affection for the product. The companies do not want the children to perceive a difference between the shows they are watching and the advertisements. By using this strategy, these companies take advantage of the fact that children are often not able to discriminate between the cartoons and the ads and do not understand that these things offered come at a cost. Often the advertising is about sugary snacks or fatty foods, leading the children down a path to bad health. Advertising geared towards children should be regulated—just as there are regulations now about tobacco and alcohol ads targeted at children.

Passage 3

Should the public be shown actual courtroom trials on television? It seems as though the system can easily be corrupted by having cameras in the courtroom. Victims are hesitant enough when testifying in front of a small crowd, but their knowledge that every word is being sent to countless homes would increase the likelihood that they would simply refuse to testify. There is little to no assumed innocence for the accused when their trial is put on television. People do not watch court television because they are concerned about our country's ability to effectively carry out the proceedings of the judicial system; instead, they are looking for the drama in witness testimony: entertainment. Thus, leave the cameras out of the courtrooms, and let the public view sitcom drama based off of the legal system.

Sample Responses To Passage 1 and 2

Passage 1

- *Sometimes the issue is easy to find because it's explicitly stated in an argument. I don't think that this argument explicitly mentions the issue because the author never mentions the question that sparked the argument. My next move should be to find the conclusion. Then I'll be able to easily find the issue. I will simply ask what question that conclusion attempts to answer. Asking the Right Questions said that the surest way to find an issue that is not explicitly mentioned in the text is to find the conclusion.*

- *Looking for indicator words may help me find the conclusion. "The truth of the matter" was listed as an indication of a conclusion and is used in the argument. Maybe the conclusion is "few parents who home school their child are capable of doing do so."*

- *This statement really could be the conclusion. Another suggestion for finding the conclusion was to look in the introduction and conclusion. And the sentence is in the introduction.*

- *Asking the Right Questions provided me with a list of components of arguments that are not the conclusion. I should check to make sure that the statement "few parents who home school their child are capable of doing do so" is not a statistic, an example, a definition, background information, or other evidence. It is not.*

- *At this point, I am mostly certain that the conclusion is that "few parents who home school their child are capable of doing so." The indicator words suggested it, the location confirmed this belief, and it did not fall into the list of components of arguments sometimes mistaken for the conclusion.*

- *At this point, I need to figure out what question stimulated this discussion, or the issue. If the conclusion is that "few parents who home school their child are capable of doing so," the issue that stimulated this discussion might be, "are parents capable of home schooling their children?" This issue can be inferred from the conclusion, and all the subsequent sentences that discuss whether parents are capable of home schooling their children.*

- *Before I conclude, I want to figure out whether this issue is prescriptive or a descriptive. To do so, I need to ask myself whether the author is describing a situation or advocating an ethical position—a position about right and wrong, desirable and undesirable, good and bad. The author details some of the problems with home school and suggests that society needs to know that these children are receiving "the education and treatment that they deserve." These statements raise questions about whether a situation—home schooling—is desirable. The issue, therefore, must be a prescriptive issue.*

Passage 2

There are no indicator words to point towards the conclusion, but a good place to look for the conclusion is either at the beginning or end of the excerpt. In this case, the very last statement is the conclusion, and you can tell it is the conclusion because it gives finality to the passage using the phrase "should be." This phrase also indicates that this is a prescriptive issue. It is not talking about the way things are or are not, but how they ought to be. The issue is assumed from the conclusion and from the preceding statements explaining why the author came to her conclusion.

Issue: *Should advertisements geared towards children be regulated?*
Conclusion: *Advertisements geared toward children should be regulated.*

Passage 4. Expanding Practice and Feedback

Read the following lengthy practice passage, an editorial. Try to locate the issue and conclusion. As you search, be sure to look for indicator words. When you are done, compare your thinking process with the step-by-step walkthrough provided by the authors at the end of the passage.

Copyright Silliness on Campus

Fred von Lohmann

Washington Post (2007)

What do Columbia, Vanderbilt, Duke, Howard and UCLA have in common? Apparently, leaders in Congress think that they aren't expelling enough students for illegally swapping music and movies.

The House committees responsible for copyright and education wrote a joint letter May 1 scolding the presidents of 19 major American universities, demanding that each school respond to a six-page questionnaire detailing steps it has taken to curtail illegal music and movie file-sharing on campus. One of the questions—"Does your institution expel violating students?"—shows just how out-of-control the futile battle against campus downloading has become.

As universities are pressured to punish students and install expensive "filtering" technologies to monitor their computer networks, the entertainment industry has ramped up its student shakedown campaign. The Recording Industry Association of America has targeted more than 1,600 individual students in the past four months, demanding that each pay $3,000 for file-sharing transgressions or face a federal lawsuit. In total, the music and movie industries have brought more than 20,000 federal lawsuits against individual Americans in the past three years.

History is sure to judge harshly everyone responsible for this absurd state of affairs. Our universities have far better things to spend money on than bullying students. Artists deserve to be fairly compensated, but are we really prepared to sue and expel every college student who has made an illegal copy? No one who takes privacy and civil liberties seriously can believe that the installation of surveillance technologies on university computer networks is a sensible solution.

It's not an effective solution, either. Short of appointing a copyright hall monitor for every dorm room, there is no way digital copying will be meaningfully reduced. Technical efforts to block file-sharing will be met with clever countermeasures from sharp computer science majors. Even if students were completely cut off from the Internet, they would continue to copy CDs, swap hard drives and pool their laptops.

Already, a hard drive capable of storing more than 80,000 songs can be had for $100. Blank DVDs, each capable of holding more than a first-generation iPod, now sell for a quarter apiece. Students are going to copy what they want, when they want, from whom they want.

So universities can't stop file-sharing. But they can still help artists get paid for it. How? By putting some cash on the bar.

Universities already pay blanket fees so that student a cappella groups can perform on campus, and they also pay for cable TV subscriptions and site licenses for software. By the same token, they could collect a reasonable amount from their students for "all you can eat" downloading.

The recording industry is already willing to offer unlimited downloads with subscription plans for $10 to $15 per month through services such as Napster and Rhapsody. But these services have been a failure on campuses, for a number of reasons, including these: They don't work with the iPod, they cause downloaded music to "expire" after students leave the school, and they don't include all the music students want.

The only solution is a blanket license that permits students to get unrestricted music and movies from sources of their choosing.

At its heart, this is a fight about money, not about morality. We should have the universities collect the cash, pay it to the entertainment industry and let the students do what they are going to do anyway. In exchange, the entertainment industry should call off the lawyers and lobbyists, leaving our nation's universities to focus on the real challenges facing America's next generation of leaders.

The writer is a senior staff attorney with the Electronic Frontier Foundation. He represented one of the defendants in MGM v. Grokster, a landmark case concerning peer-to-peer file sharing.

Step-by-Step Walkthrough

Did you find the issue and conclusion? Not sure? The following is a step-by-step walkthrough of the process outlined in the chapter. Notice how the tools and suggestions from the chapter have been implemented.

- The editorial begins with a question. I know that issues and conclusions often come early and late in arguments, and that the issue is that initial question. But when I read through the editorial, I notice that it is not addressing the question of what these major universities have in common. Thus, the opening question is NOT the issue.

- I can tell by his heated language that the author is upset about something. He states repeatedly that universities have better things to do than operate surveillance programs to identify those who download music illegally. But every expressed opinion in an argument is not necessarily the conclusion toward which all of the paragraphs point. Hence, I have to read through the entire editorial to get a more complete appreciation for the point he wants to make.

- After stating the belief that colleges have better things to do than try to catch students engaging in digital downloading, the author claims that universities would never be able to stop such illegal downloading even were they to try. The issue is starting to look more and more like: Should universities be in the business of catching students who engage in illegal digital downloading? The conclusion at this stage of the article seems to be that universities should not be in the business of trying to catch the offending students. But I need to read the entire argument before settling on that conclusion because the conclusion needs to be the single point that the author is trying to make in the entire editorial, not just a part of it.

- The latter part of the article suggests something that universities could and should do that would reward those who make music and films, while not ignoring the illegal use of the property rights involved in these artistic creations. Universities should pay a license fee to the entertainment industry that gives them their compensation, while allowing students to do the downloading that they would do anyway.

- So I want to ask what issue and conclusion would cover both the critique of universities who try to catch students who engage in illegal downloading of music and films and the suggestion of an alternative behavior that universities could engage in to provide the entertainment industry with the compensation they seek? The conclusion indicator words "only solution" and "should" in the last two paragraphs help alert me to the answer to my question.

- Issue: What role should universities play in preventing the illegal downloading of films and music?

- Conclusion: They should pay the industry a license fee that would permit their students to do the downloading they will do anyway.

CRITICAL QUESTION SUMMARY: WHY THIS QUESTION IS IMPORTANT

What Are the Issue and the Conclusion?

Before you can evaluate an author's argument, you must clearly identify the issue and conclusion. How can you evaluate an argument if you don't know exactly what the author is trying to persuade you to believe? Finding an author's main point is the first step in deciding whether you will accept or reject it.

CHAPTER 4

What Are the Reasons?

Reasons provide answers about why someone makes a particular decision or holds a particular opinion.

1. Every class should conclude with student evaluations.
2. A pig is smarter than a mule.
3. Employers should be able to fire any employee who refuses to take a drug test.

Those three claims are each missing something. We may or may not agree with them, but in their current form they are neither weak nor strong. None of the claims contains an explanation or rationale for *why* we should agree. Thus, if we heard someone make one of those three assertions, we would be left hungry for more.

What is missing is the reason or reasons responsible for the claims. *Reasons* are beliefs, evidence, metaphors, analogies, and other statements offered to support or justify conclusions. They are the statements that form the basis for creating the credibility of a conclusion. Chapter 3 gave you some guidelines for locating two very important parts of the structure of an argument—the issue and the conclusion. This chapter focuses on techniques for identifying the third essential element of an argument—the reasons.

When a writer has a conclusion she wants you to accept, she must present reasons to persuade you that she is right and to show you *why*.

It is the mark of a rational person to support her beliefs with adequate proof, especially when the beliefs are of a controversial nature. For example, when someone asserts that we should exclude certain lawyers from representing those charged with felonies, this assertion should be met with the challenge, "Why do you say such a thing?" You should raise this question whether you agree or disagree.

The person's reasons may be either strong or weak, but you will not know until you have asked the question and identified the reasons. If the answer is "because I think so," you should be dissatisfied with the argument, because the "reason" is a mere restatement of the conclusion. However, if the answer is evidence concerning serious mistakes made by inexperienced lawyers in felony cases, you will want to consider such evidence when you evaluate the conclusion. *Remember:* **You cannot determine the worth of a conclusion until you identify the reasons.**

Identifying reasons is a particularly important step in critical thinking. An opinion cannot be evaluated fairly unless we ask why it is held and receive a satisfactory response. Focusing on reasons requires us to remain open to and tolerant of views that might differ from our own. If we react to conclusions rather than to reasoning, we will tend to stick to the conclusions we brought to the discussion or essay, and those conclusions that agree with our own will receive our rapid agreement. If we are ever to re-examine our own opinions, we must remain curious, open to the reasons provided by those people with opinions that we do not yet share.

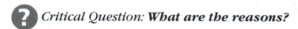 *Critical Question:* ***What are the reasons?***

The combination of the reasons and the conclusion result in what we defined in Chapter 2 as the "argument."

REASONS + CONCLUSION = ARGUMENT

Sometimes, an argument will consist of a single *reason* and a conclusion; often, however, several reasons will be offered to support the conclusion. So when we refer to someone's argument, we might be referring to a single reason and its related conclusion or to the entire group of reasons and the conclusion it is intended to substantiate.

> **Attention:** *Reasons are explanations or rationales for why we should believe a particular conclusion.*

As we use the terms, *argument* and *reasoning* mean the same thing—the use of one or more ideas to support another idea. Thus when a communication lacks reasons, it is neither an argument nor an example of reasoning. Consequently, only arguments and reasoning can be logically flawed. Because a reason *by itself* is an isolated idea, it cannot reflect a logical relationship.

Several characteristics of arguments grab our attention:

- They have intent. Those who provide them hope to convince us to believe certain things or act in certain ways. Consequently, they call for a reaction. We can imitate the sponge or the gold prospector, but we ordinarily must respond somehow.
- Their quality varies. Critical thinking is required to determine the extent of quality in an argument.

- They have two essential visible components: a conclusion and reasons. Failure to identify either component destroys the opportunity to evaluate the argument. We cannot evaluate what we cannot identify.

That last point deserves some repetition and explanation. There is little purpose in rushing critical thinking. Taking the time to locate arguments before we assess what we think might have been said is only fair to the person providing the argument.

INITIATING THE QUESTIONING PROCESS

The first step in identifying reasons is to approach the *argument* with a questioning attitude, and the first question you should ask is a *why* question. You have identified the conclusion; now you wish to know why the conclusion makes sense. If a statement does not answer the question, "Why does the writer or speaker believe that?" then it is not a reason. To function as a reason, a statement (or group of statements) must provide support for a conclusion.

Let us apply the questioning attitude to the following paragraph. First we will find the conclusion; then we will ask the appropriate *why* question. Remember your guidelines for finding the conclusion. (The indicator word for the conclusion has been italicized.)

> (1) Should metal detectors be in place at every public school? (2) Teachers were surveyed about their opinions. (3) Many indicated that they never know what to expect from their students and thought that metal detectors would be a safe solution to unexpected circumstances. (4) Fifty-seven percent of teachers agreed that metal detectors would help the school become a safer environment. (5) *Therefore*, public schools should install metal detectors for safety.

What follows "*Therefore*" answers the question raised in statement (1). Thus, the conclusion is statement (5) ". . . public schools should install metal detectors for safety." *Highlight the conclusion!*

Attention: An argument consists of a conclusion and the reasons that allegedly support it.

We then ask the question, "Why does the writer or speaker believe the conclusion?" The statements that answer that question are the reasons. In this particular case, the writer provides us with evidence as reasons. Statements (3) and (4) jointly provide the evidence; that is, together they provide support for the conclusion. Together they serve as the reason for the conclusion. Thus, we can paraphrase the reason as: *A majority of surveyed teachers believe that metal detectors would help the school's level of safety.*

Now, try to find the reasons in the following paragraph. Again, first find the conclusion, highlight it, and then ask the *why* question.

(1) Genetic screening of embryos is morally wrong. (2) People do not have the right to terminate a potential life just because it might not be the right sex, or may have a defect of some kind. (3) It cannot be said that a person's quality of life is severely changed by birth defect, or that parents should get to choose the sex of their baby.

There is no obvious indicator word for the conclusion in the paragraph, but the author is against genetic screening of embryos. The conclusion is: "Genetic screening of embryos is morally wrong." Why does the author believe this? The major reason given is that "People do not have the right to decide to terminate a potential life based on a set of their preferred criteria." Sentence (3) provides additional support for this reason.

One of the best ways for you to determine whether you have discovered a reason is to try to play the role of the communicator. Put yourself in her position and ask yourself, "Why am I in favor of this conclusion that I am supporting?" Try to put into your own words how you believe the communicator would answer this question. If you can paraphrase the answer, you have probably discovered her reasons.

As you determine a communicator's reasoning structure, you should treat any idea that seems to be used to support her conclusion as a reason, even if you do not believe it provides support for the conclusion. At this stage of critical thinking, you are trying to identify the argument Because you want to be fair to the person who made the argument, it makes good sense to assume that she believes the idea supports the conclusion and thus should at least consider the reasoning. There will be plenty of time later to evaluate the reasoning carefully.

WORDS THAT IDENTIFY REASONS

As was the case with conclusions, there are certain words that will typically indicate that a reason will follow. *Remember:* **The structure of reasoning is this, because of that**. Thus, the word *because*, as well as words synonymous with and similar in function to it, will frequently signal the presence of reasons. A list of indicator words for reasons follows:

as a result of	for the reason that
because of the fact that	in view of
is supported by	because the evidence is

KINDS OF REASONS

There are many different kinds of reasons, depending on the kind of issue. Many reasons will be statements that present evidence. By *evidence*, we mean specific information that someone uses to furnish "proof" for something she is trying to claim is true. Communicators appeal to many kinds of evidence to "prove their point." These include "the facts," research findings, examples from real life, statistics, appeals to experts and authorities, personal testimonials, metaphors, and analogies. Different kinds of evidence are more appropriate in some situations than in others, and you will find it helpful to develop rules for yourself for determining what kinds of evidence are appropriate on given occasions.

You will often want to ask, "What kind of evidence is needed to support this claim?" and then determine whether such evidence has been offered. You should know that there are no uniform "codes of evidence" applicable to all cases of serious reasoning. A more detailed treatment of evidence appears in Chapters 8–11.

When a speaker or writer is trying to support a descriptive conclusion, the answer to the *why* question will typically be evidence.

The following example provides a descriptive argument; try to find the author's reasons.

> (1) The number of people in the United States that are obese is growing quickly. (2) Studies indicate that over 25 percent of Americans are obese, not to mention the numbers of simply overweight Americans.

You should have identified the first statement as the conclusion. It is a descriptive statement about the large number of Americans who are obese. The rest of the paragraph presents the evidence—the reason for the conclusion. *Remember:* **The conclusion itself will not be evidence; it will be a belief supported by evidence or by other beliefs**.

In prescriptive arguments, reasons are typically either general, prescriptive statements or descriptive beliefs or principles. The use of these kinds of statements to support a conclusion in a prescriptive argument is illustrated in the following:

> (1) In today's society, there are all sorts of regulations on media, such as television ratings. (2) Do these ratings allow for people to make educated decisions about what they will or will not watch? (3) Do these ratings entice some people to watch a show even though they know they are not supposed to? (4) How many parents actually go by the television ratings to deter their children from watching a show? (5) More often than not, the television ratings do not prevent children from watching shows society believes that they are not mature enough to watch. (6) Television ratings are unenforceable guidelines. (7) If one believes in the censorship of media for minors, items such as the V-chip should be used for this purpose rather than the simple tagged rating at the top of the screen.

The conflict here is about whether television ratings are desirable. The author argues that if society really is concerned about what children are watching, then it should implement the use of items such as the V-chip, as stated in sentence (7). Let us look for sentences that answer the question, "Why does the author believe this conclusion?" First, note that no evidence is presented. Sentences (2) and (3) jointly form one reason, a descriptive belief: The television ratings are not significant enough to affect change, and they may even encourage some to watch more harmful shows than they would have otherwise watched. The warnings are vague and can leave people thinking that the show may not be that "bad."

Sentences (4) and (5) add a second reason: The television ratings do not really affect the choice of television shows for either parents or children. Sentence (6) provides a third reason: Television ratings cannot be enforced. There is no officer on duty other than parents, and if they do not agree with the ratings or are not around, the ratings are useless. These last two reasons are general beliefs. If the argument were expanded by the author, the beliefs themselves might be supported by evidence in some form.

KEEPING THE REASONS AND CONCLUSIONS STRAIGHT

Much reasoning is long and not very well organized. Sometimes a set of reasons will support one conclusion, and that conclusion will function as the main reason for another conclusion. Reasons may be supported by other reasons. In complicated arguments, it is frequently difficult to keep the structure straight in your mind as you attempt to critically evaluate what you have read. To overcome this problem, try to develop your own organizing procedure for keeping the reasons and conclusions separate and in a logical pattern.

We have mentioned a number of techniques for you to use in developing a clear picture of the reasoning structure. If some other technique works better for you, by all means use it. The important point is to keep the reasons and conclusions straight as you prepare to evaluate.

USING THIS CRITICAL QUESTION

Once you have found the reasons, you need to come back to them again and again as you read or listen further. Their quality is crucial to a strong argument. The conclusion depends on their merit. *Weak reasons create weak reasoning!*

Clues for Identifying and Organizing the Reasoning of a Passage

1. Circle indicator words.
2. Underline the reasons and conclusion in different colors of ink, or highlight the conclusion and underline the reasons.
3. Label the reasons and conclusion in the margin.
4. After reading long passages, make a list of reasons at the end of the essay.

Reasons First, Then Conclusions   The first chapter warned you about the danger of weak-sense critical thinking. A warning signal that can alert you to weak-sense critical thinking should go off when you notice that reasons seem to be created (on the spot, even) only because they defend a previously held opinion. When someone is eager to share an opinion as if it were a conclusion, but looks puzzled or angry when asked for reasons, weak-sense critical thinking is the probable culprit.

Certainly, you have a large set of initial beliefs, which act as initial conclusions when you encounter controversies. As your respect for the importance of reasons grows, you will frequently expect those conclusions to stand or crumble on the basis of their support. Your strongest conclusions follow your reflection about the reasons and what they mean.

Be your own censor in this regard. You must shake your own pan when looking for gold. Try to avoid "reverse logic" or "backward reasoning," whereby reasons are an afterthought, following the selection of your conclusion. Ideally, reasons are the tool by which conclusions are shaped and modified.

CRITICAL THINKING AND YOUR OWN WRITING AND SPEAKING

When you are writing or speaking, you will want to keep your audience foremost in your plans. They need to be clear about what you conclude and why you are concluding it. Do not hide your conclusion and reasons; display them openly. Give the audience a clear opportunity to see what you intend. Thus, your task is to use words, sentences, paragraphs, and indicator words to illuminate the logical relationships in your argument.

Practice Exercises

 Critical Question: **What are the reasons?**

First survey the passage and highlight its conclusion. Then ask the question, "Why?" and locate the reasons. Use indicator words to help. Keep the conclusions and the reasons separate. Try to paraphrase the reason; putting the reasons in your own words helps clarify their meaning and function.

Passage 1

Public swimming pools can be a health hazard. Many public pools are not able to obey the sanitation regulations and therefore allow for the contraction of waterborne bacteria. Studies have shown that only 60 percent of public pools are able to maintain the proper amount of chlorine in the water, allowing for those who use the pool to be infected. Many pool users have become ill after the use of a public swimming pool.

Passage 2

Schools all around the nation are forming community service programs. Should students be required to do community service? There are many drawbacks to requiring such service.

Students will not be able to understand the concept of charity and benevolence if it is something they have to do. Forced charity seems contradictory to the concept of charity. If this concept loses value for the students because the service was not a choice, they will then resent the idea of community service and not volunteer to do so at a later time in life.

Furthermore, because this community service would be coerced, the students may not perform at a high level. They may feel they will do the bare minimum of what is required. The students may also be resentful or rude to the people they are helping, which would also hamper the progress of the community service. As you can see, forced community service may not be the best programming choice for schools.

Passage 3

In high school men's basketball and men's football usually dominate the Friday night schedule. Should it be that way? These games are significant to the high school experience, but not at the cost of the other sports in the school. Just because it has been a tradition does not mean that the format has to remain that way.

It is easier for most parents and other fans to make it out to the game on Friday nights. Therefore, it is easier for them to come and see the men's basketball or men's football games. What about the girl's basketball team, or the swim team? Their games should not always be stuck on weekday afternoons and evenings. Their families often are not able to make it out to see them because most are working during the afternoons. The students who play these "secondary" sports are not getting a fair share of the spotlight; the schedule should change to accommodate these other sports.

Sample Responses To Practice Passages 1 and 2

Passage 1

ISSUE: *What makes public pools a health hazard?*
CONCLUSION: *Inadequate sanitation.*

REASONS: 1. *Sixty percent of public pools are not able to maintain proper chlorination levels.*
2. *Many people have gotten sick after using public pools.*

Recall that we are looking for the support system for the conclusion. We ask ourselves: Why does this person claim that sanitation is causing a health hazard in pools? The conclusion is justified by two research findings; these findings constitute the reasons. An indicator word for the first reason is "studies have shown."

Passage 2

Issue: *Should schools require community service?*

Conclusion: *No, schools should not require community service.*

Reason: *Forced charity makes little sense.*

(Supporting Reasons)

1. *Required community service is a self-contradiction.*
2. *Students will resent the idea of community service and choose not to volunteer to do so later in life.*
3. *Students will not perform at a high level.*
   a. *The students will only do the bare minimum, not what would most benefit the recipient.*
   b. *Students may be rude to those they are helping.*

Why are we told that schools should not require community service? The answer to that question will be the author's reasons. The first reason is supported by a collection of examples and claims, all showing us that forced community service is a contradiction. *Furthermore* is the indicator word calling our attention to the third supporting reason.

Passage 4. Expanding Practice and Feedback

Read the following longer practice passage. Then locate the reasons for Horowitz's conclusion and compare your reasons to those derived in the step-by-step walkthrough provided for the passage.

College Professors Should Be Made to Teach, Not Preach

David Horowitz

USA Today March (2005)

1. By now, we've all heard how Harvard President Lawrence Summers, a former member of President Clinton's Cabinet and a distinguished scholar in his own right, made a politically incorrect point at a faculty seminar recently.
2. One feminist professor stormed out of the room, and before you knew it, activists were clamoring for the resignation of

Summers. Soon after, he embarked on an apology tour for even raising the point that aroused them.

3. If the president of Harvard cannot raise intellectual questions in a university setting without jeopardizing his job, what does that tell you about the state of higher education in America? It tells you that American universities are in trouble. They are less free than they were in the McCarthy era (when I was in school), and something must be done to rectify the situation.

4. Two years ago, I drafted an Academic Bill of Rights that would defend "intellectual diversity" on college campuses and remove politics from the classroom. The idea has steadily gained traction as the public and, indeed, legislators hear what's happening at universities across the country.

Interest across the USA

5. Last month, I met with Minnesota legislators who have agreed to sponsor an Academic Bill of Rights based on my model. Similar legislation is before legislatures in Ohio, Pennsylvania, Florida, Tennessee, Missouri, Georgia and a dozen other states this spring.

6. Why do we need legislation? There are too many people like Ward Churchill—the University of Colorado professor who compared 9/11 victims with Nazi war criminal Adolf Eichmann—on faculties across the nation. They confuse their classrooms with a political soap box.

7. The issue is not one of their free speech as citizens, but what is appropriate to an education.

8. We don't go to our doctor's offices expecting to get political lectures. That is because doctors are professionals who have taken an oath to treat all, regardless of political belief. To introduce divisive matters into a medical consultation would injure the trust between doctor and patient that is crucial to healing. Why is the profession of education any different? It isn't.

9. Examples dot the U.S. higher education landscape:

    - It is not an education when a midterm examination contains a required essay on the topic, "Make the argument that the military action of the U.S. attacking Iraq was criminal." Yet a criminology final exam at the University of Northern Colorado did just that.
    - It is not an education when a professor of property law tells his class that the "R" in Republican stands for "racist," and devotes an entire class hour to explaining why Americans deserved to die on 9/11. But that happened at the Colorado University Law School.

- It is not an education when professors try to get their students to vote against President Bush or to demonstrate against the war in Iraq, but that has happened in classrooms across the country.

10. The Academic Bill of Rights says that a university "shall provide its students with a learning environment in which the students have access to a broad range of serious scholarly opinion pertaining to the subjects they study." It's not so revolutionary.

11. The leading opponent of my bill is the American Association of University Professors, the oldest and largest organization of faculty members. The AAUP contends that the bill would restrict professors' free speech rights. It wouldn't. Professors can still express their political opinions, but outside the classroom. In the classroom, they must distinguish between their official responsibilities as teachers and their private rights as citizens.

Once upon a time . . .

12. Ironically, the AAUP once recognized this distinction. In 1940, a year when the nation was also divided over a war, the AAUP warned: "Teachers . . . should be careful not to introduce into their teaching controversial matter which has no relation to their subject."

13. The Academic Bill of Rights uses identical language.

14. Too many professors indoctrinate students, while university administrators are intimidated from enforcing their own guidelines. It is because of this that legislatures are the last resort for providing a remedy and setting universities back on their intended course: educating our kids, not brainwashing them.

Step-by-Step Walkthrough

- First, I want to read through the entire essay to get a sense of what Mr. Horowitz wants to conclude and then try to determine his supporting reasons. It seems clear from paragraphs such as 4 and 5 and 11 through 14 that he wants an Academic Bill of Rights that would defend "intellectual diversity" on college campuses and remove politics from the classroom. (Paragraphs 4 and 14 jointly make this conclusion stand out.) This conclusion suggests that the issue he is addressing is: How can universities best support their traditional loyalty to intellectual diversity, a loyalty that presently seems to be threatened?

- As I again scan the full structure of the essay, I sense that most of the rest of it makes claims supportive of this conclusion; thus, I want to paraphrase these paragraphs into the major reasons.
- He uses his first three paragraphs to present an anecdote of an event to which he seems to be reacting strongly—an attack on a professor of Harvard for making a politically incorrect point at a recent faculty seminar.
- Thus his initial reason is suggested in the first three paragraphs of the essay. The logic here is that if someone as important as the President of Harvard can be threatened with loss of employ-ment because he expressed a particular point of view, then surely similar threats would be typical on lesser campuses and thus universities are less free than they were in the McCarthy era (see paragraph 3).
- Paragraphs 4 and 5 suggest a second reason: his Academic Bill of Rights has received support from legislators. In other words, he is claiming that his idea must be pretty strong because his Bill of Rights has attracted support by several elected officials. He is saying to us that if such people support his conclusion, then the conclusion itself is a strong one.
- I note a key indicator word "why" in paragraph 5 and that para-graphs 5 through 10 provide more reasons for his conclusion. This next part of the essay demonstrates that Mr. Horowitz does not want to protect every opinion on campus. In fact, he is very critical of Ward Churchill and others whom he sees as imposing left-wing political views on campus, as evidenced by the three "It is not an education" classroom attacks of the political right wing and the accompanying argument that doctors don't give political lectures for good reasons, so why shouldn't professors refrain from doing so for those same reasons? Another way of thinking about this reason is that we should support his Bill of Rights because students are now being treated unfairly by professors. Paragraph 10 spells out more explicitly his proposed solution to the unfairness. The university "shall provide its stu-dents with a learning environment in which the students have access to a broad range of serious scholarly opinion pertaining to the subjects they study."

The final section about the AAUP (paragraphs 12–14) contains another reason. I know that there is probably some purpose for this material, plus, I know the conclusion he is trying to dis-pense. So I ask myself: now how can the AAUP material assist in leading to the conclusion? Historically, according to Horowitz, the AAUP has made the same defense of intellectual diversity that the Academic Bill of Rights supports. Hence, even those who seem to oppose the Bill of Rights are in favor of the principles contained in it. Thus, because even my opponents support the basics in the Bill of Rights, you too should support it.

CRITICAL QUESTION SUMMARY: WHY THIS QUESTION IS IMPORTANT

What Are the Reasons?

Once you have identified the issue and conclusion, you need to understand *why* an author has come to a certain conclusion. Reasons are the *why*. If the author provides good reasons, you might be persuaded to accept her conclusion. However, right now, we are simply concerned with identifying the reasons. Identifying the reasons is the next step in deciding whether you should accept or reject the author's conclusion.

CHAPTER 5

What Words or Phrases Are Ambiguous?

Chapters 3 and 4 of this book help you identify the basic structural elements in any message. At this point, if you can locate a writer's or speaker's conclusion and reasons, you are progressing rapidly toward the ultimate goal of forming your own rational decisions. Your next step is to put this structural picture into even clearer focus.

While identifying the conclusion and reasons gives you the basic visible structure, you still need to examine the precise *meaning* of these parts before you can react fairly to the ideas being presented. Now you need to pay special attention to the details of the language.

Identifying the precise meaning of key words or phrases is an essential step in deciding whether to agree with someone's opinion. If you fail to check for the meaning of crucial terms and phrases, you may react to an opinion the author never intended.

Let's see why knowing the meaning of a communicator's terms is so important.

> Tourism is getting out of control. Tourism can be good for the economy, but it can also harm the locale and its residents. We need to do more to regulate tourism. If we keep allowing these people to do whatever they please, surely we as residents will suffer.

Notice that it is very hard to know what to think about this argument until we know more about the kinds of regulations that the person has in mind. A quota for tourists? A set of rules about the behavior expected of tourists? We just do not know what to think until we know more about these regulations the person is suggesting.

This example illustrates an important point: You cannot react to an argument unless you understand the meanings (explicit or implied) of crucial terms and phrases. How these are interpreted will often affect the acceptability of the reasoning. Consequently, before you can determine the extent to which you wish to accept one conclusion or another, you must first attempt to discover the precise meaning of the conclusion and the reasons. While their meaning typically *appears* obvious, it often is not.

The discovery and clarification of meaning require conscious, step-by-step procedures. This chapter suggests one set of such procedures. It focuses on the following question:

? *Critical Question:* **What words or phrases are ambiguous?**

THE CONFUSING FLEXIBILITY OF WORDS

Our language is highly complex. If each word had only one potential meaning about which we all agreed, effective communication would be more likely. However, most words have more than one meaning.

Consider the multiple meanings of such words as *freedom, obscenity,* and *happiness*. These multiple meanings can create serious problems in determining the worth of an argument. For example, when someone argues that a magazine should not be published because it is *obscene,* you cannot evaluate the argument until you know what the writer means by "obscene." In this brief argument, it is easy to find the conclusion and the supporting reason, but the quality of the reasoning is difficult to judge because of the ambiguous use of *obscene*. A warning: *We often misunderstand what we read or hear because we presume that the meaning of words is obvious.*

Whenever you are reading or listening, force yourself to search for *ambiguity*; otherwise, you may simply miss the point. A term or phrase is

Clarify First; Then Reason and Evaluate

ambiguous when its meaning is so uncertain in the context of the argument we are examining that we need further clarification before we can judge the adequacy of the reasoning.

When any of us is ambiguous, we have not necessarily done something either unfair or improper. In fact, many documents, like constitutions, are intentionally left ambiguous so that the document can evolve as different meanings of key terms become practical necessities. Indeed, because we rely on words to get our points across when we communicate, there is no way to avoid ambiguity. But what can and should be avoided is ambiguity in an argument. When someone is trying to persuade us to believe or do something, that person has a responsibility to clarify any potential ambiguity before we consider the worth of the reasoning.

LOCATING KEY TERMS AND PHRASES

The first step in determining which terms or phrases are ambiguous is to use the stated issue as a clue for possible key terms. Key terms or phrases will be those terms that may have more than one plausible meaning within the context of the issue—that is, terms that you know must be clarified before you can decide to agree or disagree with the communicator. To illustrate the potential benefit of checking the meaning of terminology in the stated issue, let's examine several issues:

1. Does TV violence adversely affect society?
2. Do reality shows create a misleading picture of how we live?
3. Is the incidence of rape in college residence halls increasing?

Attention: Ambiguity refers to the existence of multiple possible meanings for a word or phrase.

Each of these stated issues contains phrases that writers or speakers will have to make clear before you will be able to evaluate their response to the issue. Each of the following phrases is potentially ambiguous: "TV violence," "adversely affect society," "misleading picture," and "incidence of rape." Thus, when you read an essay responding to these issues, you will want to pay close attention to how the author has defined these terms.

The next step in determining which terms or phrases are ambiguous is to identify what words or phrases seem crucial in determining how well the author's reasons support her conclusion—that is, to identify the *key* terms in the reasoning structure. Once you locate these terms, you can then determine whether their meaning is ambiguous.

When searching for key terms and phrases, you should keep in mind why you are looking. Someone wants you to accept a conclusion. Therefore, you are looking for only those terms or phrases that will affect whether you accept the conclusion. *So, look for them in the reasons and conclusion.* Terms and phrases that are not included in the basic reasoning structure can thus be "dumped from your pan."

Summary of Clues for Locating Key Terms

1. Review the issue for possible key terms.
2. Look for crucial words or phrases within the reasons and conclusion.
3. Keep an eye out for abstract words and phrases.
4. Use reverse role-playing to determine how someone might define certain words and phrases differently.

Another useful guide for searching for key terms and phrases is to keep in mind the following rule: The more abstract a word or phrase, the more likely it is to be susceptible to multiple interpretations.

To avoid being unclear in our use of the term *abstract*, we define it here in the following way: A term becomes more and more abstract as it refers less and less to particular, specific instances. Thus, the words *equality, responsibility, pornography,* and *aggression* are much more abstract than are the phrases "having equal access to necessities of life," "directly causing an event," "pictures of male and female genitals," and "doing deliberate physical harm to another person." These latter phrases provide a much more concrete picture and are therefore less ambiguous.

You can also locate potential important ambiguous phrases by *reverse role-playing*. Ask yourself, if you were to *adopt a position contrary to the author's*, would you choose to define certain terms or phrases differently? If so, you have identified a possible ambiguity. For example, someone who sees beauty pageants as desirable is likely to define "demeaning to women" quite differently from someone who sees them as undesirable.

CHECKING FOR AMBIGUITY

You now know where to look for ambiguous terms or phrases. The next step is to focus on each term or phrase and ask yourself, "Do I understand its meaning?" In answering this very important question, you will need to overcome several major obstacles.

One obstacle is assuming that you and the author mean the same thing. Thus, you need to begin your search by avoiding "mind reading." You need to get into the habit of asking, "What do you mean by that?" instead of, "I know just what you mean." A second obstacle is assuming that terms have a single, obvious definition. Many terms do not. Thus, always ask, "Could any of the words or phrases have a different meaning?"

You can be certain you have identified an especially important unclear term by performing the following test. If you can express two or more alternative meanings for a term, each of which makes sense in the context of the argument, and if the extent to which a reason would support a conclusion is affected by which meaning is assumed, then you have located a significant ambiguity. Thus, a good test for determining whether you have identified an important ambiguity is to *substitute* the alternative meanings into the reasoning structure and see whether changing the meaning *makes a difference* in how well a reason supports the conclusion.

USING THIS CRITICAL QUESTION

The preceding paragraph deserves your full attention. It is spelling out a procedure for putting this critical question about ambiguity to work. Once you have followed the procedure, you can demonstrate to yourself or anyone else why the reasoning needs more work. Try as you might want to believe what is being said, you just cannot, as a critical thinker, agree with the reasoning until the ambiguity that affects the reasoning is repaired.

DETERMINING AMBIGUITY

Let's now apply the above hints to help us determine which key terms a communicator has left unclear. *Remember*: **As we do this exercise, keep asking, "What does the author mean by that?" and pay particular attention to abstract terms**.

    We will start with a simple reasoning structure: an advertisement.

Our Brand Sleep Aid: Works great in just 30 min.

Issue: *What sleep aid should you buy?*

Conclusion: (implied): *Buy Our Brand Sleep Aid.*

Reason: *Works great in 30 min.*

The phrases "Buy Our Brand Sleep Aid" and "in 30 min" seem quite concrete and self-evident. But, how about "works great"? Is the meaning obvious? We think not. How do we know? Let's perform a test together. Could "works great" have more than one meaning? Yes. It could mean the pill makes you drowsy. It could mean the pill completely knocks you out such that you will have difficulty waking up the next morning. Or it could have many other meanings. Isn't it true that you would be more eager to follow the advice of the advertisement if the pill worked great, meaning it works precisely as you want it to work? Thus, the ambiguity is significant because it affects the degree to which you might be persuaded by the advertisement.

    Advertising is often full of ambiguity. Advertisers intentionally engage in ambiguity to persuade you that their products are superior to those of their competitors. Here are some sample advertising claims that are ambiguous. See if you can identify alternative, plausible meanings for the italicized words or phrases.

No-Pain is the *extra-strength* pain reliever.

Here is a book at last that shows you how to find and keep a *good man*.

In each case, the advertiser hoped that you would assign the most attractive meaning to the ambiguous words. Critical reading can sometimes protect you from making purchasing decisions that you would later regret.

Let's now look at a more complicated example of ambiguity. Remember to begin by identifying the issue, conclusion, and reasons. Resist the temptation to make note of the unclear meaning of any and all words. Only the ambiguity **in the reasoning** is crucial to critical thinkers.

We absolutely must put limits on tanning. Tanning is a substantial health risk with severe consequences. Studies have shown that those who tan are at a higher risk of skin diseases as a result of tanning.

Let's examine the reasoning for any words or phrases that would affect our willingness to accept it.

First, let's inspect the issue for terms we will want the author to make clear. Certainly, we would not be able to agree or disagree with this author's conclusion until she has indicated what she means by "tanning"; does she mean tanning outdoors or artificial tanning? Thus, we will want to check how clearly she has defined it in her reasoning.

Next, let's list all key terms and phrases in the conclusion and reasons: "health risk," "severe consequences," "studies have shown," "those who tan are at a higher risk," "skin diseases," and "we should put limits on tanning." Let's take a close look at a few of these to determine whether they could have different meanings that might make a difference in how we would react to the reasoning.

First, her conclusion is ambiguous. Exactly what does it mean to "put limits on tanning"? Does it mean to prevent people from using artificial tanning devices, or might it mean putting a limit on the amount of time spent tanning? Before you could decide whether to agree with the speaker or writer, you would first have to decide what it is she wants us to believe.

Next, she argues that "those who tan are at a higher risk of skin diseases." We have already talked about how we are not sure what she means by "those who tan," but what does she mean by "skin diseases"? She could mean any number of irritations that can occur from sun exposure, or she could be talking about something as severe as skin cancer. It is significant to know which of these she was addressing if she wanted to convince you of the dangers of tanning and her conclusion to limit it. Try to create a mental picture of what these phrases represent. If you can't, the phrases are ambiguous. If different images would cause you to react to the reasons differently, you have identified an important ambiguity.

Now, check the other phrases we listed above. Do they not also need to be clarified? You can see that if you accept this writer's argument without requiring her to clarify these ambiguous phrases, you will not have understood what it is you agreed to believe.

CONTEXT AND AMBIGUITY

Writers and speakers only rarely define their terms. Thus, typically your only guide to the meaning of an ambiguous statement is the context in which the words are used. By *context*, we mean the writer's or speaker's background, traditional uses of the term within the particular controversy, and the words and statements preceding and following the possible ambiguity. All three ele-ments provide clues to the meaning of a potential key term or phrase.

If you were to see the term *human rights* in an essay, you should immediately ask yourself, "What rights are those?" If you examine the context and find that the writer is a leading member of the Norwegian government, it is a good bet that the human rights she has in mind are the rights to be employed, receive free health care, and obtain adequate housing. An American senator might mean something very different by human rights. She could have in mind freedoms of speech, religion, travel, and peaceful assembly. Notice that the two versions of human rights are not necessarily consistent. A country could guarantee one form of human rights and at the same time vio-late the other. You must try to clarify such terms by examining their context.

Writers frequently make clear their assumed meaning for a term by their arguments. The following paragraph is an example:

> The amusement park has given great satisfaction to most of its cus-tomers. More than half of the people surveyed agreed that the park had a wide variety of games and rides and that they would return to the park soon.

The phrase "give great satisfaction" is potentially ambiguous, because it could have a variety of meanings. However, the writer's argument makes clear that in this context, "give great satisfaction" means having a variety of games and rides.

Note that, even in this case, you would want some further clarification before you travel to this park, because "having a variety of games" is ambigu-ous. Wouldn't you want to know perhaps how many rides or games there were, or what some of them were? It is possible that although there is a wide variety of games, all of them are outdated or not popular anymore?

USING THIS CRITICAL QUESTION

The critical question focusing on ambiguity provides you with a fair-minded basis for disagreeing with the reasoning. If you and the person trying to per-suade you are using different meanings for key terms in the reasoning, you would have to work out those disagreements first before you could accept the reasoning being offered to you.

Examine the context carefully to determine the meaning of key terms and phrases. If the meaning remains uncertain, you have located an impor-tant ambiguity. If the meaning is clear and you disagree with it, then you should be wary of any reasoning that involves that term or phrase.

AMBIGUITY, DEFINITIONS, AND THE DICTIONARY

It should be obvious from the preceding discussion that to locate and clarify ambiguity, you must be aware of the possible meanings of words. Meanings usually come in one of three forms: synonyms, examples, and what we will call "definition by specific criteria." For example, one could offer at least three different definitions of *anxiety*:

1. Anxiety is feeling nervous (*synonym*).
2. Anxiety is what the candidate experienced when he turned on the television to watch the election returns (*example*).
3. Anxiety is a subjective feeling of discomfort accompanied by increased sensitivity of the autonomic nervous system (*specific criteria*).

For critical evaluation of most controversial issues, synonyms and examples are inadequate. They fail to tell you the specific properties that are crucial for an unambiguous understanding of the term. Useful definitions are those that specify criteria for usage—and the more specific the better.

Where do you go for your definitions? One obvious and very important source is your dictionary. However, dictionary definitions frequently consist of synonyms, examples, or incomplete specifications of criteria for usage. These definitions often do not adequately define the use of a term in a particular essay. In such cases, you must discover possible meanings from the context of the passage, or from what else you know about the topic. We suggest you keep a dictionary handy, but keep in mind that the appropriate definition may not be there.

Let's take a closer look at some of the inadequacies of a dictionary definition. Examine the following brief paragraph.

> The quality of education at this university is not declining. In my interviews, I found that an overwhelming majority of the students and instructors responded that they saw no decline in the quality of education here.

It is clearly important to know what is meant by "quality of education" in the above paragraph. If you look up the word *quality* in the dictionary, you will find many meanings, the most appropriate, given this context, being *excellence* or *superiority*. *Excellence* and *superiority* are synonyms for quality—and they are equally abstract. You still need to know precisely what is meant by *excellence* or *superiority*. How do you know whether education is high in quality or excellence? Ideally, you would want the writer to tell you precisely what *behaviors* she is referring to when she uses the phrase "quality of education." Can you think of some different ways that the phrase might be defined? The following list presents some possible definitions of *quality of education*:

average grade-point average of students

ability of students to think critically

number of professors who have doctoral degrees

amount of work usually required to pass an exam

Each of these definitions suggests a different way to measure quality; each specifies a different criterion. Each provides a concrete way in which the term could be used. Note also that each of these definitions will affect the degree to which you will want to agree with the author's reasoning. For example, if you believe that "quality" should refer to the ability of students to think critically, and most of the students in the interviews are defining it as how much work is required to pass an exam, the reason would not *necessarily* support the conclusion. Exams may not require the ability to think critically.

Thus, in many arguments you will not be able to find adequate dictionary definitions, and the context may not make the meaning clear. One way to discover possible alternative meanings is to try to create a mental picture of what the words represent. If you cannot do so, then you probably have identified an important ambiguity. Let's apply such a test to the following example:

> Our company has had many competent employees. If you join our staff, you will start immediately at the rate we discussed with, of course, added benefits. I hope you consider all these factors in making your employment decision.

This is clearly an argument to persuade someone to work at his or her place of employment. The reasons are the salary and "added benefits." Can you create a single clear mental picture of "added benefits?" We each have some such idea, but it is highly unlikely that the ideas are identical; indeed, they may be quite different. Do "added benefits" refer to health care insurance or a new corner office? For us to evaluate the argument, we would need to know more about the meaning the writer has for "added benefits." Thus, we have located an important ambiguity.

AMBIGUITY AND LOADED LANGUAGE

> If you owned a Las Vegas casino, would you want to promote *Gaming* or *Gambling* in your publicity materials?
>
> Would you be more likely to vote for *tax relief* than for a *tax cut?*
>
> Would you be more willing to vote for the reduction of *death taxes* than *estate taxes?*
>
> When national parks are asked to close visitor centers on weekends and eliminate all guided ranger tours, are you more likely to complain to your representatives if these changes are referred to as *cuts* or as *service level adjustments?*

Research shows that people have different emotional reactions to the italicized terms above even though the terms have similar definitions. Las Vegas now is more likely to tout gaming than gambling in its casinos. American citizens respond more positively to tax relief than to tax cut and are more likely to support the reduction of death taxes than estate taxes. Different emotional reactions to selected terms and phrases can greatly influence how we respond to arguments.

Terms and phrases have both *denotative* and *connotative* meanings. The denotative meaning refers to the agreed-upon explicit *descriptive referents* for use of the word, the kinds of meanings we have emphasized thus far in this chapter. There is another important meaning, however, that you need to attend to. The *connotative meaning* is the emotional associations that we have to a term or phrase. For example, the phrase "raising taxes" may have similar denotative meanings to people but trigger very different emotional reactions.

Ambiguity is not always an accident. Those trying to persuade you are often quite aware that words have multiple meanings. Furthermore, they know that certain of those meanings carry with them heavy emotional baggage. Words like *sacrifice* and *justice* have multiple meanings, and some of those meanings are loaded in the sense that they stimulate certain emotions in us. Anyone trying to use language to lead us by the heart can take advantage of these probable emotions. They can do so by using language that heightens our positive emotional reactions or "cools" our negative emotional reactions to ideas.

For example, the American military officials who control prisons in Afghanistan and Guantanamo are eager to avoid the appearance that these prisons encourage a large number of suicides among the prisoners. Yet a large number of prisoners do take their own lives. The military have to count those deaths somehow. So they have created categories like "Self-inflicted Hazardous Incidents" that permit them to acknowledge the deaths without putting them into the category of suicides. Here the ambiguity of "Self-inflicted Hazardous Incidents" is far from accidental; it is meant to defuse emotional reactions to the ideas it references.

Political language is often loaded and ambiguous. For example, *welfare* is often how we refer to governmental help to those we don't like; when help from the government goes to groups we like, we call it *assistance to the poor.* The following table consists of political terms and the intended emotional impact.

Ambiguous Political Language

Term	Emotional Impact
Revenue enhancement	Positive response to tax hikes
Tax and spend democrats	Irresponsible and wasteful
Restoring fairness	Approval of proposed tax changes
Drilling for oil	Undesirable, unreasonable
Energy exploration	Desirable
Terrorist	Wild, crazy, uncivilized
Defense spending	Protective, required
Company challenges	Optimistic
Company problems	Pessimistic
Reform	Desirable changes

All the terms in the table are ambiguous and potentially influential emotional associations. As critical thinkers, we must be sensitive to their intended emotional impact and the role of ambiguity in encouraging that impact. Be alert to how terms make you FEEL! Are those feelings blinding you to some important feature of the term? By clarifying the denotative meaning and searching for alternative meanings of terms such as *reform*, we can safeguard ourselves against easy emotional commitments to arguments we would otherwise question. After all, even the most dangerous political change is in some sense a "reform."

Norman Solomon's *The Power of Babble* provides a colorful illustration of how successful politicians use ambiguous language to persuade others. Note that Mr. Solomon has conveniently placed key ambiguous terms in alphabetical order for us.

> America is back, and bipartisan—biting the bullet with competitiveness, diplomacy, efficiency, empowerment, end games, and environmentalism, along with faith in the founding Fathers, freedom's blessings, free markets and free peoples, and most of all, God. Our great heritage has held the line for human rights, individual initiative, justice, kids, leadership, liberty, loyalty, mainstream values, the marketplace, measured responses, melting pots, the middle class, military reform, moderates, modernization, moral standards, national security, and Old Glory. Opportunity comes from optimism, patriotism, peace through strength, the people, pluralism, and points of light. Pragmatism and the power of prayer make for principle while the private sector protects the public interest. Realism can mean recycling, self-discipline, and the spirit of '76, bring stability and standing tall for strategic interests and streamlined taxation. Uncle Sam has been undaunted ever since Valley Forge, with values venerated by veterans; vigilance, vigor, vision, voluntarism, and Western values. (p. 3)

LIMITS OF YOUR RESPONSIBILITY TO CLARIFY AMBIGUITY

After you have attempted to identify and clarify ambiguity, what can you do if you are still uncertain about the meaning of certain key ideas? What is a reasonable next step? We suggest you ignore any reason containing ambiguity that makes it impossible to decide whether you agree or disagree with the reason. It is your responsibility as an active learner to ask questions that clarify ambiguity. However, your responsibility stops at that point. It is the writer or speaker who is trying to convince you of something. Her role as a persuader requires her to respond to your concerns about possible ambiguity.

You are not required to react to unclear ideas or options. If a friend tells you that you should enroll in a class because it "really is different," but cannot tell you how it is different, then you have no basis for agreeing or disagreeing with the advice. No one has the right to be believed if he cannot provide you with a clear picture of his reasoning.

AMBIGUITY AND YOUR OWN WRITING AND SPEAKING

Although most of this chapter is addressed to you as a critical reader and listener, it is also extremely relevant to improved writing and speaking. Effective communicators strive for clarity. They review what they intend to say several times, looking for any statements that might be ambiguous.

Look back at the section on "Locating Key Terms and Phrases" (p. 46). Use the hints given there for finding important ambiguity to revise your own efforts to communicate. For instance, abstractions that are ambiguous can be clarified by providing specific criteria for the use of the abstraction or by concrete illustrations, conveying the meaning you intend. Pay special attention to your own reasons and conclusions; try to rid them of ambiguity out of respect for your audience. When you fear ambiguity of expression, carefully define your terms.

Thinking about the characteristics of your intended audience can help you decide where ambiguities need to be clarified. A specialized audience may adequately understand jargon or specific abstractions that would be very ambiguous to a general audience. Remember that your audience will probably not struggle for a long time with your meaning. If you confuse a member of your audience, you will probably lose him quickly. If you never regain his attention, then you have failed in your task as a communicator.

Take another look at the previous section discussing the burden of responsibility surrounding the use of ambiguity. It is you the writer or speaker who must bear that burden; it is you who is attempting to convince someone else.

Summary

You cannot evaluate an essay until you know the communicator's intended meaning of key terms and phrases as well as alternative meanings they could conceivably have had in the context of the argument. You can find important clues to potential ambiguity in the statement of the issue and can locate key words and phrases in the reasons and conclusions. Because many authors fail to define their terms and because many key terms have multiple meanings, you must search for possible ambiguity. You do this by asking the questions, "What *could* be meant?" and "What *is* meant by the key terms?" Once you have completed the search, you will know four very important components of the reasoning:

1. the key terms and phrases;
2. which of these are adequately defined;
3. which of these possess other possible definitions, which if substituted would modify your reaction to the reasoning; and
4. which of these are ambiguous within the context of the argument.

Practice Exercises

 Critical Question: ***What words or phrases are ambiguous?***

In the following passages, identify examples of ambiguity. Try to explain why the examples harm the reasoning.

Passage 1

School dress codes are limits put on inappropriate clothing to help keep the learning environment focused. It can be quite a distraction for students if a classmate has inappropriate clothing. The use of a dress code during school is not preventing freedom of expression. The dress code still allows for students to choose what they wear as long as it is not deemed inappropriate, unlike required uniform dress codes.

Passage 2

We should treat drug use in the same way we treat speech and religion, as a fundamental right. No one has to ingest any drug he does not want, just as no one has to read a particular book. The only reason the state assumes control over such matters is to subjugate its citizens—by shielding them from temptations as befits children.

Passage 3

Note: This passage is adapted from an opinion delivered by Chief Justice Warren Burger in a Supreme Court response concerning the constitutionality of a Georgia obscenity statute.

We categorically disapprove the theory, apparently adopted by the trial judge, that obscene, pornographic films acquire constitutional immunity from state regulation simply because they are exhibited for consenting adults only. This holding was properly rejected by the Georgia Supreme Court. . . . In particular, we hold that there are legitimate state interests at stake in stemming the tide of commercialized obscenity, even assuming it is feasible to enforce effective safeguards against exposure to juveniles and passersby. Rights and interests other than those of the advocates are involved. These include the interest of the public in the quality of life and the total community environment, the tone of commerce in the great city centers, and possibly, the public safety itself . . .

The sum of experience, including that of the past two decades, affords an ample basis for legislatures to conclude that a sensitive, key relationship of human existence, central to family life, community welfare and the development of human personality, can be debased and distorted by crass commercial exploitation of sex.

Sample Responses To Passages 1 and 2

For the first practice passage, our sample response shares with you an in depth "thinking aloud" model of the critical thinking process we have been describing in this chapter and the previous two chapters.

Passage 1

- *If this passage has any significant ambiguity, Asking the Right Questions said that I'll find it in the issue, conclusion, or reasons. So my first step will be to find those parts of the argument. Neither the issue nor the conclusion is explicitly stated in this passage. No indicator words are present. I'll have to try other tools to identify the issue and conclusion. To find the issue, Asking the Right Questions suggests that I ask "What is the author reacting to?" Dress codes, I guess. Whether they are a good idea. Okay, so I'll word that idea as a question: "Should schools have a dress code?" All of the sentences in this passage are trying to convince me that we should have a dress code, so the conclusion must be, "Yes, schools should have a dress code."*

- *Again, there are no indicator words to help me find the reasons. So I'll try something else. To find the reasons, I need to put myself in the author's shoes and ask: "Why should schools have a dress code?" I can deduce two reasons from the passage: first, inappropriate clothing distracts from learning. Second, dress codes do not violate freedom of expression.*

- *Now that I have broken the argument down into its most basic parts, I can start the process of finding significant ambiguity. I'll start by identifying the key words or phrases in the issue, conclusion, and reasons. These words are crucial to the argument, and they may have more than one plausible meaning within the context. For instance, they could be abstract terms or loaded language. "Inappropriate clothing" is definitely an important element of the argument. And the author never tells me what qualifies as inappropriate. I wonder if there are other possible meanings for the term. . .*

- *"Inappropriate clothing," as far I'm concerned, is clothing with text that's hurtful or insulting. I'd prohibit such clothing from schools too! T-shirts that make fun of people are definitely inappropriate. It's pretty clear to me. Of course, Asking the Right Questions said that I might think the definition of a term is obvious, even if it's not. So I should keep questioning. Could this phrase have a different meaning?*

- *One of the clues that Asking the Right Questions suggested was to pay attention to abstract words, like obscenity and responsibility. These words are abstract—and also ambiguous—because they don't have a specific definition or set of criteria for us. "Inappropriate" similarly does not have a specific definition or set of criteria in this passage. The author never says that inappropriate means hurtful text on t-shirts. I just assumed that meaning because I think those T-shirts are inappropriate. The author also doesn't say that inappropriate means skirts of a certain length or wearing pants so low I can see a guy's boxers. The term is starting to seem a little less obvious than I originally thought.*

- *Before I can be sure, I want to try the reverse role-playing suggestion. How would an opponent of this conclusion define the term "inappropriate clothing"? Opponents of this argument would probably argue that dress codes DO prohibit freedom of expression. What might students want to express with their clothing? Political messages are often T-shirts. I've seen teenagers wearing antiwar T-shirts or T-shirts for their favorite presidential candidate. An opponent of dress codes probably would fear that students would be denied the right to voice their opinions about important issues.*

- *Wow. Now I'm stuck. If the author is talking about messages on T-shirts that hurt people, I agree. Let's prohibit them. But if the author's talking about limiting students' ability to voice their political opinions, I strongly disagree. I can't come to a decision about this issue until the ambiguity is resolved.*

Passage 2

Issue: *Should the state regulate drug use?*

Conclusion: *Drug use should not be regulated by the state.*

Reasons: 1. *Just as with freedom of speech and religion, drug use is a fundamental right.*
2. *State control subjugates citizens by not permitting them to take responsibility for voluntary acts.*

What are the key phrases in this reasoning? They are: "drug use," "fundamental right," and "subjugate citizens." You would first want to determine the meaning of each of these phrases. Is it clear what is meant by drug use? No. The limited context provided fails to reveal an adequate definition. If drug use refers to the ingestion of drugs that are not considered highly addictive, such as marijuana, wouldn't you be more likely to accept the reasoning than if the author included heroin within her definition of drugs? Can you tell from the argument whether the author is referring to all drugs or only to a subset of currently regulated drugs? To be able to agree or to disagree with the author requires in this instance a more careful definition of what is meant by "drug use." Notice that "fundamental right" and "subjugate citizens" need further clarification before you can decide whether to agree with the author.

Passage 4. Expanding Practice and Feedback

Read the following editorial. Try to identify examples of ambiguity and explain why the examples harm the reasoning.

Juvenile Injustice

The New York Times (2007)

The United States made a disastrous miscalculation when it started automatically trying youthful offenders as adults instead of handling them through the juvenile courts. Prosecutors argued that the policy would get violent predators off the streets and deter further crime. But a new federally backed study shows that juveniles who do time as adults later commit more violent crime than those who are handled through the juvenile courts.

The study, published last month in *The American Journal of Preventive Medicine*, was produced by the Task Force on Community Preventive Services, an independent research group with close ties to the Centers for Disease Control and Prevention. After an exhaustive survey of the literature, the group determined that the practice of transferring children into adult courts was counterproductive, actually creating more crime than it cured.

A related and even more disturbing study by Campaign for Youth Justice in Washington finds that the majority of the more than 200,000 children a year who are treated as adults under the law come before the courts for nonviolent offenses that could be easily and more effectively dealt with at the juvenile court level.

Examples include a 17-year-old first-time offender charged with robbery after stealing another student's gym clothes, and another 17-year-old who violated his probation by stealing a neighbor's bicycle. Many of these young nonviolent offenders are held in adult prisons for months or even years.

The laws also are not equally applied. Youths of color, who typically go to court with inadequate legal counsel, account for three out of every four young people admitted to adult prison.

With 40 states allowing or requiring youthful offenders to spend at least some time in adult jails, state legislators all across the country are just waking up to the problems this practice creates. Some states now have pending bills that would stop juveniles from being automatically transferred to adult courts or that would allow them to get back into the juvenile system once the adult court was found to be inappropriate for them.

Given the damage being done to young lives all over the country, the bills can't pass soon enough.

Step-by-Step Walkthrough

How did you do? Don't be discouraged if you struggled to identify the ambiguity in this editorial. Larger, more complex arguments can, at first, seem overwhelming. The following is a step-by-step walk-through, explaining the process of identifying the significant ambiguity in this editorial. Follow along and model your next search for ambiguity after this one:

- Before I can identify ambiguities in this editorial, I need to identify the conclusion and the reasons. After all, only terms that will affect whether I accept the conclusion are significantly ambiguous. These terms are found in the reasons and the conclusion.
- The conclusion in this article is that we should not have laws that automatically try juveniles in adult courts. The author supported this conclusion with three reasons: (1) Laws that permit courts to try juveniles as adults have led to an increase in violent crime. (2) The majority of children treated as adults under the law come before courts for nonviolent offenses that could be easily and more effectively dealt with at the juvenile court level, and (3) These laws resulting in trying juveniles in adult courts are unequally applied, as youths of color account for three out of four young people admitted to adult prison.
- The conclusion and reasons seem fairly self-explanatory to me\at first. Maybe there are no importantly ambiguous terms . . . This chapter warned me, though, that I might think terms and phrases are obvious, even when they are not. I need to force myself to ask if any of the words or phrases could have a different meaning that might influence how I would react to the argument. I am going to start by asking: what key words and phrases are crucial to the argument? To help this process, I have tried to be sure to include what I believe to be crucial words in my above summary of the reasoning structure. "Juveniles," "laws," "adult courts," "juvenile courts," "increase in violent crime," "non-violent offenses," "majority of children" and "unequally applied" are all central to the argument.
- I can probably narrow down this list; only some of these terms or phrases are likely to make a big difference in how I react to

the reasoning. Asking the Right Questions suggested that the more abstract a word is, the more I should be suspicious of an important ambiguity. So I want to ask which of these phrases are least concrete or self-evident. Which of these could have more than one meaning that could make a difference? The terms and phrases juveniles, increase in violent crime, non-violent offenses, and majority of children all seem to be subject to the possibility of more than one likely definition in this context. At first, I also considered unequally applied to possibly be importantly ambiguous, but the author provides a context by which I can derive its meaning. From this context, I can conclude that the inequality lies in the lack of adequate counsel and the disproportionate number of youths of color in adult prison.

- So I now want to determine whether different definitions of the above listed terms and phrases might lead me to have different reactions to the argument. Let's turn to the word juvenile. The author frequently used the words juveniles, children, and youths throughout the editorial. In fact, the author uses these words interchangeably. But the words don't mean the same thing to me. A child, for me, is under the age of 13. A juvenile, on the other hand, is 13 or older. Plus, when the author uses the word child, I feel worse about the laws. I think about little kids. I wonder whether the author used that word on purpose, as loaded language, to try to convince me of the argument. I think I should pursue these words.

- Asking the Right Questions recommended that I reverse role-play and consider how somebody else might define this word. Some people think these laws affect all people younger than 18-, even 13- and 14-year-olds. I bet other readers might assume that the laws only affect 16- and 17-year-olds. After all, some people might think that 16- and 17-year-olds should be responsible for the decisions, but 13- and 14-year-olds are still too young to know better. I looked through the article, and it doesn't say who's a juvenile and affected by these laws.

- I am starting to think that "juveniles" is significantly ambiguous. I am cautious, though, because Asking the Right Questions said that a term with multiple definitions is significantly ambiguous ONLY when these possible definitions, if substituted, would change my reaction to the conclusion and reasons. I need to ask myself if the argument is more or less persuasive if I switch definitions. I think it is. I would be more likely to accept the conclusion if the author is talking about laws that affect 13- and 14-year-olds, along with 16- and 17-year-olds. The idea of a 13-year-old going to prison is just awful to me. On the other hand, if the author is talking about laws that affect only 16- and

17-year olds, I would be less likely to accept the conclusion. I think 16- and 17-year-olds are practically adults. They may need to be held more responsible for their decisions. That settles it: "juveniles" is significantly ambiguous in this editorial.

- These questions and critical thinking techniques helped me reach the conclusion that "juvenile" is significantly ambiguous. Next, I think I'll apply the same process to the term "nonviolent offenses." in the second reason. I wonder whether I will agree with the author's reason if I have a different definition of violent offenses than he has.

HOPEFULLY, THAT STEP-BY-STEP WALKTHROUGH OF THE CRITICAL THINKING PROCESS HELPED YOU SEE THE SIGNIFICANT AMBIGUITY IN THIS READING.

CRITICAL QUESTION SUMMARY: WHY THIS QUESTION IS IMPORTANT

What Words or Phrases Are Ambiguous?

Once you have identified an author's argument, you need to identify key words or phrases within that reasoning that might have alternative meanings. More importantly, you need to determine whether the author explicitly uses one of those definitions. If she does not, and if one of those meanings alters your acceptance of the conclusion, you have identified an important ambiguity. Identifying ambiguous words and phrases is the next important step in determining whether you will accept or reject the conclusion.

CHAPTER 6

What Are the Value and Descriptive Assumptions?

Anyone trying to convince you to agree with a particular position will make an attempt to present reasons consistent with that position. Hence, at first glance almost every argument appears to "make sense." The visible structure looks good. But the visible, stated reasons are not the only ideas that serve to prove or support the conclusion. Hidden or unstated beliefs may be at least as significant in understanding the argument. Let's examine the importance of these unstated ideas by considering the following brief argument.

> Local law enforcement needs to do more to impose consequences for littering. Obviously, people are not taking enough initiative on their own to follow the laws; therefore, city police have to do something. How can we expect change without enforcement?

The reason—at first glance—supports the conclusion. If the city expects change in the behavior of its citizens, it follows that the city's law enforcement should have to enforce that change. But it is also possible that the reason given can be true and yet not *necessarily* support the conclusion. What if you believe that it is the individual's responsibility—not the collective responsibility of government—to take responsibility for the extent of littering? If so, from your perspective, the reason no longer supports the conclusion. This reasoning is convincing to you only if you agree with certain unstated ideas that the writer has taken for granted. In this case, one idea taken for granted is that the value, collective responsibility, is more desirable than individual responsibility.

In all arguments, there will be certain ideas taken for granted by the writer. Typically, these ideas will not be stated. You will have to find them by reading between the lines. These ideas are important invisible links in the reasoning structure, the glue that holds the entire argument together. Until you supply these links, you cannot truly understand the argument.

If you miss the hidden links, you will often find yourself believing something that, had you been more reflective, you would never have accepted. *Remember:* The visible surface of an argument will almost always be dressed in its best clothes because the person presenting the argument wishes to encourage you to make the argument your own. This chapter can be particularly useful to you as a critical thinker because it prepares you to look at the full argument, not just its more attractive features.

As another illustration, consider why you should work hard to master the skills and attitudes contained in this book. There are all kinds of reasons why you should not learn critical thinking. Careful thought is much more demanding of our energies than would be another decision-making approach like flipping a coin or asking the nearest self-confident expert what you should think and do. But this text is encouraging you to learn critical thinking. We are telling you that critical thinking is advantageous for you.

But our advice is based on some invisible beliefs, and if you do not share those beliefs, our advice should not be followed. Critical thinkers believe that such values as autonomy, curiosity, and reasonableness are among the most important of human objectives. The end-product of critical thinking is someone who is open to multiple points of view, assesses those perspectives with reason, and then uses that assessment to make decisions about what to believe and what actions to take. We trust that you like that portrayal of life and, consequently, that you will want to be a critical thinker.

When you are trying to understand someone, your task is similar in many ways to having to reproduce a magic trick without having seen how the magician did the trick. You see the handkerchief go into the hat and the rabbit come out, but you are not aware of the magician's hidden maneuvers. To understand the trick, you must discover these maneuvers. Likewise, in arguments, you must discover the hidden maneuvers, which, in actuality, are unstated ideas. We shall refer to these unstated ideas as *assumptions*. To fully understand an argument, you must identify the assumptions.

Assumptions are:

1. hidden or unstated (in most cases);
2. taken for granted;
3. influential in determining the conclusion; and
4. potentially deceptive.

This chapter will show you how to discover assumptions. But identifying assumptions is more valuable than just the positive impact it has on your own reasoning. Critical thinking necessarily involves other people who are concerned about the same issues as you. When you identify assumptions and make them explicit in your interactions with others, you make a tremendous contribution to the quality of the reasoning in our community as well.

For instance, the Associated Press recently ran an account of a study from the St. Louis Federal Reserve Bank. The study concluded that good-looking people tend to make more money and get promoted more often than those who are just average looking. As a critical thinker, you can question the assumptions behind such a report and, in so doing, prevent us from quickly embracing arguments that use such data to support their conclusions. Democracy badly needs just this kind of cautious reflection.

 Critical Question: ***What are the value and descriptive assumptions?***

GENERAL GUIDE FOR IDENTIFYING ASSUMPTIONS

When you seek assumptions, where and how should you look? Numerous assumptions exist in any book, discussion, or article, but you need to be concerned about relatively few. As you remember, the visible structure of an argument consists of reasons and conclusions. Thus, you are interested only in assumptions that affect the quality of this structure. You can restrict your search for assumptions, therefore, to the structure you have already learned how to identify.

In particular, there are two places to look for assumptions. Look for assumptions needed for the reason(s) to support the conclusions (linkage assumptions) and look for ones necessary for a reason to be true. We first introduce you to value assumptions and then to descriptive assumptions. Both are extremely influential in shaping arguments. **Look for both kinds of assumptions in the movement from reasons to conclusion!**

Note that the reasons and conclusion are also the place where we search for significant ambiguity. Once again, we are showing great respect for the importance in a speech or an essay of the reasons and the conclusion.

> *Attention: An assumption is an unstated belief that supports the explicit reasoning.*

VALUE CONFLICTS AND ASSUMPTIONS

Why is it that some very reasonable people shout that abortion is murder, while other equally reasonable observers see abortion as humane? Have you ever wondered why every U.S. president, regardless of his political beliefs, eventually gets involved in a dispute with the press over publication of government information that he would prefer not to share? How can some highly intelligent observers attack the publication of sexually explicit magazines and others defend their publication as the ultimate test of our Bill of Rights?

One extremely important reason for these different conclusions is the existence of *value conflicts*, or the differing values that stem from different frames of reference. For ethical or prescriptive arguments, an individual's values influence the reasons he provides and, consequently, his conclusion. In fact, the reasons will logically support the conclusion only if the *value assumption* is added to the reasoning. The brief argument below illustrates the role of a value assumption in a prescriptive argument.

> We should not legalize recreational drugs. Illegal drugs cause too much street violence and other crimes.

Value assumptions are very important assumptions for such arguments because they are directing the reasoning from behind a screen. The person trying to communicate with you may or may not be aware of these assumptions. You should make it a habit to identify the value assumptions on which the reasons are based.

By *value assumption*, we mean a taken-for-granted belief about the *relative desirability* of certain competing values. When authors take a position on a social controversy, they typically prefer one value over another value—they have value *priorities or preferences*. To identify these priorities you need to have a good grasp of what is meant by "values." Consequently, this is a good time to review the introduction of values in Chapter 2.

 Critical Question: **What are the value assumptions**

FROM VALUES TO VALUE ASSUMPTIONS

To identify value assumptions, we must go beyond a simple listing of values. Others share many of your values. Wouldn't almost anyone claim that flexibility, cooperation, and honesty are desirable?

Look again at the definition, and you will immediately see that, *by definition*, most values will be on everyone's list. Because many values are shared, values by themselves are not a powerful guide to understanding. What leads you to answer a prescriptive question differently from someone else is the relative intensity with which you hold specific values.

That we attach different levels of intensity to specific values can be appreciated by thinking about responses to controversies when pairs of values collide or conflict. While it is not very enlightening to discover that most people value both competition and cooperation, we do gain a more complete understanding of prescriptive choices as we discover who *prefers* competition to cooperation when the two values conflict.

A person's preference for particular values is often unstated, but that value preference, nevertheless, will have a major impact on her conclusion and on how she chooses to defend it. These unstated assertions about value priorities function as *value assumptions*. Some refer to these assumptions as *value judgments*. Recognition of relative support for conflicting values or sets of values provides you with both an improved understanding of what you are reading and a basis for eventual evaluation of prescriptive arguments.

> **Attention:** *A value assumption is an implicit preference for one value over another in a particular context. We use value preferences and value priorities as synonyms.*

When you have found a person's value preference in a particular argument, you should not expect that same person to necessarily have the same value priority when discussing a different controversy. A person's value assumptions are greatly affected by the context in which they are being applied. The context and factual issues associated with a controversy also greatly influence how far we're willing to go with a particular value preference. We hold our value preferences *only up to a point.* Thus, for example, those who prefer freedom of choice over the welfare of the community in most situations (such as wearing clothing that displays an image of the flag) may shift that value preference when they see the possibility of too much damage to the welfare of the community (such as in the case of the right of a person to give a racist speech).

In other words, value assumptions are very contextual; they apply in one setting, but we may make quite a different value priority when the specifics of the prescriptive issue change. Critical thinking plays a major role in thinking deeply about whether we want to assign priority to particular values in a given instance. Because our minds tend to like to put things in neat compartments, you have to work hard to tolerate the complexity of a person's value preferences.

TYPICAL VALUE CONFLICTS

If you are aware of typical conflicts, you can more quickly recognize the assumptions being made by a writer when she reaches a particular conclusion. We have listed some of the more common value conflicts that occur in ethical issues and have provided you with examples of controversies in which these value conflicts are likely to be evident. We anticipate that you can use this list as a starting point when you are trying to identify important value assumptions.

As you identify value conflicts, you will often find that there are several value conflicts that seem important in shaping conclusions with respect to particular controversies. When evaluating a controversy, try to find several value conflicts, as a check on yourself. Some controversies will have one primary value conflict; others may have several.

Typical Value Conflict and Sample Controversies

1. loyalty–honesty	Should you tell your parents about your sister's drug habit?
2. competition–cooperation	Do you support the grading system?
3. freedom of press–national security	Is it wise to hold weekly presidential press conferences?
4. equality–individualism	Are racial quotas for employment fair?
5. order–freedom of speech	Should we imprison those with radical ideas?
6. rationality–spontaneity	Should you check the odds before placing a bet?

THE COMMUNICATOR'S BACKGROUND AS A CLUE TO VALUE ASSUMPTIONS

We suggested earlier that a good starting point in finding assumptions is to check the background of the author. Find out as much as you can about the value preferences usually held by a person like the writer. Is she a corporate executive, a union leader, a Republican Party official, a doctor, or an apartment tenant? What interests does such a person naturally wish to protect? There is certainly nothing inherently wrong with pursuing self-interest, but such pursuits often limit the value assumptions a particular writer will tolerate. For example, it is highly unlikely that the president of a major automobile firm would place a high value on efficiency when a preference for efficiency rather than stability would lead to his losing his job. Consequently, you as a critical reader or listener can often quickly discover value preferences by thinking about the probable assumptions made by a person like the writer.

One caution is important. It isn't necessarily true that because a person is a member of a group she shares the particular value assumptions of the group. It would be a mistake to presume that every individual who belongs to a given group thinks identically. We all know that business people, farmers, and firefighters sometimes disagree among themselves when discussing particular controversies. Investigating the writer's background as a clue to her value assumptions is only a clue, and, like other clues, it can be misleading unless it is used with care.

CONSEQUENCES AS CLUES TO VALUE ASSUMPTIONS

In prescriptive arguments, each position with respect to an issue leads to different consequences or outcomes. Each of the potential consequences will have a certain likelihood of occurring, and each will also have some level of desirability or undesirability.

How desirable a consequence is will depend on a writer's or reader's personal value preferences. The desirability of the conclusions in such cases will be dictated by the probability of the potential consequences and the importance attached to them. Thus, an important means of determining an individual's value assumptions is to examine the reasons given in support of a conclusion and then to determine what value priorities would lead to these reasons being judged as more desirable than reasons that might have been offered on the other side of the issue. Let's take a look at a concrete example.

> Nuclear power plants should not be built because they will pollute our environment.

The reason provided here is a rather specific potential consequence of building nuclear plants. This writer clearly sees environmental pollution as very undesirable. Why does this consequence carry so much weight in this person's thinking? What more general value does preventing pollution help achieve? We are only guessing, but probably health or conservation is being weighted especially heavily by this person. Someone else might stress a different consequence in this argument, such as the effect on the supply of electricity to consumers. Why? Probably because he values efficiency very highly! Thus, this reason supports the conclusion *if* a value assumption is made that conservation is more important than efficiency.

One important means of determining value assumptions, then, is to ask the question, "Why are the particular consequences or outcomes presented as reasons so desirable to the person?"

Remember: **When you identify *value assumptions*, you should always try to state *value priorities*.** With controversial topics, stating value assumptions in this way will be a continual reminder both of what the writer is *giving up* and of what she is gaining. Try to resist the temptation to stop your analysis prematurely by just identifying the values of the speaker or writer. Identifying those values is a step on the way to finding the value assumptions, but by itself it provides very little assistance in understanding an argument. Values, by their nature, are possessed by us all.

MORE HINTS FOR FINDING VALUE ASSUMPTIONS

Another useful technique for generating value conflicts is to *reverse role-play*. Ask the question, "What do those people who would take a different position from the writer's care about?" When someone argues that we should not use monkeys in experimental research, you should ask yourself, "If I wanted to defend the use of monkeys, what would I be concerned about?"

Finally, you can always check to see whether the disagreement results from a value conflict concerning the *rights of an individual* to behave in a particular fashion and the *welfare of the group* affected by the behavior in question. Many arguments rest implicitly on a stance with respect to this enduring value conflict. Like other common value conflicts, we can all recall numerous instances when our thinking required us to weigh these two important values and their effects.

For example, when we wonder about the use of metal detectors in the public schools, we often begin to construct our arguments in terms of thinking

---

Clues for Identifying Value Assumptions

1. Investigate the author's background.
2. Ask "Why do the consequences of the author's position seem so important to her?"
3. Search for similar social controversies to find analogous value assumptions.
4. Use reverse role-playing. Take a position opposite the author's position and identify which values are important to that opposite position.
5. Look for common value conflicts, such as individual responsibility versus community responsibility.

about the privacy rights of the individual students *and* the threats to the student body if a student were to bring a weapon to school. Then, we try to balance those values against other values: Does the individual's right to privacy deserve greater protection than the welfare of the other students in the school in this instance? What other issues involve this value conflict? What about the request of "skinheads" to parade through ethnic neighborhoods?

FINDING VALUE ASSUMPTIONS ON YOUR OWN

Let's work on an example together to help you become more comfortable with finding value assumptions.

> Different workplaces have different working environments. Some offer competitive wages, where performance is evaluated and compared with that of others and employees may or may not get a pay raise accordingly. Some places like to encourage an environment where everyone works together as a group. Pay raises in this environment are usually done by amount of education or experience. This type of workplace allows for workers to form good relationships and work together as a team. Which work environment would really have the best productivity? One where everyone was pitted against everyone else and productivity was the only basis for pay raises, or one where the environment fosters a team that works together to up the productivity?

The structure of the two positions is outlined here for you:

CONCLUSION: *The workplace should offer competitive wages.*

REASONS: *The only basis for salary increases is productivity—therefore, this type of workplace creates optimal incentives for hard work.*

CONCLUSION: *The workplace should offer a team environment.*

REASONS: *If the staff respects each other, they create an environment that can be healthy and effectively productive.*

Notice that the work environment where wages are based on individual productivity values competition. Those who organize that kind of environment believe that competition would create more productivity because it motivates the individual. Thus, they contend that a team environment would get in the way of the productivity of the competitive environment.

VALUE ASSUMPTION: *In this context, competition is valued over cooperation.*

On the other hand, those who think the team environment would be the most productive value cooperation. They believe that working together helps the group become motivated to be more productive, not just for themselves, but for the company (the team). They think that the group work would create a better working environment than one that offered competitive wages.

VALUE ASSUMPTION: *In this situation, cooperation is valued over competition.*

Therefore, the major value conflict is cooperation versus competition. A supporter of the competitive wage environment believes the value assumption that competition among coworkers over pay, rather than cooperation among them, will create the most productive environment. Her stance on this issue does not mean that she does not value cooperation; both values are probably very important to her. In the instance of the workplace, however, competition has taken over.

Remember that complete reasoning with respect to prescriptive issues requires reasons *and* value assumptions.

USING THIS CRITICAL QUESTION

Once you have found a value assumption, what do you do with it? First, recall the purpose of every critical question—to move you toward the evaluation of reasoning! Because you know that thoughtful people have different value assumptions, you have the right to wonder why any single value assumption is being made. Thus, as a critical thinker, you would want to point out the need for anyone making an argument to offer some explanation as to why you should accept the particular value assumption that is implicit in that argument.

VALUES AND RELATIVISM

We do not want to give the impression in this chapter that value preferences are like ice cream, such that when I choose blueberry cheesecake as my flavor, you have no basis for trying to persuade me that the lemon chiffon is a better choice. Ice cream is just a matter of personal preference—end of story!

However, the choice of value preferences requires reasoning. That reasoning, like any other, can be informed, thoughtful, and caring. But it can also be sloppy and self-absorbed. Hence, value preferences require some justification that critical thinkers can consider. A value preference requires supporting reasons just as does any other conclusion. Then each of us can study the reasoning to form our own reaction.

IDENTIFYING AND EVALUATING DESCRIPTIVE ASSUMPTIONS

When you find value assumptions, you know pretty well what a writer or speaker wants the world to be like—what goals she thinks are most important. But you do not know what she takes for granted about the nature of the world and the people who inhabit it. Are they basically lazy or achievement oriented, cooperative or competitive, rational or whimsical? Her visible reasoning depends on these ideas, as well as upon her values. Such unstated ideas are descriptive assumptions, and they too are essential hidden elements of an argument.

The following brief argument about a car depends on hidden assumptions. Can you find them?

> This car will get you to your destination, whatever it may be.
> I have driven this model of car on multiple occasions.

? *Critical Question:* **What are the descriptive assumptions?**

Descriptive assumptions are beliefs about the way the world is; prescriptive or value assumptions, you remember, are beliefs about how the world should be.

Illustrating Descriptive Assumptions

Let's examine our argument about the car to illustrate more clearly what we mean by a descriptive assumption.

The reasoning structure is:

CONCLUSION: *This particular car will get you where you want to go.*

REASONS: *This model of car has functioned well on multiple occasions.*

The reasoning thus far is incomplete. We know that, *by itself,* a reason just does not have the strength to support a conclusion; the reason must be connected to the conclusion by certain other (frequently unstated) ideas. These ideas, if true, justify treating the reason as support for the conclusion. Thus, whether a reason supports, or is relevant to, a conclusion depends on whether we can locate unstated ideas that logically connect the reason to the conclusion. When such unstated ideas are descriptive, we call them *descriptive assumptions.* Let us present two such assumptions for the above argument.

> ASSUMPTION 1: *From year to year a particular model of car has a consistent quality.*

First, no such statement was provided in the argument itself. However, if the reason is true and if this assumption is true, then the reason provides some support for the conclusion. But if not all model years have the same level of dependability (and we know they do not), then experience with a model in previous years cannot be a reliable guide to whether one should buy the car in the current model year. Note that this assumption is a statement about the way things are, not about the way things *should be.* Thus, it is a *descriptive connecting assumption.*

> ASSUMPTION 2: *The driving that would be done with the new car is the same kind of driving that was done by the person recommending the car.*

When we speak about "driving" a car, the ambiguity of driving can get us into trouble if we do not clarify the term. If the "driving" of the person recommending the car refers to regular trips to the grocery store on a quiet suburban street with no hills, that driving experience is not very relevant as a comparator when the new car is to be driven in Colorado, while pulling a heavy trailer. Thus, this conclusion is supported by the reason only if a certain definition of driving is assumed.

We can call this kind of descriptive assumption a *definitional assumption* because we have taken for granted one meaning of a term that could have more than one meaning. Thus, one important kind of descriptive assumption to look for is a *definitional assumption*—the taking for granted of one meaning for a term that has multiple possible meanings.

Once you have identified the connecting assumptions, you have answered the question, "On what basis can that conclusion be drawn from that reason?" The next natural step is to ask, "Is there any basis for accepting the assumptions?" If not, then, for you, the reason fails to provide support for the conclusion. If so, then the reason provides logical support for the conclusion. Thus, you can say reasoning is sound when you have identified connecting assumptions and you have good reason to believe those assumptions.

> **Attention:** *A descriptive assumption is an unstated belief about how the world was, is, or will become.*

When you identify assumptions, you identify ideas the communicator *needs* to take for granted so that the reason is supportive of the conclusion. Because writers and speakers frequently are not aware of their own assumptions, their conscious beliefs may be quite different from the ideas you identify as implicit assumptions. When you then make the hidden connecting tissue of an argument visible, you also contribute to their understanding of their own argument and may thereby guide them to better beliefs and decisions.

USING THIS CRITICAL QUESTION

After you have found descriptive assumptions, you want to think about whether there is a strong basis for accepting them. It is certainly fair for you to expect the person making the argument to provide you with some justification for why you should accept these particular assumptions. Finally, if the assumption is not supported and you find it questionable, you are behaving responsibly when you decide not to buy the argument. Your point in rejecting it is not to disagree with the conclusion. Instead, you are saying that you cannot accept the conclusion *based on the reasons offered so far*. In other words, you are quite willing to believe what you are being told, but as a critical thinker you are in the business of personal development. That development can take place only when you accept only those conclusions that have persuasive reasons.

CLUES FOR LOCATING DESCRIPTIVE ASSUMPTIONS

Your task in finding assumptions is to reconstruct the reasoning by filling in the missing links. You want to provide ideas that help the communicator's reasoning "make sense." Once you have a picture of the entire argument, both the visible and the invisible parts, you will be in a much better position to determine its strengths and weaknesses.

How does one go about finding these important missing links? It requires hard work, imagination, and creativity. Finding important assumptions is a difficult task.

Earlier in this chapter, we gave you several hints for finding value assumptions. Here are some clues that will make your search for descriptive assumptions successful.

Keep thinking about the gap between the conclusion and reasons.   Why are you looking for assumptions in the first place? You are looking because you want to be able to judge how well the reasons support the conclusions. Thus, look for what the writer or speaker would have had to take for granted to link the reasons and conclusion. Keep asking, "*How do you get from the reason to the conclusion?*" Ask, "*If the reason is true, what else must be true for the conclusion to follow?*" And, to help answer that question, you will find it very helpful to ask, "*Supposing the reason(s) were true, is there any way in which the conclusion nevertheless could be false?*"

Searching for the gap will be helpful for finding both value and descriptive assumptions.

Look for ideas that support reasons.   Sometimes a reason is presented with no explicit support; yet the plausibility of the reason depends on the acceptability of ideas that have been taken for granted. These ideas are descriptive assumptions. The following brief argument illustrates such a case:

> CONCLUSION: *All high-school English classes will go see at least one Shakespeare play.*
>
> REASONS: *It is beneficial to experience Shakespeare's works first hand.*

What ideas must be taken for granted for this reason to be acceptable? We must assume:

a. The performance will be well done and reflective of what Shakespeare would encourage, and

b. students will understand the play and be able to relate it to Shakespeare.

Both (a) and (b) are ideas that have to be taken for granted for the reason to be acceptable and, thus, supportive of the conclusion.

Identify with the writer or speaker.   Locating someone's assumptions is often made easier by imagining that you were asked to defend the conclusion. If you can, crawl into the skin of a person who would reach such a conclusion.

Discover his background. When an executive for a coal company argues that strip mining does not significantly harm the beauty of our natural environment, he has probably begun with a belief that strip mining is beneficial to our nation. Thus, he may assume a definition of beauty that would be consistent with his arguments, while other definitions of beauty would lead to a condemnation of strip mining.

Identify with the opposition.   If you are unable to locate assumptions by taking the role of the speaker or writer, try to reverse roles. Ask yourself why anyone might disagree with the conclusion. What type of reasoning would prompt someone to disagree with the conclusion you are evaluating? If you can play the role of a person who would not accept the conclusion, you can more readily see assumptions in the explicit structure of the argument.

Recognize the potential existence of other means of attaining the advantages referred to in the reasons.   Frequently, a conclusion is supported by reasons that indicate the various advantages of acting on the author's conclusion. When there are many ways to reach the same advantages, one important assumption linking the reasons to the conclusion is that the best way to attain the advantages is through the one advocated by the communicator.

Let's try this technique with one brief example. Experts disagree about how a person should establish financial stability. Many times young people are encouraged to establish credit with a credit card. But aren't there many ways to establish financial stability? Might not some of these alternatives have less serious disadvantages than those that could result when a young person spends too much on that credit card? For example, investing some money in a savings account or establishing credit by maintaining a checking account are viable routes to establishing financial stability. Thus, those who suggest that people get credit cards to help establish financial stability are not taking into account the risks involved with their solution or the possibility of fewer risks with an alternative.

Avoid stating incompletely established reasons as assumptions.   When you first attempt to locate assumptions you may find yourself locating a stated reason, thinking that the reason has not been adequately established, and asserting, "That's only an assumption. You don't know that to be the case." Or you might simply restate the reason as the assumption. You may have correctly identified a need on the part of the writer or speaker to better establish the truth of her reason. While this clarification is an important insight on your part, you have not identified an assumption in the sense that we have been using it in these two chapters. You are simply labeling a reason "an assumption."

Do you see that when you do this, all you are doing is stating that the author's reason is her assumption—when what you are probably really trying to stress is that the author's reason has not been sufficiently established by evidence?

AVOIDING ANALYSIS OF TRIVIAL ASSUMPTIONS

Writers and speakers take for granted, and should take for granted, certain self-evident things. You will want to devote your energy to evaluating important assumptions, so we want to warn you about some potential trivial assumptions. By trivial, we mean a descriptive assumption that is self-evident.

You as a reader or listener can assume that the communicator believes his reasons are true. You may want to attack the reasons as insufficient, but it is trivial to point out the writer's or speaker's assumption that the reasons are true.

Another type of trivial assumption concerns the reasoning structure. You may be tempted to state that the writer believes that the reason and conclusion are logically related. Right—but trivial. What is important is how they are logically related. It is also trivial to point out that an argument assumes that we can understand the logic, that we can understand the terminology, or that we have the appropriate background knowledge.

Avoid spending time on analyzing trivial assumptions. Your search for assumptions will be most rewarding when you locate hidden, debatable missing links.

ASSUMPTIONS AND YOUR OWN WRITING AND SPEAKING

When you attempt to communicate with an audience, either by writing or speaking, you will be making numerous assumptions. Communication requires them. But, once again out of respect for your audience, you should acknowledge those assumptions, and, where possible, provide a rationale for why you are making those particular assumptions.

The logic of this approach on your part is to assist the audience in accepting your argument. You are being open and fair with them. An audience should appreciate your willingness to present your argument in its fullness.

Clues for Discovering Descriptive Assumptions

1. Keep thinking about the gap between the conclusion and reasons.
2. Look for ideas that support reasons.
3. Identify with the opposition.
4. Recognize the potential existence of other means of attaining the advantages referred to in the reasons.
5. Learn more about the issues.

Practice Exercises

 Critical Question: ***What are the value and descriptive assumptions?***

For each of the three passages, locate important assumptions made by the author. Remember first to determine the conclusion and the reasons.

Passage 1

Sometimes it is not always best to be completely honest. Some conclusions are better left unsaid. For instance, if you are talking to a friend and he asks for your opinion about something, the truth should be avoided if there is no way to deliver it without harming the relationship.

The truth is not always necessary. If you were a doctor and you had to give your patient bad health news, then it is important to maintain honesty. However sometimes, in the case of friendship, the honesty may need some buffering.

Passage 2

Everyone should consider playing poker to win money. It has gained great popularity. You can see people play on television daily, and there are many opportunities to play against real people online. This trend is an exciting opportunity for people everywhere to try and win money. Poker is simple to learn after one understands the rules and concepts behind the game. It is a game that people of all ages and experience can play!

Passage 3

Adopted children should have the right to find out who their biological parents are. They should be able to find out for personal and health reasons. Most children would want to know what happened to these people and why they were given up for adoption. Even though this meeting may not be completely the way the child had imagined it, this interaction could provide a real sense of closure for adopted children. There are people who believe that it does not matter who the biological parents are as long as the child has loving parents. It is true that having a supportive environment is necessary for children, but there will always be nagging questions for these children that will be left unanswered if they are not able to find out their biological parents. There are also health risks that can be avoided by allowing a child to find out who their parents are. A lot of diseases have hereditary links that would be useful for the child and the new family to know.

Sample Responses To Passages 1 and 2

In presenting assumptions for the following arguments, we list only some of the assumptions being made—those which we believe are among the most significant.

Passage 1

CONCLUSION: *Lying to spare someone's feelings is appropriate in certain situations.*

REASONS: *Telling the truth could harm a friendship.*

One value conflict that relates to this argument is that between honesty and harmony. Of course, others would argue that honesty is the best foundation for the kind of friendship they seek. A value preference for harmony over honesty links the reason to the conclusion.

As with most prescriptive controversies, more than one value conflict is involved in this dilemma. For example, this controversy also requires us to think about comfort over courage.

Passage 2

CONCLUSION: *Everyone should play poker to win money.*

REASONS: 1. *It is a popular game.*
2. *People of all ages and experience can play.*

In looking at the first reason, there is a missing link between that reason and the conclusion. The author omits two main assumptions. One, poker is enjoyable because many people play this game. And second, that "enjoyable" means profitable. The author needs these two assumptions for him to make the jump to the idea that we should all join the poker craze.

The second reason should leave the reader wondering whether it makes sense to assume that because something can happen, it should happen. Yes, we can all certainly play poker; we can also all start forest fires, but our capacity to do so is not exactly an endorsement of the activity.

Passage 4. Expanding Practice and Feedback

Read the following long blog while applying the critical thinking questions that you have thus far learned, and focusing on the question, What are the value and descriptive assumptions? Then attend to our step-by-step walkthrough evaluation and compare your thoughts to ours.

Should We Legalize Marijuana?

religionnewsblog.blogspot.com (2007)

I have met many intellectual-types who smoke pot, and they are often keen to justify their habit. They love to point out that no one has ever overdosed on pot and that they would rather be in a room full of high people than a room full of drunk people. Whether those claims are true or not, pot is hardly harmless. Two recent studies of note are pin-pointing pot's role in causing a great deal of harm to our brains, not only to our memory and thinking ability, but also to our very sanity. I hope these studies will shut up those idiot potheads who keep repeating the lie that marijuana doesn't cause any harm. Please pass this along to anyone you know who might be on the fence about this, or anyone who has children, who need to know how dangerous pot can be when the brain is forming.

Most fascinating to me is the fact noted in one of the studies that the schizophrenics did not realize how negatively and severely the drug was affecting their brain, and they usually kept using it, for some reason thinking it helped them. I have seen this effect on friends and family members who smoke pot. They become increasingly withdrawn, more quiet, more private, more awkward, less able to communicate with anyone outside of their little circle of drug users. Much like other drugs, it creates a dependency cycle, because continued usage unbalances their sober mind, leading them to use the drug more, which then further harms their mind, and on and on in a vicious cycle. Like we have long suspected, pot is now proven to fry the memory and reduce the ability to learn as well.

Should pot be legalized? I have a strong libertarian streak in me, so I am sympathetic to the pro-legalization arguments. The main advantage I see would be in the reduction of government power, especially the federal government's, which mushroomed under the War on Drugs. However, my studies of religion and culture have forced me to conclude that libertarianism doesn't work on the cultural level.

The main problem with libertarian cultural ideals is the fact that we are all in this together, we are bound in a community. The line between the personal and the social is extremely fuzzy, if it exists at all. Everything you do, even just to yourself, will end up affecting the community. Individual choices are magnified into communal benefit or burden through countless avenues, such as insurance pools, socialized medicine, law enforcement, and public works of all kinds. For example, say you commit suicide. You are hurting others by the cost you impose upon them to clean up the death scene, to dispose of your body, to do the official investigation of your demise, to conclude the legal status of your belongings, and so on. And those are just the direct and easily quantifiable costs. What about the emotional devastation on those who are close to you or to traumatized strangers who saw it happen or heard about it? What about the hidden opportunity costs of your untimely death? You might have done great things if you had lived. You would have helped others working at your job and contributing taxes, at the least.

Overall, your presence strengthens society. Unless, of course, you are a burden on society because you are chronically ill, not working, or living as a criminal. What is the one best predictor of whether you will be chronically ill, not working, or living as a criminal? No surprise here: drug use! Laws against drug use are rational and justifiable attempts to prevent people from becoming burdens on society. The libertarian solution to drug use would only work in an imaginary society where there was no social contract, no welfare system, and no external enemies. In the real world, we depend on each other, we care for one another, and communal strength is an important aspect of survival.

In short, what you do affects me, and therefore we all have the obligation to look out for one another, and the right to influence each other's actions. Definitely, anti-drug laws should be kept light-handed, lest the governmental cure become worse than the cultural disease, the cure leading to a disease in its own right, which, as with all government powers, is an ever-present danger. However, we know conclusively that marijuana is not harmless, and pot-heads should stop proclaiming it so.

The studies referenced in the article can be found at:

http://www.livescience.com/humanbiology/070501_ap_pot_ bad.html and http://www.livescience.com/humanbiology/060313_ pot_brain.html

Step-by-Step Walkthrough

Were you able to find some assumptions in the article? Below is a step-by-step walkthrough of how to search for value and descriptive assumptions in arguments. You can use hints from the model on your next search for assumptions. Remember, the best way to strengthen your critical thinking skills is to practice.

- Before I can find the hidden assumptions in the article, I need to first identify the conclusion and the reasons. I'm interested only in assumptions affecting the quality of the structure of the argument. I want to look for assumptions needed for the reasons to support the conclusions and look for ones necessary for a reason to be true.

- The conclusion in this article is that the United States should not legalize marijuana use. The author supported the conclusion with two main reasons: (1) Marijuana harms our brains, memory, and thinking ability. and users are not aware of the harmful effect. The evidence for this concern includes a study of schizophrenics as well as the author's personal experience. (2) Marijuana use would be a burden on society and harm the overall community.

- At first glance, it appears that the reasons support the conclusion. However, it is possible the reasons given can be true and not necessarily support the conclusion. Upon further consideration, it appears the reasoning is only convincing if I agree with certain unstated ideas the writer takes for granted. I'll start by identifying possible value assumptions that could affect the reasoning of the author by looking for clues about what the author seems to care strongly.

- It's important for me to remember value assumptions mean the preference of one value over another. I'll look back over the reasoning in the article and find situations in the text where it appears the author prefers one value over another. I'll start with common value preferences found in many arguments. For example, the third through fifth paragraphs in the article demonstrate the conflict between individual rights and collective responsibility. In this case, the author values the collective safety of the community through reliance on lawmakers over the personal freedom of smoking marijuana.

- When looking for value assumptions, I also want to consider consequences as clues to finding the assumptions. An apparent consequence of marijuana usage involves the author's first reason: marijuana is damaging to the human brain, and therefore undesirable. Within this reasoning, I can guess the author values health very highly. Asking the Right Questions suggest I reverserole-play to determine value conflicts. In this case, someone with the opposite belief of the writer might value the pursuit of fun, pleasure, or relaxation over health.

- Now I've identified some of the possible value assumptions in the article, but my evaluation does not stop there. I have to take the value assumptions a step further and remember that different thoughtful people often have different value assumptions. If someone with different value assumptions read the article, it

would not necessarily follow that the reasons support the author's conclusion to keep marijuana use illegal. To effectively
reason in his argument, the author should have offered some
sort of explanation for why readers should accept the value assumptions he makes. I do note that he provides some support
for his value preference of collective responsibility over individual responsibility in his discussion in paragraphs 3 through 5, in
which he reflects on some of the pros and cons of a libertarian
philosophy.

• After identifying value assumptions, I can now move on to
unearthing any descriptive assumptions in the article and
remember that descriptive assumptions (just like value assumptions) should be assumptions that directly affect the reasons and
conclusion in the article.

• After focusing on the likely truth of the reasons and the credibility of their link to the conclusions, I am able to identify descriptive assumptions the author makes. If these assumptions are not
true, then the author's conclusion does not necessarily follow
from the reasons. For example, the author believes marijuana
should be illegal because it causes harm to people's sanity.
However, he assumes that marijuana adversely affects almost
everyone's sanity, and not just a select few. If marijuana affects
the sanity of only a select group of people, then by the author's
reasoning it follows that marijuana use should only be illegal for
that group of people. If indeed marijuana does cause serious
harm to only a small segment of users, then it need not be illegal for everyone.

• Also, in making the claim that marijuana causes harm. The
author takes for granted that the evidence he cites to make this
claim is reliable generalizable evidence. It is possible that the
research support is not well conducted or not representative of
the body of research done on effects of marijuana.

• After finding the descriptive assumptions and understanding the
opposite assumptions other knowledgeable people may hold
about the issue, I want to think about whether there is a strong
basis for accepting the assumptions. It is clear to me the author
has provided little justification of why the readers should believe
the assumptions he makes. I find many of the descriptive assumptions in the article to be wholly unsupported and questionable; therefore I have difficulty believing the conclusion follows
from the reasons the author provides. I am not disagreeing with
the conclusion, but rather saying I desire stronger reasons for the
conclusion.

These are some of the questions and methods you should consider when evaluating the value and descriptive assumptions in an

article. When you read the article, did you engage in the similar methods to discover the assumptions before reading the step-by-step guide? Did you find additional assumptions not discussed here? If so, you are well on your way to becoming a critical thinker!

CRITICAL QUESTION SUMMARY: WHY THIS QUESTION IS IMPORTANT

What Are the Value and Descriptive Assumptions?

When you identify assumptions, you are identifying the link between a reason and the author's conclusion. If this link is flawed, the reason does not necessarily lead to the conclusion. Consequently, identifying the assumptions allows you to determine whether an author's reasons lead successfully to a conclusion. You will want to accept a conclusion only when there are good reasons that lead to the conclusion. Thus, when you determine that the link between the reasons and conclusion is flawed, you should be reluctant to accept the author's conclusion.

CHAPTER 7

Are There Any Fallacies in the Reasoning?

Thus far, you have been working at taking the raw materials a writer or speaker gives you and assembling them into a meaningful overall structure. You have learned ways to remove the irrelevant parts from your pan as well as how to discover the "invisible glue" that holds the relevant parts together—that is, the assumptions. All these things have been achieved by asking critical questions. Let's briefly review these questions:

1. What are the issue and the conclusion?
2. What are the reasons?
3. What words or phrases are ambiguous?
4. What are the value and descriptive assumptions?

Asking these questions should give you a clear understanding of the communicator's reasoning as well as a sense of where there might be strengths and weaknesses in the argument. Most remaining chapters focus on how well the structure holds up after being assembled. Your major question now is, "How acceptable is the conclusion in light of the reasons provided?" You are now ready to make your central focus *evaluation. Remember:* **The objective of critical reading and listening is to judge the acceptability or worth of conclusions.**

Although answering our first four questions has been a necessary beginning to the evaluation process, we now move to questions requiring us to make judgments more directly and explicitly about the worth or the quality of the reasoning. Our task now is to separate the "Fools Gold" from the genuine gold. We want to isolate the best reasons—those that we want to treat most seriously.

Your first step at this stage of the evaluation process is to examine the reasoning structure, to determine whether the communicator's reasoning has depended on false or highly doubtful assumptions or has "tricked" you through either a mistake in logic or other forms of deceptive reasoning.

Chapter 6 focused on finding and then thinking about the quality of assumptions. This chapter, on the other hand, highlights those reasoning "tricks" called *fallacies*.

Three common tricks are:

1. providing reasoning that requires *erroneous or incorrect assumptions*;
2. *distracting us* by making information seem relevant to the conclusion when it is not; and
3. providing support for the conclusion that depends on the conclusion's already being true.

Spotting such tricks will prevent us from being unduly influenced by them. Let's see what a fallacy in reasoning looks like.

> Dear editor: I was shocked by your paper's support of Senator Spendall's arguments for a tax hike to increase state money available for improving highways. Of course the Senator favors such a hike. What else would you expect from a tax and spend liberal.

Note that the letter at first appears to be presenting a "reason" to dispute the tax-hike proposal, by citing the senator's liberal reputation. But the reason is *not relevant* to the conclusion. The question is whether the tax hike is a good idea. The letter writer has ignored the senator's reasons and has provided no specific reasons against the tax hike; instead, she has personally attacked the senator by labeling him a "tax and spend liberal." The writer has committed a fallacy in reasoning, because her argument requires an absurd assumption to be relevant to the conclusion and shifts attention from the argument to the arguer—Senator Spendall. An unsuspecting reader not alert to this fallacy may be tricked into thinking that the writer has provided a persuasive reason.

This chapter gives you practice in identifying such fallacies so that you will not fall for such tricks.

 *Critical Question: **Are there any fallacies in the reasoning?***

Attention: A fallacy is a reasoning "trick" that an author might use while trying to persuade you to accept a conclusion.

A QUESTIONING APPROACH TO FINDING REASONING FALLACIES

There are numerous reasoning fallacies. And they can be organized in many different ways. Many are so common that they have been given formal names. You can find many lengthy lists of fallacies in numerous texts and Web sites. Fortunately, you don't need to be aware of all the fallacies and their names to be able to locate them. If you ask yourself the right questions, you will be able to find reasoning fallacies—even if you can't name them.

Therefore, we have adopted the strategy of emphasizing self-questioning strategies rather than asking you to memorize an extensive list of possible kinds of fallacies. We believe, however, that knowing the names of the most common fallacies can sensitize you to fallacies and also act as a language "short cut" in communicating your reaction to faulty reasoning to others familiar with the names. Thus, we provide you with the names of fallacies as we identify the deceptive reasoning processes and encourage you to learn the names of the common fallacies described on page 98 at the end of the chapter.

We have already introduced one common fallacy to you in our Dear Editor example above. We noted that the writer personally attacked Senator Spendall instead of responding directly to the senator's reasons. The Dear Editor reasoning illustrates the Ad Hominem fallacy. The Latin phrase *ad hominem* means "against the man or against the person." Arguing ad hominem is a fallacy because the character or interests of individuals making arguments usually are not relevant to the quality of the argument being made. It is attacking the messenger instead of addressing the message.

Here is another brief example of ad hominem reasoning.

Sandy: "I believe that joining sororities is a waste of time and money."

Julie: "Of course you would say that, you didn't get accepted by any sorority."

Sandy: "But what about the arguments I gave to support my position?"

Julie: "Those don't count. You're just a sore loser."

You can start your list of fallacy names with this one. Here is the definition:

F: Ad Hominem: An attack, or an insult, on the person rather than directly addressing the person's reasons.

EVALUATING ASSUMPTIONS AS A STARTING POINT

If you have been able to locate assumptions (see Chapter 6)—especially descriptive assumptions—you already possess a major skill in determining questionable assumptions and in finding fallacies. The more questionable the assumption is, the less relevant the reasoning will be. Some "reasons," such as ad hominem arguments, will be so irrelevant to the conclusion that you would have to supply blatantly erroneous assumptions to provide a logical link. Such reasoning is a fallacy, and you should immediately reject it.

In the next section, we take you through some exercises in discovering other common fallacies. Once you know how to look, you will be able to find most fallacies. We suggest that you adopt the following thinking steps in locating fallacies:

1. Identify the conclusions and reasons.
2. Always keep the conclusion in mind and consider reasons that you think might be relevant to it; contrast these reasons with the author's reasons.
3. If the conclusion supports an action, determine whether the reason states a specific and/or concrete advantage or a disadvantage; if not, be wary!
4. Identify any necessary assumption by asking yourself, "If the reason were true, what would a person have to believe for it to logically support the conclusion, and what does one have to believe for the reason to be true?"
5. Ask yourself, "Do these assumptions make sense?" If an obviously false assumption is being made, you have found a fallacy in reasoning, and that reasoning can then be rejected.
6. Check the possibility of being distracted from relevant reasons by phrases that strongly appeal to your emotions.

To demonstrate the process you should go through to evaluate assumptions and thus recognize many fallacies, we will examine the quality of the reasoning in the following passage. We will begin by assembling the structure.

> The question involved in this legislation is not really a question of whether alcohol consumption is or is not detrimental to health. Rather, it is a question of whether Congress is willing to have the Federal Communications Commission make an arbitrary decision that prohibits alcohol advertising on radio and television. If we should permit the FCC to take this action in regard to alcohol, what is there to prevent it from deciding next year that candy is detrimental to the public health in that it causes obesity, tooth decay, and other health problems? What about milk and eggs? Milk and eggs are high in saturated animal fat and no doubt increase the cholesterol in the bloodstream, believed by many heart specialists to be a contributing factor in heart disease. Do we want the FCC to be able to prohibit the advertising of milk, eggs, butter, and ice cream on TV?
>
> Also, we all know that no action by the federal government, however drastic, can or will be effective in eliminating alcohol consumption completely. If people want to drink alcoholic beverages, they will find some way to do so.
>
> CONCLUSION: *The FCC should not prohibit alcohol advertising on radio and television.*
>
> REASONS: 1. *If we permit the FCC to prohibit advertising on radio and television, the FCC will soon prohibit many kinds of advertising, because many products present potential health hazards.*
>
> 2. *No action by the federal government can or will be effective in eliminating alcohol consumption completely.*

First, we should note that both reasons refer to rather specific disadvantages of the prohibition—a good start. The acceptability of the first reason, however, depends on a hidden descriptive assumption that once we allow actions to be taken on the merits of one case, it will be impossible to stop actions on similar cases. We do not agree with this assumption, because we believe that there are plenty of steps in our legal system to prevent such actions if they appear unjustified. Thus, we judge this reason to be unacceptable. Such reasoning is an example of the *Slippery Slope Fallacy*.

F: Slippery Slope: Making the assumption that a proposed step will set off an uncontrollable chain of undesirable events when procedures exist to prevent such a chain of events.

The relevance of the second reason is questionable because even if this reason were true, the assumption linking the reason to the conclusion—the major goal of prohibiting alcohol advertising on radio and television is to *eliminate alcohol consumption completely*—is false. A more likely goal is to *reduce consumption*. Thus we reject this reason. We call this fallacy the *Searching For Perfect Solution Fallacy*. It takes the form: A solution to X does not deserve our support unless it destroys the problem entirely. If we ever find a perfect solution, then we should adopt it. But because the fact that part of a problem would remain after a solution is tried does not mean the solution is unwise. A particular solution may be vastly superior to no solution at all. It may move us closer to solving the problem completely.

If we waited for perfect solutions to emerge, we would often find ourselves paralyzed—unable to act. Here is another example of this fallacy: It's a waste of money to add a security system to your home. If a thief wants to break into your house, they will find a way to do so, regardless of any security system.

F: Searching for Perfect Solution: Falsely assuming that because part of a problem would remain after a solution is tried, the solution should not be adopted.

DISCOVERING OTHER COMMON REASONING FALLACIES

We are now going to take you through some exercises in discovering more common fallacies. As you encounter each exercise, try to apply the fallacy-finding hints that we listed above. Once you have developed good fallacy-detection habits, you will be able to find most fallacies. Each exercise presents some reasoning that includes fallacies. We indicate why we believe the reasoning is fallacious and then name and define the fallacy.

Exercise A

It's about time that we make marijuana an option for people in chronic severe pain. We approve drugs when society reaches a consensus about their value, and there is clearly now a consensus for such approval. A recent survey of public opinion reported that 73 percent thought medical marijuana should be allowed. In addition, the California Association for the Treatment of AIDS Victims supports smoking marijuana as a treatment option for AIDS patients.

As a first step in analyzing for fallacies, let's outline the argument.

CONCLUSION: *Smoking marijuana should be a medical option.*

REASONS: 1. *We approve drugs when a consensus of their medical value has been reached, and a recent survey shows a consensus approving marijuana as a medical treatment.*

2. *A California association supports medical marijuana use.*

First, we should note that none of the reasons points out a specific advantage of medical marijuana; thus we should be wary from the start. Next, a close look at the wording in the first reason shows a shift in meaning of a key term, and this shift tricks us. The meaning of the word consensus shifts in such a way that it looks like she has made a relevant argument when she has not. Consensus for drug approval usually means the consensus of scientific researchers about its merits, which is a very different consensus than the agreement of the American public on an opinion poll. Thus the reason fails to make sense, and we should reject it. We call this mistake in reasoning the *Equivocation Fallacy.* Whenever you see a key word in an argument used more than once, check to see that the meaning has not changed; if it has, be alert to the equivocation fallacy. Highly ambiguous terms or phrases are especially good candidates for the equivocation fallacy.

See whether you can detect the equivocation in the following example:

Ronda: Curtis is not a real man. He looked scared to death when that drunk at the bar threatened to punch him.

Ellen: If he's not a real man, how do you account for those incredibly bulging biceps?

F: Equivocation: A key word is used with two or more meanings in an argument such that the argument fails to make sense once the shifts in meaning are recognized.

Well, even if there is tricky use of the word "consensus," don't the survey results by themselves still support the conclusion? They do *only if* we accept the assumption that when something is popular; then it must be good—a mistaken assumption. The public often has not sufficiently studied a problem to provide a reasoned judgment. Be wary of appeals to common opinion or to popular sentiment. We label this mistake in reasoning the *Appeal to Popularity Fallacy*.

F: Appeal to Popularity (Ad Populum):   An attempt to justify a claim by appealing to sentiments that large groups of people have in common; falsely assumes that anything favored by a large group is desirable.

Now, carefully examine the author's second reason. What assumption is being made? To prove that medical marijuana is desirable, she *appeals to questionable authorities*—a California Association. A position is not good just because the authorities are for it. What is important in determining the relevance of such reasoning is the evidence that the authorities are using in making their judgment. Unless we know that these authorities have special knowledge about this issue, we must treat this reason as a fallacy. Such a fallacy is called the *Appeal to Questionable Authority fallacy*.

F: Appeal to Questionable Authority: Supporting a conclusion by citing an authority who lacks special expertise on the issue at hand.

Now let's examine some arguments related to another controversy: Should Congress approve a federally funded child-development program that would provide day-care centers for children?

Exercise B

I am against the government's child-development program. First, I am interested in *protecting the children* of this country. They need to be protected from social planners and *self-righteous ideologues* who would disrupt the normal course of life and *tear them from their mothers and families* to make them *pawns* in a universal scheme designed to produce infinite happiness in 20 years. Children should grow up with their mothers, not with a series of caretakers and nurses' aides. What is at issue is whether parents shall continue to have the right to form the characters of their children or whether the State with all its power should be given the tools and techniques for forming the young.

Let's again begin by outlining the argument.

CONCLUSION: *The government's child development program is a mistake.*

REASONS: 1. *Our children need to be protected from social planners and self-righteous ideologues, who would disrupt the normal course of life and tear them from their families.*

2. *The parents, not the State, should have the right to form the characters of their children.*

As critical readers and listeners, we should be looking for specific facts about the program. Do you find any specifics in the first reason? No. The reason is saturated with undefined and emotionally loaded generalities. We have italicized several of these terms in the passage. Such terms will typically generate negative emotions, which the writer or speaker hopes readers and listeners will associate with the position he is attacking.

The writer is playing two common tricks on us. First, she is *appealing to our emotions* with her choice of words, hoping that our emotional reactions will get us to agree with her conclusion. When communicators try to draw emotional reactions from people and then use that reaction to get them to agree to their conclusion, they commit the fallacy of an *Appeal to Emotion*. This fallacy occurs when your emotional reactions should not be relevant to the truth or falsity of a conclusion. Three of the most common places for finding this fallacy are in advertising, in political debate, and in the courtroom. A common form of this fallacy is *name calling*, which is an attempt to discredit individuals by labeling them with words that have unfavorable emotional associations. The phrase "self-righteous ideologues" illustrates name calling.

Second, she has set up a position to attack which in fact does not exist, making it much easier to get us on her side. She has extended the opposition's position to an "easy-to-attack" position. The false assumption in this case is that the position attacked is the same as the position actually presented in the legislation. Will children really be pawns in some universal scheme? The lesson for the critical thinker is: When someone attacks aspects of a position, always check to see whether she is fairly representing the position. If she is not, you have located the *Straw-Person Fallacy*.

A straw person is not real and is easy to knock down—as is the position attacked when someone commits the straw-person fallacy. The best way to check how fairly a position is being represented is to get the facts about all positions.

F: Appeals to Emotions: The use of emotionally charged language to distract readers and listeners from relevant reasons and evidence. Common emotions appealed to are fear, hope, patriotism, pity, and sympathy.

F: Straw Person: Distorting our opponent's point of view so that it is easy to attack; thus we attack a point of view that does not truly exist.

Let's now look closely at the second reason. The writer states that either parents have the right to form the characters of their children, or else the State should be given the decisive tools. For statements like this to be true, one must assume that there are only two choices. Are there? No! The writer has created a *false dilemma*. Isn't it possible for the child-development program to exist and also for the family to have a significant influence on the child? Always be cautious when controversies are treated as if only two choices are possible; there are usually more than two. When a communicator oversimplifies an issue by stating only two choices, the error is referred to as an *Either-Or* or *False Dilemma* fallacy. To find *either-or* fallacies, be on the alert for phrases like the following:

either . . . or

the only alternative is

the two choices are

because A has not worked, only B will.

Seeing these phrases does not necessarily mean that you have located a fallacy. Sometimes there *are* only two options. These phrases are just caution signs causing you to pause and wonder: "But are there more than two options in this case?"

Can you see the false dilemma in the following interchange?

Citizen: I think that the decision by the United States to invade Iraq was a big mistake.

Politician: Why do you hate America?

F: Either-Or (or False Dilemma):   Assuming only two alternatives when there are more than two.

The following argument contains another fallacy involving a mistaken assumption. Try to locate the assumption.

Exercise C

Student: It doesn't make sense for you to give pop quizzes to your class, Professor Jones. It just makes a lot of extra work for you and makes the students nervous. Students should not need pop quizzes to motivate them to prepare for each class.

The advice to Professor Jones requires a faulty assumption to support the conclusion. That something *should* be true—students should not need pop quizzes to motivate them to prepare for class—in no way guarantees that what *is* true will conform to the prescription. Reality, or "what is," is often in conflict with "what should be."

Another common illustration of this reasoning error occurs when discussing proposals for government regulation. For instance, someone might argue that regulating advertising for children's television programs is undesirable because parents *should* turn the channel or shut off the television if advertising is deceptive. Perhaps parents in a perfect world would behave in this fashion. Many parents, however, are too busy to monitor children's programming.

When reasoning requires us to assume incorrectly that what we think *should be* matches *what is*, or *what will be*, it commits the *Wishful Thinking fallacy*. We would hope that what *should* be the case would guide our behavior. Yet many observations convince us that just because advertisers, politicians, and authors should not mislead us is no protection against their regularly doing so. The world around us is a poor imitation of what the world should be like.

Here's a final example of wishful thinking that might sound familiar to you.

> I can't wait for summer vacation time, so I can get all those books read that I've put off reading during the school year.

F: Wishful Thinking: Making the faulty assumption that because we wish X were true or false, then X is indeed true or false.

Another confusion is responsible for an error in reasoning that we often encounter when seeking explanations for behavior. A brief conversation between college roommates illustrates the confusion.

> Dan: I've noticed that Chuck has been acting really weird lately. He's acting really rude toward others and is making all kinds of messes in our residence hall and refusing to clean them up. What do you think is going on?
>
> Kevin: That doesn't surprise me. He is just a jerk.

To *explain* requires an analysis of why a behavior occurred. Explaining is demanding work that often tests the boundaries of what we know. In the above example, "jerkhood" is an unsatisfactory explanation of Chuck's behavior. When asked to explain why a certain behavior has occurred, it is frequently tempting to hide our ignorance of a complex sequence of causes by labeling or naming the behavior. Then we falsely assume that because we know the name, we know the cause.

We do so because the naming tricks us into believing we have identified something the person *has* or *is* that makes her act accordingly. For example, instead of specifying the complex set of internal and external factors that lead a person to manifest an angry emotion, such as problems with relationships, parental reinforcement practices, feelings of helplessness, lack of sleep, and life stressors, we say the person *has* a "bad temper" or that the person *is* hostile. Such explanations oversimplify and prevent us from seeking more insightful understanding.

The following examples should heighten your alertness to this fallacy:

(1) In response to Dad's heavy drinking, Mom is asked by her adult daughter, "Why is Dad behaving so strangely?" Mom replies, "He's *having* a midlife crisis."

(2) A patient cries every time the counselor asks about his childhood. An intern who watched the counseling session asks the counselor, after the patient has left, "Why does he cry when you ask about his youth?" The counselor replies, "He's neurotic."

Neither respondent satisfactorily explained what happened. For instance, the specifics of dad's genes, job pressures, marital strife, and exercise habits could have provided the basis for explaining the heavy drinking. "A midlife crisis" is not only inadequate; it misleads. We think we know why dad is drinking heavily, but we don't.

A common example of the fallacy of *explaining by naming* is arguing that individuals commit violent acts because they are evil. But this naming prevents us from recognizing common causes of violent acts. Much research on violence demonstrates that people rarely hurt others for the sheer joy of hurting someone. Instead, something else, such as a major threat to inflated self-esteem or a belief that they are fighting for their God, may be stimulating the violent behavior.

Be alert for the fallacy of explaining by naming when people claim that they have discovered a cause for the behavior when all they have actually done is named it.

F: Explaining by Naming: Falsely assuming that because you have provided a name for some event or behavior you have also adequately explained the event.

LOOKING FOR DIVERSIONS

Frequently, those trying to get an audience to accept some claim find that they can defend that claim by preventing the audience from taking too close a look at the relevant reasons. They prevent the close look by diversion tactics. As you look for fallacies, you will find it helpful to be especially alert to reasoning used by the communicator that *diverts your attention* from the most relevant reasons. For example, the Ad Hominem fallacy can fool us by diverting our attention too much to the nature of the person and too little to the legitimate reasons. In this section, we present exercises that illustrate other fallacies that we are likely to detect if we ask the question, "Has the author tricked us by diverting our attention?"

Exercise D

Political speech: In the upcoming election, you have the opportunity to vote for a woman who represents the future of this great nation, who has fought for democracy and defended our flag, and who has been decisive, confident, and courageous in pursuing the American Dream. This is a caring woman who has supported our children and the environment and has helped move this country toward peace, prosperity, and freedom. A vote for Goodheart is a vote for truth, vision, and common sense.

Sounds like Ms. Goodheart is a wonderful person, doesn't it? But the speech fails to provide any specifics about the senator's past record or present position on issues. Instead, it presents a series of *virtue words* that tend to be associated with deep-seated positive emotions. We call these virtue words "*Glittering Generalities*," because they have such positive associations and are so general as to mean whatever the reader wants them to mean. The glittering generality device leads us to approve or accept a conclusion without examining relevant reasons, evidence, or specific advantages or disadvantages. Expressing a glittering generality is much like name-calling in reverse because name-calling seeks to make us form a negative judgment without examining the evidence. The use of virtue words is a popular ploy of politicians because it serves to distract the reader or listener from the specifics of actions or policies, which can more easily trigger disagreement.

F: Glittering Generality: The use of vague, emotionally appealing virtue words that dispose us to approve something without closely examining the reasons.

Let's examine another very common diversionary device.

Exercise E

I don't understand why everyone is so upset about drug companies distorting research data in order to make their pain-killer drugs seem to be less dangerous to people's health than they actually are. Taking those drugs can't be that bad. After all, there are still thousands of people using these drugs and getting pain relief from them.

What is the real issue? Is the public being misled about the safety of pain-killer drugs? But if the reader is not careful, his attention will be diverted to the issue of whether the public wants to use these drugs. When a writer or speaker shifts our attention from the issue, we can say that she has drawn a *red herring* across the trail of the original issue. Many of us are adept at committing the Red Herring Fallacy, as the drawing on the next page illustrates.

If the daughter is successful, the issue will become whether the mother is picking on her daughter, not why the daughter was out late.

You should normally have no difficulty spotting red herrings as long as you keep the real issue in mind as well as the kind of evidence needed to resolve it.

F: Red Herring: An irrelevant topic is presented to divert attention from the original issue and help to "win" an argument by shifting attention away from the argument and to another issue. The fallacy sequence in this instance is as follows: (a) Topic A is being discussed; (b) Topic B is introduced as though it is relevant to topic A, but it is not; and (c) Topic A is abandoned.

This sort of "reasoning" is fallacious because merely changing the topic of discussion hardly counts as an argument against a claim.

SLEIGHT OF HAND: BEGGING THE QUESTION

Our last illustrated fallacy is a particularly deceptive one. Sometimes a conclusion is supported by itself; only the words have been changed to fool the innocent! For example, to argue that dropping out of school is *undesirable* because it is *bad* is to argue not at all. The conclusion is "proven" by the conclusion (in different words). Such an argument *begs the question* rather than answering it. Let's look at an example that is a little less obvious.

> Programmed learning texts are clearly superior to traditional texts in learning effectiveness because it is highly advantageous for learning to have materials presented in a step-by-step fashion.

Again, the reason supporting the conclusion restates the conclusion in different words. By definition, programmed learning is a step-by-step procedure. The writer is arguing that such a procedure is good because it is good. A legitimate reason would be one that points out a specific advantage to programmed learning such as greater retention of learned material.

Whenever a conclusion is *assumed* in the reasoning when it should have been proven, begging the question has occurred. When you outline the structure of an argument, check the reasons to be sure that they do not simply repeat the conclusion in different words and check to see that the conclusion is not used to prove the reasons. In case you are confused, let's illustrate with two examples, one argument that begs the question and one that does not.

> (1) To allow the press to keep their sources confidential is very advantageous to the country because it increases the likelihood that individuals will report evidence against powerful people.

> (2) To allow the press to keep their sources confidential is very advantageous to the country because it is highly conducive to the interests of the larger community that private individuals should have the privilege of providing information to the press without being identified.

Paragraph (2) begs the question by basically repeating the conclusion. It fails to point out what the specific advantages are and simply repeats that confidentiality of sources is socially useful.

F: Begging the Question: An argument in which the conclusion is assumed in the reasoning.

USING THIS CRITICAL QUESTION

When you spot a fallacy, you have found a legitimate basis for rejecting the argument. But in the spirit of constructive critical thinking, you want to continue the discussion of the issue. Unfortunately, the author of a book or article is unavailable for more conversation. But in those instances where the fallacy occurred in an oral argument, your best bet for an enduring conversation is to ask the person who committed the fallacy if there is not a better reason for the conclusion. For example, if a red herring fallacy occurs, ask the speaker if it would be possible to return to the original issue.

SUMMARY OF REASONING ERRORS

We have taken you through exercises that illustrate a number of ways in which reasoning may be faulty. We have not listed all the ways, but we have given you a good start. We have saved some additional fallacies for later chapters because you are most likely to spot them when you focus on the particular question central to that chapter. As you encounter each additional fallacy, be sure to add it to your fallacy list.

To find reasoning fallacies, keep in mind what kinds of reasons are good reasons—that is, the evidence and the moral principles relevant to the issue.

Clues for Locating and Assessing Fallacies in Reasoning

You should reject reasoning when the author:

- attacks a person or a person's background, instead of the person's ideas
- uses slippery slope reasoning
- reflects a search for perfect solutions
- equivocates
- inappropriately appeals to common opinion
- appeals to questionable authority
- appeals to emotions
- attacks a straw person
- presents a faulty dilemma
- engages in wishful thinking
- explains by naming
- diverts attention from the issue
- distracts with glittering generalities
- begs the question

Reasoning should be *rejected* whenever you have found mistaken assumptions, distractions, or support for the conclusion that already assumes the truth of the conclusion. Reasoning should be *approached cautiously* when it appeals to group-approved attitudes and to authority. You should always ask, "Are there good reasons to consider such appeals as persuasive evidence?" A precautionary note is in order here: Do not automatically reject reasoning that relies on appeals to authority or group-approved attitudes. Carefully evaluate such reasoning. For example, if most physicians in the country choose to take up jogging, that information is important to consider in deciding whether jogging is beneficial. Some authorities do possess valuable information. Because of their importance as a source of evidence, we discuss appeals to authority in detail in the next chapter.

EXPANDING YOUR KNOWLEDGE OF FALLACIES

We recommend that you consult texts and some Web sites to expand your awareness and understanding of reasoning fallacies. Damer's *Attacking Faulty Reasoning* is a good source to help you become more familiar with reasoning fallacies. There are dozens of fallacy lists on the Web, which vary greatly in quality. A few of the more helpful sites, which provide descriptions and examples of numerous fallacies, are listed below:

The Nizkor Project: Fallacies. http://www.nizkor.org/features/fallacies/

The Fallacy Zoo, by Brian Yoder: (list of basic fallacies with examples) http://www.goodart.org/fallazoo.htm

The Fallacy Files by Gary Curtis http://www.fallacyfiles.org/

Stephen's Guide to the Logical Fallacies http://www.datanation.com/fallacies/

FALLACIES AND YOUR OWN WRITING AND SPEAKING

When you communicate, you necessarily engage in reasoning. If your purpose is to present a well-reasoned argument, in which you do not want to "trick" the reader into agreeing with you, then you will want to avoid committing reasoning fallacies. Awareness of possible errors committed by writers provides you with warnings to heed when you construct your own arguments. You can avoid fallacies by checking your own assumptions very carefully, by remembering that most controversial issues require you to get specific about advantages and disadvantages, and by keeping a checklist handy of possible reasoning fallacies.

Practice Exercises

 Critical Question: ***Are there any fallacies in the reasoning?***

Try to identify fallacies in the reasoning in each of the following three practice passages. Compare your responses to Passages 1 and 2 with the provided feedback. You will be on your own for Passage 3. Then, apply what you have learned in this chapter to Passage 4, a lengthy article, and compare your thoughts to the step-by-step walkthrough that follows.

Passage 1

The surgeon general has overstepped his bounds by recommending that explicit sex education begin as early as third grade. It is obvious that he is yet another victim of the AIDS hysteria sweeping the nation. Unfortunately, his media-influenced announcement has given new life to those who favor explicit sex education—even to the detriment of the nation's children.

Sexuality has always been a topic of conversation reserved for the family. Only recently has sex education been forced on young children. The surgeon general's recommendation removes the role of the family entirely. It should be up to parents to explain sex to their children in a manner with which they are comfortable. Sex education exclusive of the family is stripped of values or any sense of morality and should thus be discouraged. For years families have taken the responsibility of sex education, and that's the way it should remain.

Sex education in schools encourages experimentation. Kids are curious. Letting them in on the secret of sex at such a young age will promote blatant promiscuity. Frank discussions of sex are embarrassing for children, and they destroy the natural modesty of girls.

Passage 2

Pit bulls are unfairly discriminated against by the public because of hysterical overreactions to a few cases of the dogs acting violently. Only an idiot would ban this dog breed. Most of the complaints about pit bulls come from dog haters, people who tend to be frightened of dogs. I've had my loyal and loving pit bull Andy for over seven years and he has always been well-behaved. I am confident that he could never attack a human being. Also, Dr. Overopt, director of a local dog clinic, has stated that most pit bulls are not unusually aggressive. Clearly placing some kind of ban on pits bulls would be a futile gesture. I have seen other dogs, such as golden retrievers, attack people. Thus, banning pit bulls would not totally prevent dog attacks on humans. And once outlawing pit bulls is permissible, the next step will be to ban any dog that has the potential for violence. Also, a recent survey found that most of the public does not believe most pit bulls are likely to attack human beings without provocation.

Passage 3

Bill: Countries that harbor terrorists who want to destroy the United States must be considered enemies of the United States. Any country that does not relinquish terrorists to the American justice system is clearly on the side of the terrorists. This sort of action means that the leaders of these countries do not wish to see justice done to the terrorists and care more about hiding murderers, rapists, thieves, and anti-democrats.

Taylor: That's exactly the kind of argument that I would expect from someone who has relatives who have worked for the CIA. But it seems to me that once you start labeling countries that disagree with America on policy as enemies, then eventually almost all countries will be considered our enemies, and we will be left with no allies.

Bill: If that's the case, too bad. America stands for freedom, for democracy, and for truth. So it can stand against the world. Besides, the United States should be able to convince countries hostile to the United States of the error of their ways because our beliefs have a strong religious foundation.

Taylor: Do you really think most religious people are in favor of war? A Gallup poll last week found that 75 percent of highly religious people didn't think we should go to war with countries harboring terrorists.

Bill: I think that's an overestimate. How many people did they survey?

Taylor: I'm not sure. But getting back to your original issue, the biggest problem with a tough stand against countries that harbor terrorists is that such a policy is not going to wipe out terrorism in the world.

Bill: Why do you keep defending the terrorists? I thought you were a patriot. Besides, this is a democracy, and most Americans agree with me.

Sample Responses To Passages 1 and 2

Passage 1

CONCLUSION: *Sex education should not be taught in schools.*

REASONS: 1. *The Surgeon General's report reflects hysteria.*
2. *The report removes the role of the family entirely.*
3. *It is the job of parents.*
4. *Education encourages promiscuity.*

The author begins the argument by attacking the surgeon general rather than the issue. She claims that the recommendation is a by-product of the AIDS hysteria rather than the extensive research. Her suggestion that the surgeon general issues reports in reaction to hot topics in the media undermines his credibility and character and is therefore ad hominem.

The second paragraph is a straw-person fallacy because it implies that the goal of sex education is to supply all the child's sex education.

Her third reason confuses "what is" with "what should be." Just because sex education *should be* up to the parents does not mean that they *will* provide education.

The fourth reason presents a false dilemma—either keep sex education out of the schools or face morally loose, value-free children. But isn't it possible to have morally loose children even when sex education is taking place in the home? Isn't it also a possibility that both parents and the schools can play a role in sex education? Might not education result in children who are prepared to handle the issue of sex in their lives rather than morally deficient delinquents?

Passage 2

CONCLUSION: *Pitbulls should not be banned*

REASONS: 1. *Desire to ban results from hysterical public reaction to just a few cases.*
2. *Most complaints come from dog haters.*
3. *Owner knows pit bull would never attack anyone.*
4. *Banning pit bulls wouldn't solve the problem; there would still be attacks by other breeds.*
5. *Banning pit bulls would lead to banning other breeds.*
6. *Survey shows that most owners of pit bulls believe their dogs are not likely to attack human beings.*

This essay begins with Ad Hominen and Name Calling fallacies, attacking the character of those who want to ban bull dogs rather than addressing any specific arguments. Wishful thinking appears to influence the writer's third reason, and the fourth reason commits the fallacy of Search for a Perfect Solution. Reducing the number of violent dog attacks would solve SOME of the problem, even if not ALL the problem of violent dog attacks. His next reason illustrates the Slippery Slope fallacy, as it is clearly possible to make laws that ban one breed of dog without extending such laws to other breeds. In his last reason, the author commits the Ad Populum fallacy by mistakenly assuming that because many people have such a belief about dogs, then that belief is true.

Passage 4. Expanding Practice and Feedback

Read the following blog. Try to locate fallacies in the reasoning, and reflect about how the fallacies influence your reaction to the essay's persuasiveness.

Gun Control Non Sequiturs

Jacob Sullum

reason.com/blog (2008)

While researching my column for this week (about Barack Obama's position on gun control), I came across this lame response from Paul Helmke, president of the Brady Campaign to Prevent Gun Violence, to the recent shootings at Northern Illinois University (NIU):

> Do we give up and say we can't do anything about these tragedies? Or do we take common-sense steps today to make it harder for dangerous people to get dangerous weapons? . . .

> Over the years, the Brady Campaign has proposed numerous common-sense measures to reduce and prevent gun violence. It may be difficult to stop "suicide shooters" like the Northern Illinois University killer, but there are steps we can take as a nation.

> We can require background checks for every gun transaction in America. Current Federal law requires that only Federally licensed gun dealers do a computer check on the criminal backgrounds of purchasers who buy guns from them. Yet there is no such restriction on unlicensed sellers who sell guns at gun shows, from the trunk of their cars, or at their kitchen

tables. If we want to make it harder to dangerous people to get dangerous weapons, we must close this loophole and require that all gun buyers undergo a background check.

We can limit bulk purchases of handguns to cut down on the illegal gun trade. Gun buyers currently have no Federal limits on the number of guns they can buy at one time. Gun traffickers take advantage of the unlimited number of guns they can purchase at a time in order to sell guns to criminals and gangs. . . .

We can also ban the sale of military-style assault weapons and high capacity ammunition magazines. One thing the Virginia Tech and Northern Illinois University shooters had in common was that they both used high-capacity ammunition magazines that would have been prohibited under the Federal Assault Weapons Ban that expired in 2004.

The NIU murderer, Steven Kazmierczak, legally purchased the shotgun and three handguns he used, which did not qualify as "assault weapons," from a licensed dealer on three trips over seven months, and there does not seem to have been anything about his background that disqualified him from owning firearms. So the only possibly relevant suggestion offered by Helmke is to reimpose a 10-round federal limit on the size of magazines. But considering that Kazmierczak fired the shotgun six times and the handguns 48 times; that it takes just a few seconds to switch magazines; and that police arrived about six minutes after the attack started, by which time Kazmierczak already had killed himself, it is doubtful that the death toll was any higher than it would have been had he been carrying 10-round magazines. In fact, I cannot recall reading an account of a mass murder in the U.S. where "high capacity" magazines made a demonstrable difference.

The rest of Helmke's "common-sense steps" could not possibly have stopped this attack. So why trot them out and pretend otherwise? Because that's what gun controllers routinely do, as I noted in a 1994 article for reason. Their lobbying, publicity, and fundraising imperatives prevent them from admitting the truth: With something like 200 million guns in circulation and no reliable way of predicting which quiet graduate student will go on a rampage one day, this sort of thing is bound to happen occasionally. No policy short of wholesale firearm confiscation can prevent such incidents, although (as I've argued) allowing law-abiding people to carry concealed weapons in heretofore "gun-free zones" might help reduce the number of injuries and deaths after an attack starts.

Step-by-Step Walkthrough

- The first thing that I notice is that the article is a reaction to a recent shooting at a university and that the structure of the argument is a summary of someone else's argument (Paul Helmke) followed by the writer's criticism of that argument. Thus, I want to look at both arguments closely.

- Helmke's first argument responds to the issue of what should be done in response to the shootings at Northern Illinois University and concludes that perhaps we can't stop "suicide shooters" like the one in this case, but there are steps we can take as a nation to make it harder for dangerous people to get dangerous weapons?(paragraph 3). He then lists several possible steps. One characteristic that I notice is that he states the solution as having only two possibilities: giving up or taking common sense steps to make it harder for dangerous people to get dangerous weapons? Such wording suggests the possibility of an **either-or fallacy** as well as the use of **question begging** language, by the use twice of the phrase "common sense." Are there not other options than the two suggested, such as seeking innovative or non common sense, solutions, such as better ways to detect disturbed individuals and confront the disturbance? And the phrase common sense makes it seem as though the solutions are obvious when they are not; they need to be better supported.

- Although the thrust of this blogger's argument is to counter the original argument, I will keep these fallacies in mind as I try to identify fallacies in the blogger's rebuttle and evaluate the entire argument.

- I now take a closer look at Jacob Sullum's reasons and notice two that are related. In his first paragraph, he cites problems with Helmke's prescriptions being of adequate assistance to the NIU murders and concludes that it is doubtful that the death toll was any higher than it would have been had Kazmierczak been carrying 10-round magazines. To support his argument of the futility of banning the sale of military style assault weapons, he states: "In fact, I cannot recall reading an account of a mass murder in the U.S. where "high capacity" made a demonstrable difference. I recall that Asking the Right Questions encourages me to look for faulty assumptions as a sign of a fallacy, and I detect a faulty assumption with this reasoning leading to a non-sequitor: if one is not aware of some event, then no evidence exists for the event. Obviously, we can be unaware of many important events despite their actual existence.

- In his second paragraph, he argues that Helmke's suggestions could not have stopped the Northern Illinois attack and thus are not relevant. As mentioned in Asking the Right Questions, the presentation of specific disadvantages of another's prescriptions helps to avoid fallacies. But a close reading shows that Sullum misrepresents Helmke's conclusion. Helmke agrees that it may be difficult to stop "suicide shooters," but there are steps to take to make it harder for dangerous people to get dangerous weapons. Thus, Sullum has committed the fallacy of **attacking a straw person** when he concludes in the final paragraph that no policy short of wholesale firearm confiscation can prevent such an incident. Why do I think this? Because Helmke didn't argue that his steps could PREVENT such incidents.

- Also, when I reflect further on what assumptions Sullum must make for his criticisms to support his conclusion, I note that he assumes that if the steps prescribed by Helmke don't stop ALL attacks like the Northern Illinois one, then they have no value. But what if such steps help reduce the number of violent incidents? Such reasoning suggests the fallacy of a **search for perfect solutions**. Isn't some decrease in violence better than none?

- In addition, in his last paragraph, Sullum attacks the "gun controllers" rather than their arguments with his comment that "their lobbying, publicity and fund raising imperatives prevent them from admitting the truth." He attacks their background rather than the ideas—an **ad hominem** fallacy. Thus, we should ignore this attack in making judgments about the quality of Helmke's ideas.

CRITICAL QUESTION SUMMARY: WHY THIS QUESTION IS IMPORTANT

Are there Any Fallacies in the Reasoning?

Once you have identified the reasons, you want to determine whether the author used any reasoning tricks or fallacies. If you identify a fallacy in reasoning, that reason does not provide good support for the conclusion. Consequently, you would not want to accept an author's conclusion on the basis of that reason. If the author provides no good reasons, you would not want to accept her conclusion. Thus, looking for fallacies in reasoning is another important step in determining whether you will accept or reject the author's conclusion.

CHAPTER 8

How Good Is the Evidence: Intuition, Personal Experience, Testimonials, and Appeals to Authority?

In the last chapter, you made major inroads into the process of evaluating persuasive communications by learning how to detect some fallacies in reasoning. In the following chapters, we continue our focus on evaluation as we learn to ask critical questions about a specific part of the reasoning structure: claims about the "facts." Let's see what such claims look like.

Practicing yoga reduces the risk of cancer.

Playing video games increases hand-eye coordination.

More college students are coming to classes with hangovers. *Time* Magazine reports that 24 percent of college students report attending a class at least once in the last two weeks while experiencing a hangover from drinking too much the night before.

What do we make of these claims? Are they legitimate? Most reasoning includes claims such as these. In this chapter, we begin the process of evaluating such claims.

? *Critical Question:* **How good is the evidence: intuition, personal experience, testimonials, and appeals to authority?**

THE NEED FOR EVIDENCE

Almost all reasoning we encounter includes beliefs about the way the world is, was, or is going to be that the communicator wants us to accept as "facts." These beliefs can be conclusions, reasons, or assumptions. We can refer to such beliefs as *factual claims*.

> The first question you should ask about a factual claim is, *"Why should I believe it?"*
>
> Your next question is, *"Does the claim need evidence to support it?"* If it does, and if there is no evidence, the claim is a *mere assertion*. You should seriously question the dependability of mere assertions!
>
> If there is evidence, your next question is, *"How good is the evidence?"*

To evaluate reasoning, we need to remember that some factual claims can be counted on more than others. For example, you probably feel quite certain that the claim "most United States senators are men" is true, but less certain that the assertion "practicing yoga reduces the risk of cancer" is true.

Because it is extremely difficult, if not impossible, to establish the *absolute* truth or falsity of most claims, rather than ask whether they are *true*, we prefer to ask whether they are *dependable*. In essence, we want to ask, *"Can we count on such beliefs?"* The greater the quality and quantity of evidence supporting a claim, the more we can *depend on it*, and the more we can call the claim a *"fact."*

For example, abundant evidence exists that George Washington was the first president of the United States of America. Thus, we can treat that claim as a fact. On the other hand, there is much conflicting evidence for the belief "alcoholism is a disease." We thus can't treat this belief as a fact. The major difference between claims that are *opinions* and those that are *facts* is the present state of the relevant evidence. The more supporting evidence there is for a belief, the more "factual" the belief becomes.

Before we judge the persuasiveness of a communication, we need to know which factual claims are most dependable. How do we determine dependability? We ask questions like the following:

What is your proof?	*How do you know that's true?*
Where's the evidence?	*Why do you believe that?*
Are you sure that's true?	*Can you prove it?*

You will be well on your way to being among the best critical thinkers when you develop the habit of regularly asking these questions. They require those making arguments to be responsible by revealing the basis for their arguments. Anyone with an argument that you should consider will not hesitate to answer these questions. They know they have substantial support for their claims and, consequently, will want to share their evidence in the hope that you will learn to share their conclusions. When people react to simple requests for evidence with anger or withdrawal, they usually do so because they are embarrassed as they realize that, without evidence, they should have been less assertive about their beliefs.

When we regularly ask these questions, we notice that for many beliefs there is insufficient evidence to clearly support or refute them. For example, much evidence supports the assertion that taking an aspirin every other day reduces the risk of heart attack, although some other evidence disputes it. In such cases, we need to make judgments about where the *preponderance of evidence* lies as we decide on the dependability of the factual claim.

Making such judgments requires us to ask the important question, *"How good is the evidence?"* The next three chapters focus on questions we need to ask to decide how well communicators have supported their factual claims. The more dependable the factual claims, the more persuasive the communications should be.

LOCATING FACTUAL CLAIMS

We encounter factual claims as (a) *descriptive conclusions,* (b) *reasons* used to support either descriptive or prescriptive conclusions, or (c) *descriptive assumptions.* Let's examine an example of each within brief arguments.

> (a) *Frequent use of headphones may cause hearing loss.* Researchers studied the frequency and duration of head phone use among 251 college students and found that 49 percent of the students showed evidence of hearing impairment.

Note that "frequent headphone use may cause hearing loss" is a factual claim that is a descriptive conclusion supported by research evidence. In this case, we want to ask, "Is that conclusion—a factual claim—justified by the evidence?"

> (b) This country needs tougher gun regulations. *Recent crime statistics report an increase in the number of gun-related crimes over the last 10 years.*

Note that the factual claim here is the statistic reporting *"an increase in the number of gun-related crimes over the last 10 years,"* and it functions as a reason supporting a prescriptive conclusion. In this case, we want to ask, "Is that reason—a factual claim—justified by the evidence?"

> (c) Our country needs to decrease its dependency on fossil fuels. Although hybrid cars are expensive, they are an excellent means to lower gas and oil consumption in America. Also, our government needs to pursue alternative energy sources at all costs because our oil dependency is leading our country to unfavorable international actions. (Unstated descriptive assumption linking the reasons to the conclusion: *The monetary costs of switching to*

hybrid cars and alternative energy sources are far less than the political benefits to decreasing dependency on fossil fuels.)

This factual claim is a descriptive assumption, which may or may not be dependable. Before we believe the assumption, and thus the reason, we want to ask, "How well does evidence support the assumption?" You will find that while many communicators perceive the desirability of supporting their reasons with evidence, they don't see the need to make their assumptions explicit. Thus, evidence for assumptions is rarely presented, even though in many cases such evidence would be quite helpful in deciding the quality of an argument.

SOURCES OF EVIDENCE

When should we accept a factual claim as dependable? There are three instances in which we will be most inclined to agree with a factual claim:

1. when the claim appears to be undisputed common knowledge, such as the claim "weight lifting increases muscular body mass";
2. when the claim is the conclusion from a well-reasoned argument;
3. when the claim is adequately supported by solid evidence in the same communication or by other evidence that we know.

Our concern in this chapter is the third instance. Determining the adequacy of evidence requires us to ask, *"How good is the evidence?"* To answer this question, we must first ask, "What do we mean by *evidence?*"

> *Attention: Evidence is explicit information shared by the communicator that is used to back up or to justify the dependability of a factual claim (see Chapter 4). In prescriptive arguments, evidence will be needed to support reasons that are factual claims; in descriptive arguments, evidence will be needed to directly support a descriptive conclusion.*

The quality of evidence depends on the kind of evidence it is. Thus, to evaluate evidence, we first need to ask, *"What kind of evidence is it?"* Knowing the kind of evidence tells us what questions we should ask.

Major kinds of evidence include:

- intuition
- personal experiences or anecdotes
- testimonials
- appeals to authorities or experts
- personal observations
- case examples
- research studies
- analogies.

When used appropriately, each kind of evidence can be "good evidence." It can help support an author's claim. Like a gold prospector closely examining the gravel in her pan for potentially high-quality ore, we must closely examine the evidence to determine its quality. We want to know, "Does an author's evidence provide dependable support for her claim?" Thus, we begin to evaluate evidence by asking, "*How good is the evidence?*" Always keep in the back of your mind that no evidence will be a slam dunk that gets the job done conclusively. You are looking for better evidence; searching for altogether wonderful evidence will be frustrating.

In this chapter and the next one, we examine what kinds of questions we can ask of each kind of evidence to help us decide. Kinds of evidence examined in this chapter are intuition; personal experiences and anecdotes; testimonials; and appeals to authority.

INTUITION AS EVIDENCE

"I just sense that Janette is the right girl for me, even though my friends think we're a bad match."

"I just have this feeling that Senator Goodall will surprise the pollsters and win the election."

"I can tell immediately that this slot machine is going to be a winner for me today."

When we use intuition to support a claim, we rely on "common sense" or on our "gut feelings" or on hunches. When a communicator supports a claim by saying "common sense tells us" or "I just know that it's true," she is using intuition as her evidence. Intuition refers to a process in which we believe we have direct insights about something without being able to consciously express our reasons.

A major problem with intuition is that it is private; others have no way to judge its dependability. Thus, when intuitive beliefs differ, as they so often do, we have no solid basis for deciding which ones to believe. Also, much intuition relies on unconscious processing that largely ignores relevant evidence and reflects strong biases. Consequently, we must be very wary of claims backed up only by intuition.

However, sometimes "intuition" may in fact be relying on some other kind of evidence, such as extensive relevant personal experiences and readings that have been unconsciously accessed from somewhere in our mind. For example, when an experienced pilot has an intuition that the plane doesn't feel right as it taxis for takeoff, we might be quite supportive of further safety checks of the plane prior to takeoff. Sometimes "hunches" are not blind, just incapable of explanation. As critical thinkers, we would want to find out whether claims relying on intuition have any other kinds of evidential support.

DANGERS OF APPEALING TO PERSONAL EXPERIENCE AND ANECDOTES AS EVIDENCE

The following arguments use a particular kind of evidence to support a factual claim.

> "My friend Judy does really well on her tests when she stays up all night to study for them; so I don't see the need for getting sleep before taking tomorrow's test."

> "I always feel better after having a big slice of chocolate cake, so I think that anyone who is depressed just needs to eat more chocolate cake."

Both arguments appeal to personal experiences as evidence. Phrases like "I know someone who . . . ," and "In my experience, I've found . . ." should alert you to such evidence. Because personal experiences are very vivid in our memories, we often rely on them as evidence to support a belief. For example, you might have a really frustrating experience with a car mechanic because she greatly overcharges you for her services, leading you to believe that most car mechanics overcharge. While the generalization about car mechanics may or may not be true, relying on such experiences as the basis for a general belief is a mistake! Because a single personal experience, or even an accumulation of personal experiences, is not enough to give you a *representative* sample of experiences, personal experiences often lead us to commit the *Hasty Generalization* fallacy. A single striking experience or several such experiences can demonstrate that certain outcomes are *possible*; for example, you may have met several people who claim their lives were saved because they were not wearing their seat belts when they got into a car accident. Such experiences, however, cannot demonstrate that such outcomes are *typical* or *probable*. Be wary when you hear yourself or others arguing, "Well, in my experience . . ."

F: Hasty Generalization Fallacy: A person draws a conclusion about a large group based on experiences with only a few members of the group.

We will revisit this fallacy in Chapter 9 when we discuss research evidence and issues of sampling.

TESTIMONIALS AS EVIDENCE

> Note on service station wall: "Jane did a wonderful job fixing the oil leak my car had. I strongly recommend that you take your car to Jane to fix any engine problem you have."

> This book looks great. On the back cover comments from readers say, "I could not put this book down."

> Let's check out that new movie at the Fox Theatre. Several fraternity brothers have raved about the quality of the acting.

Commercials, ads for movies, recommendations on the backs of book jackets, and "proofs" of the existence of the paranormal or other controversial or extraordinary life events often try to persuade by using a special kind of appeal to personal experience; they quote particular persons, often celebrities, as saying that a given idea or product is good or bad, or that extraordinary events have occurred, based upon their personal experiences. Such quoted statements serve as *personal testimonials*. You may have listened to personal testimonials from college students when you chose your college. Testimonials are thus a form of personal experience in which someone (often a celebrity) provides a statement supporting the value of some product, event, or service, and the endorsement lacks any of the information we would need to decide just how much we should let it influence us.

How helpful is such evidence? Usually, it is not very helpful at all. In most cases, we should pay little attention to personal testimonials until we find out much more about the expertise, interests, values, and biases behind them. We should be especially wary of each of the following problems with testimonials:

- **Selectivity.** People's experiences differ greatly. Those trying to persuade us have usually carefully selected the testimony they use. What we are most likely to see on the back of a book jacket is the BEST PRAISE, not the most typical reaction. We should always ask the question, "What was the experience like for those whom we have not heard from?" Also, the people who provide the testimonials have often been selective in their attention, paying special attention to information that confirms their beliefs and ignoring disconfirming information. Often, *believing is seeing!* Our *expectancies* greatly influence how we experience events. If we believe that aliens live among us, or that humans never really landed on the moon, then we are more likely to see ambiguous images as aliens or as proof of the government conspiracy regarding the moon landing.
- **Personal interest.** Many testimonials such as those used for books, movies, and television products come from people who have something to gain from their testimony. For example, drug companies often give doctors grants to do research as long as they prescribe the drug company's brands of medication. Thus, we need to ask, "Does the person providing the testimony have a relationship with what he is advocating such that we can expect a strong bias in his testimony?"
- **Omitted information.** Testimonials rarely provide sufficient information about the basis for the judgment. For example, when a friend of yours encourages you to go see this new movie because it is the "best

Who We Are Affects Our Vision

movie ever," you should ask, with warmth, about what makes the movie so impressive. Our standards for judgment may well differ from the standards of those giving the testimony. We often have too little information to decide whether we should treat such claims seriously.

- ***The human factor.*** One reason that testimonials are so convincing is that they come from human beings and they are very vivid and detailed, a marked contrast to statistics and graphs, which tend to be very abstract. They are often provided by very enthusiastic people, who seem trustworthy, well-meaning, and honest. Such people make us *want* to believe them.

APPEALS TO AUTHORITY AS EVIDENCE

"According to my doctor, I should be taking anti-depressant drugs to help me cope with my recent episodes of depression and I don't need to worry about side effects."

The speaker has defended his claim by *appealing to authority*—sources that are supposed to know more than most of us about a given topic—so-called experts. When communicators appeal to authorities or experts, they appeal to people who they believe are in a position to have access to certain facts and to have special qualifications for drawing conclusions from the facts. Thus, such appeals potentially provide more "oomph" to an argument than testimonials, depending on the background of the authority. You encounter appeals to many forms of authority on a daily basis. And you have little choice but to rely on them because you have neither the time nor the knowledge to become adept in more than a few dimensions of our very complicated lives.

Movie reviewers: "One of the ten best movies of the year." Valerie Viewer, *Toledo Gazette.*

Talk show pundits: "The economy is heading for a recession."

Organizations: "The American Medical Association supports this position."

Researchers: "Studies show . . ."

Relatives: "My grandfather says . . ."

Religion: "The Koran says . . ."

Magazines: "According to *Newsweek* . . ."

College professors: "The appropriate interpretation of Plato is . . ."

Expert witnesses: "It is my belief that the defendant . . ."

Health Web sites: "The best present treatment for migraine headaches is . . ."

You can easily add to our list. It should be obvious that some appeals to authority should be taken much more seriously as evidence than others. Why? Some authorities are much more careful in giving an opinion than others. For example, *Newsweek* and *Time* are much more likely to carefully evaluate the available evidence prior to stating an opinion than is *The National Enquirer.* Articles on schizophrenia are more likely to be based on carefully collected evidence if they are posted on the National Institute of Mental Health Web site than if they are posted on a personal Web page. Our relatives are much less likely than editorial writers for major newspapers to have systematically evaluated a political candidate.

You should remember that *authorities are often wrong.* Also, they often disagree. The following examples, taken from *The Experts Speak,* are clear reminders of the fallibility of expert opinion (Christopher Cerf and Victor Navasky, 1998, Rev. Ed., Villard Books, New York).

"It is once and for all clear . . . that the earth is in the middle of the world and all weights move towards it." Ptolemy, *The Almagest,* second century A.D., p. 5.

"I think there is a world market for maybe five computers." Thomas Watson, chairman of IBM, 1943.

"Video won't be able to hold onto any market it captures after the first six months. People will soon get tired of staring at a plywood box every night." Darryl F. Zanuck (Head of Twentieth Century Fox Studios), ca. 1946, p. 41.

> "If excessive smoking actually plays a role in the production of lung cancer, it seems to be a minor one." Dr. W. C. Heuper (National Cancer Institute), quoted in *The New York Times*, April 14, 1954, p. 228.

These quotes should remind us that we need to ask critical questions when communicators appeal to authority. We need to ask, "*Why should we believe this authority?*" More specifically, we should ask the following questions of authorities.

How much expertise or training does the authority have about the subject about which he is communicating? Is this a topic the person has studied for a long time? Or, has the person had extensive experience related to the topic?

Was the authority in a position to have especially good access to pertinent facts? For example, was she a firsthand observer of the events about which she makes claims? Or, has a newspaper reporter, for example, actually witnessed an event, or has she merely relied upon reports from others? If the authority is not a firsthand observer, whose claims is she repeating? Why should we rely on those claims? In general, you should be more impressed by *primary sources*—or direct observers—than by *secondary sources*, those who are relying on others for their evidence. *Time* and *Newsweek*, for example, are secondary sources, while research journals such as the *Journal of the American Medical Association* are primary sources.

Is there good reason to believe that the authority is relatively free of distorting influences? Among the factors that can influence how evidence is reported are personal needs, prior expectations, general beliefs, attitudes, values, theories, and ideologies. These can subconsciously or deliberately affect how evidence is presented. For example, if a public university president is asked whether cuts in funding for education are bad for the university, he will in all probability answer "yes" and give a number of good reasons. He may be giving an unbiased view of the situation. Because of his position, however, we would want to be concerned about the possibility that he has sought out only those reasons that justify his own biases. Similarly, consider how the biases of the owners of various media outlets, such as Fox, CNN, or ABC, might influence the nature of the arguments of invited experts.

By having bias and prejudice, we mean the existence of a strong personal feeling about the goodness or badness of something up front, before we look at the evidence, such that it interferes with our ability to evaluate evidence fairly. Because many factors bias us in virtually all our judgments, we cannot expect any authority to be *totally* unbiased. We can, however, expect less bias from some authorities than from others and try to determine such bias by seeking information about the authority's personal interest in the topic. For example, we want to be especially wary when an authority stands to benefit financially from the actions she advocates.

Because an authority can have a personal interest in an issue and still make dependable claims, we should not reject a claim simply because we suspect that the authority's personal interests may interfere with her fairness. One helpful step we can take is to check to see whether authorities with diverse attitudes, prior expectations, values, and interests agree. Thus we need to ask the questions: *"Has the authority developed a reputation for frequently making dependable claims? Have we been able to rely on this authority in the past?"*

You will want to be especially concerned about the quality of authorities when you encounter factual claims on the Internet. When we go online, virtually everyone becomes a potential "authority" because people are free to claim whatever they wish, and there is no built-in process to evaluate such claims. It is clearly a "buyers beware" situation!

Because so many Web sites exist and are so free of constraints, you need to be especially vigilant for credibility and accuracy problems. You should strive to learn as much as you can about the purpose of the sites, the credentials and experience of the contributors associated with them, and the nature of the reasoning support provided for their conclusions. Pay very close attention to the reasoning structure. Check to see whether the site is associated with or linked to highly reputable sites.

Further clues that the site may be undependable include a lack of dates associated with postings, an unprofessional look to the site, claims that are vague, sweeping (e.g. "always," "never") and emotional, rather than carefully qualified, a totally one-sided view, the absence of primary source evidence, and the presence of hearsay evidence and numerous reasoning fallacies. Finally, seek out evidence on the same topic from other sites.

Problems with Citers Citing Other Citers

A particularly troublesome kind of appeal to authority that has become increasingly frequent as the sizes of many news staffs has dwindled is a situation in which one authority supports an opinion by citing another authority. For example, one paper (e.g. *The New York Times*) cites another paper (e.g. *The Washington Post*), or one news service (e.g. Reuters) cites another news service (e.g. the Associated Press). Such citations give an illusion of supportive evidence but bypass the most basic question: How dependable was the original authority's claim to begin with? A related problem is the citing of "unnamed sources" or the reference to "some say . . ." Be especially cautious when you encounter appeals to authority that make it very difficult to pin down the basis for the original claims.

USING THIS CRITICAL QUESTION

When you identify problems with intuition, personal experience, testimonials, and appeals to authority as evidence, you then have a proper basis for hesitating to accept the conclusion based on that evidence. Knowing these problems gives you some protection against bogus reasoning. However, you do want to work hard to be fair to the arguments that people present for your consideration. So it makes sense to ask those who provide you with insubstantial evidence whether they can give you some better evidence. Give arguments every chance they deserve.

Summary

Clues for Evaluating the Evidence

Use the following questions to help assess the various kinds of evidence.

Intuition

- Does the intuition have any other kind of evidential support?

Authority

- How much expertise or training does the authority have on this particular subject?
- Was the authority in a position to have especially good access to pertinent facts?
- Is there good reason to believe that the authority is relatively free of distorting influences?
- Has the authority developed a reputation for frequently making dependable claims?
- Have we been able to rely on this authority in the past?

Testimony

- What biases or interests might be affecting the person's testimony?
- Does the person have any expertise to assist his or her judgment?
- How do the person's value assumptions affect his or her testimony?
- Whose personal testimony might be helpful in assessing this person's testimony?

In this chapter, we have focused on the evaluation of several kinds of evidence used to support factual claims: intuition; personal experience and anecdotes; testimonials; and appeals to authorities. Such evidence must be relied on with caution. We have provided you with some questions you should ask to determine whether such evidence is *good evidence.* In the next chapter, we discuss other kinds of evidence, as we continue to ask the question, "*How good is the evidence?*"

Practice Exercises

 Critical Question: ***How good is the evidence: intuition, personal experience, testimonials, and appeals to authority?***

Evaluate the evidence in the following three passages.

Passage 1

Consumers are constantly being cheated by big corporations and marketing departments. People are finding themselves paying more and more for the same product just so the corporation can make more money. To make matters worse, big corporations work with their marketing departments to find ways to make their products desirable while not actually increasing the quality of the product.

Consumers are angry about being cheated and they are clamoring for a change. A recent survey elicited the following comments:

Michelle K., mother: "It seems that every time I open a bag of potato chips there is more air than chips. I remember when the bag used to be mostly full. Now you are lucky to get a bag a third full of chips. Not to mention the price! When will these things stop costing so much?"

George Z., truck driver: "I like nothing better than eating a box of crackers and drinking pop while on the road. Yet, every time I am in the store buying more snacks I feel like I am spending a fortune. How much can it possibly cost to make crackers and pop?"

Sarah L., attorney: "The price of bread has risen substantially over the last 12 years. Every year the price has gone up, and yet it is the same old bread. The bread manufacturers have done absolutely nothing to increase the quality of the bread, but the price is still rising. The bread does not last longer. It is not softer. Yet, the price is still rising! Someone should sue the bread manufacturers.

Passage 2

Are Botox injections a safe alternative to face lifts? According to an interview with Dr. N. O. Worries published in *Cosmo*, there are no dangerous side effects associated with Botox injections. Dr. Worries performs hundreds of Botox injections each month, is well established as a physician in New York City, and has her own private practice. She claims she has never had a serious problem with any of her injections and her patients have never reported side effects. Furthermore, Hollywood's

Association for Cosmetic Surgeons officially stated in a press release that Botox has never been shown to cause any negative effects, despite what other physicians might argue.

Passage 3

Are Macs really better than PCs? The answer is a resounding yes! *Computer Nerds Quarterly* recently ran an article thoroughly outlining every advantage that Macs have over PCs. Furthermore, just ask Mac users and they will quickly explain how Macs are superior to PCs. For example, Sherry, a Mac user, states, "My Mac is the best thing I ever purchased. It is fast and easy to use. Plus, it has never crashed on me. All of my friends who have PCs have complained about all kinds of problems my Mac has never had." More importantly, a recent report in *Consumer Affairs* states that more new businesses are using Mac-based systems than PC-based systems. Clearly, Macs are a cut above the PCs.

Sample Responses To Passages 1 and 2

Passage 1

CONCLUSION: *Consumers are angry at big corporations because of rising prices of their products without an increase in quality.*

REASON: *Three people had voiced their dissatisfaction with rising prices and corporate practices.*

Although the general conclusion may or may not be accurate, we should not rely on these testimonials as good "proof." This passage illustrates well the weaknesses of testimony as evidence. How typical are these "horror stories"? Would other consumers have voiced no complaint about products' prices? How were the interviews conducted? Is the author's selection of interview comments biased? Did the individuals know what the interviewer was trying to prove and thus try to please the interviewer? Have prices of other products remained constant while some have risen? Before we conclude that consumers are being cheated by big corporations, we would want much better evidence than just a few testimonials. What the testimonials do tell us, however, is that it is possible for consumers to be upset about the cost of certain products.

Passage 2

CONCLUSION: *Botox injections are safe.*

REASON: *A cosmetic surgeon and a state professional organization claim Botox is safe.*

How much should we depend on these appeals to authority? Not much. First, both authorities are likely to be very biased. They stand to gain financially by making safety claims. Dr. Worries' testimony is especially suspect because it is based on her experiences only. She has probably not sought out evidence of failures. The claims of the professional organization are as questionable as those of Dr. Worries because the organization is comprised of cosmetic surgeons, who probably perform Botox injections. If the organization were to have offered some sort of systematic research for why Botox is safe, perhaps its claims would be less suspect.

Practice Passage 4. Expanding Practice and Feedback

We have provided a lengthy passage below that was posted on a Web site and followed it with a model of a step-by-step approach to asking the question *How Good is the Evidence: Intuition, Personal Experience, Testimonials, and Appeals to Authority?* We recommend that you first try to evaluate the evidence in the article and then compare your response to our think-aloud model. We hope that the model provides you with some helpful hints for future evaluations of evidence.

Homeschooling Comes of Age

Isabel Lyman

Mises Daily (2007)

In the late 1960s and early 1970s, the modern home education movement was in its infancy. At that time, most Americans viewed home-styled education as a quaint tourist attraction or the lifestyle choice of those willing to endure more hardship than necessary.

What a difference a few decades makes.

Homeschooling has undergone an extreme makeover. From maverick to mainstream, the movement has acquired a glamorous, populist sheen.

Flip through a few issues of *Sports Illustrated*, circa 2007, and there's no shortage of news about photogenic homeschoolers who make the athletic cut. Like Jessica Long who was born in Russia, resides in Baltimore, and is an accomplished swimmer. At 15, Jessica became the first paralympian to win the prestigious Sullivan Award, which honors the country's top amateur athlete. Then there's the dashing Joey Logano who, at 17, has already won a NASCAR race.

Even presidential hopefuls and their spouses have jumped on the school-thine-own bandwagon. Congressman Ron Paul (R-Texas) has offered enthusiastic support for homeschooling families, and Elizabeth Edwards, wife of Senator John Edwards (D-North Carolina) told the *Wall Street Journal* that this fall she plans to home-educate the couple's two youngest children "with the help of a tutor."

As for scholastic achievements, this national competition season was remarkable, seeing home scholars crowned as champs in three major events. A twelve-year-old New Mexican named Matthew Evans won the National Word Power competition, sponsored by *Reader's Digest*. Thirteen-year-old Evan O'Dorney of California won the Scripps National Spelling Bee, and fourteen-year-old Caitlin Snaring of Washington was christened the National Geographic Bee champ.

Then there's Micah Stanley of Minnesota who has yet to receive any lessons in a brick-and-mortar classroom building. For the past few years, he's been enrolled in the Oak Brook College of Law, a distance learning law school headquartered in Sacramento. This past February, he took the grueling, three-day California general bar examination (California allows correspondence law students to sit for the bar), and he can now add "attorney" to his resume. In his spare time, he's finishing up a book titled, *How to Escape the Holding Tank: A Guide to Help You Get What You Want.*

Micah is 19.

A teenage lawyer/budding author, however, wouldn't surprise John Taylor Gatto, an outspoken critic of compulsory education laws and a former New York State Teacher of the Year. Writing in *Harper's Magazine*, Gatto forthrightly argued that "genius is as common as dirt."

Perhaps. But it's also understandable that when everyday folks hear about the homeschooled Joeys and Caitlins and Micahs, they become a tad intimidated—as if this educational choice were the exclusive domain of obsessive-compulsive moms and dads with money to burn, time to spare, and a brood of driven, Type-A offspring.

Although it's commendable when the young achieve Herculean goals, homeschooling has always been more about freedom and personal responsibility than winning an Ivy League scholarship or playing at Wimbledon. In general, it has attracted working-class families of all ethnicities and faiths, who have been eager to provide a nurturing, stimulating learning experience.

Of course, the unabashedly adventuresome are always an endearing staple of the movement. The Burns family, of Alaska, set out on a 36-foot sailboat this summer to travel the world for three years. Chris Burns (the dad) told the *Juneau Empire* he hopes "to connect with Juneau classrooms and host question-and-answer sessions while at sea," as well as homeschool the two Burns children.

In a legal sense, homeschools serve as a glaring reminder of a complex issue that has become the stuff of landmark Supreme Court cases: does the state have the authority to coerce a youngster to attend school and sit at a desk for 12 years? Whether said child has the aptitude and maturity for such a long-term contract (or is it involuntary servitude?) remains an uncomfortable topic because, in the acceptable mantra of the day, "education is a right."

Such a national conversation is long overdue, as there are plenty of signs — costly remedial education and rising dropout rates, to name two — to indicate that the status quo public school model isn't kid-friendly.

Homeschooling, after all, began to catch on with the masses because a former US Department of Education employee argued that children, like delicate hothouse plants, required a certain type of environment to grow shoots and blossoms, and that loving parents, not institutions, could best create the greenhouses.

It was 1969 when the late Dr. Raymond Moore initiated an inquiry into previously neglected areas of educational research. Two of the questions that Moore and a team of like-minded colleagues set out to answer were (1) Is institutionalizing young children a sound, educational trend? and (2) What is the best timing for school entrance?

In the process of analyzing thousands of studies, twenty of which compared early school entrants with late starters, Moore concluded that developmental problems, such as hyperactivity, nearsightedness, and dyslexia, are often the result of prematurely taxing a child's nervous system and mind with continuous academic tasks, like reading and writing.

The bulk of the research convinced Moore that formal schooling should be delayed until at least age 8 or 10, or even as late as 12. As he explained, "These findings sparked our concern and convinced us to focus our investigation on two primary areas: formal learning and socializing. Eventually, this work led to an unexpected interest in homeschools."

Moore went on to write *Home Grown Kids* and *Home-Spun Schools.* The rest, as they say, is history. The books, published in the 1980s, have sold hundreds of thousands of copies and offer practical advice to potential parent educators.

Nowadays, there's a sea of such self-help material, scores of commercial products, and online opportunities solely dedicated to encouraging families to learn together in the convenience of their homes. Homeschooling has graduated into a time-tested choice that allows children to thrive, learn at their own pace, and which frequently inspires other success stories. As our nation is famous for encouraging immigrants to reinvent themselves and achieve the American Dream, so home education does for youngsters whether they are late bloomers or are candidates for Mensa.

Above all, the merit of homeschooling is that it allows for experimentation, flexibility, and trial and error. Here is the great contrast with state-provided education. As with all systems hammered out by bureaucracies, public schools get stuck in a rut, perpetuate failures, respond slowly to changing times, and resist all reforms. Errors are not localized and contained, but all consuming and system wide. It's bad enough when such a system is used to govern labor contracts or postal service; it is a tragic loss when it is used to manage kids' minds.

Isabel Lyman, Ph.D., is the author of *The Homeschooling Revolution,* a paperback about the modern home education movement. Her articles and op-eds have appeared in the *Miami Herald, Wall Street Journal, Dallas Morning News, Pittsburgh Tribune-Review, Investor's Business Daily, Boston Herald, Los Angeles Daily Journal, National Review, Chronicles, Daily Oklahoman,* and other publications. See her Web site.

Step-by-Step Walkthrough

- As I read this article through from start to finish, it is very clear that the main conclusion that it wants to impart is that homeschooling is a desirable choice for many children. In applying Chapter 8, I want to ask the question: How good is the evidence for that conclusion? And to answer that question, I will begin my evaluation by first asking about what kind of evidence the author uses.
- I first notice that the first seven paragraphs emphasize achievements of homeschooled children, primarily athletic and scholastic achievements. In a sense, Lyman is implying, "I know many successful people who have been homeschooled, thus home schooling is a good choice." She is appealing to personal experience and anecdotes as evidence. *Asking the Right Questions* has alerted me to the dangers of such evidence, especially its power to persuade because it evokes such striking images. Although the experiences can be compelling and suggest POSSIBILITIES, I need to question just how typical or representative they are of homeschooled people in general. Thus I want to avoid the hasty generalization fallacy (mentioned in this chapter of *Asking the Right Questions).* What is the experience of MOST homeschooled children?
- Next I look for other kinds of evidence and notice several appeals to authority, and thus I need to ask questions to determine how much attention I should pay to them. One appeal that I notice is her mentioning of presidential hopefuls and their spouses as people who have chosen homeschooling for their children. This evidence also seems to be a form of testimonial, communicating the message: "I like the idea of homeschooling so much

that I'm sending my own children." I note a similar testimonial is her reference to the adventuresome Burns family engaging in homeschooling while sailboating. I find the appeals and testimonials of questionable value because of their selectivity; I know very little about the expertise, values, or biases of the people to whom she refers.

- I find a later appeal to authority in Lyman's essay, however, which does provide some specific evidence of its credibility. She discusses the work of Dr. Raymond Moore, which included an analysis of many research studies supporting the need for delay of formal schooling. Lyman additionally cites Moore's book that praises homeschooling, and she informs the reader that it has sold hundreds of thousands of copies. Although Moore seems to have intensely studied children's early learning, giving the appeal some credibility, Lyman provides no specific evidence of how well homeschooling has worked as a response to his concerns. Also, the mention of sales of thousands of books reminds me of the Ad Populum fallacy mentioned in Chapter 7 of *Asking the Right Questions*. This reasoning reflects the faulty assumption that if something is popular, then it must be good.

- I noticed that at the end of the article there is a posting of publications by the author, which suggests the likelihood that she has much more knowledge about this topic than the typical person. For the purpose, however, of judging the quality of the reasoning in this essay, I need to concentrate on how good her arguments are, not get distracted by how many books or articles she has written.

- In summary, I find that the evidence provided in Lyman's article has primarily demonstrated that increasingly large numbers of families are choosing homeschooling for their children. She has shared some evidence that it is possible for SOME children who homeschool to flourish. In addition, she has presented a list of potential benefits of homeschooling (see especially her last two paragraphs), which I believe are worth considering. Lyman, however, has presented no specific research evidence of the TYPICAL development of children who undergo homeschooling relative to those who do not. Thus, before I would want to make a judgment about her conclusion, I would want to seek out more specific research information on the impact of homeschooling on children.

How did you do evaluating the quality of the evidence in the previous article? Did you notice any strengths or weaknesses in the use of evidence that were missed by the evaluation? We hope that the practice better prepared you for subsequent evaluations of this kind of evidence.

CHAPTER 9

How Good Is the Evidence: Personal Observation, Research Studies, Case Examples, and Analogies?

In this chapter, we continue our evaluation of evidence. We focus on four common kinds of evidence: personal observation, research studies, case examples, and analogies. We need to question each of these when we encounter them as evidence.

? *Critical Question: **How good is the evidence: personal observation, research studies, case examples, and analogies?***

PERSONAL OBSERVATION

One valuable kind of evidence is personal observation, the basis for much scientific research. For example, we feel confident of something we actually see. Thus, we tend to rely on eyewitness testimony as evidence. A difficulty with personal observation, however, is the tendency to see or hear what we wish to see or hear, selecting and remembering those aspects of an experience that are most consistent with our previous experience and background.

Observers, unlike certain mirrors, do not give us "pure" observations. What we "see" and report is filtered through a set of values, biases, attitudes, and expectations. Because of such influences, observers often disagree about what they perceive. Thus, we should be wary of reliance on observations made by any single observer in situations in which we might expect observations among observers to vary.

Three illustrations should help you see the danger of relying on personal observation as evidence:

- A player says he crossed the end zone, and the referee says the player stepped out of bounds first.
- There is a car accident at a busy intersection. The drivers blame each other. Witnesses alternately blame the drivers and a third car that sped off.
- You send what you believe to be a friendly e-mail to a friend. Your friend responds to you wanting to know why you sent such a mean note to her.

While personal observations can often be valuable sources of evidence, we need to recognize that they are not unbiased "mirrors of reality"; and when they are used to support controversial conclusions, we should seek verification by other observers as well as other kinds of evidence to support the conclusion. For example, if an employee complains that certain remarks made by her boss are discriminatory, the claim is more credible if others who heard the remarks also think the comments were discriminatory. Also, remember that observational reports get increasingly problematic as the time between the observation and the report of the observation increases.

When reports of observations in newspapers, magazines, books, television, and the Internet are used as evidence, you need to determine whether there are good reasons to rely on such reports. The most reliable reports will be based on recent observations made by several people observing under optimal conditions who have no apparent, strong expectations or biases related to the event being observed.

RESEARCH STUDIES AS EVIDENCE

"Studies show . . ."

"Research investigators have found in a recent survey that . . ."

"A report in the *New England Journal of Medicine* indicates . . ."

One form of authority that relies a great deal on observation and often carries special weight is the research study—usually a systematic collection of observations by people trained to do scientific research. How dependable are research findings? Like appeals to any authority, we cannot tell about the dependability of research findings until we ask lots of questions.

Society has turned to the scientific method as an important guide for determining the facts because the relationships among events in our world are very complex and because humans are fallible in their observations and theories about these events. The scientific method attempts to avoid many of the built-in biases in our observations of the world and in our intuition and common sense.

What is special about the scientific method? Above all, it seeks information in the form of *publicly verifiable data*—that is, data obtained under conditions such that other qualified people can make similar observations and see whether they get the same results. Thus, for example, if one researcher reports that she was able to achieve cold fusion in the lab, the experiment would seem more credible if other researchers could obtain the same results.

A second major characteristic of scientific method is *control*—that is, the using of special procedures to reduce error in observations and in the interpretation of research findings. For example, if bias in observations may be a major problem, researchers might try to control this kind of error by using multiple observers to see how well they agree with one another. Physical scientists frequently maximize control by studying problems in the laboratory so that they can minimize extraneous factors. Unfortunately, control is usually more difficult in the social world than in the physical world; thus it is very difficult to successfully apply the scientific method to many questions about complex human behavior.

Precision in language is a third major component of the scientific method. Concepts are often confusing, obscure, and ambiguous. Scientific method tries to be precise and consistent in its use of language.

While there is much more to science than we can discuss here, we want you to keep in mind that scientific research, when conducted well, is one of our best sources of evidence because it emphasizes verifiability, control, and precision.

PROBLEMS WITH RESEARCH FINDINGS

Unfortunately, the fact that research has been applied to a problem does not necessarily mean that the research evidence is dependable evidence or that the interpretations of the meaning of the evidence are accurate. Like appeals to any source, appeals to research evidence must be approached with caution. Also, some questions, particularly those that focus on human behavior, can be answered only tentatively even with the best of evidence. Thus, there are a number of important questions we want to ask about research studies before we decide how much to depend on their conclusions.

When communicators appeal to research as a source of evidence, you should remember the following:

1. Research varies greatly in *quality*; we should rely more on some research studies than others. There is well-done research and there is poorly done research, and we should rely more on the former. Because the research process is so complex and subject to so many external influences, even those well-trained in research practices sometimes conduct research studies that have important deficiencies; publication

in a scientific journal does not guarantee that a research study is not flawed in important ways.

2. Research findings often contradict one another. Thus, *single* research studies presented out of the context of the family of research studies that investigate the question often provide misleading conclusions. Research findings that most deserve our attention are those that have been repeated by more than one researcher or group of researchers. We need to always ask the question: "Have other researchers verified the findings?"

3. Research findings *do not prove* conclusions. At best, they *support* conclusions. Research findings do not speak for themselves! Researchers must always *interpret* the meaning of their findings, and all findings can be interpreted in more than one way. Thus, researchers' conclusions should not be treated as demonstrated "truths."

Attention: When you encounter statements such as "research findings show . . ." you should retranslate them into "researchers INTERPRET their research findings as showing . . .".

---

4. Like all of us, researchers have expectations, attitudes, values, and needs that bias the questions they ask, the way they conduct their research, and the way they interpret their research findings. For example, scientists often have an emotional investment in a particular hypothesis. When the American Sugar Institute is paying for your summer research grant, it is very difficult to then "find" that sugar consumption among teenagers is excessive. Like all fallible human beings, scientists may find it difficult to objectively treat data that conflict with their hypothesis. A major strength of scientific research is that it tries to make public its procedures and results so that others can judge the merit of the research and then try to replicate it. However, regardless of how objective a scientific report may seem, important subjective elements are always involved.

5. Speakers and writers often distort or simplify research conclusions. Major discrepancies may occur between the conclusion merited by the original research and the use of the evidence to support a communicator's beliefs. For example, researchers may carefully qualify their own conclusions in their original research report only to have the conclusions used by others without the qualifications.

6. Research "facts" change over time, especially claims about human behavior. For example, all of the following research "facts" have been reported by major scientific sources, yet have been "refuted" by recent research evidence:

> Prozac is completely safe when taken by children.
> It is important to drink eight glasses of water a day.
> Depression is caused entirely by chemical imbalances in the brain.
> Improper attachment to parents causes anti-social behavior in children.

7. Research varies in how artificial it is. Often, to achieve the goal of control, research loses some of its "real-world" quality. The more artificial the research, the more difficult it is to generalize from the research study to the world outside. The problem of research artificiality is especially evident in research studying complex social behavior. For example, social scientists will have people sit in a room with a computer to play "games"

Clues for Evaluating Research Studies

Apply these questions to research findings to determine whether the findings are dependable evidence.

1. *What is the quality of the source of the report?* Usually, the most dependable reports are those published in peer-review journals, those in which a study is not accepted until it has been reviewed by a series of relevant experts. Usually—but not always—the more reputable the source, the better designed the study. So, try to find out all you can about the reputation of the source.
2. Other than the quality of the source, are there other clues included in the communication suggesting the research was well done? For example, *does the report detail any special strengths of the research?*
3. *Has the study been replicated?* Has more than one study reached the same conclusion? Findings, even when "statistically significant," can arise by chance alone. For example, when an association is repeatedly and consistently found in well-designed studies, like the link between smoking and cancer, then there is reason to believe it, at least until those who disagree can provide persuasive evidence for their point of view.
4. *How selective has the communicator been in choosing studies?* For example, have relevant studies with contradictory results been omitted? Has the researcher selected only those studies that support his point?
5. *Is there any evidence of strong-sense critical thinking?* Has the speaker or writer showed a critical attitude toward earlier research that was supportive of her point of view? Most conclusions from research need to be qualified because of research limitations. Has the communicator demonstrated a willingness to qualify?
6. *Is there any reason for someone to have distorted the research?* We need to be wary of situations in which the researchers *need* to find certain kinds of results.
7. *Are conditions in the research artificial and therefore distorted?* Always ask, "How similar are the conditions under which the research study was conducted to the situation the researcher is generalizing about?"
8. *How far can we generalize, given the research sample?* We discuss this question in depth in our next section.
9. *Are there any biases or distortions in the surveys, questionnaires, ratings, or other measurements that the researcher uses?* We need to have confidence that the researcher has measured accurately what she has wanted to measure. The problem of biased surveys and questionnaires is so pervasive in research that we discuss it in more detail in a later section.

that involve testing people's reasoning processes. The researchers are trying to figure out why people make certain decisions when confronted with different scenarios. However, we should ask, "Is sitting at the computer while thinking through hypothetical situations too artificial to tell us much about the way people make decisions when confronted with real dilemmas?"

8. The need for financial gain, status, security, and other factors can affect research outcomes. Researchers are human beings, not computers. Thus, it is extremely difficult for them to be totally objective. For example, researchers who want to find a certain outcome through their research may interpret their results in such a way to find the desired outcome. Pressures to obtain grants, tenure, or other personal rewards might ultimately affect the way in which researchers interpret their data.

As you can see, despite the many positive qualities of research evidence, we need to avoid embracing research conclusions prematurely.

GENERALIZING FROM THE RESEARCH SAMPLE

Speakers and writers usually use research reports to support generalizations—that is, claims about events in general. For example, "the medication was effective in treating cancer for the patients in the study" is not a generalization; "the medication cures cancer" is. The ability to generalize from research findings depends on the *number, breadth*, and *randomness* of events or people the researchers study.

The process of selecting events or persons to study is called *sampling*.

Because researchers can never study all events or people about whom they want to generalize, they must choose some way to sample; and some ways are preferable to others. You need to keep several important considerations in mind when evaluating the research sample:

1. The sample must be large enough to justify the generalization or conclusion. In most cases, the more events or people researchers observe, the more dependable their conclusion. If we want to form a general belief about how often college students receive help from others on term papers, we are better off studying 100 college students than studying 10.

2. The sample must possess as much *breadth*, or diversity, as the types of events about which conclusions are to be drawn. For example, if researchers want to generalize about college students' drinking habits in general, their evidence should be based on the sampling of a variety of different kinds of college students in a variety of different kinds of college settings. Students at a small private school in the Midwest may have different drinking habits than students at a large public school on the West Coast; thus, a study of students attending only one school would lack breadth of sampling.

3. The more *random* the sample, the better. When researchers randomly sample, they try to make sure that all events about which they want to generalize have an *equal chance* of getting sampled; they try to avoid a biased sample. Major polls, like the Gallop poll, for example, always try to sample randomly. This keeps them from getting groups of events or people that have biased characteristics. Do you see how each of the following samples has biased characteristics?

a. People who volunteer to be interviewed about frequency of sexual activity.

b. People who are at home at 2:30 P.M. to answer their phone.

c. Readers of a popular women's magazine who clip and complete mail-in surveys.

Thus, we want to ask of all research studies, "How many events or people did they sample, how much breadth did the sample have, and how random was the sample?"

A common problem that stems from not paying enough attention to the limits of sampling is for communicators to *overgeneralize* research findings. They state a generalization that is much broader than that warranted by the research. In Chapter 7, we referred to such overgeneralizing as the *Hasty Generalization* fallacy. Let's take a close look at a research overgeneralization:

> Alcohol consumption is at an all-time high at colleges nationwide. A recent survey conducted by Drinksville University found that of the 250 people surveyed, 89 percent drink on a semi-regular basis.

Sampling procedures prohibit such a broad generalization. The research report implies the conclusion can be applied to *all* campuses, when the research studied only one campus. We don't even know whether the conclusion can be applied to that campus, because we don't know how randomly researchers sampled from it. The research report is flawed because it greatly overgeneralizes. *Remember:* **We can generalize only to people and events that are like those that we have studied in the research!**

Attention: A common tendency of the news and television media is to generalize beyond what is warranted by a sample when reporting research results. Thus pay very close attention to the nature of samples used in publicized research.

BIASED SURVEYS AND QUESTIONNAIRES

It's early evening. You have just finished dinner. The phone rings. "We're conducting a survey of public opinion. Will you answer a few questions?" If you answer "yes," you will be among thousands who annually take part in surveys—one of the research methods you will encounter most frequently. Think how often you hear the phrase "according to recent polls."

Surveys and questionnaires are usually used to measure people's attitudes and beliefs. Just how dependable are they? It depends! Survey responses are subject to many influences; thus, one has to be very cautious in interpreting their meaning. Let's examine some of these influences.

First, for survey responses to be meaningful, they must be answered honestly. That is, verbal reports need to mirror actual beliefs and attitudes. Yet, for a variety of reasons, people frequently shade the truth. For example, they may give answers they think they ought to give, rather than answers that reflect their true beliefs. They may experience hostility toward the questionnaire or toward the kind of question asked. They may give too little thought to the question. If you have ever been a survey participant, you can probably think of other influences.

Remember: You cannot assume that verbal reports accurately reflect true attitudes.

Second, many survey questions are ambiguous in their wording; the questions are subject to multiple interpretations. Different individuals may in essence be responding to different questions! For example, imagine the multiple possible interpretations of the following survey question: "Do you think there is quality programming on television?" The more ambiguous the wording of a survey, the less credibility you can place in the results.

You should always ask the question: "How were the survey questions worded?" Usually, the more specifically worded a question, the more likely that different individuals will interpret it similarly.

Third, surveys contain many *built-in biases* that make them even more suspect. Two of the most important are *biased wording* and *biased context.* Biased wording of a question is a common problem; a small change in how a question is asked can have a major effect on how a question is answered. Let's examine a conclusion based on a recent poll and then look at the survey question.

> A college professor found that 86 percent of respondents believe
> that President Bush has failed the American people with respect to
> his handling of the war in Iraq.

Now let's look closely at the survey question: "What do you think about the President's misguided efforts in the war in Iraq?" Look carefully at this question. Do you see the built-in bias? The "leading" words are "the President's misguided efforts." Wouldn't the responses have been quite different if the question had read: "What do you think about the President's attempt to bring democracy, markets, and freedom to the Iraqi people?" Thus, the responses obtained here are not an accurate indicator of attitudes concerning President Bush's handling of the war in Iraq.

Survey and questionnaire data must always be examined for possible bias. *Look carefully at the wording of the questions!* Here is another example. We have emphasized the word that demonstrates the bias.

QUESTION: *Should poor people who* **refuse** *to get a job be allowed to receive welfare benefits?*

CONCLUSION: *Ninety-three percent of people responding believe poor people should not receive welfare benefits.*

The effect of *context* on an answer to a question can also be powerful. Even answers to identical questions can vary from poll to poll depending on how the questionnaire is presented and how the question is embedded in the survey. The following question was included in two recent surveys: "Do you think we should lower the drinking age from 21?" In one survey, the question was preceded by another question: "Do you think the right to vote should be given to children at the age of 18 as it currently is?" In the other survey, no preceding question occurred. Not surprisingly, the two surveys showed different results. Can you see how the context might have affected respondents?

Another important contextual factor is *length*. In long surveys, people may respond differently to later items than to earlier items simply because they get tired. *Be alert to contextual factors when evaluating survey results.*

Because the way people respond to surveys is affected by many unknown factors, such as the need to please or the interpretation of the question, should we ever treat survey evidence as good evidence? There are heated debates about this issue, but our answer is "yes," as long as we are careful and do not generalize further than warranted. Some surveys are more reputable than others. The better the quality of the survey, the more you should be influenced by the results.

Our recommendation is to examine survey *procedures* carefully before accepting survey *results*. Once you have ascertained the quality of the procedures, you can choose to generate your own *qualified generalization*—one that takes into account any biases you might have found. Even biased surveys can be informative; but you need to know the biases in order to not be unduly persuaded by the findings.

CRITICAL EVALUATION OF A RESEARCH-BASED ARGUMENT

Let's now use our questions about research to evaluate the following argument in which research evidence has been used to support a conclusion.

Parents who push their children to study frequently end up causing their children to dislike reading, a recent study argues. The researchers studied 56 children in the sixth grade and found that those who reported the greatest dislike for reading were the ones whose parents frequently forced them to read. Alternatively, students who reported enjoying reading had less domineering parents. "The more demanding the parents were with studying, the less likely the child was to enjoy reading on his or her own," claim Stanley and Livingstone in the August issue of *Educator's War Chest*. The study was conducted at Little Creek elementary school in Phoenix, Arizona. The study found that if not forced to study, children were more likely to pick up a book in their free time. "It seems that there is a natural inclination to rebel against one's parents in children, and one way to manifest this inclination is to refuse to read if the child's parents force the child to study," reported Stanley and Livingstone.

The research is presented here in an uncritical fashion. We see no sign of strong-sense critical thinking. The report makes no references to special strengths or weaknesses of the study, although it does provide some detail about the research procedures so that we can make judgments about its worth as the basis of a generalization. There is no indication of whether the study has been replicated. Also, we do not know how selective the communicator has been in choosing studies, nor how this research fits into the broader context of research on children and their enjoyment of reading. We do not know what benefits publishing this study may have had for the researchers.

Have the researchers and passage author overgeneralized? The sample is small—56—and it lacks breadth and randomness because it is restricted to one elementary school in the Southwest. We need to ask many questions about the sampling. How were these children selected? How was the study advertised to the parents? Could there have been a bias in the kind of parents willing to sign up for such a study? Would we have gotten similar results if we had randomly chosen families from a large number of schools throughout the country? This passage clearly illustrates a case of overgeneralization!

Are the questionnaires biased? Consider being a parent and completing a questionnaire about how controlling you are. Don't you think we could raise doubts about the accuracy of responses to such a questionnaire? Too little information is given about the wording of the questionnaires or about the arrangement of questionnaire items to judge the ambiguity of the item wording and the possibility of biased wording and biased context.

We have raised enough questions about the above passage to be wary of its factual claims. We would want to rely on much more research before we could conclude that these claims are dependable.

Let's now look at a very different source of evidence.

CASE EXAMPLES AS EVIDENCE

President of a large university: "Of course our students can move on to high paying jobs and further study at large universities. Why, just this past year we sent one of our students, Mary Nicexample, off to law school at Harvard. In her first year Mary remained in the top 5 percent of her class. Therefore, our students can certainly achieve remarkable success at elite universities."

A frequently used kind of evidence that contrasts markedly to the kind of research study that we have just described, which emphasized studying large representative samples, is the use of a detailed description of one or several individuals or events to support a conclusion. Such descriptions are usually based on observations or interviews and vary from being in depth and thorough to being superficial. We call such descriptions *case examples*.

Communicators often begin persuasive presentations with dramatic descriptions of cases. For example, one way to argue to increase the drinking age is to tell heart-wrenching stories of young people dying in car accidents when the driver was young and drunk.

Case examples are often compelling to us because of their colorfulness and their interesting details, which make them easy to visualize. Political candidates have increasingly resorted to case examples in their speeches, knowing that the rich details of cases generate an emotional reaction. Such cases, however, should be viewed more as *striking examples or anecdotes* than as proof, and we must be very suspicious of their use as evidence.

Dramatic cases *appeal to our emotions* and distract us from seeking other more relevant research evidence. For example, imagine a story about a man who tortured and murdered his numerous victims. The human drama of these crimes may lead us to ignore the fact that such a case is rare and that over the past 30 years 119 inmates with capital sentences were found to be innocent and released from prison.

Attention: *Be wary of striking case examples as proof!*

Although case examples will be consistent with a conclusion, do not let that consistency fool you. Always ask yourself: "Is the example typical?" "Are there powerful counterexamples?" "Are there biases in how the example is reported?"

Are there times that case examples can be useful, even if they are not good evidence? Certainly! Like personal experiences, they demonstrate important *possibilities* and put a personal face on abstract statistics. They make it easier for people to relate to an issue and thus take more interest in it.

ANALOGIES AS EVIDENCE

Look closely at the structure of the following brief arguments, paying special attention to the reason supporting the conclusion.

> Adults cannot learn all of the intricacies of new computer technology. Trying to teach adults new computer systems is like trying to teach an old dog new tricks.

> It is important for an educator to weed out problem students early and take care of the problems they present because one bad egg ruins the omelet.

These two arguments use *analogies* as evidence, a very different kind of evidence from what we have previously been evaluating. How do we decide whether it is good evidence? Before reading on, try to determine the persuasiveness of the two arguments.

Communicators often use *resemblance* as a form of evidence. They reason in the following way: "If these two things are alike in one respect, then they will probably be alike in other respects as well."

For example, when bipolar disorder (manic depression) was first identified, psychologists frequently treated it similarly to depression because both shared the common characteristics of severe depression. We reason in a similar fashion when we choose to buy a CD because a friend recommends it. We reason that because we resemble each other in a number of likes and dislikes, we will enjoy the same music.

An argument that uses a well-known similarity between two things as the basis for a conclusion about a relatively unknown characteristic of one of those things is an *argument by analogy*. Reasoning by analogy is a common way of presenting evidence to support a conclusion.

Analogies both stimulate insights and deceive us. For example, analogies have been highly productive in scientific and legal reasoning. When we infer conclusions about humans on the basis of research with mice, we reason by analogy. Much of our thinking about the structure of the atom is analogical reasoning. When we make a decision in a legal case, we may base that decision on the similarity of that case to preceding cases. For example, when judges approach the question of whether restricting pornographic material violates the constitutional protection of free speech and freedom of expression, they must decide whether the potentially obscene pornographic material is analogous to freedom of speech; thus, they reason by analogy. Such reasoning can be quite insightful and persuasive.

Identifying and Comprehending Analogies

Accurate analogies are powerful, but they are often difficult for people to evaluate. Analogies compare two known things to allow the reader to better understand the relationship to something that is unfamiliar. To be able to identify such comparisons, it is important to understand how analogies are structured. The first part of an analogy involves a familiar object or concept. That object or concept is being compared to another familiar object or concept. The second part is the relationship between the familiar objects or concepts. This relationship is used to create a principle that can be used to assist the understanding of a different object or concept. Finally, the relationship of the new or unfamiliar object or concept is described in the same format as the known object or concept.

For example, "Relearning geometry is like riding a bike. Once you start, it all comes back to you." In the preceding analogy, riding a bicycle, the known, is used to explain relearning geometry, the unknown. We are familiar with the idea of getting on a bike after a period of time and "it all coming back to us" as we start to ride again. The analogy, therefore, explains relearning geometry in the same way, arguing if one simply starts to do geometry problems, remembering how to do such problems will simply come back to the person.

Once the nature and structure of analogies is understood, you should be able to identify analogies in arguments. It is especially important to identify analogies when they are used to set the tone of the conversation. Such analogies are used to *"frame"* an argument. To identify framing analogies, look for comparisons that are used not only to explain a point but also to influence the direction a discussion will take.

For example, in the 2004 presidential election, the war in Iraq was an important issue. Opponents of the war used the analogy comparing the war in Iraq to the Vietnam War. The use of Vietnam as an analogy to the war in Iraq was not only an attempt to explain what is happening in Iraq now but also to cause people to look negatively upon the war in Iraq. Conversely, proponents of the war in Iraq used the analogy comparing the war to World War II. World War II carries with it more positive connotations than does the Vietnam War, so this analogy was used to reframe the discussion in terms more favorable to the war in Iraq. Always look for comparisons that attempt to direct the reaction to an object through framing. A careful evaluation of framing analogies will prevent you from being misled by a potentially deceptive analogy.

Framing analogies is not the only thing to be wary of when looking for analogies in arguments. One must also be careful when evaluating arguments that use overly emotional comparisons. For example, one person in arguing against the estate tax recently compared the tax to the Holocaust. Who could possibly be in favor of a tax that is the equivalent of the Holocaust? However, we must evaluate the analogy to see whether it is really accurate or simply an emotion-laden comparison intended to coerce people into agreeing with a certain perspective by making the alternative seem ridiculous. After all, regardless of what one thinks about the estate tax, it is not responsible for the deaths of millions of people. Overly emotional analogies cloud the real issues in arguments and prevent substantive discourse. Try to identify comparisons made that contain significant emotional connotations to avoid being deceived by these analogies.

Evaluating Analogies

Because analogical reasoning is so common and has the potential to be both persuasive and faulty, you will find it very useful to recognize such reasoning and know how to systematically evaluate it. To evaluate the quality of an analogy, you need to focus on two factors.

1. The number of ways the two things being compared are similar and different.
2. The *relevance* of the similarities and the differences.

A word of caution: You can almost always find some similarities between any two things. So, analogical reasoning will not be persuasive simply because of many similarities. Strong analogies will be ones in which the two things we compare possess *relevant* similarities and lack *relevant* differences. All analogies try to illustrate underlying principles. *Relevant similarities and differences are ones that directly relate to the underlying principle illustrated by the analogy.*

Let's check out the soundness of the following argument by analogy.

> I do not allow my dog to run around the neighborhood getting into trouble, so why shouldn't I enforce an 8 o'clock curfew on my 16-year-old? I am responsible for keeping my daughter safe, as well as responsible for what she might do when she is out. My dog stays in the yard, and I want my daughter to stay in the house. This way, I know exactly what both are doing.

A major similarity between a pet and a child is that both are thought of as not being full citizens with all the rights and responsibilities of adults. Plus, as the speaker asserts, he is responsible for keeping his dog and daughter safe. We note some relevant differences, however. A dog is a pet that lacks higher-order thinking skills and cannot assess right and wrong. A daughter, however, is a human being with the cognitive capacity to tell when things are right and wrong and when she should not do something that might get her (or her parents) in trouble. Also, as a human, she has certain rights and deserves a certain amount of respect for her autonomy. Thus, because a daughter can do things a dog cannot, the differences are relevant in assessing the analogy. The failure of the analogy to allow for the above listed distinctions causes it to fail to provide strong support for the conclusion.

Another strategy that may help you evaluate reasoning by analogy is to *generate alternative analogies* for understanding the same phenomenon that the author or speaker is trying to understand. Such analogies may either support or contradict the conclusions inferred from the original analogy. If they contradict the conclusion, they then reveal problems in the initial reasoning by analogy.

For example, when authors argue that pornography should be banned because it is harmful to women, as well as to all who view it, they are using a particular analogy to draw certain conclusions about pornography: Pornography is like a form of discrimination, as well as a means by which people are taught women are nothing but sex objects. Others, however, have offered alternative analogies, arguing that pornography is "a statement of women's sexual liberation." Note how thinking about this different analogy may create doubts about the persuasiveness of the original analogy.

A productive way to generate your own analogies is the following:

1. Identify some important features of what you are studying.
2. Try to identify other situations with which you are familiar that have some similar features. Give free rein to your imagination. Brainstorm. Try to imagine diverse situations.
3. Try to determine whether the familiar situation can provide you with some insights about the unfamiliar situation.

For example, in thinking about pornography, you could try to think of other situations in which people repeatedly think something is demeaning because of the way people are treated in a given situation, or because of what watching something might cause others to do. Do segregation, racist/sexist jokes, or employment discrimination come to mind? How about arguments claiming that playing violent video games, watching action movies, or listening to heavy metal music causes children to act violently? Do they trigger other ways to think about pornography? You should now be capable of systematically evaluating the two brief analogical arguments at the beginning of this section. Ask the questions you need to ask to determine the structure of the argument. Then, ask the questions to evaluate the argument. Look for relevant similarities and differences. Usually, the greater the ratio of relevant similarities to relevant differences, the stronger the analogy. An analogy is especially compelling if you can find *no* relevant difference and you can find good evidence that the relevant similarities do indeed exist.

We found a relevant difference that weakens each of our two initial sample analogies on page 135. Check your evaluation against our list.

(First example) Learning computer skills involves cognitive capabilities well within those of your average adult; teaching "an old dog new tricks" involves training an animal with lower cognitive abilities, who is set in his ways, how to obey a command he may never have heard before. Learning computer skills is not the same as classically conditioning an animal.

(Second example) The interactions of students in a classroom environment are very complex. The effect any one student might have on the group cannot easily be determined, just as the effects the group might have on the individual are difficult to predict. Conversely, a rotten egg will definitely spoil any food made from it. Also, it is problematic to think of people as unchanging objects, such as rotten eggs, that have no potential for growth and change.

Analogies that trick or deceive us fit our definition of a reasoning fallacy; such deception is called the *Faulty Analogy* fallacy.

F: Faulty Analogy: Occurs when an analogy is proposed in which there are important relevant dissimilarities.

In one sense, all analogies are faulty, because they make the mistaken assumption that because two things are alike in one or more respects, they are necessarily alike in some other important respect. It is probably best for you to think of analogies as varying from very weak to very strong. But even the best analogies are only suggestive. Thus if an author draws a conclusion about one case from a comparison to another case, then she should provide further evidence to support the principle revealed by the most significant similarity.

Summary

This chapter has continued our focus on the evaluation of evidence. We have discussed the following kinds of evidence: observation, research studies, case examples, and analogies. Each source has its strengths and weaknesses. Usually, you can rely most on those claims that writers or speakers support directly by extensive scientific research. However, many issues have not been settled by scientific research, and consequently communicators must rely on research that is not conclusive and on other sources of evidence. You should be especially wary of claims supported by biased observation, dramatic case examples, poorly designed research, or faulty analogies. When you encounter *any* evidence, you should try to determine its quality by asking, *"How good is the evidence?"*

Practice Exercises

 Critical Question: **How good is the evidence?**

Evaluate each of these practice passages by examining the quality of the evidence provided.

Passage 1

Are children of alcoholics more likely to be alcoholics themselves? In answering the question, researchers sampled 451 people in Alcoholics Anonymous to see how many would say that one, or both, of their parents were alcoholics. People in AA used in the study currently attend AA somewhere in Ohio, Michigan, or Indiana and were asked by people in charge of the local AA programs to volunteer to fill out a survey. The research found that 77 percent of the respondents had at least one parent they classified as an alcoholic. The study also surveyed 451 people randomly from the same states who claim not to be heavy drinkers. Of the non-heavy drinkers, 23 percent would label at least one of their parents as alcoholic.

Passage 2

I think California's "three strikes law" is a great idea. Why should criminals be given unlimited chances to continue to re-offend? We give a batter only three attempts to swing and hit a ball, so why does a criminal deserve any better? Three swings and misses and you are out; three offenses and convictions and you are in, jail that is.

Passage 3

One of the greatest symbols of the United States is the American flag. While cases in the past have defended desecration of the flag as symbolic speech I argue, "Where is the speech in such acts?" I do not believe allowing people to tarnish the flag and thus attack everything that America stands for is the same as allowing free speech. If you have something bad to say about the United States say it, but do not cheapen the flag with your actions. Many Americans died to keep that flag flying.

Those who want to support flag burning and other such despicable acts are outnumbered. Last month, 75 people were surveyed in a restaurant in Dallas, Texas, and were asked if they supported the unpatriotic desecration of the American flag in an attempt to express some sort of anti-American idea. Ninety-three percent responded that they were not in favor of desecration of the American flag. Therefore, our national lawmakers should pass a law protecting the American flag against such horrible actions.

Sample Responses To Passages 1 and 2

Passage 1

CONCLUSION: *Children of alcoholics are more likely to become alcoholics than are children of non-alcoholics.*

REASON: *More alcoholics than non-alcoholics reported having at least one alcoholic parent.*

Note that the results presented are from a single study without reference to how typical these results are. We also do not know where this information was published, so we can make no assessments regarding how rigorously the study was reviewed before publication. However, we can ask some useful questions about the study. The sample size is quite large, but its breadth is questionable. Although multiple states were sampled, to what extent are the people in the AA programs in these states typical of alcoholics across the nation? Also, how do alcoholics in AA compare to alcoholics who have not sought help? Perhaps the most important sampling problem was the lack of a random sample. While the self-reported non-alcoholics were randomly selected in the three states, the respondents in AA were selected on a voluntary basis. Do those who volunteered to talk about their parents differ greatly from those who did not volunteer? If there is a difference between the volunteers and non-volunteers, then the sample is biased.

How accurate are the rating measurements? First, no definition for alcoholic for those answering the survey is given beyond currently being in AA. In addition, we are not told of any criteria given to the research participants for rating parents as alcoholic. Thus we are uncertain of the accuracy of the judgments about whether someone was an alcoholic. Also, problematic is the fact that the selection of the supposed control group of non-alcoholics is based on self-assessment. We know that there is a socially acceptable answer of not being an alcoholic, and people tend to give socially acceptable answers when they are known. This response tendency could also bias the sampling in the supposed control group. We would want to know more about the accuracy of these ratings before we could have much confidence in the conclusion.

Passage 2

CONCLUSION: *Three strikes law for criminal offenses are desirable.*

REASON: *Allowing a criminal to offend three times is like allowing a batter in baseball to swing and miss three times.*

The author is arguing the desirability of the three strikes law by drawing an obvious analogy to baseball. The similarity the author is focusing on is that three chances for a batter to hit a ball is much like the three chances awarded to convicted offenders to shape up or to be put in jail for a long time. But simply saying three criminal offenses deserve harsh punishment ignores the complexity involved in criminal sentencing. For example, while a swing and a miss is a strike regardless of the type of pitch the pitcher throws, we might feel context is very important for sentencing criminals. What if the third offense is something very minor? Does it make sense to punish the criminal severely for a third offense regardless of what the other two were? Because of an important relevant difference, we conclude that this analogy is not very relevant.

Passage 4. Expanding Practice and Feedback

Read the following article from the *New York Times* and apply the critical thinking question that you have studied in this chapter. Then compare your thoughts with the "think aloud" feedback that follows the article.

Americans Change Faiths at Rising Rate, Report Finds

Neela Banerjee

The New York Times (2008)

WASHINGTON — More than a quarter of adult Americans have left the faith of their childhood to join another religion or no religion, according to a new survey of religious affiliation by the Pew Forum on Religion and Public Life.

The report, titled "U.S. Religious Landscape Survey," depicts a highly fluid and diverse national religious life. If shifts among Protestant denominations are included, then it appears that 44 percent of Americans have switched religious affiliations.

For at least a generation, scholars have noted that more Americans are moving among faiths, as denominational loyalty erodes. But the survey, based on interviews with more than 35,000 Americans, offers one of the clearest views yet of that trend, scholars said. The United States Census does not track religious affiliation.

The report shows, for example, that every religion is losing and gaining members, but that the Roman Catholic Church "has experienced the greatest net losses as a result of affiliation changes." The survey also indicates that the group that had the greatest net gain was the unaffiliated. More than 16 percent of American adults say they are not part of any organized faith, which makes the unaffiliated the country's fourth largest "religious group."

Detailing the nature of religious affiliation—who has the numbers, the education, the money—signals who could hold sway over the country's political and cultural life, said John Green, an author of the report who is a senior fellow on religion and American politics at Pew.

Michael Lindsay, assistant director of the Center on Race, Religion and Urban Life at Rice University, echoed that view. "Religion is the single most important factor that drives American belief attitudes and behaviors," said Mr. Lindsay, who had read the Pew report. "It is a powerful indicator of where America will end up on politics, culture, family life. If you want to understand America, you have to understand religion in America."

In the 1980s, the General Social Survey by the National Opinion Research Center indicated that from 5 percent to 8 percent of the population described itself as unaffiliated with a particular religion.

In the Pew survey 7.3 percent of the adult population said they were unaffiliated with a faith as children. That segment increases to 16.1 percent of the population in adulthood, the survey found. The unaffiliated are largely under 50 and male. "Nearly one-in-five men say they have no formal religious affiliation, compared with roughly 13 percent of women," the survey said.

The rise of the unaffiliated does not mean that Americans are becoming less religious, however. Contrary to assumptions that most of the unaffiliated are atheists or agnostics, most described their religion "as nothing in particular." Pew researchers said that later projects would delve more deeply into the beliefs and practices of the unaffiliated and would try to determine if they remain so as they age.

While the unaffiliated have been growing, Protestantism has been declining, the survey found. In the 1970s, Protestants accounted for about two-thirds of the population. The Pew survey found they now make up about 51 percent. Evangelical Christians account for a slim majority of Protestants, and those who leave one evangelical denomination usually move to another, rather than to mainline churches.

To Prof. Stephen Prothero, large numbers of Americans leaving organized religion and large numbers still embracing the fervor of evangelical Christianity point to the same desires.

"The trend is toward more personal religion, and evangelicals offer that," said Mr. Prothero, chairman of the religion department at Boston University, who explained that evangelical churches tailor many of their activities for youth. "Those losing out are offering impersonal religion and those winning are offering a smaller scale: mega-churches succeed not because they are mega but because they have smaller ministries inside."

The percentage of Catholics in the American population has held steady for decades at about 25 percent. But that masks a precipitous decline in native-born Catholics. The proportion has been bolstered by the large influx of Catholic immigrants, mostly from Latin America, the survey found.

The Catholic Church has lost more adherents than any other group: about one-third of respondents raised Catholic said they no longer identified as such. Based on the data, the survey showed, "this means that roughly 10 percent of all Americans are former Catholics."

Immigration continues to influence American religion greatly, the survey found. The majority of immigrants are Christian, and almost half are Catholic. Muslims rival Mormons for having the largest families. And Hindus are the best-educated and among the richest religious groups, the survey found.

"I think politicians will be looking at this survey to see what groups they ought to target," Professor Prothero said. "If the Hindu population is negligible, they won't have to worry about it. But if it is wealthy, then they may have to pay attention."

Experts said the wide-ranging variety of religious affiliation could set the stage for further conflicts over morality or politics, or new alliances on certain issues, as religious people have done on climate change or Jews and Hindus have done over relations between the United States, Israel and India.

"It sets up the potential for big arguments," Mr. Green said, "but also for the possibility of all sorts of creative synthesis. Diversity cuts both ways."

Step-by-Step Walkthrough

What are the strengths and the weaknesses of the evidence presented in this article? How does the evidence differ from the heavy use of personal experience testimonials in the article on homeschooling at the end of Chapter 8? Let's see what thinking aloud about this article might look like.

- First, I want to have a sense of the issue and the conclusion so that I can see how the evidence fits into the overall structure of the reasoning. A reading through the article shows an emphasis on describing shifts in religious affiliations and why that matters. The central issue seems to be, "How have religious affiliations changed recently and why are such changes important?" Then I note the reliance on survey data and appeals to authority to support conclusions such as the following

  Conclusions based on survey data:
  More than a quarter of adult Americans have left the faith of their childhood to join another religion or no religion.
  Forty-four percent of Americans have switched religious affiliations.
  While every religion is losing and gaining members, the Roman Catholic Church "has experienced the greatest net losses as a result of affiliation changes," and the group with the greatest net gain was the unaffiliated.
  While the unaffiliated have been growing, Protestantism has been declining.
  Immigration influences American religion greatly.

  Conclusions by the experts in response to the issue of "What are the implications of the survey findings?"
  Prof. Stephen Prothero: Politicians will be looking at this survey to see what groups they ought to target.
  Experts in general: Wide ranging variety of religious affiliation could set the stage for further conflicts over morality or politics or new alliances on certain issues; it sets up potential for big arguments and for creative synthesis.

- Next, I want to know more specifically just on what kind of evidence the author depends. This article clearly relies on research studies in the form of surveys, but it also includes appeals to authority (see Chapter 8). Because appeals to authority are not a focus of this chapter, I will concentrate only on evaluating the survey evidence.

- Thus, I will next want to ask the critical questions about surveys mentioned in *Asking the Right Questions*. The first survey mentioned is a Pew Forum on Religion and Public Life survey referred to as "U.S. Religious Landscape Survey." I need to ask, "What does the article communicate about the quality or reputation of the source?" I am aware that Pew survey studies are often cited in major publications; thus, I have the sense that they are reputable. I also checked out their Web site at http://people-press.org/about/, which indicates that it is a nonpartisan organization, whose president is the former president of the Gallup poll organization, as well as other relevant information suggesting its credibility. But as important an indicator of the quality of the particular study is information about the study itself, especially about sampling procedures and wording of questions. I know that even some of the best research often has limitations that are not acknowledged in newspaper reports.

• I note that the survey was based on interviews with more than 35,000 Americans, thus a very large sample size. Good! I view the sample size as a major strength. But the authors fail to specify the randomness or the breadth of the sample. It is an interview survey; and I wonder, for example, whether there might be biases in the kinds of individuals willing to volunteer to participate in interviews about their religious affiliations. Thus, I need to be sensitive to possible overgeneralizations in the article. Another survey is mentioned for comparison purposes, but no information is provided about that survey; so I will be cautious about reliance on its findings.

• How about the wording used in the survey? Are there important ambiguities? Very little direct information is provided about survey wording. Thus my next best clue is wording used in the statement of results, such as "More than 16 percent of American adults say they are not part of any organized faith," and "7.3 percent . . . said they were unaffiliated with a faith as children." Because the actual wording of questions, as well as the context and order of the questions is omitted, I find it difficult to judge the extent of bias in the wording and in order of questions.

• The next question of quality of the article that strikes me is the language used in stating findings. It is a language of broad generalization, such as, "More than 16 percent of American adults say they are not part of any organized faith," or "44 percent of Americans have switched religious affiliations," or "Protestants, . . . usually move to another, rather than to mainline churches." I will want to mentally note that biases in samples may make such generalizations overreaching. For example, shouldn't the generalizations be worded "Americans who volunteer to be interviewed for Pew surveys . . . " rather than Americans in general. However, because the sample size is so large and the organization has had much experience with large surveys, I wouldn't expect a major sample bias.

• Another question that I want to ask of this evidence is whether it has been replicated. Have other researchers found similar results? The author fails to cite any replications.

- I also question how selective the communicator has been in choosing the portions of the study she discusses in the article. Newspaper articles have space limitations and thus must be selective in what they highlight. Has there been any selective bias in choosing which results to emphasize?
- Is there any evidence of strong sense critical thinking? I don't note any comments about research limitations. Is there any reason for someone to have distorted the research?
- I would want to know more about the Pew Forum on Religion and Public Life in order to make judgments about how likely it is to have any kinds of biases that might have influenced how it collected the data and how it interpreted it.
- In summary, my impression is that these reports of survey results deserve my attention because (1) they address an issue that is interesting to me and relevant to other important issues, (2) they reveal interesting shifts in religious affiliation behavior in the United States, and (3) they are based on a very large sample size interview study conducted by what seems to be a reputable survey organization. But I should avoid overgeneralizing from the findings and keep in mind the limitations noted in my walkthrough.

CRITICAL QUESTION SUMMARY: WHY THIS QUESTION IS IMPORTANT

How Good Is the Evidence: Personal Observation, Research Studies, Case Examples and Analogies?

Many reasons and conclusions require evidence before we should find them very trustworthy. Also, some kinds of evidence should be much more persuasive than others. Thus, answering this question helps us determine both the need for evidence and the quality of the evidence provided. By identifying the evidence offered in support of a reason and/or a conclusion, you are taking an important step in evaluating their dependability. For example, if the evidence that supports a reason is good, the reason better supports the conclusion. Thus, you might be more willing to accept the author's conclusion if the author offers good evidence in support of a reason, which in turn provides good support for the conclusion.

CHAPTER 10

Are There Rival Causes?

We begin this chapter with a story.

> An inquisitive little boy noticed that the sun would show up in the sky in the morning and disappear at night. Puzzled by where the sun went, the boy tried to watch the sunset really closely. However, he still could not figure out where the sun was going. Then, the boy also noticed that his babysitter showed up in the mornings and left at night. One day he asked his babysitter where she went at night. The babysitter responded, "I go home." Linking his babysitter's arrival and departure with the coming of day and night, he concluded that his babysitter's leaving caused the sun to also go home.

This story clearly illustrates a common difficulty in the use of evidence: trying to figure out what caused something to happen. We cannot determine an intelligent approach to avoiding a problem or encouraging a particular positive outcome until we understand the causal pattern that gave rise to the phenomenon in the first place. For example, we want to know what caused the steady rise in oil prices in the United States over the last few years. Or, *why* the suicide rate among professionals increased over the last 10 years.

The story also shows a very common difficulty in using evidence to prove that something caused something else—the problem of *rival causes*. The fictional little boy offered one interpretation of his observations: the sun sets at night because my babysitter goes home. We expect that you can see another very plausible explanation for why the sun sets.

Although rival causes will rarely be as obvious as they are in our story, you will frequently encounter experts presenting one hypothesis to explain events or research findings when other plausible hypotheses could also explain them. Usually, these experts will not reveal rival causes to you because they do not want to detract from the sound of certainty associated with their claims; you will have to produce them. Doing so can be especially helpful as you decide "how good is the evidence?" The existence of multiple, plausible rival causes for events reduce our confidence in the cause originally offered by the author.

Searching for rival causes will always be appropriate when a speaker or writer presents you with some evidence and offers a cause to explain it.

 Critical Question: Are there rival causes?

> **Attention:** *A rival cause is a plausible alternative explanation that can explain why a certain outcome occurred.*

WHEN TO LOOK FOR RIVAL CAUSES

You need to look for rival causes when you have good reason to believe that the writer or speaker is using evidence to support a claim about the cause of something. The word *cause* means "to bring about, make happen, or affect." Communicators can indicate causal thinking to you in a number of ways. We have listed a few.

X has the effect of . . .	X deters . . .
X leads to . . .	X increases the likelihood . . .
X influences . . .	X determines . . .
X is linked to . . .	X is associated with . . .

These clues to causal thinking should help you recognize when a communicator is making a causal claim. Once you note such a claim, be alert to the possibility of rival causes.

THE PERVASIVENESS OF RIVAL CAUSES

On the afternoon of March 28, 1941, Virginia Woolf wrote two letters, sealed them, and placed them on the mantle. She quickly put on her coat, grabbed her walking stick, and headed outside. She crossed the meadows to the river Ouse, where she put large stones into her coat pocket and threw herself into the river, committing suicide.

Authors have offered numerous hypotheses to explain this event, including the following:

1. Virginia Woolf had a fear of impending madness. She had a history of mental illness and depression. Also, given the recent outbreak of World War II and her history of an inability to deal with aggression, Virginia decided it would be best if she took her own life.[1]

---

[1] Alma Halbert Bond, *Who Killed Virginia Woolf: A Psychobiography* (New York: Human Sciences Press, 1989): 15–19.

2. Some psychologists argue Virginia Woolf had an intense attachment with her father. The attachment was so strong that Virginia developed to be much like her father in many significant ways. One important event in Virginia's life, therefore, was watching her father's deteriorating health when Virginia was in her early twenties. She never forgot about her father's suffering and deterioration. So, when Virginia was 59 years old and feeling that her writing was beginning to deteriorate, she took her life in order to avoid identifying with, and in essence becoming, her dying father.[2]

3. Virginia Woolf was disillusioned with her marriage to Leonard Woolf. The two had a sexless marriage, and Virginia found companionship in an extra-marital lesbian relationship. Virginia's homosexuality put tremendous strain on the marriage that was in turn only made worse by the fact that Leonard probably had several affairs. Virginia was a very jealous person and did not take lightly to these affairs. Her dissatisfaction with the condition of her marriage led her to take her life.[3]

Woolf's own writing leads to any number of possible causes for her suicide.

Now, let's leave Virginia Woolf's suicide for a moment and examine a different event in need of explanation—the findings of a research study.

A researcher reported that eating celery helps curb aggression. A total of 151 women were surveyed, and 95 percent who reported eating celery on a regular basis also reported low levels of aggression, or overall irritability. Of the portion of women who do not eat celery on a regular basis, 53 percent reported frequent feelings of irritability, agitation, and aggression.

In this study, the researcher probably began with the hypothesis that eating celery *causes* reduction of aggressive impulses, and he found evidence consistent with that hypothesis. But let us offer several rival, or different, causes for the same findings:

1. Research participants were highly suggestible, and the *expectation of low levels of aggression* was responsible for the reported differences; like the sugar pill placebo effect in medicine, believing that eating celery lowers aggression might have stimulated a number of physical and mental processes that caused participants to feel less aggression.

2. Participants wanted to please the researchers; thus, they reported feeling low levels of aggression, even though they did experience some aggressive feelings.

3. Nothing is known about the women involved in the study. It is entirely plausible that those who eat celery are health conscious, and thus are more likely to exercise. The increased amounts of exercise can be an outlet for aggression, and thus lower feelings of aggression. Those who

[2]Ibid. pp. 59–63.
[3]Ibid. pp. 62–63.

do not eat celery regularly may not exercise as often and thus do not have an outlet for their aggression.

Now, let's leave the research laboratory for a moment and move to the national pages of our newspapers and examine an argument related to crime statistics.

Since 1993, the levels of serious violent crime in the United States have decreased steadily. It is obvious that the heavy focus we place on law enforcement is no longer necessary. People are becoming civic minded and are choosing to no longer pursue a life of crime. Money spent on law enforcement can now better be spent elsewhere.

The hypothesis offered by the writer is that people's increasing civic engagement is the cause of the decrease in violent crimes over the last 12 years. But, let's again generate some plausible rival causes:

1. Violent crime rates have decreased because of the increased focus on law enforcement the writer is specifically calling to be cut. An increased concern with law enforcement, and not the civic concerns of citizens, caused violent crime levels to decrease.
2. Recent legislative actions have increased the punishments associated with violent crimes. These increased punishments make the costs of committing a violent crime far outweigh the benefits of committing violent crimes. People are not more civic minded, rather they are looking out for their own personal interests.
3. The booming economy in the 1990s could have decreased the number of people in poverty. Given that the poor are typically the perpetrators of what we call violent crimes, fewer poor people would lower the violent crime rate.

Lessons Learned

1. Many kinds of events are open to explanation by rival causes.
2. Experts can examine the same evidence and "discover" different causes to explain it.
3. Most communicators will provide you with only their favored causes; the critical reader or listener must generate rival causes.
4. Generating rival causes is a creative process; usually such causes will not be obvious.
5. Finally, the certainty of a particular causal claim is inversely related to the number of plausible rival causes. Hence, identifying the multiple rival causes gives the critical thinker the proper sense of intellectual humility.

Now, let's examine some important lessons that can be learned from Virginia Woolf's suicide, the celery research study, and the crime statistics.

In the following sections, we explore the implications of these lessons for the critical thinker.

DETECTING RIVAL CAUSES

Locating rival causes is much like being a good detective. When you recognize situations in which rival causes are possible, you want to ask yourself questions like:

- Can I think of any other way to interpret the evidence?
- What else might have caused this act or these findings?
- If I looked at this from another point of view, what might I see as important causes?
- If this interpretation is incorrect, what other interpretation might make sense?

THE CAUSE OR *A* CAUSE

The youth are exhibiting an alarming increase in the rate of depression among elementary aged children. Talk show hosts begin to interview the experts about *the* cause. It is genetic. It is the prevalence of teasing among peer groups. It is parental neglect. It is too much TV news coverage of terrorism and wars. It is lack of religion. It is stress. The experts may *claim* to have the answer, but they are not likely to *know* it. That is because a frequently made error is to look for a simple, single cause of an event when it is really the result of a combination of many *contributory* causes—a cause that helps to create a total set of conditions necessary for the event to occur.

Multiple contributory causes occur more often than do single causes in situations involving the characteristics or activities of humans. In many cases, the best causal explanation is one that combines a considerable number of causes that *only together* are sufficient to bring about the event. So, the best answer experts can give to the talk show hosts' question is "We don't know *the* cause for such events, but we can speculate about possible causes that might have contributed to the event." Thus, when we are searching for rival causes, we need to remember that any single cause that we identify is much more likely to be a contributory cause than *the* cause.

When communicators fail to consider the complexity of causes, they commit the following reasoning fallacy:

F: Causal Oversimplification: Explaining an event by relying on causal factors that are insufficient to account for the event or by overemphasizing the role of one or more of these factors.

In some sense, almost all causal explanations are oversimplifications; thus you want to be fair to communicators who offer explanations that do not include *every* possible cause of an event. Causal conclusions, however, should include sufficient causal factors to convince you that they are not too greatly oversimplified, or the author should make clear to you that the causal factor she emphasizes in her conclusion is only one of a number of possible contributing causes—**a** cause, not **the** cause.

RIVAL CAUSES AND SCIENTIFIC RESEARCH

Scientific research attempts to isolate some of the most important contributing causes from other extraneous causes and provides a major source of hypotheses about what causes events in our world. Researchers start with tentative beliefs—hypotheses—about causes of events. For example, when a massive wave killed thousands of people, researchers generated many hypotheses about the cause of tsunamis. One hypothesis was that tsunamis are caused by massive underwater earthquakes.

Once a hypothesis has been firmly established by dependable research evidence, it changes from a hypothesis to a law. In the domain of complex human behavior, however, there are very few established general laws. Stated claims like "fundamentalism causes terrorism" and "tax cuts cause economic growth" sound like laws, but we need to remain skeptical of the generalizability of such claims. They must currently be viewed as hypotheses, not laws, and are best stated as follows: "fundamentalism may be a contributing cause in the decision to resort to terrorism," and "tax cuts may be a contributing cause in stimulating economic growth."

Then, what should you do when speakers or writers use findings from research studies to conclude that one event causes another? First, remember that their conclusion should be viewed as **a** cause, not **the** cause. Then try to find out as much as you can about the research procedures used to produce the findings that support the hypothesis. Finally, try to determine rival causes that might explain the findings. The more plausible rival causes that can account for the findings, the less faith you should have in the hypothesis favored by the communicator.

Let's use the following argument to practice detecting rival causes.

Playing violent video games for long periods of time appears to increase the likelihood that a child will physically assault another child. The results confirm the general suspicion that violent video games cause violence in children. The relevant research findings are from the Center for Preventing Youth Violence, which enrolled 1,001 male children from across the United States. One-third of the children played "violent" video games, one-third played "non-violent" video games, and the remaining third did not play any video games. The children played several hours of video games alone every day for two weeks. At the end of the two weeks, the children from the different groups were put into a room with toys so that they could play together. Those children who played violent video games were more likely to get into physical altercations with other children than were those who played "non-violent" video games or no video games at all.

Should parents take away all of their children's "violent" video games? Not until they consider rival causes! How else might one explain these group differences?

First, let's outline the reasoning:

CONCLUSION: (Researchers' hypothesis) *Playing violent video games appears to cause an increase in violence among children.*

REASON: (Researchers' evidence) *Research study showed children who played violent video games were more likely to get into physical altercations with other children than were those children who did not play violent video games.*

Note that the words *appears to cause* in the conclusion tell us the researchers are making a causal claim about the evidence. But other hypotheses can explain this evidence.

The report fails to tell us how the children were selected into the three different groups. It is possible that the children were allowed to self-select what games they play, and perhaps children who are more likely to be violent tend to choose "violent" video games. If so, it is possible the researcher has the causal link reversed. Also, nothing is revealed as to how the "play" situation was set up for the children. Perhaps the room or selection of toys was set up in such a way to encourage physical altercations among those who played the "violent" video games. We bet you can think of other reasons these groups—violent video game players and not—differ in their likelihood of resorting to physical violence.

We cannot make you aware of all possible rival causes. In the following selections, however, we provide several clues for finding common rival causes.

RIVAL CAUSES FOR DIFFERENCES BETWEEN GROUPS

One of the most common ways for researchers to try to find a cause for some event is to *compare groups*. For example, you will frequently encounter the following kinds of references to group comparisons:

Researchers compared an experimental group to a control group.

One group received treatment X; the other group didn't.

A group with learning disabilities and a group without learning disabilities.

When researchers find differences between groups, they often conclude, "Those differences support our hypothesis." For example, a researcher might compare a group of people trying to lose weight treated with a new drug with a control group of people trying to lose weight that does not get the new drug, find that the groups differ in their weight loss, and then conclude that the drug caused the difference. The problem is that *research groups almost always differ in more than one important way*, and thus group differences often are consistent with multiple causes. Thus, when you see communicators use findings of differences between groups to support one cause, always ask, "Are there rival causes that might also explain the differences in the groups?"

Let's take a look at a study that compares groups and try to detect rival causes.

In a recent research study, students who prepare for a standardized test by taking a special course designed to teach students how to take the test have scored higher than students who prepare for the same standardized test by reviewing several books about the test.

Here we have two groups: the students who take the class and the students who read a few books. The question we need to ask is, "Did these two groups differ in important ways other than the test preparation they experienced?" Did you think of either of the following possible important differences between the two groups that might account for test score differences?

- *Differences in students' academic (and economic) background.* It is possible that the course costs a substantial sum of money, and only those students who had the money could afford to take the class. Moreover, it is also possible that those students who could afford the money for the class also could afford better private school education before taking the test, and thus start off from a privileged position in comparison with the students who did not take the class.
- *Differences in motivation.* Perhaps the students who signed up for the class are the students who really want to excel in the test. Students who read a few books might be less interested in scoring really well on the standardized test. Alternatively, the students might have chosen study

methods based on how they best learn. It is possible that those who learn best in a class setting might be predisposed to do well on standardized tests.

You probably came up with other important differences. Remember: *Many factors can cause research groups to differ!*

CONFUSING CAUSATION WITH ASSOCIATION

We have an inherent tendency to "see" events that are associated, or that "go together," as events that cause one another. That is, we conclude that because characteristic X (e.g., amount of energy bars consumed) is associated with characteristic Y (e.g., performance in an athletic event), that X therefore causes Y. The following are examples of such reasoning:

1. Classes with larger numbers of students enrolled tend to experience high rates of students' skipping class.
2. More red cars than any other color are pulled over for speeding; therefore, the color of the car affects how fast it goes.

When we think this way, we are, however, often very wrong! Why? Usually multiple hypotheses can explain why X and Y "go together." In fact, there are at least four different kinds of hypotheses to account for any such relationship. Knowing what these are will help you discover rival causes. Let's illustrate each of the four with a research example.

A recent study reported that "smoking combats the flu." The researchers studied 525 smokers and found that 67 percent of the smokers did not have the flu once over the last three years. The researchers hypothesized that the nicotine in the smoke from cigarettes destroys the flu virus before it can spread and cause sickness.

Should people who are feeling under the weather run out and start smoking to prevent the onset of the flu? Not yet. Before they do, they should contemplate each of four potential explanations for the research findings.

Explanation 1: *X is a cause of Y.* (Smoking does indeed kill the flu virus.)

Explanation 2: *Y is a cause of X.* (Feeling healthy, or feeling the beginning of what might be the flu, causes people to smoke.)

Explanation 3: *X and Y are associated because of some third factor, Z.* (Smoking and being without the flu are both caused by related factors, such as frequent washing of the hands after smoking prevents the spread of the flu virus.)

Explanation 4: *X and Y influence each other.* (People who do not usually catch the flu have a tendency to smoke, and the smoke may affect some potential illnesses.)

Remember: *Association or correlation does not prove causation!*

Yet much evidence to prove causation is only based on association or correlation. When an author supports a hypothesis by pointing to an association between characteristics, always ask, "Are there other causes that explain the association?"

Test yourself on the following:

> A recent study reported that "ice cream causes crime." The researchers studied ice cream sales and crime rates over the last five years in the ten largest U.S. cities and found that as ice cream sales increase, so does the crime rate. The researchers hypothesized that the consumption of ice cream triggers a chemical reaction in one's brain causing the individual to have an inclination toward crime.

We hope you can now see that people who eat ice cream need not be concerned that they are about to commit a crime. What rival causes did you think of? Couldn't the increased summer heat account for the association between ice cream sales (X) and crime (Y)?

This confusion between correlation and causation is as understandable as it is dangerous. A cause will indeed precede its effect. But many things preceded that effect. Most of them were not causal.

If Only Having Good Ideas Were So Simple!

You should now be able to identify two common causal reasoning fallacies by attending to the above four possible explanations of why events might be associated:

F: Confusion of Cause and Effect: Confusing the cause with the effect of an event or failing to recognize that the two events may be influencing each other.

F: Neglect of a Common Cause: Failure to recognize that two events may be related because of the effects of a common third factor.

CONFUSING "AFTER THIS" WITH "BECAUSE OF THIS"

Shortly after the 2004 Summer Olympics where Michael Phelps won six gold medals and two bronze medals, the price of college tuition nationwide once again increased. Does this mean we can attribute the price of college tuition to Michael Phelps' Olympic success? No. There are many other possible causes. If we were to infer such a conclusion, we would be illustrating a very common way that people confuse causation with association.

Often, we try to explain a particular event as follows: Because event B *followed* event A, then event A *caused* event B. Such reasoning occurs because human beings have a strong tendency to believe that if two events occur close together in time, the first one must have caused the second one.

To appreciate the flaw in this reasoning, pick up today's newspaper and make a list of what is going on in the world. Then pick up yesterday's newspaper and make a similar list. Could you conclude that the events of yesterday are causing the events of today? Clearly relying only on the temporal association would be foolish . For example, yesterday's news contained more stories about the war in Iraq, and today's news reported that IBM is attempting to buy a start up firm to advance open-source software. It is highly unlikely that events in Iraq caused IBM's attempt to expand its business. Many events that occur after other events in time are not caused by the preceding events. When we wrongly conclude that the first event causes the second because it preceded it, we commit the *Post Hoc, Ergo Propter Hoc* (meaning: "after this, therefore because of this") fallacy, or, for short, the Post Hoc fallacy. Such reasoning is responsible for many superstitious beliefs. For example, you may have written an excellent paper while wearing a particular hat, so now you always insist on wearing the same hat when you write papers.

F: Post Hoc Fallacy: Assuming that a particular event, B, is caused by another event, A, simply because B follows A in time.

The following examples further illustrate the problem with this kind of reasoning.

> "The quarter I found yesterday must be lucky. Since I have found it, I got an A on a really hard test, my least favorite class was canceled, and my favorite movie was on TV last night." (Never mind the fact that I studied really hard for my test, my professor has a six-year old who recently had the flu, and the TV schedule is made far in advance of my finding a quarter.)

> Ever since September 11th, 2001, large numbers of people have been afraid to fly, and airlines are suffering financially because of it. (But perhaps it is also relevant that the economy was suffering

before, and continued to suffer after September 11, and the weak economy could mean that people have less disposable income with which to purchase airplane tickets.)

As you might guess, political and business leaders are fond of using the post hoc argument, especially when it works in their favor. For example, they tend to take credit for anything good that takes place after they assumed their leadership role and to place blame elsewhere for anything bad that happens.

Remember: The finding that one event follows another in time does not by itself prove causation; it may be only a coincidence. When you see such reasoning, always ask yourself, "Are there rival causes that could account for the event?" and, "Is there any good evidence other than the fact that one event followed the other event in time?"

EXPLAINING INDIVIDUAL EVENTS OR ACTS

Why did Mount St. Helen's erupt again in 2004? What caused the increase in alcohol prices? Why did Barack Obama win the presidential election?

Like our question about Virginia Woolf's suicide, these questions seek explanations of individual historical events. Scientific research studies cannot answer the questions. Instead, we must search the past for clues. Such a search makes us highly susceptible to reasoning errors for several reasons. A few of these are especially important to remember.

First, as we saw in Virginia Woolf's case, so many different stories for the same event can "make sense." Second, the way we explain events is greatly influenced by social and political forces, as well as by individual psychological forces. For example, men view the cause of drug abuse differently than women do, and Democrats might view the causes of poverty differently from Republicans.

Also, a common bias is "the *fundamental attribution error*," in which we typically overestimate the importance of personal tendencies relative to situational factors in interpreting the behavior of others. That is, we tend to see the cause of others' behavior as coming from within (their personal characteristics) rather than from without (situational forces.) So, for example, when someone steals something from someone else, we are likely to view the stealing initially as a result of a tendency of the person to be immoral or to be inconsiderate. However, we should also consider the role of outside circumstances, such as poverty or an honest mistake.

Another kind of common psychological error is to start with a limited number of possible causes and then to interpret additional information (even if it is irrelevant) as corroborating these existing hypotheses, rather than keeping the information separate or generating new, perhaps more complex, hypotheses. Our tendency is to simplify the world; yet often explanations require much complexity. Explaining events is not as simple as frequently portrayed by guest experts on the popular talk shows.

How can we know whether we have a "good" explanation of a particular event or set of events? We can never know for sure. But we can make some progress by asking critical questions.

Be wary of accepting the first interpretation of an event you encounter. Search for rival causes and try to compare their credibility. We must accept the fact that *many* events do not have a simple explanation.

EVALUATING RIVAL CAUSES

The more plausible the rival causes that you come up with, the less faith you can have in the initial explanation offered, at least until further evidence has been considered. As a critical thinker, you will want to assess as best you can how each of the alternative explanations fits the available evidence, trying to be sensitive to your personal biases.

In comparing causes, we suggest that you apply the following criteria:

1. their logical soundness;
2. their consistency with other knowledge that you have; and
3. their previous success in explaining or predicting events.

USING THIS CRITICAL QUESTION

Every assertion about causation should trigger immediate curiosity in the mind of a critical thinker. But are there alternative causes for the phenomenon? Asking someone to consider rival causes is constructive criticism at its finest. Your objective in doing so is to find a better causal explanation.

EVIDENCE AND YOUR OWN WRITING AND SPEAKING

The last three chapters have indirectly provided you with a clue for effective communication. Your audience will be justifiably impressed when you provide strong and sufficient evidence for your claims. But implicit in this clue is a warning: Your audience expects and should demand that your claims are supported by thorough evidence. Satisfying this demand is one of your greatest challenges as a writer and speaker.

Summary

Factual claims about the causes of events are weakened when other claims about the causes can be offered. Such claims are *rival causes.*

A common logical error in explaining observations is to confuse causation with association. Thus, always ask what other causes might explain observed associations. Be especially alert to the post hoc fallacy.

Practice Exercises

 *Critical Question: **Are there rival causes?***

Each of the following examples provides an argument to support a causal claim. Try to generate rival causes for such claims. Then try to determine how much you have weakened the author's claim by knowledge of rival causes.

Passage 1

Oranges to combat the blues. Researchers have recently revealed that eating two oranges a day can help alleviate depression. Researchers studied 13 patients who had feelings of depression. After three weeks of eating two oranges a day, 9 of the 13 people reported improvement in their condition. The researchers hypothesize that the citric acid and vitamin C in oranges helps to stimulate serotonin production, helping to combat depression.

Passage 2

Why did the corporate executive steal funds from his business? A close look at his life can provide a clear and convincing answer. The executive comes from a very successful family where his parents are doctors and his siblings are lawyers. As a corporate executive, he was not making as much money as his family members. Also, the executive believes heavily in the American dream and the idea that if one works hard enough that person will succeed. However, despite his hard work the executive has had a number of recent business failures, including losing a substantial sum of money in the stock market. To make matters worse, his children need braces. To live up to expectations, become a success, and provide for his family, the executive had to steal the money from his business.

Passage 3

According to a recent study, one of the major causes of violence in schools is listening to aggressive heavy metal music. Researchers studied more than 100 cases of "serious" violence within schools, and have found that 68% of the children involved in the violence listened to heavy metal music. These children would frequently come to school with headphones, listening to this music, as well as wearing clothing from heavy metal bands. Frequently these heavy metal songs discuss violence, and therefore are a direct cause of school violence.

Sample Responses To Passages 1 and 2

Passage 1

CONCLUSION: *Eating oranges helps alleviate depression.*

REASON: *9 of 13 patients who ate oranges experienced improvement with their depression.*

Can anything else account for the change besides eating oranges? Yes; the researcher fails to rule out many obvious alternative explanations. For example, the patients might have *expected* to get better, and these *expectancies* might have led to feeling better. Also, they knew the purpose of eating oranges, and a rival cause is that they *tried to please* the researchers by reporting that they felt better. We can also hypothesize that external events during the three-week treatment period caused the change. Perhaps during the three weeks of treatment, for example, the weather was especially good, and these people spent much more time exercising outside than usual, which could also help alleviate depression. Another possibility is that these people were suffering from a form of depression from which they could naturally expect to recover in a short period of time. Can you locate other rival causes?

Passage 2

CONCLUSION: *The executive stole money from his company to compete with his family members, to show that he is not a failure, and to provide for his family.*

REASON: *The executive was probably concerned with all of the above elements.*

It is possible that all of the above factors were important in causing the corporate executive to steal from his company. But many other people in society have the same pressures put upon them and they do not resort to illegal means to obtain money. Are there other possible causes for such behavior? As in the case of Virginia Woolf, we suspect there may be many other plausible explanations. Before we could conclude that these stresses in the executive's life are the causal factors, we would want to know more about his childhood and more about recent events in his life. For example, has the corporate executive had any recent disagreements with his boss? Had he been using drugs? Had he had any recent highly stressful experiences? Did he have a history of stealing? After the fact, we can always find childhood experiences that make sense as causes of adult behavior. Before we draw causal conclusions, however, we must seek evidence to prove that the one set of events caused the other in addition to the mere fact that one set of events preceded the other set. We must also be wary not to fall victims to the fundamental attribution error and be certain to consider external causal factors, as well as internal ones.

Passage 4. Expanding Practice and Feedback

What you learned in this chapter of *Asking the Right Questions* will help you walk through the critical thinking process of determining alternative causes. Use the step-by-step explanation at the end of the first passage as a possible example to check your work.

The World According to Disney

Cathy Arnst

Business Week—Working Parents Blog (2008)

This morning a *New York Times* profile of Michelle Obama contained something that truly shocked me. When she entered Princeton University in 1981—a mere 27 years ago—as one of 94 black freshmen in a class of 1,100, the mother of her white roommate spent months pleading with college officials to give her daughter a white roommate instead. "Mom just blew a gasket when I described Michelle," Catherine Donnelly, the roommate, says today. "It was my secret shame."

It's hard for me to imagine that happening today. I realize I live a somewhat sheltered life when it comes to racism, given that my daughter attends a diverse public school in Brooklyn. She would be mystified by raced-based objections to any of her friends. But I think she's not unusual. Survey after survey has found that most members of the under-30 generation are virtually color-blind these days, no matter where they live. And I have a feeling a lot of the credit for this racial progress goes to Disney.

I know, I know, you'd rather not give any credit to the saccharine-sweet world of Disney. But the fact is, the Disney network is a racial nirvana, where children and adults of all races, creeds and colors play, date, and work together, without an eyebrow raised. Take the wildly popular *High School Musical*: the romantic leads, Troy and Gabriela, are a white jock and a Latina brain. Their best friends are both black and the villain is a rich white girl adored by a black basketball player who also loves to bake. Or how about Corey in the House, a spin-off of the hit *That's So Raven*. African-American Corey moves into the White House when his dad is named the head chef by a Hispanic president. His best friends are a white surfer dude and a Middle East girl, who he secretly has a crush on.

This color blind casting is no accident. Disney Channel president of entertainment Rich Ross told Multichannel News four years ago that when he took over in 1996 he was determined to change the complexion of the network.

> We felt [diversity] was missing from the channel at that point, so it became mandatory to be inclusive if we were to march forward as a kid-driven brand," says Ross. "We also knew that if you wanted to send a clear message about diversity [it should include] different ethnic and religious diversities [as well as subjects like] kids with disabilities.

Too bad the rest of Hollywood hasn't followed suit. According to an *Entertainment Weekly* study of casts for the fall 2008 season, each of the five major broadcast networks is whiter than the Caucasian percentage (66.2%) of the U.S. population. And all of the networks are representing considerably lower than the Latino population percentage of 15.2%. The one big exception to this white-mostly casting is teen-focused programming:

> Color-blind casting is something teen-focused networks seem to have down pat: Nary has a show passed through ABC Family or The N without an interracial coupling or a naturally integrated cast. (ABC Family's *Greek* even has an interracial gay couple.) Those networks' execs say it's a simple matter of economics, that their Gen-Y viewers accept—nay, expect and demand—such a reflection of their multicultural lives. "They're completely color-blind," ABC Family president Paul Lee says of younger viewers. "We've done a lot of things wrong as a nation, but we've clearly done something right here. They embrace other cultures."

The millennial generation's attitude toward race was described beautifully two years ago in a *Washington Post* outlook piece, What's Wrong With This Picture?, by a member of that cohort, Justin Brett-Gibson:

> Ninety-five percent of 18-to-29 year olds have friends from different racial backgrounds, according to a Washington Post-Kaiser-Harvard poll. Many Millennials take it further: To us, differences in skin color are largely irrelevant. That's not to say that young minorities never experience racial inequality. Prejudices still exist, and serious economic gaps still yawn between racial and cultural groups. But I feel fortunate to live in an era when, in choosing friends or dates, race can be among the least of my concerns. Essentially, it's no big deal.

As we enter a campaign season featuring the nation's first black presidential candidate, let's hope the children shall lead us, and race will be a non-issue. I never want to go back to 1981.

Step-by-Step Walkthrough

Were you able to find any alternative causes within the article? I hope you did, as there are many possibilities. Follow the example below to understand one possible evaluation of rival causes in the article.

- I start by remembering that I need to look for rival causes when I have good reason to believe the writer or speaker is using evidence to support a claim about the cause of something. In this particular article, the second paragraph signals me that the author draws a causal link between the color-blindness of the under-30 generation and the diversity of race on television when she uses the phrase "I have a feeling a lot of the credit for the racial progress goes to Disney." She then follows with a paragraph depicting how the Disney network features diversity in its TV programming. In other words, the author is arguing that a main cause of a generation's racial progress is teen television programming.
- I want to consider some of the problems with attributing the cause of color-blindness to television programming. There are problems in the reasoning that tell me that there may be some alternative causes the author is not mentioning. First, the author's hypothesis assumes a significant number of the under-30 generation is watching the programming described. The article even stated the Disney Channel only started including racially diverse casts in the past four years, narrowing down the timeframe in which people could be influenced. Furthermore, no evidence was provided about the television habits of the generation; and the article even states that the rest of Hollywood does not have diverse casting. How do we know how many young Americans are even watching the television shows mentioned in the article? I also wonder why stations like the Disney channel would influence teens more than the other programming they watch that is mostly Caucasian based?
- Now that I have suspicions that alternative causes may be at play, I ask myself, "What else besides television programming might have caused the under-30 generation to be more racially color-blind?" Authors often try to provide readers with one convincing cause of a social trend, but creatively brainstorming other possible ways to explain the trend can yield multiple other possibilities.
- So I next create a list of possible rival causes through creative brainstorming. Some possible alternative causes that could lead to greater acceptance of diversity include:

The Education System—Textbooks, teachers, and educational programming shown in schools are reflecting a more diverse society than in past generations. It was only decades ago that we integrated the school systems; so it is no wonder previous generations seemed less diverse.

Changing Demographics—Perhaps one possible cause for increased diversity is the diversification of neighborhoods and school districts. Instead of separate but equal, we are seeing schools with diverse populations and neighborhoods comprised of various races. In the past, neighborhoods (and thus school districts) often were comprised of particular ethnic groups, but urban sprawl and increased population are creating environments with more variety. Perhaps just being around people of different backgrounds makes other realize they are not as different as people once believed.

Political Influences—Younger generations are seeing minorities take more positions of power in government. Women, African Americans, Hispanics, and immigrants now hold, or are contenders for, some of the highest political offices in the United States. Figures such as Barack Obama, Hillary Clinton, Arnold Schwarzenegger, and Condoleezza Rice could make diversity seem more acceptable than past political figures.

These are just three of the most obvious possible rival causes

- I shouldn't forget to consider the possibility that the author may be committing the fallacy of Confusion of Cause and Effect. Perhaps X and Y influence each other. In other words, maybe the executives at stations such as Disney were just integrating casts to meet their market's demand. If Disney saw a growing number of diverse viewers, they could potentially be catering to the needs of the audience. Perhaps viewer diversity (Y) was shaping Disney's practices (X). Furthermore, there is always the chance that a third variable is causing X and Y to seem causally associated, and the author is neglecting this common cause.
- Because the author did not provide reasons for why one should accept her explanation of the cause of the racial progress over other explanations, I should not be very willing to accept her explanation and, ultimately, her conclusion. I would like to see more evidence of consideration of other possible causes before finding her conclusion acceptable.

We hope that you were able to generate your own possible rival causes to the causal claims in the article and to follow along with the sample think aloud model. If so, you are on your way to being successful at the creative thinking involved in detecting rival causes.

CRITICAL QUESTION SUMMARY: WHY THIS QUESTION IS IMPORTANT

Are There Rival Causes?

While an author might offer an explanation for why certain events occurred, other explanations might be plausible. When you try to identify rival causes, you are finding alternative explanations for an event. If you can identify alternative explanations, you must decide whether you should believe the author's explanation or one of the other explanations. If the author does not provide reasons for why you should accept her explanation over other explanations, you should not be willing to accept her explanation and, ultimately, her conclusion. Thus, looking for rival causes is another step in deciding whether to accept or reject an argument.

CHAPTER 11

Are the Statistics Deceptive?

How much should you be persuaded by the following passage?

> The adjective "Kafkaesque," exists in more than 250 different languages, suggesting that his work has had a major impact all over the world.

You should not be very impressed by the above reasoning. The argument *deceives us with statistics*!

One of the most frequent kinds of evidence that authors present is "statistics." You have probably often heard people use the following phrase to help support their argument: "I have statistics to prove it." We use statistics (often inappropriately) to rate the performance of a new movie, to measure the sales of a new product, to judge the moneymaking capabilities of certain stocks, to determine the likelihood of the next card's being the ace, to measure graduation rates for different colleges, to measure alcohol content in a given beverage, to record frequency of different groups' having sex, and to provide input for many other issues.

Statistics are evidence expressed as numbers. Such evidence can seem quite impressive because numbers make evidence appear to be very scientific and precise, as though it represents "the facts." Statistics, however, can, and often do, lie! They do not necessarily prove what they appear to prove.

As a critical thinker, you should strive to detect erroneous statistical reasoning. In a few short paragraphs, we cannot show you all the different ways that people can "lie with statistics." However, this chapter will provide some general strategies that you can use to detect such deception. In addition, it will alert you to flaws in statistical reasoning by illustrating a number of the most common ways that authors misuse statistical evidence.

Critical Question: Are the statistics deceptive?

UNKNOWABLE AND BIASED STATISTICS

The first strategy for locating deceptive statistics is to try to find out as much as you can about how the statistics were obtained. Can we know precisely the number of people in the United States who cheat on their taxes, have premarital sex, drink and drive, run red lights, use illegal drugs, hit a car in a parking lot and left without informing anyone, buy pornographic material, or illegally download music? We suspect not. Why? Because there are a variety of obstacles to getting accurate statistics for certain purposes, including unwillingness to provide truthful information, failure to report events, and physical barriers to observing events. Consequently, statistics are often in the form of "educated guesses." Such estimates can be quite useful; they can also be quite deceiving. Always ask, "How did the author arrive at the estimate?"

One common use of unknowable statistics is to impress or alarm others with large numbers, often presenting them with a suspicious precision. For example, large numbers may be used to try to alert the public to the increasing incidence of physical or mental disorders, such as cancer, eating disorders, or childhood autism. We want to be most impressed by these numbers if we know how carefully they were determined. The issue of unknowable numbers has been a major one in efforts to establish accurate counts of deaths resulting from the conflict in Iraq. For example, the Iraq Body Count Web site reported civilian deaths since the beginning of the Iraqi war to be in the range of 81, 632 to 89,103 as of March, 2008. Other sources, however, were reporting lower and higher numbers, depending on the counting methodology. Before reacting to such statistics, we need to ask how they were determined.

CONFUSING AVERAGES

Examine the following statements:

(1) One way to make money fast is to become a professional football player. The average football player made $2.5 million in 2006.

(2) There is no reason to worry about the new nuclear power plant's being built in our city; the average amount of harm caused by nuclear accidents is rather low.

Both examples use the word *average.* But there are three different ways to determine an average, and in most cases each will give you a different average. What are the three ways? One is to add all the values and divide this total by the number of values used. The result is the *mean.*

A second way is to list all the values from highest to lowest, then find the one in the middle. This middle value is the *median.* Half of the values will be above the *median*; half will be below it. A third way is to list all the values and then count each different value or range of values. The value that appears most frequently is called the *mode*, the third kind of average.

Attention: *It makes a big difference whether a writer is talking about the mean, median, or mode.*

Consider the salaries of the "stars" vs. the average players in professional sports. The biggest stars, such as the star quarterback, will make much higher salaries than most other players on the team. The highest-paid football players for the year 2006 made more than 15 million dollars—well over the average. Such high winnings will increase the mean dramatically, but they will have no major effect on the median or mode. Thus, in most professional sports the mean salaries will be much higher than the median or modal salaries. Consequently, if one wished to make to make the salaries seem extremely high, one would choose the mean as the indicator of the average.

Now, let's look carefully at example (2). If the average presented is either the mode or the median, we may be tricked into a false sense of security. For example, it is possible that many "small" accidents happen, causing very little damage. However, we would also want to know about larger accidents. How much damage is caused by these larger accidents, and how frequently do these larger accidents occur? These are all questions we would want to have answered before we feel secure with the new nuclear power plant. If there are a few very large accidents, but most are rather minor, the mode and the median nuclear accident values could be quite low, but the mean would be very high.

When you see "average" values, always ask: "Does it matter whether it is the mean, the median, or the mode?" To answer this question, consider how using the various meanings of average might change the significance of the information.

Not only is it important to determine whether an average is a mean, median, or mode, but it is often also important to determine the gap between the smallest and largest values—the *range*—and how frequently each of the values occurs—the *distribution*. For example, assume that you are at a casino and are trying to figure out which slot machine to play. Would you be satisfied with information about the average payout for each machine? We wouldn't.

We would want to know the *range* of payout—that is, the highest and the lowest cash winnings as well as the frequency of the different levels. The average might seem impressive, but if 15 percent of people end up losing all of their money without winning once, we suspect that you would rather do something else with your money. Also, if the frequency of payoff of high money amounts is very low, you might second guess your choice of slot machine.

Let's consider another example in which knowing the range and distribution would be important.

> Doctor speaking to 20-year-old patient: The prognosis for your cancer is very poor. The median length of survival is 10 months. You should spend the next few months of your life doing those things that you have always wanted to do.

But how dire should the patient view his future after receiving such a diagnosis? First, all we know for sure is that half of the people with this diagnosis die within 10 months, and half live longer than 10 months. But we don't know the *range and distribution* of how much longer this half lives! It is possible that the range and distribution of people who live more than 10 years could reveal that some or many people live well beyond 10 more months. Some, or even many, may live past 80! Knowing the complete survival distribution could change how this cancer victim views his future.

Another factor that the patient should consider is whether different hospitals in the country have different ranges and distributions of survival for his cancer. If so, he should consider choosing treatment at the hospital with the most favorable distribution. Thus, when an average is presented, ask yourself: "Would it be important for me to know the range and distribution of values?"

CONCLUDING ONE THING, PROVING ANOTHER

Communicators often deceive us when they use statistics that prove one thing but then claim to have proved something quite different. The statistics don't prove what they seem to! We suggest two strategies for locating such deception.

One strategy is to *blind yourself to the communicator's statistics* and ask yourself, "What statistical evidence would be helpful in proving her conclusion?" Then, compare the needed statistics to the statistics given. If the two do not match, you may have located a statistical deception. The following example provides you with an opportunity to apply that strategy.

> A new weight-loss drug, Fatsaway, is effective in helping obese people lose weight. In a clinical trial, only 6 out of 100 people on Fatsaway reported any side effects with taking the drug. The company manufacturing the drug argues, "With 94 percent of people having positive results with Fatsaway, it is safe to say our pill is one of the most effective weight-loss pills in the market."

How should the company manufacturing the drug have proven its conclusion that Fatsaway is 94 percent effective as a weight-loss pill?

Shouldn't they have performed a study as to how many people lost weight with the pill, and how much weight these people lost? Instead, the company reported statistics regarding the frequency of side effects and has assumed that if the pill did not produce side effects then the pill was effective in helping them lose weight. The company proves one thing (relatively small number of people report side effects with Fatsaway) and concludes another (Fatsaway is effective at helping people lose weight). An important lesson to learn from this example is to *pay close attention to both the wording of the statistics and the wording of the conclusion* to see whether they are referring to the same thing. When they are not, the author or speaker may be lying with statistics.

It is frequently difficult to know just what statistical evidence should be provided to support a conclusion. Thus, another strategy is to examine the author's statistics *very closely* while *blinding yourself to the conclusion;* then ask yourself, "What is the appropriate conclusion to be drawn from those statistics?" Then, compare your conclusion with the author's. Try that strategy with the following example.

> Almost half of all Americans cheat on their significant others. A researcher recently interviewed people at a shopping mall. Of the 75 people responding to the survey, 36 admitted to having friends who had admitted cheating on someone they were seeing.

Did you come up with the following conclusion? Almost half of the people *in one given location* admit to *having friends* who report having cheated, *at least once*, on someone with whom they were dating or were otherwise involved. Do you see the difference between what the statistics proved and what the author concluded? If so, you have discovered how this author has lied with statistics.

Now, practice on the following.

> A recent survey asked college students, "Have you ever had a night of binge drinking during the school year?" The researcher reported that 83 percent of college students answer "yes" and concluded, "The results demonstrate that universities are overly stressing their students, causing the students to engage in dangerous drinking habits to escape the pressures of college classes."

Do you see how the writer has concluded one thing while proving another? Do you think the results might have been different if the researcher had asked, "Do you drink to escape the stress from your college classes?"

DECEIVING BY OMITTING INFORMATION

Statistics often deceive us because they are incomplete. Thus, a further helpful strategy for locating flaws in statistical reasoning is to ask, "*What further information do you need before you can judge the impact of the statistics?*" Let's look at two examples to illustrate the usefulness of this question.

> (1) Large businesses are destroying the small town feel of our "downtown" area. Just last year, the number of large businesses in the city has increased by 75 percent.
>
> (2) Despite common fears, skydiving is much safer than other activities, such as driving a car. In one particular month, in Los Angeles, 176 people died in car accidents while 3 died in skydiving accidents.

In the first example, 75 percent seems quite impressive. But something is missing: The *absolute numbers* on which this percentage is based. Wouldn't we be less alarmed if we knew that this increase was from 4 businesses to 7, rather than from 12 to 21? In our second example, we have the numbers, but we don't have the *percentages*. Wouldn't we need to know what these numbers mean in terms of percentages of people involved in both activities? After all, there are fewer total skydivers than there are people traveling in cars.

When you encounter impressive-sounding numbers or percentages, be wary. You may need to get other information to decide just how impressive the numbers are. When only absolute numbers are presented, ask whether percentages might help you make a better judgment; when only percentages are presented, ask whether absolute numbers would enrich their meaning.

Another important kind of potential missing information is *relevant comparisons*. It is often useful to ask the question, "As compared to . . . ?"

Each of the following statements illustrates statistics that can benefit from asking for comparisons:

- Medusa hair spray, now 50 percent better.
- SUVs are dangerous and should not be allowed on the road. In 2004, SUVs were responsible for 4,666 deaths. Certainly something needs to be done.
- Movie budgets are outrageous nowadays. Just look at *Harry Potter and the Goblet of Fire*; the budget for that movie alone is $150,000,000!
- More evidence that our culture is "dumbing down" is provided by the fact that a recent *New York Times* article reported that fewer than half of teenagers interviewed knew when the Civil War was fought.

With reference to the first statement, don't you need to ask, "50 percent better than what?" Other ineffective hair sprays? Previous Medusa brand hair spray? As for the second statement, wouldn't you want to know how many of those deaths would have been prevented if an SUV were not involved, how many other motor vehicle fatalities not involving an SUV there were, the number of SUVs on the road compared to how many deaths they were involved in, and how many miles SUVs travel compared to how many deaths occur in SUVs? With reference to the third statement, how does the budget of one particular movie relate to the budget of other movies, and is this one case highly unusual, or is it typical of the movie industry? As for knowledge of Civil War dates, how do these findings compare to results from a similar survey completed 20 years ago?

When you encounter statistics, be sure to ask, "What relevant information is missing?"

RISK STATISTICS AND OMITTED INFORMATION

> Daily use of Nepenthe brand aspirin will lower the chance of a second heart attack by 55 percent.

> Routine physicals have been linked to finding early cures and lowering people's likelihood of early death by 13 percent.

A common use of statistics in arguments—especially arguments about health risks—is the reporting of risk reduction as a result of some intervention. Such reports can be deceptive. The same amount of risk reduction can be reported in *relative* or *absolute* terms, and these differences can greatly affect our perceptions of the actual amount of risk reduction.

Imagine a 65-year-old woman who just had a stroke and is discussing treatment options with her doctor. The doctor quotes statistics about three treatment options:

> (1) Treatment X will reduce the likelihood of a future stroke by 33 percent,

> (2) Treatment Y will reduce the risk by 3 percent, and

> (3) With treatment Z, 94 percent of women are free of a second stroke for 10 years, compared to 91 percent of those who go untreated.

Which treatment should she choose? Our guess is that she will choose the first. But all of these options refer to the same size treatment effect. They just express the risk in different ways. The first (the 33 percent) is the *relative risk reduction*. If a treatment reduces the risk of heart attack from 9 in 100 to 6 in 100, the risk is reduced by one-third, or 33 percent. But the *absolute* change, from 9 to 6 percent, is only a 3 percent reduction, and the improvement of a good outcome from 91 to 94 is also only 3 percent. The point is that expressing risk reductions in relative, rather than absolute terms can make treatment effects seem larger than they really are, and individuals are more likely to embrace a treatment when benefits are expressed in relative rather than absolute terms. Risks presented as *ratios* can be especially misleading. Consider the potentially different impact of learning that high cholesterol doubles the rate of heart attacks versus learning that high cholesterol increases the likelihood of a heart attack from 1 percent to 2 percent. As you might expect, drug companies usually use relative risk in their ads, and media reports also tend to focus on relative risk.

> *Attention: Relative risk reduction statistics can be deceiving. When you encounter arguments using such statistics, always try to determine how the results might be different and less impressive if expressed in absolute terms.*

Summary

We have highlighted a number of ways by which you can catch people "lying" with statistics. We hope that you can now see the problem with the statistic cited at the beginning of the chapter about the widespread use of the term "Kafkaesque." *Hints*: Where did that impressive figure of more than 250 languages come from? Have Kafka's works been translated into more than 250 languages?

Clues for Evaluating the Evidence

1. Try to find out as much as you can about how the statistics were obtained. Ask, "*How does the author or speaker know?*" Be especially vigilant when the communicator may be trying to impress or alarm you with large numbers.
2. Be curious about the *type of average* being described and whether knowing the *range and distribution* of events would add a helpful perspective to the statistic.
3. Be alert to users of statistics *concluding one thing, but proving another.*
4. Blind yourself to the writer's or speaker's statistics and compare the needed statistical evidence with the statistics actually provided.
5. Form your own conclusion from the statistics. If it doesn't match the author's or speaker's conclusion, then something is probably wrong.
6. Determine what information is missing. Be especially alert for misleading numbers and percentages and for missing comparisons.

Practice Exercises

 *Critical Question: **Are the statistics deceptive?***

For each of the practice passages, identify inadequacies in the evidence.

Passage 1

Campaigns for national office are getting out of hand. Money is playing a central role in more and more elections. The average winner in a Senate race now spends over $8 million in his or her campaign, while typical presidential candidates spend more than $300 million. It is time for some serious changes, because we cannot simply allow politicians to buy their seats through large expenditures on advertisements.

Passage 2

The home is becoming a more dangerous place to spend time. The number of home-related injuries is on the rise. In 2000, approximately 2,300 children aged 14 and under died from accidents in the home. Also, 4.7 million people are bit by dogs each year. To make matters worse, even television, a relatively safe household appliance is becoming dangerous. In fact, 42,000 people are injured by televisions and television stands each year. With so many accidents in the home, perhaps people need to start spending more time outdoors.

Passage 3

Looking fashionable has never been easier! Every year the number of fashion designers increases by 8 percent, making a wider selection of fashionable objects available. Also, because the price of fashionable merchandise reflects the status the clothing brings with it, it is very easy to pick out the most fashionable articles of clothing. Furthermore, the leading fashion magazines have improved in quality by 46 percent. Certainly anyone can look fashionable if he or she wishes to do so.

Sample Responses To Passages 1 and 2

Passage 1

CONCLUSION: *A change in campaigning for national office is necessary.*
REASON: *Politicians are spending too much on campaigns. The average Senator spent more than $8 million on his or her campaign. Presidential candidates spend more than $300 million on their campaigns.*

Are campaigns costing too much money? The words *average* and *typical* should alert us to a potential deception. We need to know the kind of average used for these statistics, as well as the range and distribution of campaign costs. Was the average the mean, the median, or the mode? For example, using the mean in the Senate race data could potentially lead to a figure that is skewed toward higher numbers because of certain, particularly close, Senate races where candidates spent large sums of money. However, because many Senators are basically guaranteed re-election, these races may involve less spending. We know that only a few Senate race elections are usually close. Therefore, most may not spend as much as was reported, if the mean was used to present the average. If this were the case, the median or the mode would probably show a lower value.

Also, important comparison figures are missing. How does campaign spending compare to similar spending in the past? What about spending for other offices? It is possible that campaign spending has actually gone down in recent years.

Passage 2

CONCLUSION: *It is becoming increasingly dangerous to spend time in one's home.*

REASONS: 1. *Household-related injuries are on the rise.*
2. *In one year, 2,300 children died in household accidents.*
3. *4.7 million people are bit by dogs every year.*
4. *42,000 people are injured by televisions each year.*

To evaluate the argument, we need to first determine what the most appropriate evidence is to answer the question, "Are households more unsafe than they used to be?" In our opinion, the best statistic to use to answer the preceding question is a comparison of the rate of serious household accidents per year now and the same statistic over the past. Also relevant is the number of injuries per hour spent in the house versus the same statistic for past years. It is possible that more household injuries occur because people are spending more time in their houses than they used to spend. If they are inside the house more, it is only logical that the number of injuries occurring in the house would also rise.

The evidence presented in the argument is questionable for a number of reasons. First, no number is given at all regarding the number of household injuries. We know the author says they are on the rise, but no evidence is provided demonstrating a rise. Second, no details are given regarding the deaths of children in household accidents. How does this statistic compare to children's deaths in the home in the past? What types of accidents are causing these children's deaths? Third, the number of dog bites is deceptive. We do not know whether these dog bites occur in the home. More importantly, the number of dog bites does not seem to move us toward the conclusion that being at home is unsafe. Fourth, the statistic regarding televisions is questionable. Where does the author get the impressive sounding statistic? Also, how serious are most of these injuries?

Passage 4. Expanding Practice and Feedback

You can now practice further what you have learned in this chapter about asking the question "Are the Statistics Deceptive?" by following a step-by-step demonstration of applying that critical thinking question to statistics used in a lengthy article.

College Drinking, Drug Use Grows More Extreme

Buddy T

About.com Guide (2007)

Since 1993, the number of college students who drink and binge drink has remained about the same, but the intensity of excessive drinking and rates of drug abuse have jumped sharply, according to The National Center on Addiction and Substance Abuse at Columbia University in New York City.

A four-year study of college alcohol and drug use, *Wasting the Best and the Brightest: Substance Abuse at America's Colleges and Universities*, reveals that each month 49 percent of full-time college students, about 3.8 million, binge drink and/or abuse prescription and illegal drugs. In 2005, approximately 1.8 million of those students, 22.9 percent, met the medical criteria for substance abuse and dependence.

In the general population, an estimated 8.5 percent meet the criteria for substance abuse and dependence, making the proportion almost three times higher for college students.

Partying More Intense

Despite prevention efforts on campuses over the past several years, the report found that there has been no change in the proportion of students who drink (70 compared with 68 percent) and binge drink (40 compared with 40 percent) from 1993 to 2005.

Perhaps more disturbing, the study found that the frequency of excessive drinking has increased sharply:

- Between 1993 and 2001, the proportion of students who binge drink three or more times in the past two weeks is up 16 percent.
- Students who drink on 10 or more occasions in a month, up 25 percent.
- Students who get drunk at least three times a month increased 26 percent.
- Students who "drink to get drunk," rose 21 percent.

Drug Abuse Up Sharply

But those increases pale in comparison to the increases of the percentage of students abusing drugs between 1993 and 2005:

- 343 percent for opioids like Vicodin and OxyContin.
- 93 percent for stimulants such as Ritalin and Adderall.
- 450 percent for tranquilizers like Xanax and Valium.
- 225 percent for sedatives like Nembutal and Seconal.
- 100 percent for daily marijuana use.
- 52 percent for cocaine, heroin, and other illegal drugs.

According to the CASA report, an estimated 310,000 U.S. college students smoke marijuana daily and 636,000 students use illegal drugs (other than marijuana), such as cocaine and heroin.

Consequences of Abuse

Consequences of this trend to more extreme substance abuse on college campuses have been costly. According to the CASA report, those consequences include:

- 1,717 deaths from unintentional alcohol-related injuries in 2001, up six percent from 1998.
- A 38 percent increase from 1993 to 2001 in the proportion of students injured as a result of their own drinking.
- A 21 percent increase from 2001 to 2005 in the average number of alcohol-related arrests per campus. In 2005, alcohol-related arrests accounted for 83 percent of all campus arrests.
- 97,000 students were victims of alcohol-related rape or sexual assaults in 2001.
- 696,000 students were assaulted by a student who had been binge drinking in 2001.

Acceptance Is Inexcusable

"It's time to get the 'high' out of higher education," said Joseph A. Califano, Jr., CASA's chairman, in a news release. "Under any circumstances acceptance by administrators, trustees, professors and parents of this college culture of alcohol and other drug abuse is inexcusable. In this world of fierce global competition, we are losing thousands of our nation's best and brightest to alcohol and drugs, and in the process robbing them and our nation of their promising futures."

"College presidents, deans and trustees have facilitated a college culture of alcohol and drug abuse that is linked to poor student academic performance, depression, anxiety, suicide, property damage, vandalism, fights and a host of medical problems," said Califano.

Finding Solutions

"By failing to become part of the solution, these Pontius Pilate presidents and parents, deans, trustees and alumni have become part of the problem. Their acceptance of a status quo of rampant alcohol and other drug abuse puts the best and the brightest—and the nation's future—in harm's way."

In response to the increase in intensity of drinking and drug abuse on college campuses, The National Center on Addiction and Substance Abuse has issued Ten Key Actions for Colleges and Universities to Prevent and Reduce Student Substance Abuse.

Step-by-Step Walkthrough

Statistics can be very valuable but are often deceptive and misleading. Join us in a step-by-step journey through the above article, treating the process as a rehearsal for your future efforts at asking the critical thinking question "Are the Statistics Deceptive?"

- I know that statistics are evidence expressed as numbers. So, I first want to identify numbers in the article that seem to be used as evidence. A full reading reveals many statistics, and my first question concerns how the statistics were obtained. Virtually no information is supplied in the article concerning specifically how the statistics were arrived at. For example, how were students selected and how were reports of drinking behaviors obtained and recorded?
- Thus, before I choose to put too much faith in the meaning of any of these values, I want to seek out information about the details of how the numbers were derived. I am especially concerned about the accuracy of large, precise numbers because I know that the precision can often make them seem more striking than they really are. So I will note to myself that the following large numbers in the latter part of the article could be deceptive: about 3.8 million binge drink; approximately 1.8 million of those students met the medical criteria for substance abuse and dependence; 1717 deaths from unintentional alcohol-related injuries in 2001; 97,000 students were victims of alcohol-related rape or sexual assaults in 2001; and 696,000 students were assaulted by a student who had been binge drinking in 2001. I ask myself: How are these numbers knowable? How carefully were they determined?
- Next, I check to see whether there are any averages, such as means, medians, or modes that could be confusing. Averages are never directly referred to, but it is possible that some of the

percentage numbers might actually be in the form of averages; this would be the case, for example, if percentages for each university were collected and then averaged. Thus, I wonder how these percentages were calculated. In addition, I would like to know the range and distribution of percentages across colleges so that I could see whether the percentages varied significantly in different schools or different areas of the country.

- Next, I note the many times that percentage increases are expressed, in which case I need to ask whether important information is omitted. Especially important are the initial percentage numbers on which these changes in percentages are based. I am most suspicious of the large percentage increases mentioned under the heading "Drug Abuse Up Sharply."

- Numbers such as 343, 93, and 450 percent seem very scary, but how alarmed should I be? For example, a 300 percent increase could result from an increase from 1 percent to 4 percent usage, or alternatively from 10 percent to 40 percent; and I would be much more alarmed in the latter case. Or to take another example, 100 percent means doubling the amount; but a jump from 1 to 2 percent is far different psychologically than a jump from 10 to 20 percent. I recognize that if I were trying to diminish the importance of a change from 1 to 2 percent (a 100 percent change), I could argue that usage has only increased by 1 percent, so why be overly alarmed? Because of this potential deceptiveness of percentage figures, I would like to know the absolute percentages used in all calculations of percentage increases, the major statistic used throughout the article.

- In summary, there is much missing information that I would like to have before judging just how dire and alarming the changes are in the intensity of excessive drinking and rates of drug abuse in college students. A good way to attain that information is to seek out detailed descriptions of the actual research leading to the article.

Were you able to locate any more instances of deception with the statistics in the article? The sample walkthrough above just scratches the surface of the possibilities available when determining whether statistics are deceptive.

CRITICAL QUESTION SUMMARY: WHY THIS QUESTION IS IMPORTANT

Are the Statistics Deceptive?

Authors often provide statistics to support their reasoning. The statistics appear to be hard evidence. However, there are many ways that statistics can be misused. Because problematic statistics are used frequently, it is important to identify any problems with the statistics so that you can more carefully determine whether you will accept or reject the author's conclusion.

CHAPTER 12

What Significant Information Is Omitted?

How compelling is the following advertisement?

> Try Happyme, the number one doctor prescribed treatment for depression.

The purpose of the advertisement is, of course, to persuade you to buy more of the designated product. Even before your critical-thinking skills developed to their current level, you knew that such advertisements tell less than the whole truth. For example, if the Happyme Company gives a bigger discount to psychiatrists than do other pharmaceutical companies, provides psychiatrists with greater numbers of free samples, or provides cruises for psychiatrists who use their product, you are unlikely to see this information included in the advertisement. You will not see that information, but it is quite relevant to your decision about what to take for your depression.

Although critical thinkers are seeking the strength of autonomy, they cannot do so if they are making decisions on the basis of highly limited information. Almost any conclusion or product has some positive characteristics. Those who have an interest in telling us only the information they want us to know will tell us all of these positive characteristics in great and vivid detail. But they will hide the negative aspects of their conclusions. Thus, actual autonomy requires our persistent searching for what is being hidden, either accidentally or on purpose.

By asking questions learned in previous chapters, such as those concerning ambiguity, assumptions, and evidence, you will detect much important missing information. This chapter tries to sensitize you even more to the importance of *what is not said* and to serve as an important reminder that we react to an incomplete picture of an argument when we evaluate only the *explicit* parts. We thus devote this chapter to an extremely important additional question you must ask to judge the quality of reasoning: What significant information is omitted?

 Critical Question: **What significant information is omitted?**

THE BENEFITS OF DETECTING OMITTED INFORMATION

You should remember that almost any information that you encounter has a purpose. In other words, its selection and organization was done by someone who hoped that it would affect your thinking in some way. Hence, your task is to decide whether you wish to be an instrument of the chosen purpose. Often that purpose is to persuade you.

Advertisers, teachers, politicians, authors, speakers, researchers, bloggers, and parents all organize information to shape your decisions. It is a natural and highly predictable desire on their part. Thus, those trying to persuade you will almost always try to present their position in the strongest possible light. So when you find what you believe to be persuasive reasons—those gold nuggets for which you are prospecting—it's wise to hesitate and to think about what the author may *not* have told you, something that your critical questioning has not yet revealed.

By *significant omitted information*, we mean information that would affect whether you should be influenced by a speaker's or writer's arguments, that is, information that *shapes the reasoning*! Interspersed throughout the chapter will be examples of reasoning that are not very convincing, not because of what is said but because of what is omitted. Study the examples carefully and notice how in each case the failure to look for omitted information would have resulted in your making a premature and potentially erroneous judgment.

THE CERTAINTY OF INCOMPLETE REASONING

Incomplete reasoning is inevitable for several reasons. First, there is the limitation imposed by time and space. Arguments are incomplete because communicators do not have forever to organize them, nor do they have unlimited space or time in which to present their reasons.

Second, most of us have a very limited attention span; we get bored when messages are too long. Thus, communicators often feel a need to get their message across quickly. Advertisements and editorials reflect both these factors. For example, editorials are limited to a specific number of words, and the argument must both be interesting and make the author's point. Editorial writers, therefore, engage in many annoying omissions. Television commentators are notorious for making highly complicated issues sound as if they are simple. They have very little time to provide the degree of accurate information that you will need to form a reasonable conclusion. So our minds need to do a lot of extra work to fill in the many gaps in what they have to say in these situations.

A third reason for the inevitability of missing information is that the knowledge possessed by the person making the argument will always be incomplete.

A fourth reason why information may be omitted is because of an outright attempt to deceive. Advertisers *know* they are omitting key bits of information. If they were to describe all the chemicals or cheap component parts that go into their products, you would be less likely to buy them. Experts in every field consciously omit information when open disclosure would weaken the persuasive effect of their advice. Such omissions are particularly tempting if those trying to advise you see you as a "sponge."

A final important reason why omitted information is so prevalent is that the values, beliefs, and attitudes of those trying to advise or persuade you are frequently different from yours. You can expect, therefore, that their reasoning will be guided by assumptions different from those you would have brought to the same question. Critical thinkers value curiosity and reasonableness; those

The Virtue of Curiosity for a Critical Thinker

working to persuade you often want to extinguish your curiosity and to encourage you to rely on unreasonable emotional responses to shape your choices.

A particular perspective is like a pair of blinders on a horse. The blinders improve the tendency of the horse to focus on what is directly in front of it. Yet, an individual's perspective, like blinders on a horse, prevents that person from noting certain information that would be important to those who reason from a different frame of reference. Unless your perspective is identical to that of the person trying to persuade you, important omissions of information are to be expected.

QUESTIONS THAT IDENTIFY OMITTED INFORMATION

If you are now convinced that reasoning will necessarily be incomplete, you may ask, "What am I supposed to do?" Well, initially you have to remind yourself that regardless of how attractive the reasons supporting a particular decision or opinion may seem at first glance, it's necessary to take another look in search of omitted information.

How do you search, and what can you expect to find? You ask questions to help decide what additional information you need, and then ask questions designed to reveal that information.

There are many different kinds of questions you can use to identify relevant omitted information. Some questions you have already learned to ask will highlight important omitted information. For example, asking critical questions about ambiguity, the use of evidence, and the quality of assumptions usually identifies relevant omitted information.

In addition, to help you determine omitted information that might get overlooked by other critical questions, we provide you below with a list of some important kinds of omitted information and some examples of questions to help detect them.

Being aware of these specific types should help you a lot in locating relevant omitted information. Because there are so many kinds of important omitted information, however, you should always ask yourself the general question, "Has the speaker or writer left out any other information that I need to know before I judge the quality of his reasoning?"

Let's examine some arguments that have omitted some of the types of information just listed and watch how each omission might cause us to form a faulty conclusion. Only by asking that omitted information be supplied in each case could you avoid this danger. Initially, let's look at an advertising claim.

Zitout brand facial cleanser's commercials claim that the cleanser removes 95 percent of deep-down dirt and oil, helping to fight unsightly blemishes. Should we all run out and buy Zitout facial cleanser? Wait just a minute! Among many omissions, the advertisement fails to include any of the following pieces of information: (a) what percentage of deep-down dirt and oil other facial cleansers remove; maybe they remove 99 percent of dirt and oil; (b) amount of dirt and oil removed by washing with soap alone; it might

Clues for Finding Common Kinds of Significant Information

1. **Common counterarguments**
   a. What reasons would someone who disagrees offer?
   b. Are there research studies that contradict the studies presented?
   c. Are there missing examples, testimonials, and opinions from well-respected authorities, or analogies that support the other side of the argument?

2. **Missing definitions**
   a. How would the arguments differ if key terms were defined in other ways?

3. **Missing value preferences or perspectives**
   a. Would different values create a different approach to this issue?
   b. What arguments would flow from values different from those of the speaker or writer?

4. **Origins of "facts" referred to in the argument**
   a. What is the source for the "facts"?
   b. Are the factual claims supported by competent research or by reliable sources?

5. **Details of procedures used for gathering facts**
   a. How many people completed the questionnaire?
   b. How were the survey questions worded?
   c. Did respondents have ample opportunity to provide answers different from those reported by the person using the responses?

6. **Alternative techniques for gathering or organizing the evidence**
   a. How might the results from an interview study differ from written questionnaire results?
   b. Would a laboratory experiment have created more reliable and informative results?

7. **Missing or incomplete figures, graphs, tables, or data**
   a. Would the data look different if they included evidence from earlier or later years?
   b. Has the author "stretched" the figure to make the differences look larger?

8. **Omitted effects, both positive and negative, and both short- and long-term, of what is advocated and what is opposed**
   a. Has the argument left out important positive or negative consequences of a proposed action? What are the costs? What are the benefits?
   b. Do we need to know the impact of the action on any of the following areas: political, social, economic, biological, spiritual, health, or environmental?

be possible that faces can be cleaned adequately with normal soap; (c) potential negative consequences of using this specific product; it is possible that some of the ingredients might cause excessive dryness or pose cancer risks; (d) other sources of blemishes; perhaps dirt and oil are not the highest concerns when washing one's face; (e) how much dirt and oil is necessary to cause blemishes; maybe 5 percent will still cause a significant number of blemishes; and (f) other advantages or disadvantages of the facial cleanser, such as smell, price, and length of effective action. The advertiser has omitted much significant data that you would need if you were to buy wisely.

Do you see how advertising phrases like "4 out of 5 doctors agree," "all natural," "fat free," "low in carbs," "good for your heart," "number 1 leading brand," "ADA approved," and "no added preservatives" may all be accurate but misleading because of omitted information?

THE IMPORTANCE OF THE NEGATIVE VIEW

There is one type of omitted information that we believe is so important to identify and so often overlooked that we want to specifically highlight it for you: the *potential negative effects* of actions being advocated, such as the use of a new medication, the building of a large new school, or a proposed tax cut. We stress the negative effects here because usually proposals for such action come into existence in the context of backers' heralding their benefits, such as greater reduction of a certain medical problem, better appearance, more leisure, more educational opportunities, increased length of life, and more and/or improved commodities. However, because most actions have such widespread positive *and negative* impacts, we need to ask:

- Which segments of society do *not* benefit from a proposed action? Who loses? What do the losers have to say about it?
- How does the proposed action affect the distribution of power?
- What are the action's effects on our health?
- How does the action influence our relationships with one another? With the natural environment?

For each of these questions, we always also want to ask, "What are the potential *long-term negative effects* of the action?"

To illustrate the usefulness of asking these omitted-information questions, let's reflect upon the following question: What are some possible negative effects of building a large new school? Did you think of the following?

- *Destruction of the environment.* For example, would the building of a new school involve the removal of a wooded area? How would the local wildlife be affected by the potential loss of a habitat?
- *Shifts in quality of education provided.* What if the new school attracts skilled teachers or gifted students away from other schools? What if the new school absorbed a significant amount of the funds available to schools, depriving other schools of the same funds?
- *Effects of property values.* If the school does not do well in comparison with national standards, how will this affect the property values of the houses in the surrounding community?
- *Increased tax burden.* How would the new school be funded? If the new school is a public school, the opening of the new school could result in

an increase in property taxes for the local community to help support the new school.

- *Prevention of other potentially helpful expansion.* Is it possible that the land used for the school would have better been used for some other new building? For example, what if there were plenty of schools, but not enough jobs in the neighborhood; would the land have been better used to build new businesses?
- *Increased demand for housing.* Is there enough housing available in the community to accommodate new teachers and families that desire access to the new school?

Attention: Proposals for new societal interventions tend to empha-size their potential benefits and ignore their drawbacks. Thus when evaluating such proposals, be alert to their possible failure to con-sider negative consequences of their actions.

Questions such as these can give us pause for thought before jumping on the bandwagon of a proposed action.

OMITTED INFORMATION THAT REMAINS MISSING

Just because you are able to request important missing information does not guarantee a satisfactory response. It is quite possible that your probing ques-tions cannot be answered. Do not despair! You did your part. You requested information that you needed to make up your mind; you must now decide whether it is possible to arrive at a conclusion without the missing informa-tion. We warned you earlier that reasoning is always incomplete. Therefore, to claim automatically that you cannot make a decision as long as information is missing would prevent you from ever forming any opinions.

USING THIS CRITICAL QUESTION

Once you have thought about the existence of missing information in an argument, what should you do? The first logical reaction is to seek the infor-mation. But usually you will encounter resistance. Your options as a critical thinker are to voice your displeasure with the argument in light of the miss-ing information, keep searching for the information that you require, or cau-tiously agree with the reasoning on the grounds that this argument is better than its competitors.

When you propose an action, think about potential, relevant counterar-guments to what you are advocating and share those counterarguments with your audience. To do otherwise is to insult them. They know there are alter-native perspectives. So, in the interest of your own integrity, be open about their existence.

Practice Exercises

 Critical Question: ***What significant information is omitted?***

In each of the following examples, there is important missing information. Make a list of questions you would ask the person who wrote each passage. Explain in each case why the information you are seeking is important to you as you try to decide the worth of the reasoning.

Passage 1

Recent research has shown that eating and sleeping less can lead to a longer life. In laboratory experiments, rats fed a bare minimum and allowed to sleep much less than normal were found to be better able to recover from injuries and to live longer than rats that were fed plenty of food and slept a substantial amount. The researchers concluded that people, too, could benefit from less eating and sleeping and more physical activity.

Passage 2

Cloning technology can lead to many positive breakthroughs in the medical field. If we were to adequately develop cloning technology, there would no longer be a need for people to die because of a lack of organ donors. With cloning, researchers could artificially develop new organs for people in need of transplants. Plus, because these organs would be cloned from the person's own tissues, there would be no chance of their body rejecting the transplanted organ. The cloned organs can be made in bodies that lack a head, and thus would not involve a "death" in order to save a life. Another advantage of cloning is that it can help fight disease. Certain proteins produced by clones can be used to fight diseases such as diabetes, Parkinson's disease, and cystic fibrosis.

Passage 3

America is the policeman of the world. It is our job to go into countries that need our help and to watch over them. One effective way to limit the interactions we need to have with other countries is to encourage the development of democracy and free markets in these countries. After all, the modern Western democracies have not fought wars against one another, and they are all democratic with a free market structure. Furthermore, look at the easy transition Germany had when it was reunited. Democracy was installed and the formerly split West and East Germany came along just fine. In fact, the German economy did really well with the transition also. Germany currently has the third largest GDP of any country in the world, all because of democracy and capitalism.

Sample Responses To Passages 1 and 2

Passage 1

CONCLUSION: *People would benefit from eating and sleeping less.*

REASON: *Studies on rats have shown that when rats eat and sleep less, they recover from injuries better and live longer than other rats.*

Before we all start to cut back on our food intake and amount of sleep, we should re-evaluate the information provided leading to this conclusion. What are the counterarguments, for example? Is it possible that humans and rats differ too much to generalize from one to the other about the effects of sleep? Also, how much longer did the rats that ate and slept less live, and how much faster did these same rats recover from injuries? Is it possible that the variance is small or insignificant? Did the rats suffer any negative effects from eating and sleeping less? Would the rats have lived longer and recovered faster if instead of sleeping and eating less they ate and slept far more than the other rats?

Furthermore, just what do we know about the testing procedures? Nothing at all! These are just a few of the questions we would want to ask before we relied on the information in this passage.

Passage 2

CONCLUSION: *Cloning can provide positive medical benefits.*

REASONS   1. *Clones can be used for human transplants.*
            2. *Clones can be used to help combat certain diseases.*

First, we should note that this reasoning advocates pursuing a new technology—human cloning—and cites only its advantages. The writer omits possible disadvantages. We need to consider both advantages and disadvantages. What serious side effects might result from using cloned organs? Are cloned organs as stable as regular organs? What positive and negative effects might cloning technology have on human decision-making? Would people be less likely to take care of their bodies and their organs if they knew that new organs could be grown to replace their current ones? Would the availability of the technology lead people to misuse cloning to produce complete human clones for an insidious purpose? Would people clone themselves, helping add to the burden already placed on the Earth by the current population? The advantages of the procedure may well outweigh the disadvantages, but we need to be aware of both in judging the merits of the conclusion.

Furthermore, let's look at the missing information regarding the research. Did you notice that no research has been cited? In fact, the argument fails to tell us that no tests on human cloning have occurred in the United States. Therefore, all of the discussion on the benefits of cloning is hypothetical. Would actual research prove the hypothetical benefits to be possible? We do not know.

Passage 4. Expanding Practice and Feedback

Read the following passage. While reading, pay special attention to what the author does not tell you. Try to find examples where omitted information harms the reasoning of the article.

Back to 18?

Radley Balko

Reason Magazinen (2007)

It's been 20 years that America has had a minimum federal drinking age. The policy began to gain momentum in the early 1980s, when the increasingly influential Mothers Against Drunk Driving added the federal minimum drinking age to its legislative agenda. By 1984, it had won over a majority of the Congress.

President Reagan initially opposed the law on federalism grounds but eventually was persuaded by his transportation secretary at the time, now-Sen. Elizabeth Dole. Over the next three years every state had to choose between adopting the standard or forgoing federal highway funding; most complied. A few held out until the deadline, including Vermont, which fought the law all the way to the U.S. Supreme Court (and lost). Twenty years later, the drawbacks of the legislation are the same as they were when it was passed.

The first is that the age set by the legislation is basically arbitrary. The U.S. has the highest drinking age in the world (a title it shares with Indonesia, Mongolia, Palau). The vast majority of the rest of the world sets the minimum age at 17 or 16 or has no minimum age at all. Supporters of the federal minimum argue that the human brain continues developing until at least the age of 21.

Alcohol expert Dr. David Hanson of the State University of New York at Potsdam argues such assertions reek of junk science. They're extrapolated from a study on lab mice, he explains, as well as from a small sample of actual humans already dependent on alcohol or drugs. Neither is enough to make broad proclamations about the entire population. If the research on brain development is true, the U.S. seems to be the only country to have caught on to it. Oddly enough, high school students in much of the rest of the developed world—where lower drinking ages and laxer enforcement reign—do considerably better than U.S. students on standardized tests.

The second drawback of the federal drinking age is that it set the stage for tying federal mandates to highway funds, enabling Congress

to meddle in all sorts of state and local affairs it has no business attempting to regulate—so long as it can make a tortured argument
about highway safety.

Efforts to set national speed limits, seat belt laws, motorcycle
helmet laws and set a national blood-alcohol standard for DWI cases
have rested on the premise that the federal government can blackmail the states with threats to cut off funding.

The final drawback is pretty straightforward: It makes little
sense that America considers an 18-year-old mature enough to marry,
to sign a contract, to vote and to fight and die for his country, but not
mature enough to decide whether or not to have a beer.

So for all of those drawbacks, has the law worked? Supporters
seem to think so. Their primary argument is the dramatic drop in the
number of alcohol-related traffic fatalities since the minimum age first
passed Congress in 1984. They also cite relative drops in the percentage of underage drinkers before and after the law went into effect.

But a new chorus is emerging to challenge the conventional
wisdom. The most vocal of these critics is John McCardell Jr., the former president of Middlebury College in Vermont. McCardell's experience in higher education revealed to him that the federal age simply
wasn't working. It may have negligibly reduced total underage consumption, but those who did consume were much more likely to do
so behind closed doors and to drink to excess in the short time they
had access to alcohol. McCardell recently started the organization
Choose Responsibility, which advocates moving the drinking age
back to 18.

McCardell explains that the drop in highway fatalities often
cited by supporters of the 21 minimum age actually began in the late
1970s, well before the federal drinking age set in.

What's more, McCardell recently explained in an online chat for
the "Chronicle of Higher Education," the drop is better explained by
safer and better built cars, increased seat belt use and increasing awareness of the dangers of drunken driving than in a federal standard.

The age at highest risk for an alcohol-related auto fatality is 21,
followed by 22 and 23, an indication that delaying first exposure to
alcohol until young adults are away from home may not be the best
way to introduce them to drink.

McCardell isn't alone. Kenyon College President S. Georgia
Nugent has expressed frustration with the law, particularly in 2005
after the alcohol-related death of a Kenyon student. And former *Time*
magazine editor and higher ed reporter Barrett Seaman echoed
McCardell's concerns in 2005.

The period since the 21 minimum drinking age took effect
has been "marked by a shift from beer to hard liquor," Seaman
wrote in *Time*, "consumed not in large social settings, since that

was now illegal, but furtively and dangerously in students' residences. In my reporting at colleges around the country, I did not meet any presidents or deans who felt the 21-year age minimum helps their efforts to curb the abuse of alcohol on their campuses."

The federal drinking age has become somewhat sacrosanct among public health activists, who've consistently relied on the accident data to quell debate over the law's merits.

They've moved on to other battles, such as scolding parents for giving their own kids a taste of alcohol before the age of 21 or attacking the alcohol industry for advertising during sporting events or in magazines aimed at adults that are sometimes read by people under the age of 21.

But after 20 years, perhaps it's time to take a second look—a sound, sober (pardon the pun), science-based look—at the law's costs and benefits, as well as the sound philosophical objections to it.

McCardell provides a welcome voice in a debate too often dominated by hysterics. But beyond McCardell, Congress should really consider abandoning the federal minimum altogether, or at least the federal funding blackmail that gives it teeth. State and local governments are far better at passing laws that reflect the values, morals and habits of their communities.

Step-by-Step Walkthrough

The search for missing information requires that we think about what other information would be desirable to form a well-educated conclusion. Were you able to find instances where information was omitted in the passage? Here is one sample response.

- First, I want to look to see whether the author discusses relevant counterarguments. In this case, the author has included some of the opposition's standpoint. The author acknowledged that the opposition favors the 21 drinking age due to fewer traffic fatalities since its inception, and then he rebuked this point. However, he bases his rebuttal on appeals to authorities—two college presidents. These appeals are primarily supported by personal experiences, and I recall the limitations of such evidence from an earlier chapter in Asking the Right Questions. He has omitted significant research evidence that would better support the presidents' arguments. In addition, he acknowledges a rebuttal to his first argument by stating that supporters of the federal minimum argue that the human brain continues developing until at least the age of 21. He rebuts this reason in his next paragraph. I believe that his rebuttals to the counterarguments may omit important information; I wonder whether there are other missing arguments, studies, or opinions from well-respected authorities supporting the other side of the argument.

- Next, I want to think back to my training about value preferences. I ask, "What value preferences might have helped shape the authors arguments and would different values create a different approach to this issue?" Certain different values would. For example, if a person valued collective responsibility in the sense of federal government intervention over individual responsibility, then supporting the 21 drinking age might seem more desirable than allowing younger people to choose for themselves whether they wish to drink alcohol. Recognizing that value preferences influence his reasoning and that I might have an opposing value preference should help me better decide how convincing I find his conclusion

- I also must consider the origin of the "facts" in the argument. There is much discussion about alcohol-related auto deaths, but where did these "facts" come from? How can we be sure they are a reputable source? We know nothing about the source, method of collection, sample size, or any of the specifics of the "facts" the author provides. For all we know, the author could have completely falsified the information or skewed the data in his favor. We don't know whether there is an alternative means for gathering the information or whether other sets of more reliable facts exist. Because of the omission of information about the facts, we can't be sure how reliable the author's evidence really is.

- I notice other important omitted information when the author compares the drinking age of the United States to other countries, arguing that the U.S. drinking age is the lowest in the world. Such comparisons omit important information. For example, are there important differences between national attitudes toward alcohol consumption that might make higher minimum drinking ages make more sense in the United States?

- Lastly, the author has given no consideration to the omitted short- and long-term effects of what he is advocating. Lowering the drinking age in the United States would cause a whole chain of effects on citizens. What are some of the projected costs of allowing teenagers to drink legally? For example, would lowering the drinking age create more high school deaths in America due to alcohol? What segments of society would not benefit from allowing 18-year-olds to drink? How would this affect American high schools if some students were legally allowed to purchase alcohol for younger students? Are there studies about the long-term effects on alcohol consumers if they start drinking at a younger age? We must consider the importance of the negative view when considering any solution. Furthermore, what are the benefits of lowering the drinking age? Would the economy be better off if more Americans were consuming alcohol on a regular beverage? Would fewer people travel to Mexico or Canada to drink on vacation, thus providing more revenue to U.S. tourism? It appears the author has not even considered the possible impact of lowering the legal drinking age. Without addressing some plausible costs and benefits, the reader does not really know what is at risk in the argument about lowering the drinking age.

These examples are just some instances where missing information harmed the argument for lowering the national drinking age. Remember, by questioning the persuasiveness of the argument, you are not necessarily refuting the conclusion. Rather, as a critical thinker you desire more evidence to support the conclusion.

CRITICAL QUESTION SUMMARY: WHY THIS QUESTION IS IMPORTANT

What Significant Information Is Omitted?

When an author is trying to persuade you of something, she often leaves out important information. This information is often useful in assessing the worth of the conclusion. By explicitly looking for omitted information, you can determine whether the author has provided you with enough information to support the reasoning. If she has left out too much information, you cannot accept the reasons as support for the conclusion. Consequently, you should choose to reject her conclusion.

CHAPTER 13

What Reasonable Conclusions Are Possible?

By this stage you should be better equipped to pan for intellectual gold—to distinguish stronger reasons from weaker ones.

Consider the following argument:

> Large corporations spend far too much time and money advertising to children. Children's programming is riddled with commercials trying to sell them the latest toy, telling the children they will not be happy unless they have it. The practice of advertising to children is horrendous and should be illegal. Advertising to children, who cannot critically evaluate the ads they see, puts a strain on parents to either say "no" to their children and have them get upset, or to give in to their children's demands, ultimately spoiling the children.

Should you urge your local congressman to criminalize advertisements to children? Suppose you checked the author's reasons and found them believable. Are there other conclusions that might be equally consistent with these reasons as the author's conclusion? The chapter summary will suggest several possible alternative conclusions.

Very rarely will you have a situation in which only one conclusion can be reasonably inferred. In an earlier chapter, we discussed the importance of rival causes. The point there was that there are different possible causal bases for a particular conclusion. This chapter, however, focuses on the alternative *conclusions* that are all possible outcomes from a single set of reasons.

Consequently, you must make sure that the conclusion you eventually adopt is the most reasonable and the most consistent with your value preferences. The recognition that the reasons could provide support for conclusions different from yours should heighten your interest in any further tests or studies that would help identify the best conclusion.

 Critical Question: ***What reasonable conclusions are possible?***

ASSUMPTIONS AND MULTIPLE CONCLUSIONS

Evidence attempting to support a factual claim or a group of strong reasons supporting a prescriptive conclusion can both be interpreted to mean different things. Reasons do not generally speak for themselves in an obvious way. As we have seen many times, conclusions are reached only after someone makes certain interpretations or assumptions concerning the meaning of the reasons.

If you make a different assumption concerning the meaning of the reasons, you will reach different conclusions. Because we all possess different levels of perceptual precision, frames of reference, and prior knowledge, we repeatedly disagree about which assumptions are preferable. We form different conclusions from reasons because our diverse backgrounds and goals cause us to be attracted to different assumptions when we decide to link reasons to conclusions.

DICHOTOMOUS THINKING: IMPEDIMENT TO CONSIDERING MULTIPLE CONCLUSIONS

Very few important questions can be answered with a simple "yes" or an absolute "no." When people think in black or white, yes or no, right or wrong, or correct or incorrect terms, they engage in *dichotomous thinking.* This type of thinking consists of assuming there are only two possible answers to a question that has multiple potential answers. This habit of seeing and referring to *both* sides of a question as if there are only two has devastatingly destructive effects on our thinking. By restricting the conclusions we consider to be only two, we are sharply reducing the robust possibilities that careful reasoning can produce.

We encountered dichotomous thinking earlier when we discussed the either-or fallacy in Chapter 7. This fallacy, and dichotomous thinking in general, damages reasoning by overly restricting our vision. We think we are finished after considering two optional decisions, thereby overlooking many options and the positive consequences that could have resulted from choosing one of them.

Dichotomous thinkers often are rigid and intolerant because they fail to understand the importance of context for a particular answer. To see this point more clearly, imagine this situation: Your roommate asks you to help plan her biology paper. The paper is to address the question: Should scientists pursue stem cell research? In her mind, the paper requires her to defend a "yes" or "no" position.

Are you a SPONGE or a LIGHT BULB?

You have learned that dichotomous thinking can be avoided by qualifying conclusions, by putting them into context. This qualification process requires you to ask about any conclusion:

1. *When* is it accurate?
2. *Where* is it accurate?
3. *Why* or *for what purpose* is it accurate?

You then begin to apply this process to the paper assignment.

Would you be surprised by your roommate's growing frustration as you explained that at certain specified times, in certain situations, to maximize particular values or objectives one should allow stem cell research? She's looking for "yes" or "no"; you provided a complicated "it depends on . . ."

Rigid, dichotomous thinking limits the range of your decisions and opinions. Even worse, it overly simplifies complex situations. As a consequence, dichotomous thinkers are high-risk candidates for confusion.

The next section illustrates the restrictive effects of dichotomous thinking.

TWO SIDES OR MANY?

1. Should the United States engage in peacekeeping in other countries?
2. Is William Shakespeare the best playwright of all time?

Before we look at several arguments in which multiple conclusions are possible, let's make sure you appreciate the large number of conclusions that are

Should the United States Engage in Peacekeeping in Other Countries?

1. Yes, when the country is intricately tied to the United States, such as Saudi Arabia.
2. Yes, if the United States is to be perceived as the sole superpower responsible for maintaining world peace.
3. Yes, if the United States' role is to be limited to keeping peace and does not involve actually fighting a war.
4. Yes, when our economic interests abroad are at stake.
5. Yes, when Americans might be harmed by violence in other countries.
6. No, the United States has enough domestic problems to handle such that we should not spend time in other countries.
7. No, if peacekeeping is the goal, such actions are better left up to the UN or NATO.

possible with respect to most important controversies. Let's examine the following two controversies.

At first glance, these questions and many like them seem to call for yes or no answers. However, a qualified yes or no is often the best answer. The advantage of *maybe* as an answer is that it forces you to admit that you do not yet know enough to make a definite answer. But at the same time you avoid a definite answer; you form a tentative decision or opinion that calls for commitment and eventual action. It's wise to seek additional information that would improve the support for your opinions, but at some point you must stop searching and make a decision, even when the most forceful answer you are willing to defend is a "yes, but . . ."

Glance back at the questions that preceded the last paragraph. Ask yourself what conclusions would be possible in response to each question. Naturally, a simple "yes" or a "no" answer would be two possible conclusions. Are there others? Yes, there are many! Let's look at just a few of the possible answers to the first of these questions.

Notice that in each case we added a condition necessary before the conclusion can be justified. In the absence of any data or definitions, any of these seven conclusions could be most reasonable. These seven are just a few of the conclusions possible for the first question.

SEARCHING FOR MULTIPLE CONCLUSIONS

This section contains one argument pointing out multiple conclusions that could be created from its reasons. The intention is to give you a model to use when you search for conclusions. We will give you the structure of the argument before we suggest alternative conclusions. Study the reasons without looking at the conclusion, and try to identify as many conclusions as possible that would follow from the reasons. You can always use the *when, where,* and *why* questions to help generate alternative conclusions.

CONCLUSION: *The United States should continue to use the death penalty as a form of punishment.*

REASONS: 1. *Without the death penalty, there is no way to punish people who commit wrongs, such as harming guards or inmates, after already having a life sentence.*

2. *It is only fair that someone should die for purposely taking the life of another.*

Let's start by accepting these reasons as sensible to us. What do we then make of them? We have one answer in the conclusion of the writer: Continue the use of the death penalty.

But even when we accept these two reasons, we would not necessarily conclude the same thing. Other conclusions make at least as much sense on the basis of this support. For example, it would follow that we should continue to use the death penalty, but only in cases where someone has already been sentenced to life in prison, and the prisoner kills a guard or another inmate.

Alternatively, these reasons might suggest that we need to maintain the death penalty in cases of prisoners' harming guards or other prisoners. Not only is this alternative conclusion logically supported by the reasons, but it also leads to a conclusion quite different from the original conclusion.

PRODUCTIVITY OF IF-CLAUSES

If you went back over all the alternative conclusions discussed in this chapter, you would notice that each optional conclusion is possible because we are missing certain information, definitions, assumptions, or the frame of reference of the person analyzing the reasons. Consequently, we can create multiple conclusions by the judicious use of *if-clauses.* In an *if*-clause, we state a condition that we are assuming in order to enable us to reach a particular conclusion. Notice that the use of *if*-clauses permits us to arrive at a conclusion without pretending that we know more than we actually do about a particular controversy.

When you use *if*-clauses to precede conclusions, you are pointing out that your conclusion is based on particular claims or assumptions about which you are uncertain. To see what we mean, look at the following sample conditional statements that might precede conclusions.

1. If the tax cut is targeted toward those at the lower end of the economic spectrum, then . . .
2. If a novel contains an easily identifiable protagonist, a clear antagonist, and a thrilling climax, then . . .
3. If automakers can make cars that are more fuel efficient, then . . .

If-clauses present you with multiple conclusions that you should assess before making up your mind about the controversy, and they also broaden the list of possible conclusions from which you can choose your own position.

ALTERNATIVE SOLUTIONS AS CONCLUSIONS

We frequently encounter issues posed in the following form:

> Should we do X?
> Is X desirable?

Such questions naturally "pull" for dichotomous thinking. Often, however, posing questions in this manner hides a broader question, "What should we do about Y?" (usually some pressing problem). Rewording the question in this way leads us to generate multiple conclusions of a particular form: solutions to the problem raised by the reasons. Generating multiple solutions greatly increases the flexibility of our thinking.

> **Attention:** *A good way to help generate multiple conclusions is to change the question from "Should we do Action X?" to "What should be done about Problem Y?"*

Let's examine the following passage to illustrate the importance of generating multiple solutions as possible conclusions.

> Should we close the bars downtown? The answer is a resounding yes! Since the bars opened, a dozen young college students have suffered from alcohol poisoning.

Once we change this question to, "What should we do about the number of college students suffering from alcohol poisoning?" a number of possible solutions come to mind, which help us formulate our conclusion to the issue. For example, we might conclude: "No, we should not close the bars downtown; rather, we should strictly enforce the drinking age and fine bars that sell alcoholic beverages to minors."

When reasons in a prescriptive argument are statements of practical problems, look for different solutions to the problems as possible conclusions.

Clues for Identifying Alternative Conclusions

1. Try to identify as many conclusions as possible that would follow from the reasons.
2. Use *if-clauses* to qualify alternative conclusions.
3. Reword the issue to "What should we do about Y?"

THE LIBERATING EFFECT OF RECOGNIZING ALTERNATIVE CONCLUSIONS

If logic, facts, or studies were self-explanatory, we would approach learning in a particular manner. Our task would be to have someone else, a teacher perhaps, provide the beliefs that we should have. Specifically, we would seek that single identifiable set of beliefs that logic and facts dictate.

While we have tremendous respect for logic and facts, we cannot exaggerate their worth as guides for conclusion formation. They take us only so far; then we have to go the rest of the way toward belief, using the help that facts and logic have provided.

A first step in using that help is the search for possible multiple conclusions consistent with logic and the facts as we know them. This search liberates us in an important way. It frees us from the inflexible mode of dichotomous thinking sketched above. Once we recognize the variety of possible conclusions, each of us can experience the excitement of enhanced personal choice.

ALL CONCLUSIONS ARE NOT CREATED EQUAL

We want to warn you that the rewarding feeling that often comes with generating multiple conclusions may tempt you to treat them as equally credible and to believe your job is done after you've made your list. But remember that some conclusions can be better justified than others, and the most believable ones should be the ones that most affect your reaction to the author's reasoning. Indeed, one clever way to weaken strong reasoning about global warming or the cause of the war in Iraq or the wisdom of distance learning is to make the claim that experts disagree.

The implication of such a statement is that once disagreement is identified, one argument is as good as the next. Therefore, there is no basis for new action to address the problem. But such an approach is insulting to careful critical thinking. Critical thinkers have standards of careful reasoning that they can apply to identify the strongest reasoning.

Summary

Very rarely do reasons mean just one thing. After evaluating a set of reasons, you still must decide what conclusion is most consistent with the best reasons in the controversy. To avoid dichotomous thinking in your search for the strongest conclusion, provide alternative contexts for the conclusions through the use of *when*, *where*, and *why* questions.

Qualifications for conclusions will move you away from dichotomous thinking. *If*-clauses provide a technique for expressing these qualifications.

For instance, let's take another look at the argument at the beginning of the chapter for restricting advertisements aimed at children. What alternative conclusions might be consistent with the reasons given?

AUTHOR'S CONCLUSION: *Advertisements aimed at children should be illegal.*

ALTERNATIVE CONCLUSIONS: 1. *If corporations are to be treated as persons, then they have a right to free speech that includes advertisements; thus, their right to advertise should not be limited.*

2. *If it can be demonstrated that children are unable to assess what they view, and thus are heavily influenced by the advertisements they see, then advertisements aimed at children should be illegal.*

3. *If the purpose of the proposed legislation is to limit the content of advertisements aimed at children, then the government should not make such ads illegal, but rather take a more proactive role in regulating the content of advertisements aimed at children.*

Many additional alternative conclusions are possible in light of the author's reasons. We would shrink the quality of our decision-making if we did not consider those alternative conclusions as possible bases for our own beliefs.

Practice Exercises

 Critical Question: **What reasonable conclusions are possible?**

For each of the following arguments, identify different conclusions that could be drawn from the reasons.

Passage 1

Feeding large numbers of people is not easy. However, dining halls on campus should try to accommodate a larger variety of tastes. Students all across campus consistently complain not only about the quality of food, but the lack of selection they find in the dining halls. All the dining halls need to do is offer a wider range of food to better please more students, and thus keep more of them eating on campus as opposed to off campus. Dining services is failing its duty to the students when it does not provide a large selection of food options every day.

Passage 2

I have never been that strong of a runner, but when I bought my new training shoes, Mercury, my time greatly improved. Now I can run faster, longer, and am less sore afterward. *Runner's Digest* also says the Mercury is one of the best shoes on the market. Therefore, all people who want to run should buy Mercury shoes.

Passage 3

Many people feel it is a good idea to legalize prostitution. A substantial number of people visit prostitutes now even though the practice is generally illegal. So proponents argue that it makes sense to legalize prostitution. Are these people right? Absolutely not! Prostitution is a horribly immoral practice, and it should not be legalized. Prostitution helps spread sexually transmitted infections. Also, the legalization of prostitution will cause more men to cheat on their wives with prostitutes with the consequent negative fallout for families. Nothing good could possibly come from the legalization of prostitution.

Sample Responses To Passages 1 and 2

Passage 1

CONCLUSION: *Dining services are not doing an adequate job of providing food on campus.*

REASONS: 1. *Students are upset about the quality of the food.*
2. *There are not enough options provided every day.*
3. *More options would keep students happy and keep them eating on campus.*

To work on this particular critical-thinking skill, we need to assume that the reasons are strong ones. If we accept these reasons as reliable, we could also reasonably infer the following conclusions:

If dining services' goal is to provide a wide selection of food while ensuring the least amount of wasted food at the end of the day, then they are not letting students down with the current selections offered to students.

If dining services aim to keep the price of on-campus food down, and a more expansive menu would cause an increase in prices, they are not failing in their duty to students.

Notice that the alternative conclusions put dining services in quite a different light compared to the negative portrayal they received in the original conclusion.

Passage 2

CONCLUSION: *All potential runners should buy Mercury brand shoes.*

REASONS: 1. *When the author bought Mercury brand shoes, her time greatly improved.*
2. *Runner's Digest stated that Mercury brand shoes are some of the best running shoes on the market.*

On the basis of these reasons, we could infer several alternative conclusions:

Runners who are similar to the author should buy Mercury brand running shoes.

If one can afford Mercury brand shoes, the shoes are a great resource for people who are trying to run faster and longer.

If a runner is unhappy with the shoes she currently uses for training, then she should buy Mercury brand running shoes.

Passage 4. Expanding Practice and Feedback

Read the following article paying special attention to instances of dichotomous thinking. What other reasonable conclusions are possible on the issue discussed in the article? Then compare your critical thinking to the think aloud example. Try to use the comparison to provide clues for improving your next effort to ask this critical thinking question.

Should We Stop Eating Meat to Help the Planet?

Maryann Bird

chinadialogue.net (2008)

The global food crisis has put a new focus on the debate over the benefits of a vegetarian diet. Apart from the usual arguments about animal rights, healthy eating, chemical residues, food-borne illnesses, pollution and waste, dwindling fish populations and more, there is the question of feeding the livestock raised for slaughter.

Cows, sheep, pigs, chickens and other animals destined for our dinner tables need to be fed—indeed, fattened up—before they are killed. As more countries around the world develop their economies and their people become wealthier—especially in Asia and Latin America—the demand for meat is booming. At a time when a steadily climbing global human population needs food, more grain is being used as animal feed.

Additionally, more and more forested land (even in unique places such as the Amazon rainforest) is being cleared for pasture and plantation. And while humans and animals both now require more grain—wheat, corn and rice—and soybeans for food and food products, there is now a further hungry mouth demanding grain supplies: the biofuels industry. All of this has driven grain prices up in places where hungry people can least afford it, and provoked protests—some violent—in countries across the global south.

The World Food Programme (WFP) recently announced that high food prices are creating the biggest challenge that the United Nations agency has faced in its 45-year history, a silent tsunami threatening to plunge more than 100 million people on every continent into hunger. "This is the new face of hunger—the millions of people who were not in the urgent hunger category six months ago but now are," the agency's executive director, Josette Sheeran, said in April 2008. The prices of grain and dairy products—including bread, pasta, tortillas, flour, milk and eggs—are on the rise everywhere, in addition to the direct cost of meat itself.

As Lester R Brown of the Earth Policy Institute in Washington has written: "The stage is now set for direct competition for grain between the 800 million people who own automobiles, and the world's 2 billion poorest people. The risk is that millions of those on the lower rungs of the global economic ladder will start falling off as higher food prices drop their consumption below the survival level."

As well as the grain-price and grain-competition aspects of the meat-producing industry, the United Nations Food and Agriculture Organisation (FAO) reported in 2006 that: "The livestock sector emerges as one of the top two or three most significant contributors to the most serious environmental problems, at every scale from local to global."

In a report entitled *Livestock's Long Shadow: Environmental Issues and Options*, researchers concluded that the impact of the sector—while socially and politically very significant—was so environmentally massive that its impact needed to be urgently reduced. According to the report, livestock—while providing a third of humanity's protein intake and creating livelihoods for one billion of the world's poor—also:

- has degraded about 20% of the world's pastures and rangeland (and 73% of rangelands in dry areas);
- is responsible for 18% of greenhouse-gas emissions measured in carbon dioxide (CO_2) equivalent—more than transport's share;
- accounts for more than 8% of the world's human water use;
- contributes to eutophication, "dead" zones in coastal areas and degradation of coral reefs;
- adds to health-harming pollution in water, through animal wastes, antibiotics and hormones, chemicals from tanneries, fertilisers and pesticides;
- affects the replenishment of freshwater by compacting soil, reducing infiltration, degrading the banks of watercourses, drying up floodplains and lowering water tables;
- pre-empts land that once was habitat for wildlife, thereby reducing biodiversity.

Chiefly among wealthy nations, "high intakes of animal-source foods, in particular, animal fats and red meat", are linked to cardio-vascular disease, diabetes and some types of cancer.

In addition, vast amounts of energy are expended in transporting animals to slaughterhouses, killing them, refrigerating their carcasses and distributing their flesh. Producing one calorie of meat protein, according to research at the University of Chicago, means burning far more fossil fuel and outputting far more CO_2 than does a calorie of plant protein.

Musician Paul McCartney, a longtime vegetarian, recently urged the world to turn vegetarian in the fight against global warming. "The biggest change anyone could make in their own lifestyle would be to become vegetarian," the former Beatle said in April. "I would urge everyone to think about taking this simple step to help our precious environment and save it for the children of the future."

Maryann Bird is associate editor of chinadialogue.

Step-by-Step Walkthrough

While reading the article were you able to consider the large number of conclusions possible? Below is a step-by-step method one critical thinker used when evaluating other possible conclusions.

- First, I want to identify the author's conclusion and her reasons because I know that ultimately I'm going to want to try to identify multiple conclusions that can be derived from those reasons. I don't find the author's conclusion to be very explicit in the body of her essay, but I think that the title of her essay captures well her implicit question: Should we stop eating meat to help the planet? Throughout her essay, she stresses the negative societal and environmental impact of the meat producing industry, and she begins her essay with alluding to ceasing the raising of livestock for slaughter as a possible new benefit of a vegetarian diet. The author implicitly concludes that we should stop eating meat all-together to help the environment, and she provides a number of reasons why we should eliminate meat from our diets. The issue appears to be framed black and white: we either eat meat or we do not. However, maybe someone with different assumptions could generate different conclusions.
- Now, I'll want to be conscious of her reasons as I move toward the process of identifying other conclusions. Two reasons stand out. The second through fifth paragraphs highlight how meat production is increasing grain prices, which is having a major

negative effect on the poorest people in the world. The following four paragraphs provide a list of negative environmental consequences of the meat production industry. Her seventh paragraph captures this second reason very well when it states "the impact of the sector . . . was so environmentally massive that its impact needed to be urgently reduced."

- Now I'll search for multiple conclusions to the issue. I'll start by accepting these reasons as sensible to me. I will use my imagination to generate a list of conclusions that are not overly dichotomous. Perhaps we should reach a middle ground and eliminate a portion of meat from our diet, such as cutting meat intake in half. Perhaps we should invest in finding more sustainable ways to raise livestock that are less taxing on the environment. These are just two examples of conclusions that fall in the gray area on the spectrum of meat consumption.

- I can always generate if-clauses to form possible conclusions. For example, "If we are able to affordably gain protein and nutrients from other source, we should not eat meat" or "If we can make meat production more efficient for the environment we should allow ourselves to eat meat." Generating if-clauses such as these broaden the list of possible conclusions from which we can choose our own position.

- If the author wanted to present an argument with multiple possible conclusions, perhaps the title should be reworded from "should we stop eating meat?" to "what could we do about meat consumption to help the planet?" By creating an either-or situation, the author has limited one's ability to think more broadly about solutions to the problem raised. I realize that the issue is more in-depth than the author presents it; and when I evaluate the author's argument, I will consider the other possible conclusions available.

Were you able to identify some alternative conclusions of your own? Did you identify the dichotomy presented in the article?

CRITICAL QUESTION SUMMARY: WHY THIS QUESTION IS IMPORTANT

What Reasonable Conclusions Are Possible?

When you are deciding whether to accept or reject an author's conclusion, you want to make sure that the author has come to the most reasonable conclusion. An author often oversteps his reasoning when he comes to a conclusion. By identifying alternative reasonable conclusions, you can determine which alternative conclusions, if any, you would be willing to accept in place of the author's conclusion. This step is the final tool in deciding whether to accept or reject the author's conclusion.

CHAPTER 14

Overcoming Obstacles to Critical Thinking

Critical thinking liberates us from believing something just because someone says it is true. The primary values of a critical thinker liberate us even more because they push us to question and seek insights from anyone within our vicinity. But you must have noticed that as wonderful as critical thinking is for our mental health and development, it is not a common occurrence for most of us. We just see very few people who regularly ask the right questions.

Why? What is there about people or about critical thinking that provides a barrier to critical thinking? This chapter is based on the assumption that the first important step in overcoming these barriers is realizing that they exist. We cannot defeat invisible enemies; we need to expose them.

REVIEWING FAMILIAR OBSTACLES

While we have not focused on barriers to critical thinking so far in this book, we already *have* encountered a few serious roadblocks to critical thinking. For example, in Chapter 2, we learned about the ease with which we can be encouraged to go along with the crowd as a substitute for critical thinking. We have an understandable desire to be regarded highly by those we surround ourselves with. Hence, when they seem to be leaning toward a conclusion as a group, we can easily, unless we are very careful to remember the virtues of critical thinking, convince ourselves that any misgivings we have about the reasoning that led to the conclusion are insignificant.

Groupthink is a regular part of our world. To *go along* with the team or the club, is to *get along* with those people. This very desire to be accepted or to fit is responsible for the bandwagon fallacy. Anyone selling an idea knows how susceptible we are to testimonials that make us think everyone in her right mind is starting to hold a particular conclusion. We are pushed along by the force of the group's opinion. As with any of these obstacles, we want to recognize the tendency and then reflect in each instance whether the torrent of voices saying we should do or buy something has substantial reasons for its conclusion.

A second social obstacle to habitual critical thinking is our relative unwillingness to listen to people we do not like. The material in Chapter 2 encourages critical thinkers to consider how they can come across so as to keep the conversation going because we are more likely to listen to those we feel warmly toward. Put that tendency together with our frequent desire to hang around with other people who share our viewpoints, and the result is reduced critical thinking. We can hardly grow unless we tolerate and listen to a broad spectrum of people and viewpoints. Stretching ourselves, requiring ourselves to seek and consider conflicting bundles of reasons, is a powerful antidote to mental stagnation.

A third obstacle consists of the fallacies we have already examined in Chapter 7. The reason we gave individual attention to several of them is because they are so common. Pick any of them; think about why it is so common. Usually, we are in a rush to judgment; we want our conclusions fast and clean. Consequently, for example, when somebody teaches us a name for some problem we see around us, we think, "Aha, now I understand why that problem arises." We explain by naming because we are not careful to ask, "But now that we have the name for that mental disorder, are we any closer to understanding WHY it occurs?"

Our impatience to settle on a conclusion gets us in trouble again and again. In a later chapter we spoke about the confusion between correlation and causation. Once we hear the difference, we think to ourselves, "Well, I would hardly make that kind of silly error." But then we do, and we do so because we see a time relationship between two events and instead of wondering whether there is any explanatory link, we simply rush to see a causal link that is not present. In almost all instances, conclusions should be reached after systematic, relaxed reasoning.

MENTAL HABITS THAT BETRAY US

Cognition refers to the process of thinking. Our cognitive capabilities are numerous, but we are limited and betrayed by a series of mental habits. These cognitive biases push and pull us, unless we rope and tie them to make them behave. They move us in the direction of conclusions that we would never accept were we exercising the full range of critical thinking skills. While this section touches on only a few of them, understanding and resisting the ones we discuss will make a major contribution to the quality of your conclusions.

The Seductive Quality of Personal Experience

When something happens to us, we experience it directly and intensely. We tend to trust ourselves and our observations. Consequently, in any conversation we have a tendency to stress personal experiences. Furthermore, whenever those experiences differ from those of others, we have an inclination to weight personal experience more highly, even when it disagrees with the more scientific observations of others.

The average person who cites "personal experience" as a basis for belief is unfortunately running a great risk of several practical errors. Perhaps the most obvious of these errors is captured by checking the sample size of the group claiming to have observed reality. It's *one*, isn't it? Although you are, as an individual, capable of great insight, would you really want to rely on just one person's observations, even your own?

Now combine this tendency with the *choice-supportive bias*, and you can surely see how we need to strive to associate with a broad range of diverse people. The choice-supportive bias is the habit of looking backward at our previous choices and recalling them as being of much higher quality than they actually were. Our defense mechanisms seem well-defined and powerful. We want to look good in our own eyes. What a useful guarantee of that effect is identifying what we have done in our life with multiple positive characteristics.

Belief in a Just World

When an issue arises, our reactions may too often be guided by our deep psychological needs. If certain things are true we feel better. For instance, when someone discusses the relative emotional stability of men and women, intelligence of citizens from various countries, or the impact of aging on competence, each of us has a vested interest in the result of the discussion. We "need" certain conclusions to be true, for we belong to a category of people who look better if certain conclusions are reached.

Because we wish certain conclusions to be true, we may reason *as if* they are true, despite strong evidence to the contrary. Not only do we want our vested interests to prevail, but we also wish for a comfortable, fair world. The wish for a just world is often transformed in our minds into the belief in a just world.

This belief in a just world can distort our reasoning in numerous regards. Suppose for instance, we bring the belief in a just world to an evaluation of the need for governmentally regulating the extent of radon gas in dwellings. We might erroneously presume that no one would ever build a dwelling that contained dangerous amounts of radon gas; to do so would not be just.

Another painful example of the danger of the belief in a just world occurs sometimes when people believe someone who is actually manipulating them with expressions of deep love. In a just world, no one would play with our emotions like that. Thus, some assume we can automatically trust expressions of love. Can we?

Stereotypes

One approach to thinking about biases is to see them as potentially distorting assumptions. You approach any topic with certain preliminary beliefs or habits of mind. The previous section discussed one such habit—a preference for using personal experience to guide choices and adjustments. Another assumption or bias that can distort your decisions is the tendency to stereotype. When we stereotype we allege that a particular group has a specific set of characteristics.

Stereotypes are substitutes for thought. Here are a few examples:

1. Men with facial hair are wise.
2. Overweight individuals are jolly.
3. Japanese are industrious.
4. Young people are frivolous.
5. Women make the best secretaries.
6. Welfare recipients are lazy.

All six of these illustrations pretend to tell us something significant about the quality of certain types of people. If we believe these stereotypes, we will not approach people and their ideas with the spirit of openness necessary for strong sense critical thinking. In addition, we will have an immediate bias toward any issue or controversy in which these people are involved. The stereotypes will have loaded the issue in advance, *prior to* the reasoning.

Imagine, for instance, that you considered politicians to be manipulative and greedy. You possess that stereotype and approach political conversations with that assumption. Would you then be able to "pan for gold" with the aid of the critical questions you have learned? Isn't it more likely that you would not give an honest, caring politician a fair chance to convince you of her virtue? There seems to be something basically unfair about letting a stereotype prevent our giving someone or his arguments an opportunity to convince us.

Stereotypes are used so commonly because when they are true, they save us lots of time. If all politicians were indeed manipulative and greedy, it would make us more efficient readers and listeners to bring the stereotype with us when participating in a political conversation.

BUT, rarely is a stereotype safe. Nor is it fair! Each person deserves our respect, and their arguments deserve our attention. Stereotypes get in the way of critical thinking because they attempt to short circuit the difficult process of evaluation. As critical thinkers, we want to model curiosity and openness; stereotypes cut us off from careful consideration of what others are saying. They cause us to ignore valuable information by closing our minds prematurely.

The Urge to Simplify

Most of us prefer simplicity to complexity. Decisions and situations with simple answers permit us to move on rapidly and confidently to the next topic or life event. We don't have to wrestle so hard and invest so much mental energy in simple situations.

This bias for simplification was discussed earlier when we introduced dichotomous thinking. One reason for the attractiveness of dichotomous thinking for many of us is its simplicity. We can handle or master two potential alternatives with less anxiety than would emerge were we to see choices in terms of a continuum of possible choices.

Suppose we were to ask you whether drugs should be legalized. If you think of the question as one requiring a "yes" or "no" answer, it appears to be a manageable question you can handle after some initial reflection.

But there are many types of drugs; legalization takes many forms; potential drug users are various ages; legalization could contribute or detract from many potential social objectives. This issue is so complex it makes our heads hurt to consider it.

Critical thinking, though, forces us to consider an issue as it is, with all the complexity it possesses. To take the easy way out and dichotomize the issue is to miss out on the rich number of possible responses to drugs and other human dilemmas.

The urge to simplify can also limit our search for hypotheses about the meaning of evidence or for alternative conclusions flowing from a set of reasons. Whenever we restrict our perspective we cut ourselves off from potential insight.

For instance, when we choose a spouse, religion, or value assumption, we want to push ourselves to think broadly from alternative perspectives. Consider the obvious deficiencies of choosing your religion solely on the basis of your understanding of what it means to be a Baptist, Methodist, or Presbyterian. The alternatives to these three are incredibly numerous. By not considering these alternatives, by giving in to the desire to simplify the decision, you would have been unnecessarily sloppy in your choice.

While it is frequently unrealistic to consider all possible alternatives, hypotheses, or conclusions, compel yourself to resist the bias for simplification. Work on yourself to look further before making important judgments. You cannot evaluate every possible spouse, for example, but you should look beyond your neighborhood.

Belief Perseverance

You bring to any conversation or test a set of preconceptions. You start with opinions. To return to the panning for gold metaphor, *before* you even dip your pan into the gravel you think you have gold in the pan. Your beliefs are valuable because they are yours. Understandably you want to hold onto them.

This tendency for personal beliefs to persevere is a tough obstacle to critical thinking. We are biased from the start of an exchange in favor of our current opinions and conclusions.

If I prefer the Democratic candidate for mayor, regardless of how shallow my rationale is, I may resist your appeal on behalf of the Republican candidate. I might feel bad about myself if I were to admit that my previous judgment had been flawed. This exaggerated loyalty to current beliefs is one of the sources of *confirmation bias*. Because of belief perseverance, we might study the mayoral election searching only for information consistent with our belief that the Democratic candidate is meritorious and the Republican candidate is weak. In this manner, belief perseverance leads to weak sense critical thinking.

Part of what is going on with belief perseverance is our exaggerated sense of our own competence. Some 85 percent of college teachers, for instance, say in surveys that they are better than average teachers, and 90 percent of them say they are improving each year. It is not just in Lake Wobegon, home of the *Lake Wobegon Effect*, where all the children are better than average, or so their parents say. This unfortunate habit of mind is probably responsible also for our sense that we are living in the midst of incredibly biased people, while we are unbiased. We tell ourselves that we see things as they are, while others look at the world through foggy, colored lens.

To counter belief perseverance, it's helpful to remember that strong sense critical thinking requires the recognition that judgments are tentative or contextual. We can never permit ourselves to be so sure of anything that we stop searching for an improved version. The struggle to remain open and full of questions requires us to fight against belief perseverance.

> The human understanding when it has once adopted an opinion . . .
> draws all things else to support and agree with it.
> —Francis Bacon, *Novum Organum* (1620).

When we change our minds in light of a superior argument, we deserve to be proud that we have resisted the temptation to remain true to long-held beliefs. Such a change of mind deserves to be seen as reflecting a rare strength. Foolish consistency in the face of persuasive counterarguments is intellectually dishonest.

Availability Heuristic

Critical thinking is hard, systematic work. We are always searching for ways to avoid its rigors. Each bias in this chapter can be seen as an attempt to avoid mental effort. I may rely on personal experience, stereotyping, simplification, and my current beliefs because in each case the alternative requires more rigorous "panning."

Another misleading bias that promises to help us reach sound judgments without critical thinking is the availability heuristic. A *heuristic* is a guide for understanding or discovery. The availability heuristic refers to our tendency to rely on information and memories that are easily retrieved as a basis for our decisions and judgments. The weight attached to a particular piece of evidence therefore depends more on its availability than its appropriateness as a reason.

You can observe the dangers of the availability heuristic all around you. Newspaper headlines about a particularly brutal slaying convince residents that more police must be hired. Reservoirs are built because a recent drought suggested to residents that we may be entering an era with less rainfall. Parents warn their children not to associate with people who dress in a bizarre fashion because the parents vividly remember the trouble caused in their youth by people who wore those kinds of clothes.

To recognize the power of the availability heuristic, imagine that you were asked to compare the safety of airplanes and automobiles. There are volumes of comparative data that you *could* use to form your judgment. Would you consult them or would you rely on the availability heuristic? Alternatively, think back over the last two weeks. How often have you invited someone to lunch so she could present a viewpoint diametrically opposite to your current perspective?

Recent events, for instance, tend to have a disproportionate impact on our perceptions. While the recency of plane crashes in Tokyo, Detroit, or Dallas should not distort your comparison, the resulting tendency to exaggerate the occurrence of plane crashes is common. We may remember better those instances that just occurred even though they may have been exceptions to what normally occurs. The availability of recent events in our memory bank must be consciously checked by asking, "Were those recent events typical?"

Another factor affecting the availability of evidence is its vividness. Striking examples tend to overwhelm typical examples in our memory. One fiery plane crash with dozens of casualties can etch powerful images in our mind. These images may be vastly disproportionate to typical experiences on airplanes. Statistics describing what is typical can often be very dry; typical experiences can be dull *and* safe.

Because we have a tendency to remember startling and unusual events, we must struggle to place available information into a broader context. Our desire to engage in strong sense critical thinking requires us to process "available" information by asking, "Is it typical?" Answering that question forces us to study evidence, compiled more systematically. "Available" evidence must be diluted with evidence collected from perspectives different from our own.

In a sense, critical thinkers must censor themselves. They must recognize that they will begin conversations or thought with certain tendencies inconsistent with critical thinking. What distinguishes strong sense critical thinkers is their drive to resist these biases, to keep searching for improved beliefs, and to conduct that search in diverse streams.

WISHFUL THINKING

In 2005 Stephen Colbert reminded us of the dangerous mental habit of *truthiness*. A person is loyal to truthiness when he prefers concepts or facts he wishes to be true, rather than concepts or facts known to be true. In other words, many of us just form beliefs through a form of wish fulfillment. What we wish to be true, we simply declare IS true. That way the facts conform to our beliefs rather than fitting our beliefs to the facts. We are sure you can see the problem here.

We WANT our presidents and politicians to be honest. We don't want to believe corporations don't care about the environment. When wishes collide with reality, we have difficulty relinquishing the wishes. Because we think things should be different than they are, we then believe indeed they are different. Once we recognize this tendency in ourselves, we need to keep asking, "Is that true because I want it be true, or is there convincing evidence that it's true?"

Wishful thinking has staying power because of the frequency of our denial patterns. Quite unconsciously, we fight with the facts, trying to reinforce visions of the world that are rosy beyond the bounds of reality. Anxieties and fears about the problems we face together and individually serve as a protective shield against seeing the actual world in which we live. Think of how frequently over the course of your life you will hear leaders of nations declare that the war they are fighting will soon be over, and victory will be won. But such predictions usually turn out to be hollow promises. To have to face the facts that the war may go on and on or that it will not result in a clear victory for the home team is just too painful to consider. So the mind erases it.

Attention: A form of wishful thinking is magical thinking. People tend to rely on magic as a causal explanation for explaining things that science has not acceptably explained, or to attempt to control things that science cannot. Much of the world is beyond our control and we know we are up against forces and dilemmas that seem to exceed our reach to solve. We react by replacing the Tooth Fairy and the Easter Bunny with some new source of alleged power and influence who can bring optimism and security to our thoughts. Magical thinking tends to be greatest when people feel most powerless to understand or alter a situation. In the face of great need, any belief in the randomness or accidental aspects of life are set aside as grim and replaced with the promise of magical causal relationships.

The antidote to wishful thinking, like the antidote for each of the obstacles in this chapter, is the active use of critical questions to cut through as many of these obstacles as possible. The obstacles will always be part of us; we cannot ignore them, but we can surely resist them with curiosity and a deep respect for the principles of critical thinking.

CHAPTER 15

READINGS CLUSTER 1

Should We Protect Children from Advertising?

We often protect the innocence of children. We place regulations on what children are allowed to do and the rights they are given before they reach adulthood. We require children to be educated and cared for domestically. Furthermore, the government places age restrictions on the purchasing of alcohol, cigarettes, and pornography. One of the most heated issues in the discussion about children is how much protection society and the government should extend to children. Do we have a collective responsibility to assure children the best conditions possible, or are parents individually responsible for the well-being of their offspring? One area under constant debate is the regulation of advertising directed at children. The articles in this chapter introduce the various arguments for and against regulating advertising directed at children. Using the knowledge you gained from *Asking the Right Questions,* read the passages and answer the questions through critical evaluation.

Advertising to Children: Is It Ethical?

Rebecca A. Clay

Monitor On Psychology (2000)

Ever since he first started practicing, Berkeley, Calif., psychologist Allen D. Kanner, PhD, has been asking his younger clients what they wanted to do when they grew up. The answer used to be "nurse," "astronaut" or some other occupation with intrinsic appeal.

Today the answer is more likely to be "make money." For Kanner, one explanation for that shift can be found in advertising.

"Advertising is a massive, multi-million dollar project that's having an enormous impact on child development," says Kanner, who is also an associate faculty member at a clinical psychology training program called the Wright Institute. "The sheer volume of advertising is growing rapidly and invading new areas of childhood, like our schools."

According to Kanner, the result is not only an epidemic of materialistic values among children, but also something he calls "narcissistic wounding" of children. Thanks to advertising, he says, children have become convinced that they're inferior if they don't have an endless array of new products.

Now Kanner and several colleagues are up-in-arms about psychologists and others who are using psychological knowledge to help marketers target children more effectively. They're outraged that psychologists and others are revealing such tidbits as why 3- to 7-year-olds gravitate toward toys that transform themselves into something else and why 8- to 12-year-olds love to collect things. Last fall, Kanner and a group of 59 other psychologists and psychiatrists sent a controversial letter protesting psychologists' involvement to APA.

In response, at its June meeting, APA's Board of Directors acted on a recommendation from the Board for the Advancement of Psychology in the Public Interest and approved the creation of a task force to study the issue. The task force will examine the research on advertising's impact on children and their families and develop a research agenda. The group will look at the role psychologists play in what some consider the exploitation of children and consider how psychology can help minimize advertising's harmful effects and maximize its positive effects.

The group will also explore implications for public policy. Task force members will be chosen in consultation with Div. 37 (Child, Youth and Family Services) and other relevant divisions.

Unethical Practices?

The letter protesting psychologists' involvement in children's advertising was written by Commercial Alert, a Washington, D.C., advocacy organization. The letter calls marketing to children a violation of APA's mission of mitigating human suffering, improving the condition of both individuals and society, and helping the public develop informed judgments.

Urging APA to challenge what it calls an "abuse of psychological knowledge," the letter asks APA to:

• Issue a formal, public statement denouncing the use of psychological principles in marketing to children.

- Amend APA's Ethics Code to limit psychologists' use of their knowledge and skills to observe, study, mislead or exploit children for commercial purposes.
- Launch an ongoing campaign to investigate the use of psychological research in marketing to children, publish an evaluation of the ethics of such use, and promote strategies to protect children against commercial exploitation by psychologists and others using psychological principles.

"The information psychologists are giving to advertisers is being used to increase profits rather than help children," says Kanner, who helped collect signatures for the letter. "The whole enterprise of advertising is about creating insecure people who believe they need to buy things to be happy. I don't think most psychologists would believe that's a good thing. There's an inherent conflict of interest."

Advertisers' efforts seem to work. According to marketing expert James U. McNeal, PhD, author of "The Kids Market: Myths and Realities" (Paramount Market Publishing, 1999), children under 12 already spend a whopping $28 billion a year. Teenagers spend $100 billion. Children also influence another $249 billion spent by their parents.

The effect this rampant consumerism has on children is still unknown, says Kanner. In an informal literature review, he found many studies about how to make effective ads but not a single study addressing ads' impact on children. Instead, he points to research done by Tim Kasser, PhD, an assistant professor of psychology at Knox College in Galesburg, Ill. In a series of studies, Kasser has found that people who strongly value wealth and related traits tend to have higher levels of distress and lower levels of well-being, worse relationships and less connection to their communities.

"Psychologists who help advertisers are essentially helping them manipulate children to believe in the capitalistic message, when all the evidence shows that believing in that message is bad for people," says Kasser. "That's unethical."

Driving Out Psychologists

Psychologists who help companies reach children don't agree. Take Whiton S. Paine, PhD, an assistant professor of business studies at Richard Stockton College in Pomona, N.J. As principal of a Philadelphia consulting firm called Kid2Kid, Paine helps Fortune 500 companies market to children.

Paine has no problem with launching a dialogue about psychologists' ethical responsibilities or creating standards similar to ones used in Canada and Europe to protect children from commercial exploitation. Such activities will actually help his business, he says, by giving him leverage when clients want to do something that would inadvertently harm children. What Paine does have a problem with is driving psychologists out of the business.

"If you remove ethical psychologists from the decision-making process in an ad's creation, who's left?" he asks. "People who have a lot less sensitivity to the unique vulnerabilities of children."

Others who have read the proposal point out that psychological principles are hardly confidential.

"We can't stop alcohol or tobacco companies from using the basic research findings and theories found in textbooks and academic journals," says Curtis P. Haugtvedt, PhD, immediate past president of Div. 23 (Consumer Psychology) and an associate professor of marketing at Ohio State University in Columbus. "The same issue exists for all sciences: the information is available in public libraries."

The problem with trying to regulate the use of psychological principles is that "people acting in ways psychologists find objectionable probably aren't members of APA anyway," says Haugtvedt, who received a copy of the Commercial Alert letter. He believes that having general guidelines as to appropriate uses and areas of concern would be beneficial to all parties.

Daniel S. Acuff, PhD, for example, draws on the child development courses he took during his graduate schooling in education to advise such clients as Disney, Hasbro and Kraft. His book "What Kids Buy and Why: The Psychology of Marketing to Kids" (Free Press, 1997) draws on child development research to show product developers and marketers how to reach children more effectively.

To Acuff, the letter to APA is not only an "unconstitutional" attempt to limit how professionals make their living but also a misguided overgeneralization.

Since Acuff and his partner started their business in 1979, they have had a policy guiding their choice of projects. As a result, they turn down assignments dealing with violent video games, action figures armed with weapons and other products they believe are bad for children. Their work focuses instead on products that they consider either good for children or neutral, such as snacks and sugary foods parents can use as special treats. The letter to APA fails to acknowledge that psychological principles can be used for good as well as bad, he says.

"I don't agree with black-and-white thinking," says Acuff, president of Youth Market Systems Consulting in Sherman Oaks, Calif. "Psychology in itself is neither good nor bad. It's just a tool like anything else."

Rebecca A. Clay is a writer in Washington, D.C.

CRITICAL THINKING QUESTIONS

1. In this article, the author's reasoning relies on assumptions about human nature and children. What assumptions does Clay make about the nature of children? Do you agree with the author's assumptions about children? What might the opposite assumptions about the nature of children be? How could believing the opposite assumptions affect Clay's argument?

2. One reason against advertising to children states, "Thanks to advertising . . . children have become convinced that they're inferior if they don't have an endless array of new products." Can you identify rival causes for a child's feeling of inferiority?

3. Ask yourself if there is any significant omitted information in the author's reasoning. What critical thinking questions do you ask when determining whether there is any omitted information? For example, does Clay provide substantial reasons that someone who disagrees with her conclusion would offer? How would further addressing the counterargument enhance Clay's argument?

Television Advertising Leads to Unhealthy Habits in Children; Says APA Task Force

Dale Kunkel

American Psychological Association Online (2004)

WASHINGTON – Research shows that children under the age of eight are unable to critically comprehend televised advertising messages and are prone to accept advertiser messages as truthful, accurate and unbiased. This can lead to unhealthy eating habits as evidenced by today's youth obesity epidemic. For these reasons, a task force of the American Psychological Association (APA) is recommending that advertising targeting children under the age of eight be restricted.

The Task Force, appointed by the APA in 2000, conducted an extensive review of the research literature in the area of advertising media, and its effects on children. It is estimated that advertisers spend more than $12 billon per year on advertising messages aimed at the youth market. Additionally, the average child watches more than 40,000 television commercials per year.

The six-member team of psychologists with expertise in child development, cognitive psychology and social psychology found that children under the age of eight lack the cognitive development to understand the persuasive intent of television advertising and are uniquely susceptible to advertising's influence.

"While older children and adults understand the inherent bias of advertising, younger children do not, and therefore tend to interpret commercial claims and appeals as accurate and truthful information," said psychologist Dale Kunkel, Ph.D., Professor of Communication at the University of California at Santa Barbara and senior author of the task force's scientific report.

"Because younger children do not understand persuasive intent in advertising, they are easy targets for commercial persuasion," said psychologist Brian Wilcox, Ph.D., Professor of Psychology and Director of the Center on Children, Families and the Law at the University of Nebraska and chair of the task force. "This is a critical concern because the most common products marketed to children are sugared cereals, candies, sweets, sodas and snack foods. Such advertising of unhealthy food products to young children contributes to poor nutritional habits that may last a lifetime and be a variable in the current epidemic of obesity among kids."

The research on children's commercial recall and product preferences confirms that advertising does typically get young consumers to buy their products. From a series of studies examining product choices, say Drs. Kunkel and Wilcox, the findings show that children recall content from the ads to which they've been exposed and preference for a product has been shown to occur with as little as a single commercial exposure and strengthened with repeated exposures.

Furthermore, studies reviewed in the task force report show that these product preferences can affect children's product purchase requests, which can put pressure on parents' purchasing decisions and instigate parent-child conflicts when parents deny their children's requests, said Kunkel and Wilcox.

Finally, in addition to the issues surrounding advertising directed to young children, said Kunkel, there are concerns regarding certain commercial campaigns primarily targeting adults that pose risks for child-viewers. "For example, beer ads are commonly shown during sports events and seen by millions of children, creating both brand familiarity and more positive attitudes toward drinking in children as young as 9–10 years of age. Another area of sensitive advertising content involves commercials for violent media products such as motion pictures and video games. Such ads contribute to a violent media culture which increases the likelihood of youngsters' aggressive behavior and desensitizes children to real-world violence," said Dr. Kunkel.

According to the findings in the report, APA has developed the following recommendations:

- Restrict advertising primarily directed to young children of eight years and under. Policymakers need to take steps to better protect young children from exposure to advertising because of the inherent unfairness of advertising to audiences who lack the capability to evaluate biased sources of information found in television commercials.
- Ensure that disclosures and disclaimers in advertising directed to children are conveyed in language clearly comprehensible to the intended audience (e.g., use "You have to put it together" rather than "some assembly required").
- Investigate how young children comprehend and are influenced by advertising in new interactive media environments such as the internet.
- Examine the influence of advertising directed to children in the school and classroom. Such advertising may exert more powerful influence because of greater attention to the message or because of an implicit endorsement effect associated with advertising viewed in the school setting.

APA Task Force on Advertising and Children: Dale Kunkel, Ph.D., University of California, Santa Barbara; Brian Wilcox, Ph.D., University of Nebraska; Edward Palmer, Ph.D., Davidson College; Joanne Cantor, Ph.D., University of Wisconsin, Madison; Peter Dowrick, Ph.D., University of Hawaii; Susan Linn, Ed.D., Harvard University.

The American Psychological Association (APA), in Washington, DC, is the largest scientific and professional organization representing psychology in the United States and is the world's largest association of psychologists.

Critical Thinking Questions

1. Walk through the panning-for-gold approach with Clay's article. Why would the author want you to believe the passage? Take notes about the potential problems in the article. Critically evaluate the passage using your arsenal of tools from *Asking the Right Questions*. Lastly, form your own conclusion based on the reasonableness of what was said.
2. As a result of the research findings, the APA developed a series of recommendations regarding advertising to children. As we know, many reasonable conclusions are often possible in a given situation. After reviewing the findings, what are some other possible solutions the APA could have recommended

instead? Can you create any other possible solutions through the use of *if*-clauses?

3. Evaluate your own solutions alongside the APA's solutions. Remember, all conclusions are not created equal. Are you willing to accept one of your own solutions over the APA's recommendation? How do your own solutions affect your willingness to accept the author's conclusion?

4. Now consider how your own value preferences affect your alternate solutions. For instance, someone who values individual responsibility over collective responsibility would probably recommend that individuals should take actions to protect themselves from advertising, rather than have the government or organizations take responsibility. What other values could influence possible alternative solutions?

Taking Responsibility for Our McActions

Cam Beck

MarketingProfs Daily Fix (2007)

Stanford University researcher Tom Robinson recently published a study linking brands with the perception of quality in children. Apparently kids think McDonald's-branded products taste better than its unbranded (but identical) counterparts. This "revelation" is supposed to make us think that McDonald's is evil because their marketing is responsible for making kids fat.

In anticipation of the backlash, McDonald's promised to reduce the amount of money it spends on advertising to kids, and this MSNBC article says, "The study will likely stir more debate over ***the movement to restrict ads to kids***." [emphasis mine].

First of all, that extraneous details influence our perception is nothing new. The authors of *Made to Stick* cited a study conducted in 1986 that demonstrated how irrelevant details can make ideas appear more credible. At a wine-tasting gala in Germany back in 1991, our host explained that the reason a yellow tablecloth was used was because it gave customers the sense that the chardonnay tasted better.

Second, and most important, when are we going to stop looking to government to fix our inability to say "no" to our kids? I really don't care how much money McDonald's spends on advertising to children, because three things are true:

1. One Big Mac or Happy Meal, when consumed properly, is not going to kill me or my kids;
2. Thus, marketing them is not an inherently immoral act; and
3. I can always say "No" to prevent excess.

Coincidentally, my son asked me just this weekend if he could have McDonald's (or Chick-fil-A, Wendy's, or Whataburger) for dinner, and I simply said we wouldn't. We had good, healthy food waiting for us at home, and there was simply no reason to buy and eat fast food, no matter how tasty it might have seemed to either of us at that time.

Note to parents: It wasn't difficult.

I understand that a diet consisting solely of Big Macs and Happy Meals is a sure path to obesity, and I understand that obesity is a serious problem. But I don't know of any advertising that advocates obesity. Ads, as they should, advocate the consumption or use of a product or service. Sometimes they work, and sometimes they don't, but in the end, there is no mystery about what we're getting when we buy fast food. It is our responsibility to make sound decisions concerning our own diets and lives, and the diets and lives of our children.

When we ask Congress or any other regulatory agency to interfere, we are admitting the people do not have the capacity to make sound decisions about their own lives (We rarely, if ever, apply the same logic to ourselves—It's always the "other people" who have the problem and thus must be governed by outside sources). This creates an interesting paradox, since those same people who can't make sound decisions when confronted with a convincing ad are responsible for electing members of Congress, who appoint the regulatory authorities to which we must answer.

How can we claim the capacity to make decisions about our laws and representatives while at the same time claim that we don't have the capacity to make good decisions about how we react to advertising? If we cannot resist the temptation to eat fatty foods (or say "No" to our children) because the advertising makes it too appealing, we cannot logically claim that we have the discernment to preserve the very liberty that puts the reins of power within our reach.

I do believe companies have a responsibility to not only create products and services that are not innately harmful, but also to market them ethically. But at some point all of us, as consumers and as citizens, have to take responsibility to govern our own decisions. The implications of behaving otherwise go far beyond how we market Big Macs, Happy Meals, or anything else.

It means we can't be trusted with anything at all.

CRITICAL THINKING QUESTIONS

1. As you read, you should have created a list of the issue, conclusion, and reasons presented by Beck. Now consider the effectiveness of the evidence presented in the reasoning. When reading an article such as this, what questions should you ask yourself to critically evaluate the strength of the type of evidence presented?

2. Consider the ambiguity of key words and phrases within the passage. Are there any abstract ideas? What are the most important words and phrases within the passage? Explain how having an alternative definition for an ambiguous term directly affects Beck's conclusion.

3. The author takes a very decided stance on the issue of whether advertising should be regulated due to obesity in children. What value preferences influence the author's argument? How could a reader holding opposite value preferences reach a different conclusion when reading the passage?

4. Ask yourself, "What significant information is omitted in Beck's article?" One type of omitted information to consider is the *potential negative effects* of the government not regulating advertising. What are some possible negative effects of unregulated freedom for advertisers on television? Take your analysis one step further and consider more possible negative effects of regulating advertising. Which effects do you find more compelling?

How to Inoculate Your Children Against Advertising

Lisa Tiffin

Get Rich Slowly: Personal Finance that Makes Cents (2008)

I have a confession to make: I like commercials. Even though they can be boring, insulting, and just plain bothersome, on some level they intrigue me. I often wonder why certain ads fail miserably while others succeed in catapulting a brand to the forefront of store shelves. I like commercials because I enjoy guessing which will sink the product and which marketing genius will get a promotion. But what I hadn't considered until I had children was how much power commercials seem to have over us.

Out of the Mouth of Babes

What changed my perception was a routine shopping trip a few years ago with my then four-year-old boys. As I paused my shopping cart in front of the cleaning supplies, Andy said, "Mom, aren't we going to buy some Clorox?" I stared in surprise at my child because, although he was pointing straight at the Clorox, I knew he wasn't able to read.

I puzzled over the bleach incident for some time because not only were the boys unable to read, but I didn't generally buy bleach. Eventually, my husband and I realized that commercials were to blame. While I had been dismissing commercial-watching as a mildly amusing pastime, marketers were subtly invading my home and impressing their values on my captivated and trusting children.

Shortly after we saw how easily we had been replaced as the value-shapers in our home, we also began to notice just how much allure commercials held for our children. And as soon as we began to hear choruses of, "Can we buy this?" and "We need to have that!" from the lips of our twins, we realized we needed to act.

If You Want to Defeat Your Enemy, Sing His Song

Our first option was simply to turn the television off, but since our kids were only watching one or two shows per week in addition to a nightly game show we watched as a family, it was hard to believe they were watching too much. Also, if the commercials during those short hours were having this much effect, we had to consider what growing up in our media-saturated culture would do to them if they weren't properly armed.

What we decided to do was slightly unconventional, but it made sense to us. We inoculated our boys using a principle I had learned in a college communications course. Little by little, we taught them about basic economics and simple marketing techniques used by companies to encourage people to part with their hard-earned money. The theory was that if they could recognize the tactics companies used to market a product to people, then our children would become resistant to the claims presented in commercials and slowly learn to be discerning about their validity.

We didn't sit the boys down for long lectures; rather, every time we noticed that a commercial or a print ad caught their attention, we asked them if they thought the product really did what the commercial claimed. This introduced the idea that sometimes people say things that aren't true and that it was okay for them to question what they saw and heard. It also taught the boys that what they think is important and valuable.

At the same time, we explained to them how companies need money to pay their workers and themselves, and how those companies try to convince others to buy their products in order to make money. Slowly, we began to see a change in their behavior.

Raising Savvy Consumers

We knew our approach was working when, only a few months later, the boys asked me which paper towels we used. Soon after I answered them, I heard the sounds of running water and giggling coming from the downstairs bathroom. When I went to investigate, I saw Andy and Matt busily soaking paper towels and loading them with various toys. The explanation? They were testing the assertion that the towels were so strong they could carry heavy loads even when wet. The twins were so pleased the claims were true that Matt insisted we use nothing but this particular brand of towel in the future.

Eventually, the lessons of trusting your own judgment, testing the claims of others, and discovering true value began to have an effect on our kids' everyday lives. Instead of whining for toys they saw in a magazine, Andy and Matt would show me the ad and ask if I thought the toy lived up to its claims, whether I thought it was a good price or not, and how long I thought it would last. They began to check the piece count on building sets before they spent their birthday money on them, and they would ask store clerks for more information before making purchases.

Recently, a mattress commercial came on. We adults filtered out the woman falling sound asleep as soon as her head hit the pillow until Andy matter-of-factly piped up, "It doesn't work. I tried it." Smiling at the picture of my son trying to fall instantly asleep, I realized that while the mattress test hadn't worked, the inoculation had.

Ready for Anything

By introducing just a little bit of the marketing germ, we gave Andy and Matt a tool for wading through the thousands of ads that will clamor for their attention as they grow up in our consumer-driven society. Eventually, they will be able to use this process to decide if a product falls in line with their own values. For now, I am proud to hear my children constantly question the broad claims made by marketers, and I am pleased that we have been able to pass on to them our values of critical thinking and careful consideration.

This piece originally appeared in The Polishing Stone in slightly different form.

CRITICAL THINKING QUESTIONS

1. At the end of the article, the author declares she is glad she was able to pass on her critical thinking ability to her children. What examples of critical thinking from *Asking the Right Questions* were you able to determine Tiffin used when inoculating her children from the media? What other critical thinking tools would you suggest that Tiffin recommend using when evaluating television advertisements? For example, explaining the problems with improper appeals to authority is a critical thinking tool highly relevant to television advertisements.

2. Pretend you had the opportunity to respond to this passage. Explain to the author how the argument would be improved with evidence. What specific parts of the article require more or better evidence? Why is evidence important when considering the issue of advertising to children?

3. Identify significant descriptive assumptions Tiffin makes within the argument. Ask, *"If the reason is true, what else must be true for the conclusion to follow?"* Does connecting the hidden tissue of an argument through exposing assumptions strengthen or weaken the argument as a whole?

4. Suppose a classmate reads the above passage and says, "We shouldn't believe the argument because explaining deceptive marketing tactics will not work on EVERY SINGLE child. Even if we adopted Tiffin's method, part of the problem would still be there." What fallacy from Chapter 7 of *Asking the Right Questions* is your classmate committing? Why is it particularly important to keep this particular fallacy in mind when determining solutions for advertising?

Food Marketing to Children in the Context of a Marketing Maelstrom

Susan E. Linn

Journal of Public Health Policy (2004)

Childhood obesity is a major public health problem in the United States, yet U.S. children are targeted as never before with marketing for foods high in sugar, fat, salt, and calories. The advertising industry's stance is that parents should bear sole responsibility for what and how much their children eat—a simplistic view. We take a close look at the nature, depth, and breadth of food marketing aimed at children.

Marketing Maelstrom: The Escalation of Marketing to Children

While food comprises a large portion of what is marketed to children, food marketing occurs in the context of a myriad of other marketing messages to them as well, including advertising for toys, clothing, accessories, movies, television programs, video games, and countless other consumer goods. Even products traditionally purchased by adults such as automobiles, dog food, and air travel are now being marketed to children. While children have been targets for advertising since the advent of mass marketing, the intensity and frequency of children's current exposure to commercial messages is unprecedented.

Today, children between the ages of 2 and 18 spend almost forty hours a week outside of school engaged with media, defined in this article as including television, films, video and computer games, radio, and print materials, most of which is commercially driven. In spite of the growing popularity of the Internet and computer games, television is still the primary electronic medium with which children engage. Children are often alone when they watch television, meaning that no adult is present to help them process the marketing messages permeating the medium. Thirty-two percent of children ages two to seven have televisions in their rooms, as do 65% of children eight to eighteen and 26% of children under two.

While television is the most prevalent medium in children's lives, their access to the Internet—where the lines between content and marketing can be blurred—is growing. Companies lure children with "advergaming," in which products are incorporated into computer and video games as a means of advertising. Companies keep children's attention focused on specific brands much longer than with a traditional commercial. One site, called Candystand, consists of games featuring products from the food conglomerate Kraft, such as Lifesavers, Crème Savers, and Jello Pudding Bites.

Nor is marketing limited to the time children spend outside of school. In 2000, a report from the federal government's General Accounting Office (GAO) called marketing in schools a "growth industry." Exclusive beverage contracts, corporate-sponsored teaching materials, book covers featuring ads, and corporate-sponsored newscasts are just a few of the ways that marketing infiltrates educational settings.

The advertising industry spin is that parents should bear sole responsibility for protecting children from marketing and that parents are to blame for the unhappy consequences of commercialism.

In the 1970s, the changing needs of families outstripped the services provided by public institutions. Children's advocates observed the phenomenon of "latchkey kids." Millions of elementary school children were home alone from the time they finished school until a parent returned from work. By the 1980s, the phenomenon sparked studies of their school performance, calls for after-school programs, hotlines for kids to call if they were frightened, and books written to help children survive on their own at home. Parents at work worried that their children were going to be prey for all kinds of predators, and instructed them not to answer the door, or to tell people who telephoned that their parents were busy in the next room.

These children did not go unnoticed by the advertising industry, and a new marketing demographic reflected the vulnerability of children alone at home, unsupervised. As Alan Toman, president of The Marketing Department, an advertising agency, explained in the Chicago Tribune in 1988, "Latchkey kids are a natural for a lot of consumer products. . . . We are just beginning to see companies approaching this particular kids' market, taking seriously how many purchases kids control and calculating how much potential they represent."

That same year, the Thomas J. Lipton Company (now owned by Unilever) put out a magazine called *Kidsmart*, aimed at latchkey kids and their parents. The magazine contained safety tips and fun projects as well as four pages of ads for Lipton packaged foods such as Cup of Soup, Fun Fruit snacks, and fruit drinks.

For children whose parents felt safer with them at home than roaming the streets, the major housebound activity was watching television. In 1988, the *New York Times* reported that 80 percent of American kids were watching TV after school. According to the *Times*, "Marketers have been responding. The value of commercial time sold to national advertisers for syndicated children's programs, primarily between 3 p.m. and 5p.m. on weekdays, grew from nothing in 1982 to $107 million last year."

The eighties also saw marketers flocking to newly created cable television stations. Campbell's, for instance, created a soup music video to sell Chunky Soup on the popular teen-oriented cable station, MTV. In a prescient twist on the refrain of the day, a vice president of research at the children's cable television station Nickelodeon announced, "The latest European research shows that product preferences develop at a much earlier age than anyone had ever thought. . . . As people begin to understand this, to see how brand loyalty transfers to adulthood, *there is almost nothing that won't be advertised as for children"* (italics added).

The sheer volume of child-targeted marketing is stressful for families. As experts on child rearing urge parents to "pick their battles," parents are overwhelmed by commercially created battles to fight. If they are strict about food, should they also be strict about violent toys, media programs, and music? What about precociously sexualized clothing? Computer, video game, and TV time? Materialism?

As most parents struggle to set limits, corporations often undermine parental authority by encouraging children to nag. They inundate children with images that tend to portray adults as incompetent, mean, or absent and that encourage children to engage in behaviors that are troublesome to parents. A 1999 article in *Advertising Age* begins, "Mothers are known for instructing children not to play with their food. But increasingly marketers are encouraging them to." Instead of acquiescing to parents' concerns, the marketing industry often sees parental disapproval as a strong selling point with kids. When discussing the strategy for selling Kraft Lunchables, a marketing expert put it this way, "Parents do not fully approve—they would rather their child ate a more traditional lunch—but this adds to the brand's appeal among children because it reinforces their need to feel in control."

The amount of money spent on marketing to children doubled during the 1990s and was estimated at about $15 billion annually in 2002. In general, food companies spend enormous sums on marketing. In 2002, McDonalds spent over $1.3 billion on advertising in the United States alone, making Burger King's $650 million seem paltry by comparison. PepsiCo spent more than $1.1 billion, outspending Coca-Cola by about $544,000. Kraft Foods (owned, incidentally, by tobacco giant Phillip Morris—now called Altria Group), maker of Kraft Macaroni and Cheese, Oreos, and Kool-Aid, spent about $465 million in 2001. The year before, Burger King spent $80 million on advertising just to children and Quaker Oats spent $15 million pitching Cap'n Crunch. When it comes to food, children are targets for everything from edible checkers to battery-operated lollipops.

How Food Marketers Insinuate Their Brands into Children's Lives

Television Commercials

In spite of the growing popularity of the Internet and computer games, television is still the primary medium advertisers use to reach children. Two hours of programming on the Cartoon Network, between 5:30 and 7:30 p.m. on a weekday evening (prime viewing time for children) contained twenty food commercials, or one every six minutes. Almost all of the food commercials children see on television are for foods high in calories, fat, salt, and/or sugar. Television food advertising is effective. Children's requests for food products, misperceptions about nutrition, and increased caloric intake have been shown to be linked to television advertising. So have parental purchases. One 30-second food commercial can affect the brand choices of children as young as two, and repeated exposure has even greater impact.

Beyond Commercials: Tie-ins, Brand Licensing, and Product Placement

When considering the degree to which food advertising permeates television viewing for children, we also have to consider brand licensing (when an image or logo is leased for use on products other than the one it was created for) and product placement (when products are inserted into the content of programming). Along with most children's movies, many of the TV programs children watch partner with food companies. For instance, in 2003, six hours of programming on Nickelodeon one Sunday afternoon contained 40 food commercials, or about one every nine minutes. However, that did not include all of the programs whose characters are now icons for food products. Nickelodeon's hit program SpongeBob SquarePants was Kraft's top selling Macaroni and Cheese in 2002 and the number one "face" shaped Good Humor Ice Cream Bar. Once a program is associated with a particular brand, the program itself becomes an ad for that food. Visit any supermarket and you'll find shelves filled with examples of these links between media programs and food manufacturers.

Take another Nickelodeon's hit program, *Rugrats*—Chucky, Angelica, and the other Rugrats tykes now grace packages of Kraft Macaroni and Cheese, as well as Farley's Fruit Rolls, a peanut-butter-and-jelly flavored Good Humor ice cream sandwich, and Amurol bubble gum with comics printed on the gum itself ("view & chew"). Nickelodeon itself has a line of fruit snacks featuring Nicktoons characters.

Tie-ins like these are designed to lure children into selecting foods associated with favorite movie or TV characters. They are also designed to keep children continually reminded of products. As one marketing expert says, corporations are "trying to establish a situation where kids are exposed to their brand in as many different places as possible throughout the course of the day or the week, or almost anywhere they turn in the course of their daily rituals."

Children's introduction to TV-linked calories often begins in earnest with juice. According to Lisa Rant, a beverage industry writer, "The beverage aisle is brimming with brews for babies, and mom can take her pick from a plethora of multi- and single-serve solutions with products packaged specifically for the pediatric set. Apple & Eve travels down Sesame Street with Elmo's Punch, Big Bird's Apple, Grover's Grape and Bert & Ernie's Berry juices . . ."

Sesame Street isn't the only children's program to cash in on juice boxes for the littlest children. Libby's offers juice boxes adorned with Arthur characters, and because "toddlers are naturally drawn to colorful graphics and familiar characters, Mott's made its move with juice boxes that have featured Nickelodeon's *Rugrats* and, more recently, PBS' *Dragon Tales*. The innovative *Dragon Tales* promotion ran for six months, with changes in graphics every 45 days to 'refresh' the campaign."

From a juice company's point of view—and that of many parents—little juice boxes or containers make sense: they're small enough for a young child to handle (both physically and with regard to appetite), easy to transport, and relatively unspillable. As Julie Halpin, CEO of the Gepetto Group, explained, "Companies often find it difficult to generate enough volume with a product designed only for infants and toddlers. . . . Because this is a relatively short life-stage, the product needs to encourage enough purchase frequency to make sense as a business proposition. If the line of products can be broad and appropriate for different times of day and drinking occasions, a brand for this consumer can work." Yet the form of juice packaging the article above extols is exactly the type that the American Academy of Pediatrics has voiced concern over, suggesting that babies and toddlers may be drinking too much juice, citing as a factor its easy portability, in the form of covered cups and juice boxes. In addition to providing babies with too many calories, sipping juice throughout the day may be harmful to young children's teeth.

Parents can "just say no" to a toddler's grocery aisle requests. But toddlers, going through the developmental phase of differentiating themselves from their parents, are prone to do so by actively and tenaciously asserting their voice, needs, and wants. For media- or brand-saturated little ones and their parents—even for families who restrict television viewing to public television—a trip to the grocery store may turn into a struggle.

Product placement—when a company pays to have its products inserted in the content of media—is prohibited by law in children's television programming, but is rampant in the prime time programs that are children's favorites. According to *Business Week*, Coca-Cola paid $20 million for product placement in the TV show

American Idol, a favorite of teens and pre-teens. On *The Gilmore Girls,* another popular show with children, characters eat Kellogg's Pop Tarts for breakfast.

Interestingly enough, *The Gilmore Girls* was created through a consortium of corporations, including many, such as Kellogg, from the food industry, called The Family Friendly Programming Forum. The stated mission of the Forum is to create programming that is good for families to watch together—programming that is free of excessive violence and explicit sexuality, but not free of marketing food.

Thus far, neither films, video games, nor the Internet has regulations about placing brands within the content of their media products aimed at children. For instance, McDonald's food products were embedded in the hit children's film Spy Kids. An executive of Heinz, commenting on placing EZ Squirt ketchup in the child-oriented web site NeoPets.com, said that product awareness "just went through the roof. . . . Trials of the product increased by 18 percent." Meanwhile, other fast food outlets, Pizza Hut and KFC, are destinations along the way in the video/arcade game, Crazy Taxi.

Product placement can also be found in children's books, including those for babies. Scholastic publishes *The M&M Counting Book,* and Simon and Schuster has one featuring Oreos. These cardboard books are particularly troublesome because the covers often look exactly like the packaging these foods come in. Literacy experts encourage parents to read to babies and toddlers, citing gains in literacy and the promotion of positive parent-to-baby bonding. Babies and young children whose mothers or fathers read to them—especially when their parents take them on their laps or read to them at bedtime—associate warm, snuggly feelings with reading, and reading itself becomes early on a pleasurable experience for them. However, if the books they are reading include the *Hershey Kisses: Counting Board Book* or the *Skittles Riddles Math* book, one can assume that babies are gaining equally warm, snuggly feelings about candy.

Food companies also market to children through toys. Smuckers, for instance, has a Cabbage Patch doll, Peanut Butter and Jelly Kid, designed to sell a product called Goobers. Hot-Wheels makes toy cars sporting the M&M candy logo. Barbie dolls work at both Pizza Hut and McDonald's, and the latter partners with Play Doh and Easy Bake.

Restricting Advertising to Children

The United States regulates marketing to children less than most other industrial democracies. Sweden and Norway ban marketing to children under twelve. The Province of Quebec, in Canada, bans marketing to children under 13. Greece prohibits ads for toys on television between 7 a.m. and 10 p.m. Ads for toy guns and tanks are not allowed at any time. In the Flemish speaking areas of Belgium, no advertising is allowed within five minutes of a children's television program shown on a local station. Advertising regulations proposed by the European Union would ban commercials suggesting that children's acceptance by peers is dependent on their use of a product. Finland bans advertisements that are delivered by children or by familiar cartoon characters. The French parliament government recently banned all vending machines in middle and secondary schools. New Zealand is considering a ban on junk food marketing to kids. And, in 2004, the British Broadcasting Corporation severed marketing connections between their children's programming and junk food companies.

Given their particular vulnerabilities to marketing there is a powerful argument to be made that it is in the best interest of children that companies refrain from marketing to them at all. How can this discussion proceed in the face of the current political climate in the United States that favors deregulation of corporate practices in general? Perhaps the mounting evidence linking food advertising to children's food consumption suggests that the food industry's child targeted marketing is a good place to begin. Even the advertising industry is expecting new regulations. An online poll published in *Advertising Age* found that 77 percent of respondents think that there is a direct link between TV ads and childhood obesity. In a poll of professionals involved with marketing to youth, 68 percent of the people responding agreed with the statement, "I expect there will be increased regulation of the food and restaurant industry." Therefore, any conversation about curbing childhood obesity should include a hard look at food marketing, culminating in a decision about how, and whether, those who market foods should be allowed to continue their practice of targeting children.

Corrective Actions

The public health community needs to undertake a massive campaign to educate parents, in particular new parents, about the links between commercial culture and childhood obesity. However, public education in itself is not adequate. On both state and federal levels the government should take steps to restrict the current onslaught of food marketing that targets children. The reality of drafting and bringing to fruition such legislation is both complex and cumbersome, but that should not prevent a creative and rigorous exploration of a wide range of options for restricting food marketing to children.

- Congress could pass the bill currently introduced in the Senate that would return to the Federal Trade Commission the power to regulate marketing to children.
- Corporate tax deductions for advertising and marketing junk food to children could be eliminated.
- Congress could also act to discourage links between toy and food companies that lead to food branded toys and toy giveaways by fast food companies such as McDonald's and Burger King.
- Legislation might also discourage product placement of food products in movies, video and computer games, and television programs popular with children and adolescents by requiring that such embedded advertising be identified when it occurs.
- Food companies might be prohibited from using advertising techniques that exploit children's developmental vulnerabilities such as commercials that encourage kids to turn to food for empowerment, or to be popular, or for fun. The use of cartoon characters—so appealing to young children—to market food products might be also eliminated.
- State or federal law might prohibit food companies from promotions such as child-targeted sweepstakes and contests, to which young people are particularly susceptible.
- Schools could certainly be discouraged from engaging in sale and marketing of unhealthy food products.

Conclusion

Food marketing is pervasive in children's lives and occurs in the context of a virtual bombardment of commercial messages at home, at school, and in the community. Given the intensity and pervasiveness of marketing to children, it is either cynical or naïve to assume that individual parents should bear the sole burden of shielding children from the potentially harmful effects of a $15 billion industry. Given growing alarm about childhood obesity, among other market related health concerns, we need to look at marketing to children as a societal issue, not just a familial one, and search for solutions that will alter the commercial culture surrounding children and families.

CRITICAL THINKING QUESTIONS

1. This article is mainly prescriptive rather than descriptive. What does the author conclude we should do about advertising to children? What are the main reasons supporting the author's preferred policy?
2. Now consider alternate conclusions. What are some other possible approaches to the problem that other people with

different value preferences might take? How do specific value preferences influence different conclusions?

3. Are any of the numerous statistics in the article deceptive? Pay special attention to statistics citing averages. Ask yourself, "What statistical evidence would be helpful in proving the conclusion?" Then, compare the needed statistics to the statistics given. Do they match up?

4. Who is responsible for the protection of children? How much does society and the government need to help out parents? The author of this argument answers these questions in the unstated descriptive assumptions within the argument. How might a reader who agrees with the conclusion answer these questions? How would a reader who disagrees with the argument answer these questions?

ESSAY QUESTIONS

1. This readings chapter had a common issue: how much should we protect children from advertisers? Because all of the passages discussed the same issue, it is easy to see overlapping value conflicts. Integrate the value conflicts present in the articles. Which authors held similar and opposing values?

2. By using the critical thinking methods outlined in *Asking the Right Questions,* you can easily identify faults within reasoning. However, it is often more difficult for students to identify examples of strong reasoning. Using the articles in this section, write an essay in which you choose the most persuasive of the articles. Explain what you found persuasive about the article, relying on your critical thinking skills. What did the author do properly? What evidence was most compelling? Furthermore, include where the article was deficient.

3. Much of the strong evidence regarding advertising to children was presented in favor of regulating advertising to children. Very few authors against regulation presented strong empirical evidence with large sample sizes. Use your research skills to locate stronger evidence to form an argument against regulating advertising to children. Then, construct an argument with your own evidence and reasons for why regulating advertising to children is not desirable. Which of your evidence is the strongest and weakest? Why?

What Is the Proper Role of Government in Improving the Quality of Families in Our Culture?

One of the most heated debates of contemporary American politics is the extent to which the government should be involved in the creation of families. The debate can be quite emotional because our families and family structures are personal. In addition, our preferences and opinions widely vary. Moreover, unlike some other political questions, these questions have direct implications for our daily lives. Should the government prohibit marriage to certain people? Should the government encourage its citizens to marry and have children? Should the government regulate reproduction? The articles in this readings section will introduce arguments that address this controversial set of questions. Read the articles armed with the questions and tools you've adopted through your study of *Asking the Right Questions*.

Taking Marriage Private

Stephanie Coontz

The New York Times (2007)

Why do people—gay or straight—need the state's permission to marry? For most of Western history, they didn't, because marriage was a private contract between two families. The parents' agreement to the match, not the approval of church or state, was what confirmed its validity.

For 16 centuries, Christianity also defined the validity of a marriage on the basis of a couple's wishes. If two people claimed they had exchanged marital vows—even out alone by the haystack—the Catholic Church accepted that they were validly married.

In 1215, the church decreed that a "licit" marriage must take place in church. But people who married illicitly had the same rights and obligations as a couple married in church: their children were legitimate; the wife had the same inheritance rights; the couple was subject to the same prohibitions against divorce.

Not until the 16th century did European states begin to require that marriages be performed under legal auspices. In part, this was an attempt to prevent unions between young adults whose parents opposed their match.

The American colonies officially required marriages to be registered, but until the mid-19th century, state supreme courts routinely ruled that public cohabitation was sufficient evidence of a valid marriage. By the later part of that century, however, the United States began to nullify common-law marriages and exert more control over who was allowed to marry.

By the 1920s, 38 states prohibited whites from marrying blacks, "mulattos," Japanese, Chinese, Indians, "Mongolians," "Malays" or Filipinos. Twelve states would not issue a marriage license if one partner was a drunk, an addict or a "mental defect. " Eighteen states set barriers to remarriage after divorce.

In the mid-20th century, governments began to get out of the business of deciding which couples were "fit" to marry. Courts invalidated laws against interracial marriage, struck down other barriers and even extended marriage rights to prisoners.

But governments began relying on marriage licenses for a new purpose: as a way of distributing resources to dependents. The Social Security Act provided survivors' benefits with proof of marriage. Employers used marital status to determine whether they would provide health insurance or pension benefits to employees' dependents. Courts and hospitals required a marriage license before granting couples the privilege of inheriting from each other or receiving medical information.

In the 1950s, using the marriage license as a shorthand way to distribute benefits and legal privileges made some sense because almost all adults were married. Cohabitation and single parenthood by choice were very rare.

Today, however, possession of a marriage license tells us little about people's interpersonal responsibilities. Half of all Americans aged 25 to 29 are unmarried, and many of them already have incurred obligations as partners, parents or both. Almost 40 percent of America's children are born to unmarried parents. Meanwhile, many legally married people are in remarriages where their obligations are spread among several households.

Using the existence of a marriage license to determine when the state should protect interpersonal relationships is increasingly impractical. Society has already recognized this when it comes to children, who can no longer be denied inheritance rights, parental support or legal standing because their parents are not married.

As Nancy Polikoff, an American University law professor, argues, the marriage license no longer draws reasonable dividing lines regarding which adult obligations and rights merit state protection. A woman married to a man for just nine months gets Social Security survivor's benefits when he dies. But a woman living for 19 years with a man to whom she isn't married is left without government support, even if her presence helped him hold down a full-time job and pay Social Security taxes. A newly married wife or husband can take leave from work to care for a spouse, or sue for a partner's wrongful death. But unmarried couples typically cannot, no matter how long they have pooled their resources and how faithfully they have kept their commitments.

Possession of a marriage license is no longer the chief determinant of which obligations a couple must keep, either to their children or to each other. But it still determines which obligations a couple can keep—who gets hospital visitation rights, family leave, health care and survivor's benefits. This may serve the purpose of some moralists. But it doesn't serve the public interest of helping individuals meet their care-giving commitments.

Perhaps it's time to revert to a much older marital tradition. Let churches decide which marriages they deem "licit." But let couples—gay or straight—decide if they want the legal protections and obligations of a committed relationship.

CRITICAL THINKING QUESTIONS

1. As you read this essay, consider the title of the essay as well as what controversy is taking place in our society that Professor Coontz's essay is reacting to. Try to use such speculation as a clue to help answer the question: What is the specific issue that the essay addresses and what is its conclusion?

2. Because the conclusion is prescriptive, Professor Coontz relies on several unstated value assumptions in her argument. Try to detect these assumptions by asking what would the writer have to care about in order for her reasons to

support her conclusion. To identify whether a reason relies on a value assumption, consider whether a reason would be persuasive if you held the opposite value assumption. To identify her value assumptions, you must first identify the conclusion and the reasons. This step is necessary because an assumption often links the reason to the conclusion— readers who don't share an author's assumptions may not find the reasons persuasive.

3. Readers often enter an argument with their own unstated, sometimes unrealized assumptions about the world. These assumptions influence their willingness to accept certain reasons that an author may provide. For instance, a reader of this article probably has developed beliefs as to the nature of marriage, before he or she ever read this article. What are some common beliefs about marriage? Which of these beliefs would lead the reader to reject certain reasons in this argument? In answering these questions, what other assumptions in the author's reasoning have you discovered?

4. What types of evidence does Professor Coontz employ? What questions does *Asking the Right Questions* recommend you ask to determine the quality of this evidence?

The question of whether the government should regulate marriage is a subject of interest to academics and journalists. But the interest doesn't end there. The blogosphere is also abuzz with this discussion. The following blog entry addresses the issue of whether the government should regulate a person's right to marry more than one person. Polygamy is outlawed in the United States and in most of the Western world. The anonymous author of this blog identifies as an "old-fashioned liberal" from Copenhagen, Denmark.

Swedish Top Lawyer Wants to Legalize Polygamy . . .

New Zonka Blog (2007)

One of Sweden's top lawyers, Stefan Lindskog, wants to break the marriage laws, because they "discriminate" based on sexual preference. And finds that polygamous marriages should gain the same rights, benefits and protection as a traditional marriage enjoys.

Source: Aftonbladet; hattip: I Mitt Sverige.

We have heard that argument again and again, in various shapes and forms. Whether it is homosexual marriages, polygamous marriages or some other kind of non-traditional marriage form that is being suggested. But mostly it is the two former forms that are being promoted. I can understand why such suggestions come up from time to time among common people, but I'm still amazed when it comes from highly educated people, particularly people who should know why our societies favor marriages between one man and one woman, and give such relationships their blessing and benefits over other kinds of relationships. There is nothing illegal in having a homosexual relationship or having a polyamourous relationship, whether it is one woman having several male lovers or vice versa, same for other types of relationships. But should the state (society) actively support such relationships?

There are good reasons for the state to support marriages between one man and one woman, some of these are bound in cultural morals and tradition but the overriding reason for supporting the union between man and woman, and that alone, is that it forms the most stable basic unit that the society needs to survive from generation to generation. Homosexual unions cannot reproduce (have children), and thus are "dead ends" and cannot produce the next generation of the society. Polygamous relations are not very stable, usually the polygamous relations that occurs is one man having many wives, and that leads to subjugation of women (as we see in Islamic societies) as well as a scarcity of women, which will have the young men combating each other or others for fame and fortune and a harem or two! Of course polygamous relationships the other way around are possible as well, but will exhibit similar characteristics. Only in the rare case that you could have an equal number of polygamous men and women, some kind of equilibrium could be reached, but that would be rather unlikely.

So the best solution for the state/society is to give their blessing to traditional one man/one woman marriages and the nuclear family, as that is the most stable relationship known that is able to reproduce the next generation of citizens, and that is exactly what the state has been doing until now, as such blessing in the form of benefits and rights is acting in the states best interest, and should be continued as well. If the citizens want to enter other kinds of relationships, they are free to do so, but shouldn't expect the benefits either. And a state/society has the right to use the carrot to promote behavior that is in the best interest of the state/society. But as long as it is not using the whip to outlaw behavior and different sexual behavior, I have no problem with such measures, and in fact I condone this.

CRITICAL THINKING QUESTIONS

1. Let's imagine you were going to respond to this blog entry. Most likely, you have a strong opinion of the issue. Careful. Often our own biases can distort our understanding of an argument. If we agree with an argument, we might unconsciously strengthen the argument. If we disagree with the argument, we may create a straw-man of the argument. To prevent this distortion, before you respond to the argument, you want to make sure that you understand the issue that the author is addressing and his conclusion and reasons. What are the issue, conclusion, and reasons in this blog entry?

2. Continue to imagine you had the opportunity to respond to this entry. Explain to the author how this argument would be improved with evidence. Be sure to point out specific instances in this article that call for evidence.

3. In this entry, the author's reasoning relies on several assumptions about the purpose of marriage. What are these assumptions? What are some alternative assumptions that people may hold about the purpose of marriage?

4. Chapter 12 of *Asking the Right Questions* encourages you to ask the question "What significant information is omitted?" One important type of omitted information to consider is the *potential negative effects* of actions being advocated. What are the negative effects of the conclusion advocated in this blog entry?

While the discussion of marriage, particularly same-sex marriage, is frequently discussed in American politics, the issue of whether our government should regulate parents is rarely debated in mainstream media. This next article is an exception. It was published in the *Seattle Post-Intelligencer*, one of two major newspapers in Seattle, Washington. Peg Tittle, the author, also edited a collection of essays entitled *Should Parents be Licensed? Debating the Issues.* In this editorial, she suggests a controversial solution to the problem of bad parenting.

We License Plumbers and Pilots—Why Not Parents?

Peg Tittle

The Seattle Post-Intelligencer (2004)

We have successfully cloned a sheep. It is not unreasonable, then, to believe that we may soon be able to create human life. And I'm sure we'll develop carefully considered policies and procedures to regulate the activity, perhaps if only because we have Mary Shelley's Frankenstein lurking in our minds.

For example, I doubt we'll allow someone to create his own private work force or his own little army. And I suspect we'll prohibit cloning oneself for mere ego gratification.

I imagine we'll enforce some sort of quality control, such that cloned human beings shall not exist in pain or be severely substandard with respect to basic biological or electrochemical functioning.

And I suspect one will have to apply for a license and satisfy rigorous screening standards. I assume this will include not only meeting certain requirements with regard to the lab and its equipment, but also submitting, and obtaining approval of, a detailed plan regarding the future of the cloned human being; surely we won't allow a scientist to create it and then just leave it in the lab's basement one night when he leaves.

The thing is, we can already create human life. Kids do it every day.

And although we've talked ourselves silly and tied ourselves in knots about ending life—active, passive, voluntary, coerced, premeditated, accidental, negligent—we have been horrendously silent, irresponsibly laissez-faire about beginning life. We would not accept such wanton creation of life if it happened in the lab. Why do we condone it when it happens in bedrooms and backseats?

It should be illegal to create life, to have kids, in order to have another pair of hands at work in the field or to have more of us than them. It should be illegal to create a John Doe Jr. to carry on the family name and/or business.

And it should be illegal to knowingly create a life that will be spent in pain and/or that will be severely substandard.

As for the screening process, would-be teachers are generally required to study full-time for at least eight months before the state will allow them the responsibility of educating children for six hours a day once the kids become 6 years of age. Many would say we have set the bar too low.

And yet we haven't even set the bar as high—in fact we haven't set a bar at all—for parents. Someone can be responsible not only for a child's education but for virtually everything about the child, for 24 hours a day until that child is 6 years of age—that is, for the duration of its critical, formative years—and he or she doesn't even have to so much as read a pamphlet about child development.

As Roger McIntire notes, "We already license pilots, salesmen, scuba divers, plumbers, electricians, teachers, veterinarians, cab drivers, soil testers and television repairmen. . . . Are our TV sets and toilets more important to us than our children?"

Then again, wait a minute—we have set a bar for parents: adoptive/foster parents. Those would-be parents have to prove their competence. Why do we cling to the irrational belief that biological parents are automatically competent—in the face of overwhelming evidence to the contrary? We have, without justification, a double standard.

One common response to this notion of licensing parents is dismissal with a giggle, as if I'm suggesting the presence of police in the bedroom. But there is no necessary connection between sex (whether or not it occurs in the bedroom) and reproduction (unless, of course, you reject all forms of contraception), so that response indicates an error of overgeneralization. On the other hand, sex can make you a parent only in the biological sense; since I'm proposing that we license both parentage (the biological part of being a parent—the provision of sperm, ovum, and/or uterus) and parenting (the social part of being a parent—the provision of care, very comprehensively defined), the response also indicates an error of undergeneralization.

Another response to licensing parents is a sort of goofy incomprehension, often followed with something like "Well, it's not as if people plan it, you know—usually, it just happens." Excuse me? It is not possible to create life "by accident"—men don't accidentally ejaculate into vaginas and women don't accidentally catch some ejaculate with their vaginas. (As for failed contraception, there's morning-after contraception and abortion.) "I created someone by accident" should be just as horrific, and just as morally reprehensible, as "I killed someone by accident." (At the very least, such "parents" should be charged with reckless or negligent reproduction.)

Yet another response is dismissal with indignation, because surely such a proposal violates our rights! But do we have the right to replicate ourselves, to create a person? And do we have a right to raise that, or any other, person? There are many good arguments claiming that we don't: for starters, merely having a capability doesn't entail the right to exercise that capability. (Ruth Chadwick has written a good article examining various motives for having kids—she finds them all inadequate as grounds for the right to have them.) There are also many good arguments for claiming that such "rights" are better conceived as responsibilities or even privileges.

One must also be careful about distinguishing between moral rights and legal rights. (Laura Purdy has written an excellent article investigating whether it's immoral to have children when there's a good chance they'll have a serious disease or handicap and David Resnik has written about whether genetic enhancement is immoral or unjust—neither advocates parenting licenses, but their conclusions are nevertheless relevant; for example, if it is immoral to have children with genetic defects, that might serve as a premise supporting parent licensing.)

But even if we do have the right to be a parent or to parent, no right is absolute. My rights end where your freedoms begin. The real question is under what conditions do we have those rights and, then, under what conditions are those rights violated. Why, for example, should the right to be a parent depend on the means of becoming a parent? People seeking access to new reproductive technologies are screened for genetic anomalies, infectious diseases and other "high-risk factors"; they must read and understand information about the risks, responsibilities and implications of what they are undertaking; and they must undergo counseling that addresses their values and goals.

Why should children born as a result of assisted insemination or in vitro fertilization be privileged to a higher standard of care in their creation than children born as a result of coitus? These questions about rights are not easy questions to answer, and this particular dismissal of the proposal to license parents reveals gross naiveté.

Yet another dismissal appeals to the difficulty or impossibility of implementing the idea: Who would set the requirements, what would those requirements be, how would they be assessed? . . . Often lurking beneath these concerns is one more: "and I suppose I wouldn't be good enough!" Partly, this is a paper tiger response: The more ridiculous the claim, the easier it is to mock, so people imagine all sorts of complicated and unrealistic policies and procedures that no advocate of parent licenses would ever suggest. (Read Hugh LaFollette, Covell and Howe, and Jack Westman for real proposals.)

And partly, paradoxically, this response reveals a failure of the imagination: Licensing parents could be as simple as when you turn 18, you get the book and study it or take the course, then you take the written test, and the eye test, and if you pass, you get a beginner's license, then you do some hands-on child care for maybe six months under the guidance of a licensed parent, and if you pass that part, you get your license, and if you don't, maybe you try again in a while. Sound familiar? So what's the problem?

Well, those bedrooms and backseats—we could never really control the parentage part. No, not at the moment. But what if we developed a contraceptive vaccination? (But nooo, our little boy scientists, once they'd finished snickering over the name "Dolly," developed Viagra instead.) We could administer the vaccine as a matter of routine, perhaps once puberty is reached. And then, as part of the license, the antidote could be made available.

One last objection concerns the potential for abuse. Do we really want to give the state this particular power? I have to say, seeing a theocracy coming ever closer, that this is the argument that gives me most pause.

I want to point out that just because something will be abused doesn't mean it shouldn't be tried, and I want to point out that our many other licensing policies still exist despite the occasional abuse. But I've read Margaret Atwood's "Handmaid's Tale." It's chilling. But I've also read the reports of people too drugged out to even know they're pregnant. And it's not a question of which scenario is more likely. One is already happening and has been for quite some time.

Most of us have seen broken kids, kids who didn't get what they needed at a critical stage in their development, so they go through life thinking the world owes them something. And indeed we do. But sadly, tragically, we can't give it to them because that critical window of time has passed: We can't go back and flush from the fetus the chemicals that interfered with its development; we can't go back and provide the baby with the nutrients required for growth; we can't go back and give the child the safety and attention that would have led to a secure personality. Every year, millions of the people we've created so carelessly are being starved, beaten or otherwise traumatized. Thousands die. And that doesn't count the ones still walking around.

To be succinct, the destruction of life is subject to moral and legal examination—so too should be the creation of life, whenever and however it occurs.

CRITICAL THINKING QUESTIONS

1. Much of the reasoning structure in this essay consists of the writer mentioning and then addressing counterarguments to her proposal. Do you believe that is a good argument strategy? Why? Why not?

2. After listing the authors' reasons, check to see whether some terms are importantly ambiguous. For example, the meaning of the terms *rights* and *privileges* is important in determining how one reacts to this essay. Has the author made the definitions of these terms sufficiently clear? How might different definitions lead you to different evaluations of the author's reasoning? What other terms need clarification?

3. Review your issue, conclusion, and reasons for this argument. Note how much the reasoning relies on analogies. How good is this evidence? What assumptions need to be questioned in evaluating the analogies? What other kinds of evidence would you want to provide to improve the writer's overall argument?

4. Professor Tittle's language can evoke very strong emotional responses in the reader, as illustrated in this section of the argument: "Every year, millions of the people we've created so carelessly are being starved, beaten or otherwise traumatized. Thousands die. And that doesn't count the ones still walking around." *Note other emotionally loaded language in this essay.* Why are appeals to emotion, such as this one, dangerous insertions in arguments? What can you as the reader do to minimize any undue influence from these appeals?

5. Who owns a child? Who is responsible for the well-being of a child? The author of this argument implicitly answers these questions in her unstated descriptive assumptions within the argument. How might a reader who strongly disagrees with the argument answer these questions? In answering these questions, you will identify one of the controversial descriptive assumptions in this article.

6. What are central value conflicts related to this controversy? What value assumptions influence the reasoning chosen by the writer? If one were arguing against the licensing of parents, how would the value assumptions differ?

Jens and Vita, but Molli? Danes Favor Common Names

Lizette Alvarez

The New York Times (2004)

COPENHAGEN – If Denmark somehow morphed into the celebrity epicenter of the universe, there would be no place for the baby-naming eccentricities of the world's megastars.

Apple Paltrow Martin would be rejected as a fruit, Jett Travolta as a plane (and misspelled as well), Brooklyn Beckham as a place, and Rumer Willis, as, well, Danish name investigators would not even know where to begin with that one.

"Cuba is also a problem," said Michael Lerche Nielsen, assistant professor for the Department of Name Research at Copenhagen University. "I have to decide: Is this a typical boy or girl name? And that's the problem with geographical names."

In Denmark, a country that embraces rules with the same gusto that Italy defies them, choosing a first and last name for a child is a serious, multitiered affair, governed by law and subject to the approval of the Ministry of Ecclesiastical Affairs and the Ministry of Family and Consumer Affairs.

At its heart, the Law on Personal Names is designed to protect Denmark's innocents—the children who are undeservedly, some would say cruelly, burdened by preposterous or silly names. It is the state's view that children should not suffer ridicule and abuse because of their parents' lapses in judgment or their misguided attempts to be hip. Denmark, like much of Scandinavia, prizes sameness, not uniqueness, just as it values usefulness, not frivolousness.

"You shouldn't stand out from anyone else here; you shouldn't think you are better than anyone else," said Lan Tan, a 27, Danish woman of Singaporean and Malaysian descent who is trying to win approval for her daughter's name, Frida Mei Tan-Farndsen. "It's very Scandinavian."

While other Scandinavian countries have similar laws, Denmark's is the strictest. So strict that the Danish Ministry of Justice is proposing to relax the law to reflect today's Denmark, a place where common-law marriage is accepted, immigration is growing, and divorce is routine. The measure, which would add names to the official list, is scheduled for debate in Parliament in November. "The government, from a historical point of view, feels a responsibility towards its weak citizens," said Rasmus Larsen, chief adviser at the Ministry for Ecclesiastical Affairs, discussing the law. "It doesn't want to see people put in a situation where they can't defend themselves. We do the same in traffic; we have people wear seat belts."

People expecting children can choose a pre-approved name from a government list of 7,000 mostly Western European and English names—3,000 for boys, 4,000 for girls. A few ethnic names, like Ali and Hassan, have recently been added. But those wishing to deviate from the official list must seek permission at their local parish church, where all newborns' names are registered. A request for an unapproved name triggers a review at Copenhagen University's Names Investigation Department and at the Ministry of Ecclesiastical Affairs, which has the ultimate authority. The law only applies if one of the parents is Danish.

Many parents do not realize how difficult it can be to get a name approved by the government. About 1,100 names are reviewed every year, and 15 percent to 20 percent are rejected, mostly for odd spellings. Compound surnames, like Tan-Farnsden, also pose a problem.

Parents who try to be creative by naming their child Jakobp or Bebop or Ashleiy (three recent applications) are typically stunned when they are rejected. In some cases, a baby may go without an officially approved name for weeks, even months, making for irate, already sleep-deprived, parents.

Greg Nagan, 39, and Trine Kammer, 32, thought it would be cute to name their daughter Molli Malou. To their surprise, Malou was not a problem, but Molli with an I, which they thought sounded Danish, had to be reviewed by the government. The church told Ms. Kammer she needed to state in a letter the reason for choosing Molli. She did so, and said she told the clerk, "Here's your stupid letter: The reason for naming her Molli is because we like it."

"Isn't this silly?" Ms. Kammer said. "We love to make everything a rule here. They love to bureaucratize."

The century-old law was initially designed to bring order to surnames. Before the law, surnames changed with every generation: Peter Hansen would name his son Hans Petersen. Then Hans Petersen would name his son Peter Hansen. And on it went, wreaking bureaucratic havoc. The law ended that. It also made it difficult for people to change their last names, a move that was designed to appease the noble class, which feared widespread name-poaching by arrivistes, Mr. Nielsen said.

Then in the 1960's, a furor erupted over the first name Tessa, which resembled tisse, which means to urinate in Danish. Distressed over the lack of direction in the law, the Danish government expanded the statute to grapple with first names. Now the law is as long as an average-size book.

It falls mostly to Mr. Nielsen, at Copenhagen University, to apply the law and review new names, on a case-by-case basis. In a nutshell, he said, Danish law stipulates that boys and girls must have different names, first names cannot also be last names, and bizarre names are O. K. so long as they are "common."

"Let's say 25 different people" worldwide, he said, a number that was chosen arbitrarily. How does Mr. Nielsen make that determination? He searches the Internet.

Generally, geographic names are rejected because they seldom denote gender. Cairo, if it is approved at all, may be approved for a boy, but then could not be used for a girl. Jordan is a recent exception to the one-gender rule.

In some cases, Mr. Nielsen says, he believes he is performing a vital public service. He advised the Ministry that Anus and Pluto be rejected, for example. He also vetoed Monkey. "That's not a personal name," Mr. Nielsen explained. "It's an animal. I have to protect the children from ridicule."

Leica, however, has been approved, as has Benji, Jiminico and Fee.

"People's names have become part of their identities now," Mr. Nielsen said. "And people change their names the way you change your clothes or your apartment. It has become more common."

And what about Molli Malou?

Approved, by government decree, just recently.

CRITICAL THINKING QUESTIONS

1. How did you find yourself reacting to this essay? This argument is largely descriptive. Its central aim is to inform the reader about the Law on Personal Names, not to convince the reader to support or disagree with the law and how one reacts to the desirability of this naming practice. But the article does provide reasons that could be used by those favoring and those opposing the Danish attitude toward the optimal responsibility for choosing a child's name; and how one might react to the desirability of this practice will likely be influenced by such reasons Construct the prescriptive arguments—the issues, conclusions, and reasons—for those favoring and opposing the Law on Personal Names.

2. The controversy over the Law on Personal Names has, as its core, a value conflict. What is this value conflict? On what side of the conflict do the parents of children like Molli Malou fall? On what side do advocates of the law fall?

3. Rasmus Larsen, the chief advisor at the Ministry for Ecclesiastical Affairs, offered an analogy to justify the Law on Personal Names, "[the law] doesn't want to see people put in a situation where they can't defend themselves. We do the same in traffic; we have people wear seat belts." How persuasive is this evidence? To determine the quality of this analogy, *Asking the Right Questions* suggests you identify the number of ways the two things being compared are similar and different and to consider the *relevance* of the similarities and the differences.

4. Rasmus Larsen also made this statement: "The government, from a historical point of view, feels a responsibility towards its weak citizens." What assumption does Larsen make about human nature? Do you agree with this descriptive assumption?

China's One Child Policy: The Policy That Changed the World

Malcolm Potts

British Medical Journal (2006)

The Chinese one child policy is unique in the history of the world. It was a source of great pain for one generation, but a generation later it began to yield important economic benefits. For China, and the world as a whole, the one child policy was one of the most important social policies ever implemented.

Rapid population growth is an unforgiving task master. Even with the one child policy—as a result of the high birth rate a generation before—China still has one million more births than deaths every five weeks. The Chinese State Council launched the policy in 1979, "so the rate of population growth may be brought under control as soon as possible." However, the root cause of the policy lay back in the 1960s with Mao Zedong's belief that "the more people, the stronger we are"—an ideology that prevented China from developing the highly successful voluntary family planning programmes that countries such as South Korea and Taiwan had put in place in the 1960s.

Deng Xiao-ping, the acknowledged architect of China's contemporary economic miracle, was a major sponsor of the 1979 policy. He said that unless the birth rate fell rapidly, "we will not be able to develop our economy, and raise the living standards of our people." Economists and demographers now recognise that a falling birth rate offers a demographic dividend, as the economically productive proportion of the population grows more rapidly than the general population. Without a rapid decline in fertility, China's economy would not have grown by 7–8% a year over the past decade; such growth has lifted an unprecedented 150 million people out of abject poverty.

Could China ever have achieved the same results without the one child policy? Possibly. Between 1952 and 1979, the Chinese total fertility rate fell from 6.5 to 2.75, and today all age groups and social classes prefer to have two children or fewer. Some western commentators believe China over-reacted,[6] whereas others emphasise that even small changes in the timing of a decline in fertility are important. The difference between a total fertility rate of 2.1, which might have been achieved without the policy, and a total fertility rate of 1.6 (found today) releases 24% more resources for the family and national investment. The Indian economy has begun to grow rapidly, but unlike China the decline in fertility has been uneven, and states such as Bihar and Uttar Pradesh (total fertility rates of 4.4 and 4.8) remain mired in poverty.

As well as its effect on fertility rates, China's one child policy has had a variety of other effects. Each successive birth cohort is smaller and women tend to marry men who are several years older than themselves, so fewer potential brides are available than grooms. Further, like many countries, China has a long tradition of favouring boys and the technology of ultrasound and selective abortion, although illegal, has further skewed the sex ratio. The under-registration of female births and higher mortality due to greater neglect of female babies makes exact measurement difficult, but Ding and Hesketh found a ratio of male to female births of 1.15 across the whole cohort and of 1.23 for first births between 1996 and 2001. Lastly, when birth rates fall rapidly, during their most productive years the younger generation needs to support a high ratio of old people, although as people age they may also save at a higher rate. China's new prosperity has repercussions around the world in other ways—for instance, Chinese competition for oil is one reason that the cost of petrol is so high.

Undoubtedly, the one child policy caused great individual pain and it has been heavily criticised. For people in the United States especially, the idea that society's long term interests could ever be more important than individual rights was anathema. A veritable media industry has arisen in the US criticising the one child policy, although it chooses to overlook the tens of millions of coercive pregnancies in other countries where family planning and legal abortion are not available. The Bush administration refuses to fund the United Nations Population Fund because it works in China, even though this fund has never supported the one child policy.

The Chinese demographic crisis arose because between 1960 and 1973 the population grew by 2% or more each year. Today, the whole of sub-Saharan Africa, along with Pakistan, Iraq, Afghanistan, and the Philippines, have population growth rates of at least 2%. Between now and 2050 the population of Niger, West Africa, is projected to grow fivefold from 14 to 53 million. As the World Bank acknowledges, without a rapid decline in fertility, tens of millions of Nigeriens will be uneducated, unemployed, and desperately poor; they will either starve or be fed by Western humanitarian aid.

Last month, the UK All Party Parliamentary Group on Population, Development, and Reproductive Health ended an important series of hearings on the impact of population growth on the millennium development goals. Experts from around the world called on the UK's Department for International Development and the international community to give much greater emphasis to population and family planning. Baige Zhao, vice minister of the National Population and Family Planning Commission of China offered "to share our information and also our commodities." As China reaches out to help other countries, their contribution to international family planning could prove an important additional global benefit of the sacrifices the Chinese people made to implement the one child policy.

Malcolm Potts, *Fred H Bixby endowed chair*
School of Public Health, University of California, Berkeley,
CA 94720-7360, USA (potts@berkeley.edu)

CRITICAL THINKING QUESTIONS

1. Is this article a prescriptive argument or a descriptive argument? What does this distinction tell us about the argument?
2. Describing an important value conflict in the argument, Professor Potts wrote, "for people in the United States especially, the idea that society's long term interests could ever be more important than individual rights was anathema." What value conflict was he describing?
3. This value conflict is not the only one. What other values are at odds in this argument?
4. Professor Potts supports his conclusion with several statistics. What questions does *Asking the Right Questions* suggest you consider when evaluating statistics? Are the statistics in this reading deceptive?
5. In making judgments about the desirability of China's one child policy, what information is omitted that might influence such judgments?

The Regulation of the Market in Adoption

Richard Posner

Boston University Law Review (1987)

Many married couples are unable to have children and want to adopt them. Recent advances in the treatment of fertility problems appear to have been offset by the growing tendency of women to marry later and postpone childbearing to their thirties, when they are likelier to have fertility problems and will have less time to do something about them (whether the something is medical treatment or joining the queue for adoption). Childless couples who try to adopt through an adoption agency find that they must join a long queue and that even then they may be ineligible to adopt— not because they would be unfit parents but because the agencies, having a very limited supply of babies, set demanding (and sometimes arbitrary) criteria of age, income, race, and religion to limit demand to supply. . . .

In the remainder of this article I shall describe briefly how such a market might operate, under what regulatory constraints, and with what likely consequences, and in doing so will try to respond to the most frequently expressed objections to allowing the market to function in this area.

Characteristics of and Desirable Constraints on the Baby Market

The Question of Price

For heuristic purposes (only!) it is useful to analogize the sale of babies to the sale of an ordinary good, such as an automobile or a television set. We observe, for example, that although the supply of automobiles and of television sets is rationed by price, not all the automobiles and television sets are owned by wealthy people. On the contrary, the free market in these goods has lowered prices, through competition and innovation, to the point where the goods are available to a lot more people than in highly controlled economies such as that of the Soviet Union. There is even less reason for thinking that if babies could be sold to adoptive parents the wealthy would come to monopolize babies. Wealthy people (other than those few who owe their wealth to savings or inheritance rather than to a high income) have high costs of time.

It therefore costs them more to raise a child—child rearing still being a time-intensive activity—than it costs the nonwealthy. As a result, wealthy couples tend to have few rather than many children. This pattern would not change if babies could be bought. Moreover, since most people have a strong preference for natural, as distinct from adopted, children, wealthy couples able to have natural children are unlikely (to say the least) to substitute adopted ones.

It is also unlikely that allowing people to bid for babies with dollars would drive up the price of babies, thereby allocating the supply to wealthy demanders. Today we observe a high black-market price conjoined with an artificially low price for babies obtained from adoption agencies and through lawful independent adoptions. The "blended" or average price is hard to calculate; but probably it is very high. The low price in the lawful market is deceptive. It ignores the considerable queuing costs—most people would pay a considerable premium to get their adopted baby now, not five or ten years from now. And for people unable to maneuver successfully in the complex market created by the laws against baby selling, the price is infinite. Quality-adjusted prices in free markets normally are lower than black market prices, and there is no reason to doubt that this would be true in a free market for adoptions. Thus, while it is possible that "[i]nherent in the baby black market is the unfairness that results from the fact that only the affluent can afford to pay the enormous fees necessary to procure a baby," the words "black market" ought to be italicized. It is not the free market, but unwarranted restrictions on the operation of that market, that has raised the black market price of babies beyond the reach of ordinary people.

Thus far I have implicitly been speaking only of the market for healthy white infants. There is no shortage of nonwhite and of handicapped infants, and of any children who are no longer infants, available for adoption. Such children are substitutes for healthy white infants, and the higher the price of the latter, the greater will be the demand for the former. The network of regulations that has driven up the full price (including such nonmonetary components of price as delay) of adopting a healthy, white infant may have increased the willingness of childless couples to consider adopting a child of a type not in short supply, though how much (if at all) no one knows. The present system is, in any event, a grossly inefficient, as well as covert, method of encouraging the adoption of the hard-to-place child. If society wants to subsidize these unfortunate children, the burden of the subsidies should be borne, if not by the natural parents of these children, then by the taxpaying population at large—rather than by just the nation's childless white couples, who under the present unsystematic system bear the lion's share of the burden by being denied the benefits of an efficient method of allocating healthy white infants for adoption in the hope that this will induce them to adopt nonwhite, handicapped, or older children.

The Question of Quality

As soon as one mentions quality, people's hackles rise and they remind you that one is talking about a traffic in human beings, not in inanimate objects. The observation is pertinent, and at least five limitations might have to be placed on the operation of the market in babies for adoption. The first, already mentioned and already in place, is that the buyers can have no right to abuse the thing bought, as they would if the thing were a piece of steel or electronics. This really should go without saying. The laws against child abuse have never distinguished among different methods of acquiring custody of the child. Natural parents are not permitted to abuse a child because they are natural rather than adoptive parents; and people who acquire their children illegally through the black market are no more exempt from the child-abuse laws than people with illegal income are exempt from paying income tax on it. If I were arrested for torturing my cat and charged with violation of the laws forbidding cruelty to animals, it would be no defense that I had bought the cat for forty dollars.

If the laws against child abuse were perfectly efficacious, nothing more would have to be said on the subject. But they are not. The abuse occurs in secret, and the victim may be too young and too dependent to bring it to the attention of the authorities— or indeed to know what is going on. In addition, many child abusers may be so mentally or psychologically abnormal that they cannot be deterred even by very harsh penalties. In such a setting, preventive as well as punitive measures may be justified. Today, all adoptive parents are, in theory anyway, screened for fitness. Adoption agencies are charged with this responsibility, and if we moved toward a freer market in babies the agencies could be given the additional function of investigating and certifying prospective purchasers, who would pay the price of the service. . . .

The third limitation on a baby market concerns remedies for breach of contract. In an ordinary market a buyer can both reject defective goods and, if the seller refuses to deliver and damages would be an inadequate remedy for the refusal, get specific performance of the contract. Natural parents are not permitted to reject their baby, either when it is born or afterward, because it turns out to be handicapped or otherwise not in conformity with their expectations; no more should adoptive parents who buy their babies. Nor should the adoptive parents be able to force the natural mother to surrender the baby to them if she changes her mind, unless some competent authority determines that the baby would be better off adopted. For the welfare of the baby must be considered along with that of the contracting parties. Refusing to grant specific performance in circumstances in which it appears that forcing the sale to go through would harm the baby is consistent with the basic equity principle that the third-party effects of equitable remedies must be considered in deciding whether to grant such a remedy or confine the plaintiff to damage remedies. The child is an interested third party whose welfare would be disserved by a mechanical application of the remedies available to buyers in the market for inanimate goods.

For the same reason (the child's welfare) neither natural nor adopting parents should be allowed to sell their children after infancy, that is, after the child has established a bond with its parents. Nor should the natural mother be allowed to take back the baby after adoption, any more than a seller of a conventional good or service can (except in extraordinary circumstances) rescind the sale after delivery and payment in accordance with his contract with the buyer, unless, once again, a competent authority decides that the baby's welfare would be increased. I shall not try to resolve the question whether, in any of these remedial settings, the welfare of the child should be paramount or should be balanced with that of the adult parties.

The last limitation on the baby market that I shall discuss relates to eugenic breeding. Although prospects still seem remote, one can imagine an entrepreneur in the baby market trying to breed a race of *Ubermenschen* who would command premium prices. The external effects of such an endeavor could be very harmful, and would provide an appropriate basis for governmental regulation.

I am not so sanguine about the operation of a baby market, even with the limitations I have discussed, that I am prepared to advocate the complete and immediate repeal of the laws forbidding the sale of babies for adoption. That such a market might give somewhat greater scope for child abusers and might encourage weird and potentially quite harmful experiments in eugenic breeding should be enough to give anyone pause. But to concentrate entirely on the downside would be a mistake. One million abortions a year is a serious social problem regardless of where one stands on the underlying ethical issues; so is a flourishing black market in babies combined with a severe shortage in the lawful market. The severity of the shortage is, admittedly, a matter of fair debate. In our 1978 article Dr. Landes and I estimated that about 130,000 married couples who at present are childless might adopt a child under free-market conditions. More recent research suggests this estimate is reasonable. A study conducted by the National Center for Health Statistics found that 46% of the estimated 274,000 currently married women who are between 30 and 44 years of age and sterile have adopted a child. If all those who have not adopted would like to, and would be willing to pay a free-market price, then the 148,000 married couples in the relevant population who have not yet adopted a child are unsatisfied demanders. But some unknown fraction of this number either do not want to have children at all or do not want to have adopted children. Dr. Landes and I noted that 96% of couples marrying in 1975 in which the wife was between 18 and 24 years old expected to have a child. Since most people who marry young do not know whether they have a fertility problem, it seems a fair guess that almost all of the 274,000 married couples who are sterile planned when they got married to have children, and hence that most of the 148,000 who have not yet adopted a child would like, or at some time in the past would have liked, to adopt a child. Of course, wanting something and being willing to pay for it are two different things, and it might seem that many childless couples would be unwilling or unable to pay for a baby if they had to pay free market prices. But this seems unlikely. The purchase price on the free market would probably be lower than under the present system (for reasons discussed earlier), and in any event only a small fraction of the total cost (even discounted to present value) of raising a child. Bear in mind, too, that adoptive parents save the medical and opportunity costs of pregnancy. Marrying couples who expected to have a child, notwithstanding the cost, are unlikely to be deterred by the small, probably zero or even negative, incremental cost of adopting a child in a free market.

True, some couples decide after marriage that they don't want to have a child. This is particularly likely if the couple anticipates a high probability of divorce. About half of American marriages end in divorce, and some of these divorces are anticipated before children enter the picture. Another consideration is that some couples do not consider an adopted child a good substitute for the natural child they cannot have, and they may therefore decide to remain childless even if the price of an adopted child is low and the quality high. Although these factors suggest a downward adjustment in my estimates, there are three offsetting factors to consider. First, some unknown fraction of adoptions is of babies bought in the black market, and the part of the demand for a good that is satisfied in a black market reflects the shortage in the lawful market. Second, the 148,000 figure excludes married couples who become sterile after having one or more children and who would like to adopt. In fact, 20% of married couples who become sterile after having one child go on to adopt a child, and 42% of married couples with one child say that they would adopt a second child if they became sterile. Finally, and bearing particularly on the experiment that Dr. Landes and I proposed, ten times as many premarital pregnancies end in "pregnancy loss" (miscarriage, stillbirth, and no doubt the biggest category, abortion) as in putting the baby up for adoption.

One reason people fear the operation of a free market in babies for adoption is that they extrapolate from experience with the illegal market. Critics who suggest that baby selling offers the promise of huge profits to middlemen—the dreaded "baby brokers"—fail to distinguish between an illegal market, in which sellers demand a heavy premium (an apparent, though not real, profit) in order to defray the expected costs of punishment, and a legal market, in which the premium is eliminated. Seemingly exorbitant profits, low quality, poor information, involvement of criminal elements—these widely asserted characteristics of the black market in babies are no more indicative of the behavior of a lawful market than the tactics of the bootleggers and rum-runners during Prohibition were indicative of the behavior of the liquor industry after Prohibition was repealed. . . .

So we have legal baby selling today; the question of public policy is not whether baby selling should be forbidden or allowed but how extensively it should be regulated. I simply think it should be regulated less stringently than is done today.

CRITICAL THINKING QUESTIONS

1. The first step in evaluating an argument, especially an argument of this length, is to make sure you understand the argument. Break down this argument into its essential parts: the issue, conclusion, and reasons. You can facilitate this task by attending closely to the writer's organization, especially his responses to arguments against his position. Cluster the paragraphs into major ideas and paraphrase these ideas in the margins of the essay. Keep in mind that this article has the ability to spark a very hostile response in the reader. Maybe you left the argument upset by some of Prof. Posner's suggestions. Try to be fair to the author and use language that accurately reflects his argument.

2. Prof. Posner creates an analogy in his argument when he compares the sale of babies to the sale of ordinary goods, such as television sets. He admits that there are significant differences between the subjects he analogizes, and he later addresses these differences by suggesting limitations to the adoption market that do not apply to the market of ordinary goods. Are the similarities between the two sufficiently relevant to make this evidence persuasive? Are there still significant differences he has not addressed?

3. Prof. Posner advocates for a free or, at least, freer adoption market. He recognizes that to achieve this goal the government must reduce its current regulations of this market. Prof. Posner holds several descriptive assumptions about the nature and role of the government in American life. What are these assumptions? What assumptions about government might the opposition to this argument hold?

4. Imagine you heard a classmate say, after she read this argument, "Prof. Posner is so insensitive! What an awful argument. Worse yet! He argued that we should sell babies to the highest bidder!" Your classmate just used two fallacies discussed in Chapter 7 of *Asking the Right Questions*. What fallacious tactics did she use? What differentiates these reasoning tricks from relevant reasons?

ESSAY QUESTIONS

1. The quality of several of these readings would be enhanced had the authors used more evidence. Of course, these authors had limited space, especially those writing editorials for

newspapers. Let's imagine they did not have these limitations. Choose one of these arguments. Take the opportunity
to research and strengthen the argument with more evidence. Not all evidence is of equal quality, so be sure to
review the evidence chapters in *Asking the Right Questions.*
Write an essay to convince your reader that this research
would improve the quality of the original argument.

2. Some of these articles should have been more persuasive to
you than others. Hopefully, the reasons that you found certain articles more persuasive than others were based on your
critical thinking skills. Choose an article that you did not find
very persuasive. Write an essay to the author of this article,
suggesting revisions that would improve the reasoning of the
argument. Use strong sections of the other articles as examples of the changes you are suggesting.

3. This readings chapter had a common issue: what role should
our government play in the creation of families? Because
they addressed the same issue, we should see common value
conflicts arising. These value conflicts are present in articles
about marriage and also about parenting. What are the common underlying value conflicts in the articles? How do you
know? Which authors would agree on how to resolve the
value conflict? Why do you think so?

CHAPTER 17

READINGS CLUSTER 3

What Is the Secret to Happiness?

Question any child or adult about what they desire in life and a common answer arises: I just want to be *happy*! But what exactly do we mean when we say we desire happiness? The pursuit of happiness drives people to alter their lives, work multiple jobs, change their income, start families, and find religion. A question that has been debated by psychologists, doctors, researchers, and scientists alike still puzzles us today: How do we achieve the ultimate goal of happiness? Is there a formula? Can we really become happier people? The set of articles in this chapter introduces arguments addressing the role happiness plays in our lives and theories of how we can achieve happiness. You should read carefully, paying special attention to the methods of evaluation you learned in *Asking the Right Questions*.

Researchers: Choices Spawn Happiness

Arthur Max and Toby Sterling

Associated Press, USA Today (2007)

AMSTERDAM, Netherlands—The tiny Himalayan kingdom of Bhutan long ago dispensed with the notion of Gross National Product as a gauge of well-being. The king decreed that his people would aspire to Gross National Happiness instead.

That kernel of Buddhist wisdom is increasingly finding an echo in international policy and development models, which seek to establish scientific methods for finding out what makes us happy and why.

New research institutes are being created at venerable universities like Oxford and Cambridge to establish methods of judging individual and national well-being. Governments are putting ever greater emphasis on promoting mental well-being—not just treating mental illness.

"In much the same way that research of consumer unions helps you to make the best buy, happiness research can help you make the best choices," said Ruut Veenhoven, who created the World Database of Happiness in 1999.

When he started studying happiness in the 1960s, Veenhoven used data from social researchers who simply asked people how satisfied they were with their lives, on a scale of zero to 10. But as the discipline has matured and gained popularity in the past decade, self-reporting has been found lacking.

By their own estimate, "drug addicts would measure happy all the time," said Sabina Alkire, of the Oxford Poverty and Human Development Institute, which began work May 30.

New studies add more objective questions into a mix of feel-good factors: education, nutrition, freedom from fear and violence, gender equality, and perhaps most importantly, having choices.

"People's ability to be an agent, to act on behalf of what matters to them, is fundamental," said Alkire.

But if people say money can't buy happiness, they're only partially right.

Veenhoven's database, which lists 95 countries, is headed by Denmark with a rating of 8.2, followed by Switzerland, Austria, Iceland and Finland, all countries with high per capita income. At the other end of the scale are much poorer countries: Tanzania rated 3.2, behind Zimbabwe, Moldova, Ukraine and Armenia.

The United States just makes it into the top 15 with a 7.4 index rating. While choice is abundant in America, nutrition and violence issues helped drag its rating down.

Wealth counts, but most studies of individuals show income disparities count more. Surprisingly, however, citizens are no happier in welfare states, which strive to mitigate the distortions of capitalism than in purer free-market economies.

"In the beginning, I didn't believe my eyes," said Veenhoven of his data. "Icelanders are just as happy as Swedes, yet their country spends half what Sweden does (per capita) on social welfare," he said.

In emphasizing personal freedom as a root of happiness, Alkire cited her study of women in the southern Indian state of Kerala, which showed that poor women who make their own choices score highly, compared with women with strict fathers or husbands.

Adrian G. White, of the University of Leicester, included twice as many countries as Veenhoven in his Global Projection of Subjective Well-being, which also measures the correlation of happiness and wealth. He, too, led his list with Denmark, Switzerland and Austria.

Bhutan, where less than half the people can read or write and 90% are subsistence farmers, ranks No. 8 in his list of happy nations. Its notion of GNH is based on equitable development, environmental conservation, cultural heritage and good governance.

U.S. researchers have found other underlying factors: married people are more content than singles, but having children does not raise happiness levels; education and IQ seem to have little impact; attractive people are only slightly happier than the unattractive; the elderly—over 65—are more satisfied with their lives than the young; friendships are crucial.

But the research also shows that many people are simply disposed to being either happy or disgruntled, and as much as 50% of the happiness factor is genetic. Like body weight, moods can swing only so much from their natural "set point."

So can you do anything about it? Some educators say you can.

People "can be taught emotional resilience, self control, the habits of optimism, handling negative thoughts and much else," Anthony Seldon, Tony Blair's biographer and the headmaster of Wellington College in Britain, wrote recently in the *Financial Times*.

Seldon is developing happiness courses, working with the Institute of Well-being at Cambridge which was founded last November.

One recent book seeking to cash in on the well-being craze bears the English title *Dutch Women Don't Get Depressed*, though it's written in Dutch. Veenhoven says the title is off base: statistically, women get depressed more often than men, and Dutch women aren't happier than others in the wealthy West.

Veenhoven says that with the right combination of individual choices and government policy, nations can raise their happiness quotient by as much as 5%.

In an influential 2004 academic paper, Martin Seligman, the University of Pennsylvania psychologist credited with launching the positive psychology movement in 1998, and Ed Diener of the University of Illinois at Urbana-Champaign, encouraged policymakers to consider more than economic development in their planning.

"Although economic output has risen steeply over the past decades, there has been no rise in life satisfaction during this period, and there has been a substantial increase in depression and distrust," they wrote.

British opposition leader David Cameron recently established a Quality of Life Policy Group to examine ways governments can legislate to boost national contentment levels.

"It's time we admitted that there's more to life than money, and it's time we focused not just on GDP, but on GWB—general well-being," he said in a speech last year.

Even experts acknowledge the difficulty of assigning numerical scales to feelings, and they are still grappling with how best to refine definitions.

At Cambridge's Institute of Well-being, another group has expanded the standard happiness questionnaire to 50 items, and is incorporating it into a European Social Survey of 50,000 people.

It aims to weigh not only personal feelings ("I'm always optimistic about my future"), but how people function ("I feel I am free to decide for myself how to live my life") and their relationships with others ("To what extent do you feel that people in your local area help one another?").

The idea is to find out how well-being varies across Europe, says the Cambridge proposal, acknowledging that it is more than just measuring smile time. "Happiness is more complicated than we originally thought" said Alkire.

Source: Copyright 2007 The Associated Press. All rights reserved.

CRITICAL THINKING QUESTIONS

1. As you read this essay, consider the evidence the author cites. Try to use the evidence as a clue to help answer the question, "What is the specific issue that the essay addresses and what is its conclusion?" Then, create a list of reasons supporting the conclusion. Which reasons are most compelling? Why?

2. The authors point out differing views and definitions of happiness in various studies. Do our authors ever actually define what they mean by the word *happiness*? Is the term significantly ambiguous? What are some alternative definitions for the term? Can you locate other examples of ambiguity within the passage? How does ambiguity affect the authors' reasoning?

3. The author of the article relies on the descriptive assumption that humans know what they need to be happy. However, many schools of thought, including Freudianism, assume the opposite. How could a belief in the opposite assumption of the authors' affect the reasoning and conclusion of the passage? Identify other controversial assumptions in the passage and explain how the reasoning is weakened if a reader believes the opposite assumption.

4. Remember that research findings do not *prove* conclusions, but rather *support* conclusions. Of all the research cited in the article, which research do you find most compelling and why? Does the research vary in quality? Use the framework in Chapter 9 of *Asking the Right Questions* to guide your evaluation and answer.

Money Won't Buy You Happiness

Matthew Herper

Published by Forbes.com (2004)

It's official: Money can't buy happiness.

Sure, if a person is handed $10, the pleasure centers of his brain light up as if he were given food, sex or drugs. But that initial rush does not translate into long-term pleasure for most people. Surveys have found virtually the same level of happiness between the very rich individuals on the Forbes 400 and the Maasai herdsman of East Africa. Lottery winners return to their previous level of happiness after five years. Increases in income just don't seem to make people happier—and most negative life experiences likewise have only a small impact on long-term satisfaction.

"The relationship between money and happiness is pretty darned small," says Peter Ubel, a professor of medicine at the University of Michigan.

That's not to say that increased income doesn't matter at all. There is a very small correlation between wealth and happiness—accounting for about 1% of the happiness reported by people answering surveys. And for some groups, that relationship may be considerably bigger. People who are poor seem to get much happier when their monetary prospects improve, as do the very sick. In these cases, Ubel speculates, people may be protected from negative circumstances by the extra cash. Another possibility is that the money brings an increase in status, which may have a greater impact on happiness.

Why doesn't wealth bring a constant sense of joy? "Part of the reason is that people aren't very good at figuring out what to do with the money," says George Loewenstein, an economist at Carnegie Mellon University. People generally overestimate the amount of long-term pleasure they'll get from a given object.

Sometimes, Loewenstein notes, the way people spend their money can actually make them less happy. For example, people derive a great deal of pleasure from interacting with others. If the first thing lottery winners do is quit their job and move to a palatial but isolated estate where they don't see any neighbors, they could find themselves isolated and depressed.

Other trophies simply don't bring the payoff one expects. Says Loewenstein, "If you're a single male driving around in the Ferrari with nobody next to you, it's a glaring omission."

The central problem is that the human brain becomes conditioned to positive experiences. Getting a chunk of unexpected money registers as a good thing, but as time passes, the response wears off. An expected paycheck doesn't bring any buzz at all—and doesn't contribute to overall happiness. You can get used to anything, be it hanging by your toenails or making millions of dollars a day. Mood may be set more by heredity than by anything else: Studies of twins have shown that at least half a person's level of happiness may be determined by some of the genes that play a role in determining personality.

But this raises another question. How important is happiness anyway? People with chronic illnesses describe themselves as happy, but they would still pay large sums for better health. And although healthy individuals are not much happier than quadriplegics, they would pay large sums of money to keep the use of their limbs. Some of life's most satisfying experiences don't bring happiness. For instance, having children actually makes people less happy over the short term—but that doesn't necessarily mean we should stop procreating.

"I think it's possible to way overestimate the importance of happiness," says Loewenstein. "Part of the meaning of life is to have highs and lows. A life that was constantly happy was not a good life."

However, there may be at least one important relationship between money and happiness, according to Ed Diener, the University of Illinois researcher who surveyed the Forbes 400 and the Maasai. Diener has also written that happy people tend to have higher incomes later on in their lives. So, while money may not help make people happy, being happy may help them make money.

CRITICAL THINKING QUESTIONS

1. Herper does not define what he means by the word "happiness." Once again, this could mean the term is significantly ambiguous. How can a reader determine whether the term is indeed ambiguous?

2. Many of the reasons Herper cites for his argument rely on appeals to authority. How credible are the authorities cited? In other words, should we believe the cited authorities? Recall Chapter 8 of *Asking the Right Questions*. What critical questions should you ask about the authorities presented in this article? Don't forget to consider problems with citers citing other citers.

3. Using the information provided and the Web sites suggested in Chapter 7 of *Asking the Right Questions*, identify any fallacies within Herper's article. How do any fallacies affect how you evaluate his conclusion?

4. Does any of the evidence given within the passage contradict other reported evidence? How should a reader evaluate contradictory evidence?

How to Find True Happiness

Steve Ross and Olivia Rosewood

Huffington Post (2008)

Yogis have always known there's a significant difference between pleasure and happiness. Pleasure comes from getting what you want: for example food, good sex, clothes, etc. But pleasure is short-lived and fickle. It lasts for as long as it lasts—a few hours at best. And then it's gone. Pleasure is fleeting. However true happiness is inexhaustible and permanent.

According to the yogis, pleasure and pain are two sides of the same coin. One never goes anywhere without the other, and they alternate. You may eat, but you'll be hungry again. You're lonely, then you're in love, then you're lonely, then you're in love. Then you're lonely and in love at the same time (and hopefully writing country western songs). Love and hate, war and peace, hot and cold, success and failure, rich and poor, and on and on. But true happiness transcends the pleasure/pain principle.

Everyone has isolated moments of feeling on top of the world: when you buy something you really want, achieve a long held goal, overcome a monumental challenge, or even fall in love. Yes, it feels phenomenal. In those moments, the mind is quiet, there's a sense of intense satisfaction, and a tiny sliver of happiness reveals itself. This sliver is pleasure. You might think it comes from the buying of a new house, getting a big promotion at work, finding true love, or winning a prestigious award. But the truth is that these things just assuage your desire long enough for you to experience your natural state. The happiness is the same happiness every time. The happiness is not only coming from you (as opposed to those achievements or acquisitions), it IS you. The fulfillment of desire gives you a brief glimpse of what you really are. But the yogis have realized that you don't have to merely glimpse this happiness within you through the satisfaction of desire. The material world gives you a peek at pleasure, but lasting happiness is found right where you are.

Happiness is in you, it is you, and it's not coming from an external source (including the shopping mall—and did I already mention that happiness is not at the shopping mall?). Here is the essential point: Brief happiness (pleasure) doesn't come from the object of satisfactions, it comes from you. This is where many people are erroneous in their perception, and also why people stress out, worry, and suffer: They believe happiness is out there . . . somewhere.

A wise man I met in India put it to me this way: You're living on a mountain of gold and you don't realize it. Every time it rains, the dirt and muck are washed away and the gold is revealed. And you run out into the rain, scooping up fistfuls of gold and dancing around. But you mistakingly think that the rain is bringing the gold, so you worship the rain, and you make sacrifices with your schedule to please the rain. When there's a drought, you become poor, starve, and bemoan the absence of the rain. But the gold is always there, just beneath the surface, and the rain has simply been revealing it. If you'd just dust off the mountain the slightest bit, you'd see it for what it is. Scratch the surface! Look deeper! There's no need to rely on the rain to reveal your happiness.

Now I'm not saying move out of your house, relinquish your possessions, live in the streets, and that will make you happy. That's not it at all. Living like a monk isn't necessarily going to remove your desires, either. Having is not the problem. It's wonderful to be grateful for what you do have, and it's great to have fun in the material world. You can have and enjoy all that you can manage. Suffering does not come from having, it comes from endless wanting.

Having is a necessity for survival. Having a roof over your head and food in your belly will not cause you pain. When you truly have something, you accept it as it is. There's no lofty expectation projected onto it. Will winning a trillion dollars make you happy? Well, you will have a trillion dollars. But true happiness? Nope, a trillion dollars is just a trillion dollars. Does having a roof over your head and food in your belly guarantee happiness? No, it's just food and shelter. You can have food, shelter, and even a trillion dollars, but your experience of these things has very little to do with the things themselves and everything to do with the one who is experiencing them. You can be miserable or happy. That's really up to you. Ownership and having don't rule out attaining uninterrupted happiness, but they can't promise to deliver it, either.

Remember, true happiness is independent of circumstances. Pleasure is utterly dependent on circumstance. True happiness is prior and senior to the flickering phenomena of the world. True happiness transcends the boundaries of the mind and the limitations of conditioned propriety. True happiness is uninterrupted.

CRITICAL THINKING QUESTIONS

1. From the outset, the authors provide a distinction between the terms "happiness" and "pleasure." How did a clear definition affect your understanding of the argument? Throughout the article, do the authors ever equivocate the two terms? Or rather, do the authors maintain the distinction made between the two related ideas?

2. What descriptive assumptions guide the authors' reasoning? Are these assumptions similar to or different from your own? How do differing assumptions affect the reasoning structure of the argument?

3. What type of evidence is primarily used in the authors' reasoning? How does this evidence compare to the evidence in the previous articles in this section? How could the authors strengthen their evidential claims?

Down the Tube: the Sad Stats on Happiness, Money and TV

Jonathon Clements

The Wall Street Journal (2008)

Put down the remote and back slowly away from the television.

Despite the sharp rise in our standard of living in recent decades, Americans today are little or no happier than earlier generations. Why not?

A new study suggests one possibility: Maybe we need to be smarter about how we spend our time. And, no, that doesn't mean watching more TV.

Feeling unpleasant. You can think of your happiness as having three components. First, there's your basic disposition—whether you are, by nature, a happy person or not. Clearly, there isn't a whole lot you can do about this.

Second, there are your life's circumstances, such as your age, health, marital status and income. Often, this stuff isn't nearly as important as folks imagine. If your income doubled, you would initially be delighted. But research suggests you would quickly get used to all that extra money.

That brings us to the third factor, which is how you spend your time—something you have a fair amount of control over. This is the subject of a major new study by academics Daniel Kahneman, Alan Krueger, David Schkade, Norbert Schwarz and Arthur Stone.

For the study, the five professors surveyed some 4,000 Americans, asking what they did the previous day and then quizzing them in detail about three randomly selected events from the day. Those surveyed were asked to rate the three episodes based on feelings such as pain, happiness, stress and sadness. All this was used to calculate what percentage of time people spent in an unpleasant state.

Getting involved. Result? Women, folks under age 65, those divorced or separated, lower-income earners and the less educated were likely to spend a bigger chunk of their day in an unpleasant state.

But what I found most intriguing was the study's data on which activities we enjoy. The five professors grouped activities into six clusters, based on the emotions associated with each.

The standout cluster was what the authors label "engaging leisure and spiritual activities," things like visiting friends, exercising, attending church, listening to music, fishing, reading a book, sitting in a cafe or going to a party. When we spend time on our favorite of these activities, we're typically happy, engrossed and not especially stressed.

"These are things you choose to do, rather than have to do," notes one of the study's co-authors, Prof. Schkade of the University of California, San Diego.

The obvious implication: If we devote more time to these activities, maybe we would be more satisfied with our lives. Yet the evidence suggests we've missed a huge chance to do just that—which may help explain why Americans are little or no happier than they were four decades ago.

Zoning out. Over that stretch, men reduced the amount of time they spent working. Meanwhile, women—as a group—spent more time earning income, reflecting their increased work-force participation. But this increased time at the office was more than offset by a drop in time devoted to mundane chores.

In other words, both men and women had the chance to lavish more time on "engaging leisure and spiritual activities." But in fact, time spent on these activities has actually declined over the past four decades.

Instead, there's been a significant increase in the hours devoted to what the authors call "neutral downtime," which is mostly watching television. Women now spend 15% of their waking hours staring at the tube, while men devote 17%.

Watching TV may be low-stress and moderately enjoyable. But people aren't mentally engaged the way they are when they're, say, exercising or socializing.

"I wonder whether there are self-control problems when it comes to watching television," muses Prof. Krueger, an economist at Princeton University and another of the study's co-authors. "I wonder whether people would feel better about their lives if they spent their leisure time doing something that was more interactive and more engaging."

CRITICAL THINKING QUESTIONS

1. Is the argument prescriptive or descriptive? Why? What does this characteristic tell us about the argument?

2. After determining your answer to the question above, think about whether there are reasons within the article you could use to create the other type of argument. That is, if you determined the passage was descriptive, are there any parts of the passage that could be reasons for a prescriptive argument and vice versa?

3. The article states, "Women, folks under age 65, those divorced or separated, lower-income earners and the less educated were likely to spend a bigger chunk of their day in an unpleasant state." Thus, the author implies that having these characteristics makes people less happy. However, can you identify any problems with research methodology or rival causes that may make this assertion less reliable?

4. Is evidence based on self-reports a reliable form of evidence? What questions does a reader need to ask when evaluating the worth of evidence?

Does Faith Promote Happiness?

William R. Mattox, Jr.

Policy Review (1998)

Sigmund Freud said they suffer from a form of sickness—an "obsessional neurosis" accompanied by guilt, repressed sexuality, and suppressed emotions. Former Saturday Night Live comedian Dana Carvey satirized them as frumpy, judgmental oddballs who find significance in the fact that "Santa" is an anagram of "Satan." But a number of recent research studies show that church ladies (and the men who worship alongside them) are some of the happiest and most hopeful people on the face of the earth. Now, isn't that special?

The correlation between faith and well-being can be seen both in surveys taken of the general public and in research on specific population groups. For example, a recent Gallup poll of Americans found that people with high religious involvement are twice as likely as those without to say that they are "very happy." Similarly, a literature review by psychologists Ed Diener and David Myers reported that religiousness is one of the best predictors of life satisfaction among the elderly.

David Larson, the president of the National Institute for Healthcare Research, says the link between faith and well-being is most obvious in studies that look at how people respond to adversity. For example, recently widowed women who attend church frequently report greater joy in their lives than those who are spiritually inactive. Churchgoing mothers of disabled children are less vulnerable to depression than their nonattending counterparts. And those with a devout faith are more likely than others to experience contentment in the midst of illness, marital hardships or job-related problems. Larson believes these findings about hardship groups are especially important from a research standpoint. "Apparently, the link between faith and well-being isn't because happiness leads to religious involvement so much as religious involvement leads to happiness," he says.

So why exactly does religious involvement help church ladies and men lead such happy lives? Scholars have offered—and begun testing—a variety of possible explanations. Some believe part of the answer lies in the close relationships that people frequently cultivate as members of a religious group. Others point to the greater sense of meaning, purpose, and direction that people seem to gain from finding answers to life's deepest questions. Still others posit that religious worshippers in the midst of suffering often seem to derive comfort and hope from Biblical passages.

Whatever the case, as researchers seek to learn more about the interplay of faith and happiness, they are making some fascinating discoveries. For example, social psychologist Sheena Sethi-Iyengar of the Massachusetts Institute for Technology recently presented a study at an academic conference in Philadelphia that found that people who attend liberal congregations (which have fewer restrictions on personal behavior) are significantly less happy, hopeful, and optimistic than those who attend conservative congregations.

To further test this curious finding, Sethi-Iyengar and her colleagues conducted a content analysis of the sermons, hymns, prayers, and liturgies used by conservative, moderate, and liberal congregations. The messages found in orthodox religious services proved to be the most hopeful, while those in liberal services turned out to be the least hopeful.

Sethi-Iyengar cannot say for certain why religious conservatives are happiest, but one clue her study offers is that religious conservatives are far less apt to continually blame themselves for negative life events than are religious moderates and (especially) religious liberals. "This could be a sign of smug, selfrighteousness—of 'holy rollers' feeling 'holier than thou,'" observes Larson. But given Sethi-Iyengar's content analysis, it is more likely that these findings are related in some way to religious teachings about sin, forgiveness, and being accepted by God. In other words, part of the reason for conservative churchgoers' high levels of contentment may be because it is better to have sinned and been forgiven than to wonder whether you have sinned at all.

Needless to say, there are still many unanswered questions about the relationship between faith and happiness. But as researchers continue to probe, they are finding that religious involvement seems to benefit not only church ladies, but their family members as well. For example, a recent study by psychologist Lisa Miller of Columbia University found that young women raised in a home with a devoutly religious mother are 50 percent less likely than other young women to experience depression. And in cases where the daughter chooses to adopt her mother's faith, the likelihood of depression falls another 30 percent.

No one knows where all of this research will eventually lead. But this much, at least, seems clear. Instead of being representative of the average American church lady, Dana Carvey's SNL character looks more and more like a Freudian slip.

Source: Copyright Heritage Foundation Sep/Oct 1998

CRITICAL THINKING QUESTIONS

1. When reading, you should have noticed this article contained a lot of data and statistics. As a critical thinker, you should strive to find erroneous statistical reasoning. Evaluate the statistics in the article following the framework in Chapter 11 of *Asking the Right Questions.*

2. Does the meaning of the word "faith" need to be defined in Mattox's essay? Has the author made the definition of this term sufficiently clear? Would different definitions lead you to different evaluations of the author's reasoning? How so?

3. Did this article provide all the information you needed to evaluate the data included? In other words, is any significant information omitted within the data about faith and happiness? What further information do you need before you can judge the impact of the statistics?"

4. This article expresses many associations between religious faith and happiness. Are there rival causes you might consider as possible explanations for these associations? What thinking strategies would help you to generate such causes?

Pursuing Happiness: Two scholars explore the fragility of contentment

John Lanchester

The New Yorker Magazine (2006)

It is the year 100,000 B.C., and two hunter-gatherers are out hunter-gathering. Let's call them Ig and Og. Ig comes across a new kind of bush, with bright-red berries. He is hungry, as most hunter-gatherers are most of the time, and the berries look pretty, so he pops a handful in his mouth. Og merely puts some berries in his goatskin bag. A little later, they come to a cave. It looks spooky and Og doesn't want to go in, but Ig pushes on ahead and has a look around. There's nothing there except a few bones. On the way home, an unfamiliar rustling in the undergrowth puts Og in a panic, and he freezes, but Ig figures that whatever is rustling probably isn't any bigger and uglier than he is, so he blunders on, and whatever was doing the rustling scuttles off into the undergrowth. The next morning, Og finally tries the berries, and they do indeed taste O.K. He decides to go back and collect some more.

Now, Ig is clearly a lot more fun than Og. But Og is much more likely to pass on his genes to the next generation of hunter-gatherers. The downside to Ig's fearlessness is the risk of sudden death. One day, the berries will be poisonous, the bear that lives in the cave will be at home, and the rustling will be a snake or a tiger or some other vertebrate whose bite can turn septic. Ig needs only to make one mistake. From the Darwinian point of view, Og is the man to bet on. He is cautious and prone to anxiety, and these are highly adaptive traits when it comes to survival.

We are the children of Og. For most of the time that anatomically modern humans have existed—a highly contested figure, but let's call it a million years—it has made good adaptive sense to be fearful, cautious, timid. As Jonathan Haidt, a professor of psychology at the University of Virginia, puts it in "The Happiness Hypothesis" (Basic; $26), "bad is stronger than good" is an important principle of design by evolution. "Responses to threats and unpleasantness are faster, stronger, and harder to inhibit than responses to opportunities and pleasures." This is a matter of how our brains are wired: most sense data pass through the amygdala, which helps control our fight-or-flight response, before being processed by other parts of our cerebral cortex. The feeling that a fright can make us "jump half out of our skin" is based on this physical reality—we're reacting long before we know what it is that we're reacting to.

This is one of the reasons that human beings make heavy weather of being happy. We have been hardwired to emphasize the negative, and, for most of human history, there has been a lot of the negative to emphasize. Hobbes's description of life in the state of nature as "nasty, brutish and short" is so familiar we can forget that, for most of the people who have ever lived, it was objectively true. Most humans have had little control over their fate; a sniffle, a graze, or a bad piece of meat, let alone a major emergency such as having a baby—all were, for most of our ancestors, potentially lethal. One of the first people to be given penicillin was an Oxford policeman named Albert Alexander, who, in 1940, had scratched himself on a rose thorn and developed septicemia. After he was given the experimental drug, he began to recover, but the supply ran out after five days, and he relapsed and died. That was the world before modern medicine, and it would have been familiar to Ig and Og in a crucial respect: one false move and you were dead.

We can't be sure, but it seems unlikely that our prehistoric forebears spent much time thinking about whether or not they were happy. As Darrin McMahon, a historian at Florida State University, argues in his heavyweight study of the subject, "Happiness: A History" (Atlantic Monthly Press; $27.50), the idea of happiness is not a human universal that applies across all times and all cultures but a concept that has demonstrably changed over the years. When your attention is fully concentrated on questions of survival, you don't have the time or the inclination even to formulate the idea of happiness. You have to begin to feel that you have some control over your circumstances before you begin to ask yourself questions about your own state of mind.

People who have scant control over their lives are bound to place tremendous importance on luck and fate. As McMahon points out, "In virtually every Indo-European language, the modern word for happiness is cognate with luck, fortune or fate." In a sense, the oldest and most deeply rooted philosophical idea in the world and in our natures is "Shit happens." *Happ* was the Middle English word for "chance, fortune, what *happens* in the world," McMahon writes, "giving us such words as 'happenstance,' 'haphazard,' 'hapless,' and 'perhaps.'" This view of happiness is essentially tragic: it sees life as consisting of the things that happen to you; if more good things than bad happen, you are happy.

"Call no man happy until he is dead" was the Greek way of saying this. It was only when someone had passed beyond the vicissitudes of chance, and reposed honorably in the grave, that one could finally render the verdict. The original challenge to this idea came from classical Athens, the first place where men were free and self-governing, and, not coincidentally, a culture in which a great emphasis was placed on ideas of self-reliance and self-control. Socrates seems to have been the earliest person to think critically about the conditions of happiness, and how one could be happy, and in doing so he caused a shift in the way people thought about the subject. Socrates made the question of happiness one of full accord between an individual and the good: to be happy was to lead a good life, one in keeping with higher patterns of being.

That basic idea gained considerable traction in the next two millennia; in one way or another, the philosophical investigation of happiness from Aristotle to Erasmus and on to Luther was concerned with the alignment of individual conduct and the heavenly order. McMahon explores the broad range of these ideas while pointing out the strong continuities among them. At the time the Beatitudes were written down, with their mysterious promise of blessing for the weak and the poor, "the emphasis is on the promise of future reward"; by the time of Luther, in the sixteenth century, "the experience of happiness on earth . . . was an outward sign of God's grace."

The next big turning point in the history of happiness came with the Enlightenment, and its vision of the world as a rational place, which might be governed by laws analogous to the newly discovered Newtonian laws of physics. In the words of the historian Roy Porter, the Enlightenment "translated the ultimate question 'How can I be saved?' into the pragmatic 'How can I be happy?'" With this came a new emphasis on the legitimate pursuit of pleasure. In classical and Christian thought, pleasure was seen as, at best, a distraction from the worthwhile pursuit of virtue. The Enlightenment gave pleasure much better press. "If pleasure exists, and we can only enjoy it in life, then life is happiness," argued Casanova, who was in a position to know.

This is the understanding of happiness with which the modern world begins; it is vividly captured in the second sentence of the Declaration of Independence, which asserts as self-evident a right to "Life, Liberty and the pursuit of Happiness." To non-Americans, talk of "the pursuit of happiness" can seem an amazing mixture of the simpleminded and the unexpectedly complex. What seems simple is that happiness is so straightforward that we all have a right— a right!—to seek it; what seems complex is the idea that what we're entitled to is, indeed, a pursuit, something strenuous and not necessarily successful. Some Marxists have thought that the right to pursue happiness was a last-minute substitution for a previously drafted right to property, but McMahon makes short work of that conspiracy theory. He points out that the Founding Fathers, who queried, crossed out, and haggled over every line of the Declaration, let the "pursuit of Happiness" stand unedited and unamended. But he also points out that the eighteenth-century understanding of "pursuit" was rather darker than it might seem now. Dr. Johnson's dictionary defined it as "the act of following with hostile intention," and McMahon adds that "if one thinks of pursuing happiness as one pursues a fugitive . . . the 'pursuit of happiness' takes on a somewhat different cast."

The legacy of that ambiguity is with us still. We are pursuing happiness to this day, and it is by no means clear that it is a happy process. The self-help section in any bookshop is easy to mock— indeed, it sometimes seems that the titles of self-help books are almost mocking themselves—but there is nothing to mock about the people standing in front of the shelves looking for guidance. In fact, the advice in self-help books is, by and large, pretty good. The trouble is that it is very difficult to take.

Why is this so? For the first time in human history, it's possible to give tentative answers that are based on a scientific account of mental processes. In addition to the old psych-lab tests, researchers now have access to technology such as MRI and PET scanners.

These can report where brain activity takes place, and can begin to answer questions about why our minds work in the way that they do. One example has to do with emotion, which is regulated in part by the frontal cortex of the brain, the last part to expand as mammals evolved. The orbitofrontal cortex, just above and behind the eyes, is "one of the most consistently active areas of the brain during emotional reactions," Jonathan Haidt tells us. "The neurons in this part of the cortex fire wildly when there is an immediate possibility of pleasure or pain, loss or gain." People who suffer damage to the frontal cortex can lose most of their ability to experience emotion while retaining their ability to think rationally. But they don't therefore see the world with crystalline logic, so that life suddenly becomes simple. On the contrary, Haidt reports: "They find themselves unable to make simple decisions or set goals, and their lives fall apart. When they look out at the world and think, 'What should I do now?' they see dozens of choices but lack immediate internal feelings of like or dislike. They must examine the pros and cons of every choice with their reasoning, but in the absence of feeling they see little reason to pick one or the other."

Philosophers have expounded on happiness for a long time, but only relatively recently have psychologists taken much of an interest. The study of "positive psychology," as it is called, was launched by Martin Seligman, of the University of Pennsylvania, in the late nineteen-nineties, and began with the realization that the study of psychiatry had a huge bias toward every form of illness. "The Diagnostic and Statistical Manual of Mental Disorders," the basic reference work of the psychiatric profession, was (and is) a chronicle of everything that could possibly go wrong with the human mind, from psychosis to schizoaffective disorder to mania—a harrowing catalogue. But where was the study of the mind when it was working satisfactorily? Where was the study of a healthy emotional life and successful adaptation to circumstances? In short, what had psychology to say about happiness? Haidt is a member of the positive-psychology school, and his book, which has in its packaging some of the trappings of self-help, is much more intelligent than it looks from the outside. One of the key questions—going straight to the heart of the Enlightenment ambition for us to be happy here and now, in this life—is whether happiness is a default setting of the brain. That is to say, are we, left to our own devices, and provided with sufficient food and freedom and control over our circumstances, naturally happy?

The answer proposed by positive psychology seems to be: It depends. The simplest kind of unhappiness is that caused by poverty. People living in poverty become happier if they become richer—but the effect of increased wealth cuts off at a surprisingly low figure. The British economist Richard Layard, in his stimulating book "Happiness: Lessons from a New Science," puts that figure at fifteen thousand dollars, and leaves little doubt that being richer does not make people happier. Americans are about twice as rich as they were in the nineteen-seventies but report not being any happier; the Japanese are six times as rich as they were in 1950 and aren't any happier, either. Looking at the data from all over the world, it is clear that, instead of getting happier as they become better off, people get stuck on a "hedonic treadmill": their expectations rise at the same pace as their incomes, and the happiness they seek remains constantly just out of reach.

According to positive psychologists, once we're out of poverty the most important determinant of happiness is our "set point," a natural level of happiness that is (and this is one of the movement's most controversial claims) largely inherited. We adapt to our circumstances; we don't, or can't, adapt our genes. The evidence for this set point, and the phrase itself, came from a study of identical twins by the behavioral geneticist David Lykken, which concluded that "trying to be happier is like trying to be taller." Contrary to everything you might think, "in the long run, it doesn't much matter what happens to you," Haidt writes. Consider the opposing examples of winning the lottery or of losing the use of your limbs. According to Haidt, "It's better to win the lottery than to break your neck, but not by as much as you'd think. . . . Within a year, lottery winners and paraplegics have both (on average) returned most of the way to their baseline levels of happiness."

Can that possibly be true? Here we run into one of the biggest problems with the study of happiness, which is that it relies heavily on what people tell us about themselves. The paraplegics in these studies may well report regaining their previous levels of happiness, but how can we know whether these levels really are the same? You can compare relative happiness in the course of a given day, though that's not at all the same thing. Layard cites a study, by the Nobel laureate Daniel Kahneman, reporting that people's top four favorite parts of the day feature sex, socializing after work, dinner, and relaxing. Their bottom four involve commuting, work, child care, and housework. But our absolute level of happiness is more elusive. Happiness "is something essentially subjective," Freud wrote. "No matter how much we may shrink with horror from certain situations—of a galley-slave in antiquity, of a peasant during the Thirty Years' War, of a victim of the Holy Inquisition, of a Jew awaiting a pogrom—it is nevertheless impossible for us to feel our way into such people. . . . It seems to me unprofitable to pursue this aspect of the problem any further."

That isn't, of course, the view taken by positive psychologists. Then again, the news that we're on a hedonic treadmill, so that we end up where we're always bound to end up, is so contrary to our fundamental appetites for exertion and the next new thing, that nobody can really accept it. So Lykken himself, the fellow who came up with the finding about the set point, went on to write a book about how to become happier. (It contained his favorite recipe for Key-lime pie.) Positive psychology has even devised a formula for how to be happy, where H is your level of happiness, S is your set point, C is the conditions of your life, and V is the voluntary activities you do. Ready for the secret of happiness? Here it is:

$$H=S+C+V$$

In other words, your happiness consists of how happy you naturally are, plus whatever is going on in your life to affect your happiness, plus a bit of voluntary work. Well, duh. The only vaguely surprising thing about this is how useful voluntary work can be to the person doing it—and even that isn't really news. At the end of the nineteenth century, Emile Durkheim performed a huge cross-cultural study of suicide, and found, in Haidt's words, that "no matter how he parsed the data, people who had fewer social constraints, bonds and obligations were more likely to kill themselves." The more connected we are to other people, the less likely we are to succumb to despair—a conclusion that isn't very distant from the common-sense proposition that lonely people are often unhappy, and unhappy people are often lonely.

The psychological study of happiness might seem to be something of a bust. Mainly it tells us things that people have known for a long time, except with scientific footnotes. In the end, the philosophy and the science converge on the fact that thinking about your own happiness does not make it any easier to be happy. A co-founder of positive psychology, Mihaly Csikzentmihalyi, made people carry a pager, and told them that every time it went off they should write down what they were doing and how much they were enjoying it. The idea was to avoid the memory's tendency to focus on peaks and troughs, and to capture the texture of people's lives as they were experiencing them, rather than in retrospect. The study showed that people were most content when they were experiencing what Csikzentmihalyi called "flow"—in Haidt's definition, "the state of total immersion in a task that is challenging yet closely matched to one's abilities." We are at our happiest when we are absorbed in what we are doing; the most useful way of regarding happiness is, to borrow a phrase of Clive James's, as "a by-product of absorption."

The trouble is that asking yourself about your frame of mind is a sure way to lose your flow. If you want to be happy, don't ever ask yourself if you are. A person in good health in a Western liberal democracy is, in terms of his objective circumstances, one of the most fortunate human beings ever to have walked the surface of the earth. Risk-taking Ig and worried Og both would have regarded our easy, long, riskless lives with incredulous envy. They would have regarded us as so lucky that questions about our state of mind wouldn't be worth asking. It is a perverse consequence of our fortunate condition that the question of our happiness, or lack of it, presses unhappily hard on us.

CRITICAL THINKING QUESTIONS

1. What issue does Lanchester's article address? What is his conclusion? Would you consider the argument descriptive or prescriptive? Why?
2. Remember, before taking the time to critically evaluate an issue, you should ask the question, "Who cares?" Why is the issue of happiness significant? Why do we care about the information contained in the article?
3. Use your knowledge of fallacies from Chapter 7 of *Asking the Right Questions*. Were you able to spot any red herrings within Lanchester's article? Did any sections of the piece detract from the overall argument?
4. What generalizations were made in this article? Which ones were supported by good evidence? Which ones were overgeneralizations? Did you see any evidence of strong sense critical thinking in the article?

ESSAY QUESTIONS

1. Many of the critical thinking questions after the passages address significant ambiguity of the term "happiness." Examine the different ways each author employs the idea of happiness. What are some alternative meanings of the term found within these articles? How much does substituting one author's definitions of happiness in another article modify the author's conclusion? Which author presents the most clear and concise definition of his or her meaning of happiness? How does a clear definition accept your willingness to agree with the conclusion?
2. Recall that part of being a productive critical thinker is to keep the conversation going. Suppose you are in a conversation with a classmate and you strongly agree with one of the articles in this chapter. In an effort to keep the conversation going, your classmate asks you, "Is there any evidence

that would cause you to change your mind about your argument?" In other words, pretend you are the author of an article in this section and explain what evidence would be necessary for you to change your opinion. Further, what assumptions or value preferences could lead you to changing your conclusion?

3. Choose the article you found least persuasive of all the passages in this chapter. Pretend you have the opportunity to respond to the author and explain with your critical thinking knowledge why the article was not highly persuasive. Write an essay to the author of the article. Suggest changes that could improve the reasoning of the argument. Provide examples from other more persuasive passages of strong reasoning.

CHAPTER 18

READINGS CLUSTER 4

In What Ways Can the Media Influence Society and What Can We Do About It?

With the ever-growing time people spend in front of television, computers, radios, and reading newspapers and magazines, it is no wonder various fields of study are researching the effects of the media on society. One of the most hotly debated topics in the journalism and entertainment industries is the amount of responsibility the media has to the public for their safety. Parents, public servants, and schoolteachers blame the media for the plethora of problems plaguing society today. Media moguls assert their protection of speech and desire to give the public what it wants. Do the media really influence our behavior in a major way? How biased is the press, and does the bias translate to personal views? When the well-being of society is at stake, where should we draw the line with the media? Keep these questions and your critical thinking tools in mind as you read the following articles.

The Media Doesn't Influence us . . . Except When It Does: Why Defenders and Critics of Media Violence Get It All Wrong

Carrie McLaren

Stay Free! Magazine

For anyone who teaches or writes about media, the issue of violence is hard to avoid. Both ends of the debate are represented by zealots—the censors and the free-speech absolutists. The free-speech contingent operates under two basic assumptions: first, if you express concern about media violence, you are obviously some a priori moron who sees an imaginary immediate direct causal connection between onscreen violence and the real thing. Second, since you see such a connection, it follows that you must be an advocate of censorship—you must, in other words, be the other kind of zealot, the Tipper Gores and Phyllis Schlaflys who want to suck all the pleasure out of life and turn the country into a giant, Christian nanny state.

This "censorship" vs. "free speech" debate frames the way media violence is discussed even among people who should know better. Media educators can while away days debating whether media violence even affects people at all, with many contending that there's no evidence it does. This is a curious position for them to argue. The mainstream media literacy movement is predicated on the idea that media construct reality. Media influence our views on race, gender, politics, and body image—these ideas are accepted as givens. But somehow, when it comes to violence, the effects aren't "proven."

Television executives are also quick to deny the influence of media violence. Yet the entire economy of television hinges on viewers' suggestibility. When NBC sells time to Microsoft and Toyota, it does so by hawking the tube's power to move minds. (The fact that individual commercials may fail to result in purchases is immaterial here.) Media's ability to influence people is a no-brainer for the simple fact that media is everywhere and everything; it is central to American culture. To argue that people aren't influenced by media is to argue that they aren't influenced by culture, and you don't need to be Margaret Mead to know that's insane.

We may laugh at the idiots who light their heads on fire because Beavis and Butt-head did it. Or the guys who, taking a tip from Walt Disney's The Program lie down on the highway. But all of us are swayed in one way or another. The vast majority of media-induced actions don't make the AP wire because they are, well, banal.

When Fonzie brandished a library card on Happy Days library registration shot up nationwide. After a popular Budweiser campaign, people began greeting their pals, "Whassupp!" (To capitalize on the spots' popularity with children, J. C. Penney even sold "Whassup" kiddie T-shirts.) When Ally McBeal wore a certain style of pajamas, thousands of viewers asked retailers for them. It's the same thing with movies. ET and Reese's. Tom Cruise and Ray-Bans. Dirty Harry and 44 Magnums. And it's not just companies that exploit media's influence. Many large nonprofit groups—from the NAACP to the White House drug office to the American Medical Association—hire people to lobby Hollywood for favorable coverage.

Does violence in the media influence the real world? Of course it does. Cop shows and crime reports make us scared of other people, of going out at night, of helping out strangers. That is perhaps its primary effect. But there should be no doubt that watching violence can also lead to violence. To say that it can is not to say that it does in most circumstances, with most people, in most places. Nor is it to say that violent media creates violent behavior out of nowhere.

Whether someone's violent tendencies originated with an abusive parent or with Dirty Harry is on a certain level irrelevant; the fact remains that a steady diet of media blood and guts isn't good for some people, some of the time.

To say all this is simply to acknowledge an uncomfortable truth, one for which there is no easy solution. Censorship by righteous experts or government officials is not the answer. Even if you ignore the serious First Amendment issues involved, censorship schemes could at best treat only the symptoms. The real problem with the media is not overt violence, but an unchecked market that churns out content strictly for bucks. The only solutions, then, are far more radical: the establishment of a truly public broadcasting system, as opposed to the limp vessels of PBS and NPR. Let the corporate-owned networks program whatever garbage they like. Providing true alternatives to commercial media would give viewers more choices. And even if a fraction of the audience watches the alternative channels, their presence would help put things in perspective, onscreen and off.

CRITICAL THINKING QUESTIONS

1. Is McLaren's argument mainly descriptive or prescriptive? Provide specific examples from the text that signaled you to form your conclusion.
2. What value preferences do you think McLaren holds? What value conflicts do you think are common in the debate over media influence and violence?
3. Can you find an example of a *straw person* fallacy in McLaren's article? Recall the best way to check how fairly a position is being represented is to get the facts about all positions. What facts would be helpful to reduce the constructing of a straw person?
4. Strong language can often signal the fallacies of appealing to emotion or name calling. Be careful, though. Strong language does not always denote fallacies. Evaluate examples of strong language in McLaren's article. Does the language signal any appeals to emotion or name calling? How do you know?

Children's Media Skew Gender: Imbalance Delivers a Damaging Message: Girls Don't Matter

Geena Davis

USA Today (2007)

Few people know that my first "acting" role was *The Rifleman*, from 1960s TV. As little girls, my best friend and I wanted to be brave like the characters on that show, so when we played in her backyard I was often Lucas McCain, and she would be the son, Mark.

We didn't realize at the time how odd it was that there were few female role models, or how marginalized or simply invisible female characters were, especially in children's entertainment. Today, gender distortion remains entrenched in movies and TV aimed at young children like mine.

In 2005–06, the University of Southern California's Annenberg School of Communication conducted the most comprehensive analysis of children's movies and TV programming ever done. The research was commissioned by See Jane, a program I established at the non-profit Dads & Daughters to reduce gender imbalance and stereotyping in children's media.

Analyzing the 101 top-grossing G-rated movies released from 1990 through 2004, USC's research reveals that there are three male characters for every one female.

Children's TV does better on gender balance: Shows rated TVY (for children under 7) and TVY7 (for children 7+) have a male/female ratio of roughly 2-1, while TVG (for all ages) is nearly 1-1. It is troubling, though, that the imbalance is greatest in shows for the youngest viewers.

Of course, numerical balance isn't the whole story; character portrayals also matter. In films and TV for children, male characters are half as likely as females to be parents or married, and much more likely to be violent and dumb; those disparities are even greater for male characters of color. As for females in G-rated movies, about a third are either entertainers or royalty (compared with the 0.1% of the American women who are entertainers; the USA has no royalty).

Kids learn their value by seeing themselves reflected in the culture. If their reflection is visible and common, they can say, "I must count. I see myself." But what message are we sending children with so few female characters? Or when male relationships and female accomplishments are devalued?

We're teaching them that girls and women are less valuable, while options for boys and girls are determined primarily by gender. This message damages girls *and* boys.

See Jane is working with the industry, and parents, to improve children's earliest media exposure. Our goal: ensure that children see a balance of active and complex male and female characters. That way, girls and boys will grow up to empathize with and care more about each other's stories.

Oscar and Golden Globe winning actor Geena Davis founded See Jane to engage and educate content creators and the public on gender representation and its impact, so that future entertainment media aimed at children 11 and younger will include more—and more complex—female characters. For more information visit: www.seejane.org.

CRITICAL THINKING QUESTIONS

1. How good is the evidence Davis presents? Does she rely mainly on her experience in the entertainment industry or does she rely on information from other sources? What questions should you ask and answer when evaluating the research findings cited in the article?

2. What significant information is omitted from Davis's article? Assume she had an unlimited amount of space for more evidence and reasons. What other information do you need to consider before you make an educated decision about her conclusion?

3. Throughout the article, Davis implies the way boys and girls are portrayed in the media negatively influence the way the genders emphasize with each other. Do you think there could be other factors involved in the behavior of boys and girls? In other words, what possible rival causes could be involved in the way boys and girls are perceived in society?

Media Isn't Feeding Social Ills

Katie Strickland

UCLA Daily Bruin (2008)

When you have a problem and don't feel like doing anything to solve or even understand it, one of the most effective courses of action to take is to blame the media.

The French government did just this late last week when its lower house of parliament passed a bill that makes it illegal to incite "extreme thinness."

The targets of the proposed law are "pro-anorexic" Web sites, which give tips on how to maintain the disorder anorexia nervosa. The disorder is characterized by symptoms that include a refusal to maintain a healthy weight and an intense fear of gaining weight.

But the proposed legislation, which punishes offenders with fines and even prison, could also affect the fashion industry, magazines and various other forms of print and digital media.

The faulty logic of the bill is clear: Anorexia is the media's fault.

Of course, this is almost completely impossible to prove, said Marleen S. Williams, a psychology professor at Brigham Young University who researches the relationship between the media and anorexic women.

Her comment is supported by other scientific studies on the subject, which has linked anorexia to a host of factors, including an individual's genetic makeup and personality traits such as perfectionism.

The purpose of examining this example is not to ridicule the French government for its shortsightedness, however. Their actions represent a Western trend that the U.S. engages in frequently: blaming the media for everything.

Remember those teen girls who filmed themselves beating another girl so badly she lost her ability to hear and see on the left side of her face? The attackers, according to local Sheriff Grady Judd, had planned on posting the video on YouTube and MySpace.

During a press conference, Judd said, "YouTube and MySpace (have) to make drastic changes."

Yes, drastic changes need not be made by parents or people who assault others but by networking and video-hosting Web sites.

Even more cringe-worthy, the victim's father told local media that "MySpace is the anti-Christ for children." Apparently children never fought before the inception of MySpace. This example just happens to be the most recent and talked-about, but blaming the media is versatile and has been used for many years for many different problems. Unhappy with how badly your beloved President Bush does in polls? Make like Bill O'Reilly and blame the "heavily liberal" media.

If our nation's teenagers are too promiscuous, a parent can always chalk it up to that provocative Elvis Presley.

Even the media blames itself in order to attract viewers. After the shootings at Columbine, I vividly remember watching a news program's exclusive special about which bands or singers or movies or video games were at fault.

While it would be foolish to deny that media can contribute to these problems—body image issues, violence, perceived political bias—hoisting all responsibility onto news or entertainment does more harm than good.

Ignoring the many nuances of what may cause young women to starve themselves to death does not help or heal them. Indeed, directing focus away from the complex reality of the disease only makes true understanding that much more difficult to find.

The trouble with discussing our problems is that someone will have to take responsibility. So if we find that bad parenting or lapses in our educational system are responsible for youth violence, well, we'd have to change stuff. That requires even more time than it takes to pretend it's the media's fault and probably a lot more money.

When we blame media though, we don't have to do anything except become angry when problems that are not actually the media's fault continue to occur.

Even the phrase "the media" is misleading. It sounds like one entity that is cohesively working together toward some common goal, when in fact it describes a diverse and divergent category that includes television, books, movies, games, the Internet and comic books. Surely all of these forms could not possibly be functioning as one.

But we give "the media" more power than it actually has to pretend that we are helpless to counteract anything we deem is its fault. This gives us the perfect excuse to not act in the face of compelling problems.

The next time someone—politician, friend, even ourselves—blames a form of media for anything, do your best to view their claim through a critical eye. The knee-jerk reaction of blaming the media will only work so long as it appeases the public enough to stop demanding action from those who represent us.

CRITICAL THINKING QUESTIONS

1. Remember, before you begin to evaluate an article you should identify the issue, conclusion, and reasons. What is Strickland's argument? Is it descriptive or prescriptive? How can you tell?

2. In the debate over media influence, a common value conflict arises: collective versus individual responsibility. Which type of responsibility does Strickland appear to value and advocate? Point to specific parts of the article supporting Strickland's value preference.

3. Does the author make any descriptive assumptions in the passage? If so, recall that evidence is needed for assumptions to be factual claims. Does Strickland present evidence for her assumptions? How does the amount of evidence affect the effectiveness of the argument?

4. How strong is the evidence Strickland uses to support her conclusion? How would you recommend Strickland strengthen the evidence?

Snowed: Why Is the US News Media Silent on Global Warming?

Ross Gelbspan

MotherJones Magazine (2005)

When Southern California was inundated by a foot of rain, several feet of snow, and lethal mudslides earlier this year, the news reports made no mention of climate change—even though virtually all climate scientists agree that the first consequence of a warmer atmosphere is a marked increase in extreme weather events. When four hurricanes of extraordinary strength tore through Florida last fall, there was little media attention paid to the fact that hurricanes are made more intense by warming ocean surface waters. And when one storm dumped five feet of water on southern Haiti in 48 hours last spring, no coverage mentioned that an early manifestation of a warming atmosphere is a significant rise in severe downpours.

Though global climate change is breaking out all around us, the U.S. news media has remained silent. Not because climate change is a bad story—to the contrary: Conflict is the lifeblood of journalism, and the climate issue is riven with conflict. Global warming policy pits the United States against most of the countries of the world. It's a source of tension between the Bush administration and 29 states, nearly 100 cities, and scores of activist groups working to reduce emissions. And it has generated significant and acrimonious splits within the oil, auto, and insurance industries. These stories are begging to be written.

And they are being written—everywhere else in the world. One academic thesis completed in 2000 compared climate coverage in major U.S. and British newspapers and found that the issue received about three times as much play in the United Kingdom.

Britain's *Guardian*, to pick an obviously liberal example, accorded three times more coverage to the climate story than the *Washington Post*, more than twice that of the *New York Times*, and nearly five times that of the *Los Angeles Times*. In this country, the only consistent reporting on this issue comes from the *New York Times'* Andrew Revkin, whose excellent stories are generally consigned to the paper's Science Times section, and the Weather Channel—which at the beginning of 2004 started including references to climate change in its projections, and even hired an on-air climate expert.

Why the lack of major media attention to one of the biggest stories of this century? The reasons have to do with the culture of newsrooms, the misguided application of journalistic balance, the very human tendency to deny the magnitude of so overwhelming a threat, and, last though not least, a decade-long campaign of deception, disinformation, and, at times, intimidation by the fossil fuel lobby to keep this issue off the public radar screen.

The carbon lobby's tactics can sometimes be heavy-handed; one television editor told me that his network had been threatened with a withdrawal of oil and automotive advertising after it ran a report suggesting a connection between a massive flood and climate change. But the most effective campaigns have been more subtly coercive. In the early 1990s, when climate scientists began to suspect that our burning of coal and oil was changing the earth's climate, Western Fuels, then a $400 million coal cooperative, declared in its annual report that it was enlisting several scientists who were skeptical about climate change—Patrick Michaels, Robert Balling, and S. Fred Singer—as spokesmen. The coal industry paid these and a handful of other skeptics some $1 million over a three-year period and sent them around the country to speak to the press and the public. According to internal strategy papers I obtained at the time, the purpose of the campaign was "to reposition global warming as theory (not fact)," with an emphasis on targeting "older, less educated males," and "younger, low-income women" in districts that received their electricity from coal, and who preferably had a representative on the House Energy and Commerce Committee.

The Western Fuels campaign was extraordinarily successful. In a *Newsweek* poll conducted in 1991, before the spin began, 35 percent of respondents said they "worry a great deal" about global warming. By 1997 that figure had dropped by one-third, to 22 percent.

Then as now, a prime tactic of the fossil fuel lobby centered on a clever manipulation of the ethic of journalistic balance. Any time reporters wrote stories about global warming, industry-funded naysayers demanded equal time in the name of balance. As a result, the press accorded the same weight to the industry-funded skeptics as it did to mainstream scientists, creating an enduring confusion in the public mind. To this day, many people are unsure whether global warming is real.

Journalistic balance comes into play when a story involves opinion: Should gay marriage be legal? Should we invade Iraq? Should we promote bilingual education or English immersion? For such stories an ethical journalist is obligated to give each competing view its most articulate presentation and roughly equivalent space.

But when the subject is a matter of fact, the concept of balance is irrelevant. What we know about the climate comes from the largest and most rigorously peer-reviewed scientific collaboration in history—the findings of more than 2,000 scientists from 100 countries reporting to the United Nations as the Intergovernmental Panel on Climate Change. The IPCC's conclusions, that the burning of fossil fuels is indeed causing significant shifts in the earth's climate, have been corroborated by the American Academy for the Advancement of Science, the American Geophysical Union, the American Meteorological Society, and the National Academy of Sciences. D. James Baker, former administrator of the National Oceanic and Atmospheric Administration, echoed many scientists when he said, "There is a better scientific consensus on this than on any other issue I know—except maybe Newton's second law of dynamics."

Granted, there are a few credentialed scientists who still claim climate change to be inconsequential. To give them their due, a reporter should learn where the weight of scientific opinion falls—and reflect that balance in his or her reporting. That would give mainstream scientists 95 percent of the story, with the skeptics getting a paragraph or two at the end.

But because most reporters don't have the time, curiosity, or professionalism to check out the science, they write equivocal stories with counterposing quotes that play directly into the hands of the oil and coal industries by keeping the public confused.

Another major obstacle is the dominant culture of newsrooms. The fastest-rising journalists tend to make their bones covering politics, and so the lion's share of press coverage of climate change has focused on the political machinations surrounding global warming rather than its consequences. In 1997, when the Senate overwhelmingly passed a resolution against ratifying the Kyoto Protocol, the vote was covered as a political setback for the Clinton administration at the hands of congressional Republicans. (Predictably, the press paid little attention to a $13 million industry-funded advertising blitz in the run-up to that vote.) When President Bush pulled out of the Kyoto negotiating process in 2001, the coverage again focused not on the harm that would befall the planet as a result but on the resulting diplomatic tensions between the United States and the European Union.

Prior to 2001, Bush had declared he would not accept the findings of the IPCC—it was, after all, a U.N. body. "The jury's still out," he said, and called instead for a report from the National Academy of Sciences. That report, duly produced one month later, while professing uncertainty about exactly how much warming was attributable to one factor or another, affirmed that human activity was a major contributor. In covering Bush's call for an American climate report, few reporters bothered to check whether the academy had already taken a position; had they done so, they would have found that as early as 1992, it had recommended strong measures to minimize climate impacts.

Finally, coverage of the climate crisis is one of many casualties of media conglomeration. With most news outlets now owned by major corporations and faceless investors, marketing strategy is replacing news judgment; celebrity coverage is on the rise, even as newspapers cut staff and fail to provide their remaining reporters the time they need to research complex stories.

Ultimately, however, the responsibility for the failure of the press lies neither with the carbon lobby nor with newsroom culture or even the commercialization of the news. It lies in the indifference or laziness of hundreds of editors and thousands of reporters who are betraying their professional obligation to their readers and viewers. Climate change constitutes an immense drama of very uncertain outcome. It is as important and compelling a story as any reporter could hope to work on. Perversely, for so great an opportunity, it is threatening to become the shame of the American press.

CRITICAL THINKING QUESTIONS

1. What assumptions does Gelbspan make about human nature in the article? What assumptions does Gelbspan make about the role of media in society? If a reader held the opposite assumptions, would the conclusion necessarily follow from the reasons?
2. What kinds of evidence does the author rely on? What questions do you need to ask to judge the quality of the evidence?
3. Gelbspan creates a causal link between the Western Fuels campaign and the *Newsweek* polls conducted about global

warming in 1991 and 1997. Why might this attributed causation be problematic? What should you do to determine whether rival causes are at play?

4. Did the author come to the most reasonable conclusion in the article? If so, defend the author's conclusion. If not, what other possible alternate conclusions are reasonable?

CNN's Global Warming Special Typifies Liberal Bias of Climate Coverage

Dan Gainor and Amy Menefee

Business and Media Institute (2005)

It's the end of the world as we know it—at least that's what "CNN Presents" and reporter Miles O'Brien would have us believe. CNN unveiled an hour-long, one-sided report detailing the global warming terror that could mean "a ruined world."

On Sunday night, March 27, O'Brien's "Melting Point: Tracking the Global Warming Threat" cited almost every one of the left-wing environmental movement's hot buttons about climate change: claiming it's already a fact; preaching an apocalyptic threat; blaming mankind for temperature fluctuations; bemoaning the danger to polar bears and even visiting the island of Tuvalu that is, according to O'Brien, "flooding from the inside out."

He continued: "But now the scientific debate is largely over. There is overwhelming consensus that the threat is real, that humans are at least part of the cause, and that something must be done." He repeated this declaration throughout the program in different ways. One of those was by choosing an overwhelming number of experts who agreed with him. Out of at least 25 people quoted on the show, only four expressed any skepticism about global warming even though the science is far from settled. That's a ratio of nearly 6-to-1.

At one point, he added: "Where there is fossil fuel smoke there is heat, if not fire. Here's the verdict from a United Nations report signed by more than 2,000 scientists from around the world. Most of the warming observed over the past 50 years is attributable to human activity."

While O'Brien dwelled on the numbers of the supporters for global warming theory, he didn't mention that there are thousands of opponents. Frederick Seitz, the past president of the National Academy of Sciences and president emeritus of Rockefeller University, circulated a document in 1998, the "Oregon Petition," which gathered more than 17,000 names from scientists in various fields. According to Seitz, "This [Kyoto] treaty is, in our opinion, based upon flawed ideas."

Even though Russia recently signed on to Kyoto, a treaty designed to cut emissions that allegedly contribute to global warming, it did so over the objections of its own academy of sciences.

But O'Brien didn't stop at claiming he had numbers on his side. He worked to undermine anyone who disagreed. One of the people he interviewed was former journalist Ross Gelbspan, an author of two books on climate change. O'Brien elaborated: "His latest, *Boiling Point*, documents coal and oil companies bankrolling some scientists he calls greenhouse skeptics." At least Gelbspan was honest about his own agenda: "I sort of moved from being a journalist to an advocate to an activist."

O'Brien quoted Gelbspan claiming that "the fossil fuel lobby spent huge amounts of money on a very pervasive campaign of deception and disinformation, which was designed to persuade the public and policy makers that this issue was stuck on uncertainty."

The story didn't include any background on Gelbspan. But a Web site devoted to one of his books describes him as follows: "As special projects editor of *The Boston Globe*, he conceived, directed, and edited a series of articles that won a Pulitzer Prize in 1984." That sounds great, but apparently the *Globe* didn't think so. The Pulitzer award for that year lists seven names from the *Globe* all for that one story, but Gelbspan isn't one of them.

O'Brien followed up that interview with a few quotes from Pat Michaels, a senior fellow in environmental studies at the Cato Institute, professor of environmental sciences at the University of Virginia, and author of a recent book on global warming called Meltdown. Rather than let Michaels make his points, O'Brien undermined him with an introduction as "one of the researchers who has received funding from the fossil fuel industry, more than $150,000 worth." He added the half statement/half question: "That has to taint everything you say, doesn't it?"

None of the roughly two dozen other people on the program had the sources of their funding questioned, including journalist-turned-activist Gelbspan. O'Brien didn't even mention Michaels' recent book, though he did so for Gelbspan.

After Michaels was done, O'Brien decided to undermine him one more time: "Michaels' position is in the minority. The consensus is the scientific debate is all but over." He then turned to Gus Speth, dean of the Yale School of Forestry and Environmental Studies, who continued the criticism. According to Speth, "In many cases, the same personalities have been the critics for this almost 30 years now." What Speth left out is that roughly 30 years ago, many in the scientific community were arguing the earth was in the midst of an ice age.

That was just one of many things omitted from the story, Michaels told the Business & Media Institute. He said O'Brien ignored an entire body of scientific evidence.

"When human warming starts, it continues at a constant rate, and that rate is very modest," Michaels said. "That argument has never been defeated." Michaels' book, *Meltdown*, is subtitled *The Predictable Distortion of Global Warming by Scientists, Politicians, and the Media.*

"Had I still been writing the book, this show would have been a chapter," Michaels said.

O'Brien also included some discussion of how environmentalists claim to predict the weather for the next 100 years. After describing predictive climate modeling in a highly positive fashion, he spoke with MIT climatologist Richard Lindzen, who reminded him that people "understand that forecasting weather is inaccurate beyond two or three days."

The story found little time to go into the criticisms of the analysis of temperature readings that have appeared in *The Wall Street Journal* recently. One graph, nicknamed the "hockey stick" because of its shape, has been used for years to claim that temperatures rose suddenly in the 20th century. However, some of that data was analyzed and found faulty. The statistical technique was biased and tended to draw hockey-stick forms. Even its creator, Dr. Michael Mann from the University of Virginia, admitted this according to the *Journal*. He's also corrected the other problems, but claims they didn't impact the overall result and won't release all of the data so his work can be checked.

CNN's "Melting Point" repeated several other ongoing flaws in media coverage of this environmental debate that were detailed in a November 2004 Business & Media Institute (BMI) study. That analysis, "Destroying America to Save the World," explained how the media skew the debate by claiming the "science" of Kyoto is settled when it isn't.

O'Brien's story relied overwhelmingly on "experts" who believe in global warming and didn't include an opposing view until nearly a half-hour into the program. This followed the media trend. According to the study, "Broadcast news programs presented the claims of liberal environmentalists that global warming is a given, that mankind is to blame for it, or both, 55 percent of the time (77 stories)." O'Brien only had one program, so he said it as often as he could.

In addition, he made several other typical errors covered in the BMI study, including:

- ***Blaming President Bush***: O'Brien said: "President Bush opposes Kyoto" and implied Bush is to blame for the U.S. not being part of the treaty. He never mentioned that the Senate voted 95-0 against Kyoto. While O'Brien interviewed Sen. John McCain (R-Ariz.), he didn't mention McCain voted for the resolution that opposed Kyoto along with liberal Sens. John Kerry (D-Mass.) and Barbara Mikulski (D-Md.).

- ***The Cost of Kyoto***: The story gave the projected U.S. cost of signing Kyoto as more than $400 billion each year with a possible loss of 4.9 million jobs. However, it relied on a quote from President Bush that gave the impression it was his opinion. It's actually the result of a U.S. Energy Information Administration analysis. O'Brien did fail to compare the numbers he cited for costs of Kyoto with the costs from a global warming scenario. His numbers for warming over the next 100 years: "UN estimates somewhere between $20 and $150 billion in property damage in the U.S. alone." Using his highest estimate and comparing it to the lowest figure from the Energy Department, the cost of signing the treaty would still be about 133 times more.

- ***Polar Bears Threatened***: "But the bears are in trouble, big trouble," said O'Brien, claiming they could be wiped out. "For them, it's a matter of survival." The networks trot out polar bears any time they want to tug at the heartstrings for global warming and Sunday night's broadcast was no different. In Pat Michaels' book *Meltdown*, he explained how the left-wing environmental movement takes advantage of "cute and furry" creatures to win the warming debate. "NGOs [Non-governmental organizations] know the value of a marquee species. Algae won't do. Polar bears will," he stated.

At the end of the program, the voiceover described "CNN Presents" as "separating fact from fiction." It didn't.

CRITICAL THINKING QUESTIONS

1. Recall in the last set of questions you inferred what Gelbspan's descriptive assumptions were. This article critiques Gelbspan. How do you think these authors' assumptions compare to Gelbspan's?
2. Identify common values in conflict in the debate about global warming and human actions.
3. Do the authors use any fallacious tactics in the article? What differentiates these reasoning tricks from actual reasons? How does the fallacious reasoning affect the overall argument?

4. Throughout the article, Gainor and Menefee refer to the one-sidedness of the news media and the media's inability to present both sides of the issue. Did Gainor and Menefee present or preempt a counterargument to their own article? How would preempting a counterargument strengthen Gainor and Menefee's own conclusion?

Preventing Suicide by Influencing Mass-Media Reporting: The Viennese Experience 1980–1996

Elmar Etzersdorfer and Gernot Sonneck

Archives of Suicide Research (1998)

Introduction

Since the beginning of suicide prevention very different strategies and approaches to prevent suicidal behaviour have been addressed. Apart from direct interventions with the individual (pairs, families or groups), approaches which focus on a broader level have been discussed but for a long time had a reputation of being unscientific or at least very difficult to evaluate. Concepts like primary prevention of suicidal behaviour are widely accepted as desirable, but whether it is really possible to be primarily preventive remained a different question. One area of research which investigates influences on suicidal behaviour on a macro-perspective is the possible influence of media reports on suicidal behaviour. Phillips (1974) used the term "Werther effect", which in the meantime has become widely used to describe imitative suicidal behaviour. It refers to Goethe's novel, which was blamed as having lead several young men to commit suicide in the same way as young Werther after the publication of the book.

A lot of subsequent studies dealt with the matter of media reports and suicide, and the most influential studies will be reviewed here. First, the influence of newspaper reports was investigated. Results were inconclusive (for review see Sonneck et al., 1994); nevertheless, several studies found that imitation was the best explanation to understand an increase of suicides, similar to the early study by Phillips (1974).

Later the effects of television reports were also studied, both fictional (Berman, 1988; Gould & Shaffer, 1986; Phillips, 1982) and non-fictional stories (Kessler, 1988; Phillips & Carstensen, 1986). One of the most influential studies was that by Schmidtke and Hafner (1988), finding additional suicides after a weekly serial in six episodes, dealing with the fictional suicide story of a young man, which was presented from different points of view in each film.

Phillips added studies regarding suicides hidden as car crashes (Phillips, 1977) or airplane accidents (Phillips, 1978), showing that imitational suicides did occur using these rare means also. Imitative suicidal behaviour has also been described independent from mass media, such as reports about suicide epidemics in psychiatric hospitals (e.g. Zemishlany et al., 1987), or in a school (Callahan, 1996). And, finally, imitation has also been discussed in connection with other behaviour than suicide, such as mass murder (Cantor & Sheehan, 1996).

Nevertheless, most of the above mentioned studies started after the increase of suicidal behaviour or suspected imitational behaviour had occurred and retrospectively tried to find an imitation effect. Our investigation in Vienna seems to be the only field experiment so far in this area (Phillips & Lesyna, 1995). This paper describes investigation efforts regarding media reports and imitative suicidal behaviour in the Viennese subway system and summarizes the experiences as well as the conclusions drawn from this research. At the end of the paper strategies for further research are proposed.

Methods

This study was designed as a prospective field experiment. The starting point was that after starting the subway system in 1978, it became increasingly accepted as a means to commit suicide in the eighties. Furthermore it was recognized that mass media reported about these events in a very dramatic and extensive way (headlines, pictures of the deceased, etc.). A working group of the Austrian Association for Suicide Prevention (OVSKK) was established to study mass-media reporting. Using the literature on imitative suicide then available, the actual reports in the Viennese newspapers as well as the clinical experience of the participants, hypotheses of a possible relation between media reports and imitative suicidal behaviour were formulated (Table 1). It was suggested that certain reports, that could be found after the first subway suicides and attempts, could trigger additional suicides, something Phillips and Lesyna (1995) recently called a "natural advertisement" for the idea of suicide. A differentiation was made between on the one hand aspects that could be a trigger through their expressed attitude and on the other hand aspects of a report that would increase the attention, making it more probable that someone recognizes it. We added suggestions about how to reduce the effect, which could be called an advertisement for the idea of life.

TABLE 1   Hypotheses Used for the Media Campaign
(Sonneck et al., 1994)

The trigger-effect will be the bigger:

- the more details of the special methods are reported
- the more suicide is reported as being inconceivable ("he had everything life can give")
- the more the motives are reported to be romantic ("to be forever united")
- the more simplifications are used ("suicide because of bad news")

The attention will be bigger:

- if the report is printed on the front page
- if the term "suicide" is used in the headline
- if there is a photograph of the person, who committed suicide
- if the attitude of the person is implicitly described as being heroic and desirable ("he had to do that in this situation")

The effect will be smaller:

- if more alternatives are shown (where is it possible to find help in such a situation?)
- if there are reports about a crisis that was overcome and did not result in suicide
- if readers are provided with background information on suicidal behaviour and suicide in general (such as what to do with someone who expresses suicidal thoughts)

The general assumption was twofold: A person in a suicidal crisis is ambivalent and therefore possibly prone to suggestions in both directions. A media report which allows one to identify with the person described and its suicide and to experience it as support for the (already existing and possibly urging) idea of killing oneself, may work as the last trigger for the decision to commit suicide. Another aspect was that a person who is constricted in a severe crisis and cannot think of a way out could find the solution for his unbearable situation formulated in the media report.

After formulating these hypotheses a press campaign was launched in mid-1987, informing journalists about possible negative consequences of their reporting and offering alternative ways of dealing with those issues. The effect of the campaign was that media reports changed markedly and immediately. Reports on suicidal behaviour in general became much more moderate than before, and for the first time several subway suicides were even left unreported. Continuous observation of media reporting allowed subsequent reaction in providing again and again the media with the guidelines.

Results

Figure 1 shows the number of subway suicides and attempts in Vienna from 1980 to 1996 (for half-years). In the first years following the implementation of the subway system, only a few suicides or attempts occurred; but starting about 1983, an increase of both suicides and attempts was found. After the media campaign in mid-1987 a sharp drop of suicides and attempts can be found. The decrease from the first half of 1987 to the second half is 84.2% for suicides and attempts taken together (n = 19 to n = 3). In the subsequent years the number of suicides and attempts stayed low, although up to five events per half-year can be found. The level of 1983 to 1987, nevertheless, has not been reached until 1996.

Discussion

The results show that following a media campaign in Vienna, which was launched after an increase of suicides and attempts, the subway suicides and attempts decreased and remained on a rather low level since. The preceding increase was not correlated to an extension of the transport system, nor is the drop correlated to a similar decrease in the overall number of suicides. Thus the most probable explanation is that the changed reports led to the drop of subway suicides and attempts (for more details see Sonneck et al., 1994).

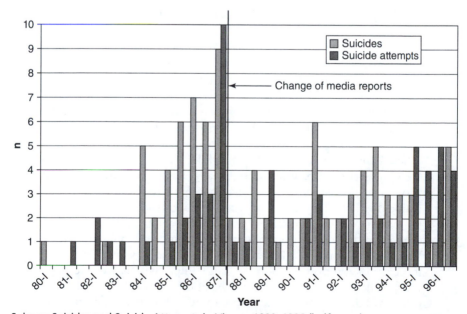

Subway Suicides and Suicide Attempts in Vienna 1980–1996 (half-years).

The overall suicide rate also slightly decreased in Vienna and in Austria in the next years, nevertheless without a sharp decline such as was seen with subway suicides. There was no increase in other methods of suicide pointing to a possible shift of method only. The further development of subway suicides and attempts suggests that some suicides at the peak have occurred additionally. The alternative explanation that they occurred earlier only but would have occurred anyway is not supported by our data, as in this case the numbers in the time before and after the drop should level (for a detailed analysis of this alternative explanation, see Phillips, 1974; or Schmidtke & Hafner, 1988).

Subway suicides are a public way to commit suicide, therefore media are more interested in it than in other methods. The subway system has to be stopped for a while after a suicide, witnesses in the station have to watch it and may be interested to read about it subsequently. A further reason for the dramatic reports in the Viennese mass-media in the eighties might have been that subway suicides and attempts had been new events, as the whole system had been started only a few years ago.

A conclusion from our study is that it is possible to change media reports, but it is necessary to state that this is not possible by forcing journalists. Journalists are used to defending their freedom to report about any issue or abstain, and of course it is not possible to forbid reports about suicide totally. Besides, it is not clear whether this really would be the most favourable way to deal with suicides in the mass media, or whether there is a preventive potential of reports as well that can be used. Our approach was to inform journalists and leave it up to them and their responsibility to make their own conclusions. Nevertheless we provided guidelines, which offer possible alternative ways of reporting (see Table 1).

Another experience in the last ten years was that it is necessary to "refresh" the knowledge or willingness of journalists from time to time. The number of subway suicides and attempts in the last years (see Figure 1) might be interpreted as a new slight increase; and, in fact, reports about subway suicides have been published again in some cases. We found that, at least in Austria, often the youngest or inexperienced journalist has to prepare the report about a suicide; someone who may be unaware about possible imitational effects. This has to do with the fact that local stories are at the bottom of the hierarchy of reporting, which again contributes to the fact that the responsibility for this issues often changes. Our strategy in Austria is to be aware of reports in newspapers and in the case of a report to send the guidelines, which are one page only, to the journalist and the newspaper and to ask for their discussion. Furthermore we are spreading the information and the guidelines among journalists, if members of the Austrian Association for Suicide Prevention get in touch with journalists for whatever reason.

Conclusions

1. It is possible to prevent suicide by influencing mass-media reports.

Although results of the studies on imitational suicides are inconclusive (e.g., Merskey, 1996), there is strong evidence that media reports about suicide may trigger additional suicides (for an overview see Phillips & Lesyna, 1995). From our study it can be concluded that it is possible to prevent imitative suicides by influencing the reports. Nevertheless many questions are up for discussion, and as our study seems to be the only field experiment in this area so far, we can only encourage to replicate it or create similar designs for further field experiments. Our study is not necessarily a proof for our hypotheses about the mechanisms of imitation, nor necessarily for all of the hypotheses used. So far it has to be concluded that we particular still do not know which reports about suicide do not trigger imitative suicides. The TV-series, which have been studied by Schmidtke and Hafner, were intended as information about suicide, tried to be not sensational and nevertheless triggered additional suicides as shown in the very sophisticated investigation (Schmidtke & Hafner, 1988).

A different strategy is to try to use media reports to spread information about help available, about alternatives to suicide and so on, which has been proposed in our media guidelines (see Table 1). Nevertheless it is well known, that only "bad news is good news", therefore a report about a crisis that has been overcome will in many cases be less interesting for mass-media than a very sensational suicide. A similar proposal is to make use of knowledge from advertising to prevent imitative suicides (Merskey, 1996), something which has been worked on already by Phillips and Lesyna (1995).

2. Methodological difficulties

It is rarely possible to explore imitational behaviour in a single case, in the way that someone would report that because he read an article he now will kill himself. Even if this were the case one would have to discuss which influence a mass-media report actually has had, and how imitation took place. Thus there are methodological difficulties.

(a) If a macro-level is studied (usually with aggregate data), it is only possible to find correlations, which, nevertheless, allow to conclude whether an influence of reports is the most probable explanation of an increase or a decrease (as in our study). There are many proposals for further studies on this level, which are needed, and we refer to the excellent review of Phillips and Lesyna (1995).

(b) On an individual level imitation is very difficult to assess, apart from the fact that this information will rarely be available. Nevertheless, all studies at least use hypotheses about the transformation of reports into behaviour, which then is individually motivated. The term "imitation" refers to the behaviour, the underlying psychological processes are more difficult to approach. Identification, particularly, is a very complex phenomenon, which in psychoanalysis is understood as a developmental as well as a pathological process (Abend & Porder, 1986). Taiminen (1992) provided one of the few studies describing intrapsychic mechanisms in an actual case of "suicide contagion", making use of the model of projective identification. In the case of media reports there is no object available of course, as it is necessary in projective identification in the strict sense. Taiminen (1992), using a intrapsychic formulation of projective identification, described that in this case an actual object was replaced by internal object representations, on which unbearable feelings were projected on.

Modelling effects have been described on work in imitation, as well as an "infectious disease model" (Hazell, 1993), consisting of host susceptibility, modes of transmission, degree of virulence, and dose dependency. Martin (1996) took a somewhat different approach, showing that adolescents who had a higher exposure to television suicide also more often had a history of suicide attempts, had higher depression scores and had more often experienced suicides. There seems to be a selective process by persons on risk, paying more attention to suicide reports (whether fictional or nonfictional) and thus increasing the exposure and facilitating imitational behaviour as well.

It remains another area of research to further elucidate how an identification takes place psychologically, what may facilitate imitational behaviour psychologically, and also what may make alternatives more attracting.

Thus there are very different areas of research involved in further studies of media reports and suicidal behaviour. Although there are many open questions, the Viennese experiences show that it is possible to prevent imitative suicides by influencing media reports.

CRITICAL THINKING QUESTIONS

1. Were you able to identify the argument (conclusion and reasons) within the article? Often multiple conclusions are present within a given article. Find another conclusion the

authors make and explain the reasoning structure behind the argument. In this case, does having multiple conclusions strengthen or weaken the article as a whole? Why do you think that is the case?

2. Is the article mainly descriptive or prescriptive? What does this approach mean for the authors' argument? What type of information or reasoning would the authors need to have to express the other form (either prescriptive or descriptive) of argument?

3. When reading an article with many statistics, what questions do you ask yourself to determine whether the statistics are reliable? Evaluate the worth of the statistics within Etzersdorfer and Sonneck's article. Is any of the data deceptive or unclear? Which statistics do you find most compelling?

4. As you further examine the statistics in the article, what significant information do you think is missing from the data provided by the authors? (Remember, significant omitted information is information that would shape your reaction to the persuasiveness of reasoning of an article.)

Essay Questions

1. Recall from Chapter 14 of *Asking the Right Questions* the dangers of belief perseverance when forming and reading arguments. Locate examples in the articles in this section that illustrate belief perseverance. How is the tendency of personal beliefs persevering an obstacle to critically strong arguments?

2. After reading all of the articles in this section about the influence of media, you should have discovered both similarities and differences among the arguments. What are some of the common value conflicts and descriptive assumptions present within the debate over the media? Which authors share similar values and assumptions? Which authors have opposite beliefs and assumptions? Support your assertions with specific examples from each text.

3. Remember, all articles are not equal in worth. By this point, you should understand the worth of an article after applying the critical thinking methods you learned in *Asking the Right Questions*. Choose the article you believe is the strongest and weakest in terms of critical thinking and write an essay explaining the strengths and weaknesses of each. Guide the reader step by step through your critical evaluation of the articles. If you could give each author one piece of advice to strengthen their arguments, what would you recommend?

CHAPTER 19

READINGS CLUSTER 5

What Role Does Physical Appearance Play in Our Lives?

Society today is drenched with "wonder products" claiming to make people more beautiful, celebrity supermodels influencing our perceptions of beauty, and increasingly high rates of plastic surgery. People are constantly altering their consumption patterns and bodies in pursuit of an elusive ideal of beauty. However, the influence of appearance in our daily lives expands far beyond a personal gratification in being beautiful. What if people treat ugly people differently? What if beautiful people live longer? What if altering our appearance to cater to societal ideals of beauty will actually make us happier people? The articles in this section introduce arguments addressing the role of beauty and appearance in our lives. Read the articles equipped with the tools and procedures you've learned through your study of *Asking the Right Questions*.

Face Value Hidden Camera Investigation: Do Looks Really Matter?

Keith Morrison

NBC News (2004)

Anybody who watches reality TV knows that when it comes to landing a date with a beautiful woman, the "Average Joe" doesn't stand much of a chance against a handsome hunk. But does the preference for physical attractiveness go deeper than just romance? Even when looks shouldn't count—for instance, at a bank or the doctor—are beautiful people treated better than everyone else? With our hidden cameras watching, Dateline set up some tests to find out.

Everybody knows how much importance we attach to beauty, maybe too much sometimes. But have you ever wondered how different life might be if you were just a little better looking?

Anthony Bernard and Allison Meiersonne are models. Good looks help them make a living. Both of them know they are lucky—it's what they were born with. But we wondered if their genetic advantage in the beauty department could be helping them in ways they never imagined?

For example, would a stranger come to their aid before assisting an average-looking person? Might they be receiving better service from repair people? Do people trust them more, just because they're good looking?

"A person's physical attractiveness—the look that they're basically born with—impacts every individual literally from birth to death," says Dr. Gordon Patzer, dean of the College of Business Administration at Roosevelt University. He's spent 30 years studying and writing about physical attractiveness. "People are valued more who are higher in physical attractiveness. As distasteful at that might be, that's the reality."

Valued more? We wondered and decided to find a group of average, nice looking individuals and super, highly attractive people to test this attractiveness phenomenon. We looked for people with similar traits: the same race, no discernible accents, similar age groups. That way the focus would be exclusively on attractiveness.

So we hired models Anthony and Allison, and asked two NBC employees, Loren and another Anthony, to hit the streets, a bank, an auto shop, and even ride the bus, all the time wearing hidden cameras to see just how much looks matter.

First, we gave our foursome folders filled with papers and had them drop the contents on a New York City street. Would anyone stop to help?

When model Allison drops her file, there seems to be a sudden change in the weather. Is it raining men? A man even uses his cane to stop the pages from flying away.

"It was just amazing how people would flock to me to clean it up," says Allison. "I have dropped my purse and wallet and people always help me pick it up. But I never really thought about if somebody else dropped their wallet, maybe they wouldn't help them. It just seems strange to me."

NBC staffer Loren is about to be that someone else. She drops the papers and people step by, rather than stop. About a dozen people pass by before, finally, a woman offers help.

But that's nothing compared to our other NBC colleague, Anthony. When he drops the folder, the sidewalk literally clears.

Even as he spreads out the papers he's supposedly collecting, people just walk on by.

"I thought, hey I'm dressed in a shirt and a tie," says Anthony. "I looked pretty professional, so maybe someone may stop and help me out. And people just kept stepping over."

"I felt embarrassed," says Loren. "You know wait a second, I think I'm somewhat attractive. Why didn't anyone help me?"

Model Anthony wouldn't know how that feels. He drops the folder and immediately an entire family stops to help. We wondered if this was just random chance, or is something else going on? We asked Dr. Patzer about our findings.

"That was a classic example of everything we find in the scholarly research that we do," says Dr. Patzer. "Those of higher physical attractiveness are automatically or immediately assisted, provided help."

And, as we saw with the family helping Anthony, it's not just about appealing to the opposite sex. While our research was not scientific, Dr. Patzer says more controlled studies do show people go out of their way to help attractive people of the same and opposite sex because they want to be liked and accepted by these good looking people.

We watched for this willingness to help when our test subjects stood on the street for five minutes seeming hopelessly lost, not asking anybody for assistance, just waiting to see if any kind soul would notice and stop.

Our NBC volunteers had no luck, but our super-attractive models were a different story. Allison had lots of helpers. A man even rolled down his car window to offer assistance. And model Anthony? He'll never be lost.

"I would hold my map and I'd be looking at the map and looking around and I'd make eye contact with someone and boom, they'd be reeled in," says Anthony.

"The lady walks past him, comes back, offers a large explanation of the layout of the city, but even does an ultimate trust . . . and offers the general part of the city in which she lives," says Dr. Patzer. "So it verifies very well again we trust more those people of higher physical attractiveness."

Trust? We watched to see what would happen when our subjects ask passersby for change of a dollar. Everyone did pretty well here, but there were differences, especially when it came to trust.

Many people did not stop or respond to NBC's Anthony. But for model Anthony, not only did more people stop, but they seemed to feel Anthony was safer, more honest. Like foreign tourists who weren't even sure how much change equals a dollar, so they held out their money and let Anthony take the correct amount.

"We had situations where people were going out of their way to try to do stuff for us that other people didn't get," he says.

For Allison, even if people couldn't find the change to give her, they would offer helpful suggestions. And she says that people just start conversations with here, something we saw when she and Loren went for a bus ride during rush hour. We wondered if anyone would offer them a seat. While sitting proved not to be an option for either of them that morning, one man, who starts out standing equidistant between Loren and Allison, strikes up a conversation with Allison for the entire bus ride.

"He did see me and he chose to speak and maybe flirt a little bit with her," says Loren. "And I felt like the third wheel."

"There are things that happen everyday in daily life and you just don't think about, wow, maybe this person did this to me because I am maybe an attractive woman and they're interested in pursuing me or something like that," says Allison. "It's very interesting."

So does the world seems like a more accommodating and friendly place to her?

"Yeah, sometimes people are just more willing to help us," says Allison. "It's strange, but you're given more credibility and you're given a lot more attention when you're attractive looking I guess."

In fact, many people seem to want to help the truly attractive on their journeys to anywhere, which we learned when we had our subjects ask for directions. They're going to approach people this time, walk right up and ask how to find a place that's actually two blocks away.

Nobody was treated rudely, but again, we saw some special treatment. People who simply overheard Allison's inquiry would come over to help. And only Allison was actually escorted to her destination.

But we wondered about something else. When time is of the essence, would people still be so accommodating to our models? It's lunch time and everyone seems to want to go to a particular sandwich shop. The goal for our group is to try to cut the line. Shockingly, everyone is able to find someone to go ahead of. But again, the reactions are different. With our NBCers they are allowed in and the interaction, the conversation just stops. But with Allison, the person she cuts continues the conversation while they wait in line. And the women model Anthony went ahead of seem thrilled to have to wait a little longer to get their lunch.

But what about when the stakes are higher, like when money is involved, or when there is a potential to be ripped off? And might good looks ever be a hindrance? Do beautiful people get better service, better deals, even better medical treatment?

We've seen that life is not necessarily fair. It's even a different world at an auto garage.

With the help of the AAA, we had cars checked over to make sure they were in good working order. Now each of our group will make a trip to the same garage asking for an oil change. Will anyone be told they needed unnecessary repairs?

Everyone receives appropriate service for an appropriate charge, but model Anthony does receive some different treatment.

"He just seemed enamored and was telling me that I should be on television that I looked like a movie star," Anthony says of the man at the shop.

"Did he give you a deal or anything?" asked Allison.

"No, he didn't," says Anthony. "He didn't even cut me any kind of a deal (you know that happens sometimes people get enamored and throw in an extra thing and say don't worry about it) but it was more that he was just so complimentary."

And good looking individuals get different treatment in some situations you might least expect it, such as a doctor's office.

"We see in medical interactions, patients who go to physicians, and those of higher physical attractiveness, the physicians will spend more time with that person and will also spend more time answering individual questions that that person asked," says Dr. Patzer.

And this special treatment starts very early on.

"For example, in a nursery, before newborn babies are released from a hospital, those babies who are higher in physical attractiveness, at this level defined as more cute, are touched more, held more and spoken to more," says Dr. Patzer, who notes the trend continues in school. "You see that those teachers when they interact with children of higher physical attractiveness, they ask more questions, they prompt them for more answers. We expect those children to do better and consequently they fulfill our expectations and they actually do do better."

And says Dr. Patzer, we are just hard wired to respond more favorably to attractive people. Even studies with babies show they will look more intently and longer at prettier faces.

"This is something anthropologically that has existed for as long as history exists," he says.

However, we did find a situation where looks did not matter. At the bank, where we inquired about rates for an auto loan, the information was punched into a computer and the same rate was given to everyone.

For the bank loan, it didn't seem to make any difference, and yet if Dr. Patzer's theory is correct, presumably it would be easier to get a loan if you're better looking.

"And that offers us a glimmer of hope," says Dr. Patzer. "Where we're taking objective data, statistics and numbers, putting them into a computer program to get a decision, when we take it out of an individuals hands, it takes the differential treatment out of the equation.

Of course though, in life, we interact all the time with people who do, however unconsciously, make judgments about us based on what we look like.

So it does make a difference, and most likely always will, no matter what we try to do about it. But it doesn't hurt to know that next time we're drawn to one human being over another, that our reasons might not be quite be quite as rational, nor even as fair, as we like to think they are.

In fact, Dr. Patzer says even justice is not blind to beauty. Studies have shown that juries find arguments more persuasive if they're made by attractive lawyers. But if beauty's in the eye of the beholder, getting 12 jurors to agree beyond a reasonable doubt on who's attractive could make for some long deliberations.

CRITICAL THINKING QUESTIONS

1. As you read the article, first consider what specific issue the essay addresses and what the conclusion of the article is. Create a list of the reasons Morrison gives to lead the reader to his conclusion on appearance. Remember, we cannot critically evaluate an article until we find a conclusion and you cannot identify the worth of a conclusion until you understand the author's reasons.

   One possible conclusion a reader can draw from the passage is "Looks are highly determinative of the way people treat others." Now compile a list of reasons supporting the author's conclusion. Take your list of reasons further by determining whether there are any reasons Morrison cites supporting the opposite conclusion.

2. Determine whether Morrison's article addresses a descriptive or prescriptive issue. That is, is the article expressing views about the way the world is or the way the world ought to be? Is the author recommending we alter our behavior in regards to the importance of appearance in society?

3. How good is the evidence the author provides for his conclusion? For example, are personal observation or eyewitness

accounts heavily relied upon for the basis of the conclusion? How large is the sample size in the referenced reasons? Are there other important questions to consider when determining the quality of evidence in the article?

4. Morrison does explain a situation where "looks did not matter." Is there any other evidence available from other sources suggesting the author's conclusion may be untrue? That is, can you find reputable sources arguing appearance does not have as great an effect on looks as Morrison argues they do? By finding evidence for counterarguments, you can better weigh the validity of Morrison's claims. How would you formulate an argument claiming beauty does not always matter?

Argentina: Ugly People Strike Back

Daniel Schweimler

BBC News, Buenos Aires (2007)

Buenos Aires is a city of beautiful people where appearances are important.

The men will tell you that Argentine women are the most attractive in the world; the women say much the same about the men.

But not everyone in Buenos Aires is beautiful. Gonzalo Otalora, for instance, is downright ugly, and he is not embarrassed to admit it.

In fact, he is fighting back on behalf of all those Argentines who don't fancy themselves as film stars or models.

I went out with him on a grey day in the Argentine capital. It was raining and windy which can cause havoc if, like many Argentines, you have spent hours dressing and making yourself up to join the ranks of the beautiful people on the streets of Buenos Aires.

But Gonzalo Otalora does not much care what he looks like. He planted himself in front of the presidential palace, the Casa Rosada or Pink House, to harangue President Nestor Kirchner to change the law.

It's not fair, he said. The beautiful people get all the breaks. Beauty is a natural advantage and he wants the good-lookers to be taxed to finance compensation for the ugly people.

Not pretty

His book, Feo (Ugly), has just been republished and is selling well. On the inside cover is a picture of Gonzalo as a youth. It is not a pretty sight.

"I was a child with thick glasses, spots and braces," he said. "The kids made fun of me at school.

"Later the girls rejected me in the discos. And then when I was looking for work, I felt so ugly and insecure that I was rejected again and left without a job.

"The great challenge in my life has been to stop being the school nerd—and thanks to my humour and bravery I've managed to overcome all that."

President Nestor Kirchner is not a typical Argentine either with his "Who cares?" attitude to clothes, hooked nose, and bags under his eyes. He should, according to Gonzalo, be sympathetic to his cause.

"The president for me is a comrade," he explained. "He's a loyal comrade because our childhoods were very similar. He also had thick glasses and spots. They also made fun of him.

"He was also very brave in overcoming his difficulties. The only difference now is that he's president of the country, and I'm not.

"And he's with an attractive woman, and I'm not."

But things in the presidential palace are about to change with Nestor Kirchner's wife, Cristina, taking over from her husband on 10 December.

She wears designer clothes, drinks a specific brand of mineral water to keep her skin looking rosy and her worst enemies say she's had her lips, you know, "resculptured".

This is no joke. Well it is, kind of. But there is a serious side to Gonzalo's campaign.

It's not about making yourself look beautiful, he says, but about coming to terms with and being positive about who you are and what nature has given you.

"The most important thing is not to feel so insecure," said Gonzalo. "The difference between being beautiful and ugly is not aesthetic but is inside. And if someone has high self-esteem then you can compete in any area in this society on equal terms with a good-looking person."

The perfect example and hero of ugly people everywhere is the Argentine and Manchester United footballer, Carlos Tevez.

Bad teeth and burn scars on his neck, he has the money for plastic surgery but does not want it.

Gonzalo wants to meet Tevez to present him with a copy of his book and get him to support his cause.

Opinion on the streets of Buenos Aires is mixed.

"I think it is totally fair, yes, yes, yes," said one woman, one of the few willing to stop in the rain and talk to Gonzalo and me.

"And also a tax on companies that help us to think that way, that beauty is only aesthetics. So whoever is ugly or doesn't fit into the social beauty parameters, suffers those invisible barriers imposed by society."

Another passer-by said: "For me, it doesn't matter. I care about people, their personality. Of course, for some people looks are important, but not for me. And you cannot put a price on beauty, there no taxes applicable. The most important is to be a good person."

Beauty big business

Elsa, a woman in her 80s, firstly tried to dodge us, then changed her mind and started talking.

"There are no advantages in life—there's just luck. My dear daughter is beautiful, she's got a good body and she's a lawyer—and she has been divorced twice.

"My beloved son-in-law left her for another woman and didn't care about their two daughters. It is matter of luck in life, there are no advantages. Luck. Everything is just luck."

Beauty around the world is big business, and huge in Argentina with a constant barrage on television and the streets exhorting consumers to buy lotions and potions, creams and shampoos, to keep them looking younger and more attractive.

As a visitor to Buenos Aires, sitting in that pavement restaurant watching the beautiful people walk by, you can succumb to the pressure, try to compete with the beautiful people and do all the work that that entails.

Or you can follow Gonzalo's example and enjoy the delights the city has to offer—and suffer the consequences.

"Waiter! Another slice of rump steak, one more bottle of wine and one of those delicious looking cream cakes to follow, if you please!"

CRITICAL THINKING QUESTIONS

1. Can you identify Schweimler's conclusion and reasons in the article? Are there any parts of the passage that do not seem to directly support the conclusion? Do the extraneous portions detract from the persuasiveness of the argument?
2. What values can you identify in the quotations in the passage? Do any of the values clash with one another? Determine the main value preferences of the author. Are they in line with your own values? If not, how will you overcome the difference in values so that you will be able to critically evaluate the article without a significant predisposed bias?
3. How strong is the evidence referencing personal experiences and the anecdotes of individuals in Argentina? Was the sample size large enough to form a well-informed conclusion? Are

there instances in which the author engages in the hasty generalization fallacy (Chapter 8 of *Asking the Right Questions*)?

4. Does Gonzalo Otalora have a strong personal interest in the topic of appearance? How so? Can we then expect a strong bias in his testimony? Could Otalora's standards of judgment differ from the standards of judgment of the reader? How might these differing standards affect the author's conclusion?

Study Credits Attractive People with Longer Life

Maggie Stehr

Daily Nebraskan (University of Nebraska) (2004)

(U-WIRE) LINCOLN, Neb.—In the survival of the prettiest, research suggests the rewards of a beautiful face include higher grades, better jobs and now, even longer lives.

Results published in the scientific journal Evolution and Human Behavior found attractive men outlast their unsightly counterparts on average by seven years, and attractive women live an average three years longer than their counterparts.

Because physical beauty invites credibility and attention, pretty people entertain additional perks and advantages, said Dawn Braithwaite, a University of Nebraska-Lincoln professor of communication studies.

Humans feel rewarded by interacting with attractive people, believing the contact raises their social status, she said. And professors, she said, are only human.

"Attractive students receive higher grades and more attention from professors," she said. "I have seen it happen. Whether it's right or wrong, it's a reality.

"But not all professors do that, so unattractive students should not drop out of college."

Molly McConkey, a freshman dance major, said attractive students exude confidence, which grabs professors' attention.

"Everyone wants to be the perfect image because life seems easier," she said. "It looks like they don't have to work as hard as everyone else."

But Braithwaite said people could be burned by their own hotness.

"People think attractive people don't earn their success and that it's based on their physical appearance," she said. "You also hear about very attractive men and women not being asked out."

People tend to think everyone is attracted to attractive people, Braithwaite said. But the myth is as fake as a set of silicone double Ds.

"We only usually date people who match us physically," she said. "We may fantasize about relationships with very attractive people, but people who are too attractive are ignored because people look for similarities when dating. We date people who are as attractive as we are."

Peter Obering, a sophomore advertising major, said guys are more likely than women to chase pretty faces because they are more attracted to physical qualities.

"Everyone just wants something as good as they can get," he said. "You want someone you can show off."

Braithwaite said paying attention to society's beauty obsession is a matter of survival.

"We are always being judged, whether at work or in the classroom," she said. "We are always putting ourselves out there. I can't make you perceive me in a certain way, but I can influence my credibility to you by making myself as attractive as possible."

Sue Bukacek, psychologist for University Health Center's Counseling and Psychological Services, said media images of idealized beauty flood American culture, fueling the emphasis on physical attractiveness.

College students especially are susceptible to pressures media weighs on appearance, she said.

"College students are figuring out who they are and dealing with the issue of identity," Bukacek said. "What we look like is a big part of the 'Who am I?' question."

Braithwaite said wide accessibility of celebrity images through Internet and TV propagate the American star culture riddled with body insecurity.

"There are 8- and 9-year-old girls worried about their appearance," Braithwaite said. "I don't remember in the second grade worrying about my weight."

Although she predicted the beauty fixation to worsen, Braithwaite said education safeguards against superficial stereotypes.

"We only think about attraction as physical," she said. "We need to took beyond the surface of our looks for what is attractive. If we only judge people on their looks we are missing a lot."

CRITICAL THINKING QUESTIONS

1. How could a reader's "belief in a just world" affect their reaction to Stehr's article? That is, do we each have a vested interest in the result of the discussion about appearance? How could a preformed belief that we live in a world where we all

are equally beautiful and unique distort the reader's reaction to the article?

2. How dependable is the "study" the article relies on? Recall that Chapter 9 of *Asking the Right Questions* provides a framework for evaluating research studies as evidence. What problems can you discover with the study referenced in Stehr's argument? Are there any aspects of the study that appear to be reliable?

3. Now imagine you have the opportunity to respond to this article. Try explaining to the author how the argument could be improved with different evidence. What types of evidence would strengthen the conclusion?

4. Within the article, Stehr often makes appeals to authority to bolster her argument. Ask yourself, "Should we believe these authorities?" Consider what authorities would be the most credible on the issue of behavior related to appearance.

5. The article draws connections between attractiveness and different outcomes. For example, the article states, "Attractive students receive higher grades and more attention from professors." This statement assumes the cause for higher grades is beauty. Do you believe this reasoning structure is critically sound? What are some possible rival causes for why people may receive higher grades?

Preparing Children for Plastic Surgery

Susan Kane

Huffington Post (2008)

At *Parenting* magazine, we receive dozens of children's books every week to review. Some are sweet and touching, some are silly and nonsensical, some illustrate important life lessons, and, of course, many are just plain bad. But in the 10 years I've been at the Parenting Group (first as the editor-in-chief of *Babytalk* magazine, now here at Parenting), I've never seen a children's book as, well, creepy as this one: *My Beautiful Mommy* by Michael Alexander Salzhauer, M.D. Have you heard about it?

You know how when you were pregnant with your second child, you bought a "Mommy's having a baby"-type book for your firstborn? And when your son started preschool, you read a "school is cool"-themed one for him? Well, *My Beautiful Mommy* is the perfect tome for . . . the next time you spend your lifes savings on new boobs and need to explain the whole thing to your 6-year-old.

To be fair, the book doesn't actually address boobs. (Though perhaps it should have; breast augmentation is the second most common type of cosmetic surgery after liposuction.) Instead, the mother in this story is seeing "Dr. Michael" (a dark-haired, broad-shouldered, and square-jawed knight in shining scrubs) for a nose job and to have her "tummy made smaller." While the illustrator, Victor Guiza, drew a comically obvious bump on the mom's nose, I'm not sure why she needs the tummy tuck; from page one, she's wearing a belly shirt that reveals a perfectly small, flat stomach (what mom of two wears a belly shirt? In fact, who wears a belly shirt, mom or not, anymore??).

For those of you who would prefer not to shell out the $19.95 (you need to save up for your eyelid surgery, after all), here's the book in a nutshell: The mom explains to her young daughter that she is having an operation, and that she may look a little different afterward. "Why are you going to look different?" the tyke asks. "Not just different, my dear," our heroine in a hospital gown responds, "prettier!" (As she says this, a thought bubble floats above her head with an image of the dashing Dr. Michael crowning her "The Prettiest Mom." Very subtle.) While her mom is recovering, the daughter eats ice cream and works on a (how convenient!) school project about cocoons and butterflies. When it's time to take the bandages off, our made-over mama, complete with her new Nicole-Kidman nose, is surrounded by swirls of pixie dust and flashes of pink.

To hammer her metamorphosis home, the next page shows the mom with butterfly wings.

And it all makes me want to run home, hug my 4-year-old daughter, and read her passages from *Our Bodies, Ourselves*. First of all, why doesn't the title character bother preparing her son (who is seen in the background), as well as her daughter, for the surgery? Is he too busy off playing baseball to notice his mom's bandages? Or is he not being groomed for a future cosmetic procedure of his own?

Because that's what this book feels like to me. Instead of preparing a child for a grown-up's plastic surgery, it seems to be preparing her for some plastic surgery of her own down the line. After all, who wouldn't want to be the "prettiest mom"? What little girl can resist fairy wings and pixie dust?

I'm not against anyone nipping and tucking and doing what it takes for them to feel comfortable with themselves. I myself often fantasize about finally getting the boobs I've never had, about tightening up my neck, and snipping off the roll of flesh above my elbows (yes, I'm telling my age with that last one). But I can't help be depressed about how the "Free to be you and me" message of my youth has been warped (free to surgically alter the flare of your nostrils!) and how our beauty-at-any-cost obsession has trickled down to our youngest and most impressionable, to the point of being packaged in a pretty pink book featuring ice cream, butterflies, and tiaras.

If we show our kids that we can't accept ourselves for who are, how will they ever believe that we accept them for who they are—buck teeth, adolescent acne, Buddha bellies, and all?

CRITICAL THINKING QUESTIONS

1. What value conflicts are present within the argument? What values do you think Kane prioritizes highly? What specific evidence from the passage supports your belief in the author's value preferences?

2. Does the juxtaposition of appearance with children create a different reaction from the reader than the previous articles that did not touch upon the idea of children? Can discussing children evoke different emotional responses in the reader than when children were not part of the argument? Is the reference to children a dangerous appeal to emotion, or in this article is the reference to children more rationally based?

3. Can you uncover any fallacies discussed in Chapter 7 of *Asking the Right Questions* in Kane's reasoning? In other words, what "tricks" does Kane use to convince you of her conclusion? Does the author try to distract us with information that seems relevant to the conclusion but is really not?

4. In the article, Kane reviews a children's book, describing the use of a comically humorous bump on a nose. Are there any instances of language within Kane's own passage signaling comedic exaggeration? Does the use of humor necessarily discredit the reliability of the argument? In this case, did the use of humor strengthen the author's reasoning or discredit the believability of her claims? In other words, do the instances of humor further the conclusion or distract from it?

Good Looks, Good Pay?

Scott Reeves

Forbes.com (2005)

"Beauty and the Beast" is the fable of a young woman who frees her prince from the body of a beast with love.

But a similar tale—call it "Beauty and the Labor Market"—finds pay differentials based on looks and doesn't have a happy ending for just plain folks.

Two university researchers say the penalty for plainness is 5% to 10% lower pay in all occupations, or slightly larger than the premium for good looks.

Daniel S. Hamermesh, an economist at the University of Texas, Austin, and Jeff Biddle, an economist at Michigan State University, held demographic and job types constant and concluded that looks are a key element in earning power.

"Better-looking people sort into occupations where beauty is likely to be more productive," the researchers conclude. "But the impact of individuals' looks on their earnings is mostly independent of occupation."

Rule of thumb for all of us who aren't fashion plates: Play to your strengths.

"I suggest that you rely on characteristics that make you productive," Hamermesh says from his office in Texas. "If you're smart, rely on brain power; if you're strong, rely on muscle; and if you're personable, rely on your personality."

The researchers controlled for variables such as experience and education. Surprisingly, looks are more important for men than women.

In the mid-1990s when the study was completed, the ugly penalty for men holding full-time jobs totaled about $2,600 in reduced pay per year, and the pretty-boy premium came to about $1,400. For women, the penalty for bad looks was $2,000, and the premium for good looks was $1,100 per year.

Unattractive women are less likely than their average or good-looking counterparts to hold jobs and are more likely to be married to men with what the researchers call "unexpectedly low human capital." That's a polite way of saying little talent, drive or prospect of success.

We like to think the meritocracy is immune to high cheekbones, button schnozzes and a good head of hair, but the researchers found that looks count even in law, a competitive, performance-based field.

In another research project, Hamermesh and Biddle reviewed the earning power of law students graduating from the same law school from 1971 to 1978 and 1981 to 1988. A panel of four people reviewed pictures of each law student, including one person younger than 35 and at least one older than 35 from each sex. The law students were ranked on a scale of one to five, with five as the best looks score. The four ratings were averaged to create a student's overall rank on the looker scale. There was no objective standard for determining good looks, but participants knew it when they saw it.

The researchers found that, five years after graduation, males who ranked one notch above average earned about 10% more than fellow students who ranked one notch below average. Fifteen years after graduation, the premium for good looks grew to 12%. The researchers say the pay differential held for lawyers working in both the private and public sectors.

In a another study, the researchers found that spending great gobs of money on makeup, haircuts and fancy duds does little to improve the perception of people with so-so looks and doesn't increase their earning power. Other researchers, using pictures of the same people as children and in middle age, found that people with a mug that could wreck a freight train in their youth didn't become better looking over the years.

However, it may be that customers prefer to work with people who are easy on the eyes. If higher earning power comes from customer taste—not employer discrimination—that would appear to undercut the premise of much employment discrimination law.

Other researchers found that young obese women earn 17% less than women within the recommended Body Mass Index range. But women who gained a significant amount of weight during the 1981 to 1988 study period earned only slightly less than women within the average weight range.

Some research has found that there's a premium for height, and that taller men generally earn higher pay than their average or short counterparts, including men in top management positions such as that of chief executive officer.

But even if you look like a toad, the key to your low pay and diminished prospects could be that you act like a toad.

In a research paper for the Federal Reserve Bank of St. Louis, researchers Kristie M. Engermann and Michael T. Owyang said, "Certain characteristics, such as appearance, might affect productivity in ways that are not as easily measured (or as obvious) as are other characteristics, like education or experience. Appearance, for example, can affect confidence and communication, thereby influencing productivity."

Height and weight might also influence productivity through health or self-esteem. Some researchers have theorized that height may increase the participation of high school students in social activities, giving them the opportunity to develop the interpersonal skills that boost productivity in the workplace. If so, it's not hard to see why such people are prized—and rewarded—by a range of companies such as **General Motors**, **Wal-Mart** or **Wells Fargo**.

Still, pay differentials could be the result of raw discrimination. Maybe employers and co-workers simply don't like being around fat, ugly people. But if fat, ugly people develop a bad attitude over time, discrimination apparently based on looks may not tell the full story.

So, remember your grandmother's wisdom: Beauty is only skin deep, but true ugliness cuts right to the bone.

Translation: A good attitude and hard work can do a lot to overcome that rutabaga nose, but nasty people are just foul.

CRITICAL THINKING QUESTIONS

1. This argument is mainly descriptive. The central focus of the article is to inform the reader about how the world reacts to appearances, not to convince the reader that the reactions to appearance are right or wrong. But the article does provide some reasons that could be used by those favoring and those opposing different treatment for different appearances. What is a possible prescriptive argument you can make using some of the reasoning in this article?

2. What are the key terms and phrases in the article? Are any of these words or phrases significantly ambiguous? Identify alternate meanings for the terms. How would a reliance on an alternative meaning for a term alter whether a reader thought the author's reasons supported the conclusion?

3. Compare the research studies cited in this article with the study used in the third article of this chapter. In what ways is the author's reliance on studies in this article more credible than in the former article? In what areas could Reeve's have strengthened his reliance on research for his argument? That is, which parts of the research study are questionable or unreliable?

4. Consider the concept of wishful thinking and Stephen Colbert's idea of *truthiness* discussed in Chapter 14 of *Asking the Right Questions*. Are there any prevalent denial patterns readers might fall prey to when considering the importance of appearance in their daily lives? As a reader, how can you minimize the effects wishful thinking may have on your critical evaluation of this article?

5. Recall the title of the article: "Good Looks, Good Pay?" Can you think of any possible rival causes for the phenomenon of higher pay noted in the article? Are good looks the only possible determinant for earning more money?

The Pursuit of Beauty: The Enforcement of Aesthetics or a Freely Adopted Lifestyle?

Henri Wijsbek

Journal of Medical Ethics (2000)

1. Introduction

Considering the amount of time, money and effort some people spend on clothes, cosmetics and their looks in general, the pursuit of beauty is a lifestyle if anything is. One feminist aptly calls it "a deeply significant existential project;" not a bad definition of "lifestyle" actually. We take an enormous interest in the way our body looks: we paint and pierce it, we keep it in shape through exercise and diet, and we take it to the cosmetic surgeon if we're really dissatisfied with some specific part of it. People do go to considerable lengths and are willing to incur serious risks, to change the appearance of their bodies for what they take to be the better.

Concern about their looks guides people's lives. So in one important sense the pursuit of beauty is clearly a lifestyle. But paradigmatically, in order to qualify as a lifestyle, a way of life should also be something you have chosen yourself. A lifestyle is a way of showing the world which things in life you deem important, what kind of life you want to live, what kind of person you want to be. This goes for men as well as for women. But the massive pressure on women to live up to some ideal standard of beauty, makes it particularly doubtful whether women's choices concerning appearance are anything but mere reflections of fashion, or worse still, of male-dominated power relations. Can women's pursuit of youth and beauty, then, ever really qualify as a freely adopted lifestyle?

2. Morgan and the technological beauty imperative

At least one feminist answers the last question with a resounding "No"! In an article entitled "Women and the knife: cosmetic surgery and the colonization of women's bodies", Kathryn Pauly Morgan sets out to investigate whether cosmetic surgery is liberating or coercive. As the title suggests, she has no doubts about the outcome. What makes her article interesting therefore, is rather what makes her think that, despite appearances to the contrary, women are coerced into cosmetic surgery. The key to her answer lies in what she calls "paradoxes of choice'" that is, situations that leave women no real options at all. She distinguishes three such paradoxes.

The first is the paradox of conformity: women do not use the medical technology to underscore their uniqueness or eccentricity, rather they all let the one and the same "Baywatch" standard determine their looks. "More often than not, what appear at first glance to be instances of choice turn out to be instances of conformity".

Secondly, women who involve themselves in the pursuit of youth and beauty do not take their body as something natural or given, but rather as raw material to be shaped and pruned to fit some external standard. Their bodies are transformed for others to exploit them. And it is men who are wielding the power, either actual men or merely imagined men who occupy the consciousness of women and make them into self-surveying subjects. This is the paradox of colonisation. It looks as if women are cultivating their own bodies, whereas in fact their bodies are being colonised by men.

Finally, there is an overwhelming pressure to undergo cosmetic surgery. The technological beauty imperative enforces itself in numerous ways: through advertising, articles in the media, in so-called success stories, in Miss America pageants. At the same time, the beauty imperative sets a new norm: those who refuse to submit to it will become stigmatised. What used to be normal is rapidly becoming deviant, problematic, inadequate and deformed. Eventually, Morgan ventures, "the 'ordinary' will come to be perceived and evaluated as the 'ugly'". The fact that women are coerced to avail themselves of these techniques and the ensuing pathological inversion of the normal constitutes the third paradox, the paradox of coerced voluntariness and the technological imperative.

Whenever a woman conforms to some single, external standard imposed on her, the conditions of genuine choice have not been met. If any of these paradoxes prevail therefore, she is not making a choice of her own, but is being forced to adapt herself to men's norms. Actually not just men's norms, nor just "white, western and Anglo-Saxon" norms, but norms that are "male-supremacist, racist, ageist, heterosexist, anti-Semitic, ableist and class-biased" and to be on the safe side, Morgan adds the ominous "eugenicist" as well.

3. Davis and the desire to be ordinary

In her very interesting book, Reshaping the Female Body, Kathy Davis offers a totally different picture of cosmetic surgery and the partial freedom women enjoy to avail themselves of its mixed blessings. Davis has investigated the actual decision process of women contemplating undergoing cosmetic surgery. Typically, they take the step of consulting a cosmetic surgeon only after having pondered the decision for years. Often they seek support from a woman who has had cosmetic surgery herself, rarely from a husband or lover. Usually they have to overcome opposition, from friends, family and colleagues. All the women Davis talked with insisted they wanted the surgery for themselves. Interestingly, even women with very bad side effects and permanent disfigurement were happy they had finally taken their lives into their own hands.

The women Davis spoke to, mostly women who had had their breasts augmented or reduced, invariably described years of suffering before even thinking about consulting a cosmetic surgeon. Their suffering, so convincingly rendered by Davis, had pervaded the whole of their lives: when buying clothes, when going to the beach, when doing sport, when having sex. They had been constantly reminded that their breasts were too big or too small.

One of the women, Sandra, complained that her breasts made her seem like somebody else: "Big breasts are supposed to be sexy. So you got to be a sex-bomb, whether you want or not". She spent years hiding her breasts under bulky sweaters and leather jackets, trying to avoid being reduced to "just a pair of tits". Ellen suffered from the opposite "problem". One story she tells is particularly poignant. She had just given birth to her first child and was lying in a hospital bed, on top of the world, feeling one hundred per cent woman. Then the nurse came in to sponge her off. She started washing Ellen's face, then her breasts, and she blurted out: "Gee, you're flat as a pancake, aren't you?" Even as she was telling this to Davis she began to cry. "It was like being stabbed with a knife; it was, it was so awful, just really awful".

Sandra and Ellen didn't want to become beautiful, they wanted to become ordinary. They wanted to put an end to their suffering, and cosmetic surgery had come to be the only way to achieve their goal.

In the last chapter of her book, Davis takes issue with Morgan about the nature of cosmetic surgery and the freedom of choice. Davis does not deny that there is pressure on women to have their bodies altered, but throughout her book she stresses women's agency. Cosmetic surgery is not simply imposed, it is fervently desired by its recipients. Women having cosmetic surgery are knowledgeable and responsible agents, no "more duped by the feminine beauty-system than women who do not see cosmetic surgery as a remedy to their problems with their appearance". At the same time, she regrets the fact that women are willing to undergo risky operations. She wishes that circumstances would be otherwise and that women would choose a different course of action.

4. The problem

I find this controversy between Morgan and Davis fascinating. Who is right? And if either is, how can it be established which one? On the face of it, Davis's conclusions seem to be by far the more plausible. They are based on sound, empirical research, whereas Morgan has done little more by way of empirical investigation than skim a few glossy magazines featuring interviews with knife-happy surgical dopes. Moreover, Davis, somewhat to her own surprise and against her own will, comes up with a balanced, not to say ambiguous view of cosmetic surgery. She weighs the pros and cons carefully and draws a conclusion that is almost shocking to the feminist she considers herself to be, let alone to more orthodox feminists with whom she has indeed experienced some troubling and unpleasant confrontations because of her liberal outlook. In that sense, her book is open-minded and courageous. Morgan's article on the other hand, smacks of lopsided exaggeration. She knew all along what she thought about cosmetic surgery, and drives home the politically correct analysis with force once again.

I'm afraid, however, that the controversy cannot be so easily settled in favour of Davis. It is not at all an easy job to decide how the data should be interpreted. Morgan could acknowledge all of Davis's results and yet stick to her own theory. Women may well say or think they make their own choices, whereas in fact they are only doing what the sexist, anti-Semitic, ageist, etc, etc, system requires them to do. It is hard to see how this disagreement about the interpretation of the empirical data could be solved empirically.

One of Davis's main objectives is to find a way of being critical of a beauty-system that treats women as inferior, without blaming the women who partake in it. But how can she do so, while at the same time stressing women's agency? Her formula—own choice, bounded circumstances—is not very satisfactory, because choices are always made with less than complete information, under conditions not wholly of the agent's own making, and with few if any ideal options available. It seems to follow from her assumptions that women are blameable after all. How could anyone choose to partake in a blameable practice, without her- or himself incurring any blame?

Actually, Morgan's views seem to be more condoning of women. If they do not choose to undergo cosmetic surgery, but are rather coerced into compliance by an oppressive beauty-system, they can hardly be blamed for being so coerced. It is the system that should be blamed, not its victims. But Morgan's views have some nasty implications as well. Not only are women victims, they are duped victims at that, surgical dopes, not real agents responsible for their own doings.

Underlying the disagreement between Morgan and Davis is a conceptual problem about freedom and responsibility. Before we can answer the question whether women who participate in the beauty-system are blameable agents or innocent zombies, or whether yet a third characterisation is more appropriate, we must become clear about the conditions of freedom, agency and blame.

5. Freedom, agency and blame

Neither Morgan nor Davis makes it very clear how the beauty-system actually sustains its coercive influence. Morgan has not empirically investigated the matter, but she makes two suggestions. In the first place, its evil influence is spread by men, "brothers, fathers, male lovers, male engineering students who taunt and harass their female counterparts, and by male cosmetic surgeons". And if not by actual men, then by "hypothetical men" who live "ghostly but powerful lives in the reflective awareness of women".

Davis, who has painstakingly investigated women's actual decision process, concludes that contrary to what is assumed by Morgan and many others, women are not pressed into the operation by actual men. As a matter of fact, husbands and boyfriends more often than not try to talk their partners out of it. For that reason, some women even concealed that they were planning to have an operation from their husbands or boyfriends. Actually, when Davis describes what makes women try cosmetic surgery as a last resort, other women figure prominently not only as support, but also as catalysts. Many of the painful remarks about their appearance were made by other women, either out of jealousy, or condescension or mere thoughtlessness. I have already mentioned the nurse's remark about Ellen, but Davis quotes some others as well, for instance: "Gosh, I thought you had more than that!" and "Big breasts are so-o-o uncomfortable dear. I wish I had yours".

However, Davis does think a considerable pressure is being exerted by something much more abstract and far less tangible than real men or women, something she calls "the beauty-system" or "the gender society", and sometimes still less specific "the social order", without elaborating on the content or working of this "social order". I suppose this is the same as what Morgan refers to when she uses the more picturesque phrase "hypothetical men". But according to Davis this pressure is not so strong as actually to coerce women into cosmetic surgery. They are left with a choice. Her formula for this ambiguous situation was: choice, constrained by circumstances which are not of the agent's own making. The constraints she refers to are the relative lack of information about the operation and its possible consequences and secondly, the lack of viable alternatives for women in a society organised by gender and power hierarchies.

Lack of information is something that is inherent in all choice situations. People do not have perfect foresight: some options are apt to be overlooked, and the ones considered can always turn out to be different from what was being imagined. Notoriously this holds for medical interventions. But only if the surgeon withholds available and relevant information on purpose could the situation be called coercive. In that case, women would be forced to make a decision on a skewed set of data. If this actually happens, they cannot make a free decision and therefore they cannot be held responsible for it. But this is hardly a controversial case. I take it that literally everybody agrees that the surgeon should give the woman all the relevant data. If he does not, he is to be blamed, not she.

The complaint about lack of viable options is much more difficult to deal with. What options are lacking, what circumstances should be different? I have no reliable figures, and they would be very hard to come by, but the number of women who do opt for cosmetic surgery is almost negligible compared to the number who do not. In order to make the claim that women have no viable options except cosmetic surgery at all plausible, the category of women to whom it applies has to be made much more precise. Suppose such a category could be defined: women with characteristics a, b and c all opt for cosmetic surgery under circumstances x, y and z. Even if this claim could be vindicated, nothing as yet would have been established as to what actually causes them to do so. Physical and psychological characteristics such as size of breasts and lack of self assurance would presumably figure on the one side, and stereotypes and role models are among the things that would figure on the other side of some such explanation.

Causal explanation

Suppose then that the statistically significant correlation could be dressed up to a causal explanation for this well-defined category of women, would that make them into the unfree and irresponsible zombies Morgan takes them to be? Not necessarily. Being caused to do something is not in itself a threat to either freedom or responsibility. It would only be so if you hold that free and responsible agency implies the ability to act in defiance of the causal network that makes up the rest of the world. It is a wildly implausible claim that people have such a contracausal metaphysical power and I have nothing to say to its credit. If you were to trace the antecedents of any act far enough, you would always find that its causes lie outside the agent. Usually acts are considered to flow from some combination of beliefs and desires. But of course one can always push the inquiry one step further back and ask where these beliefs and desires come from. Ultimately, they will be caused by something the person is not in control of. If being the ultimate cause of one's actions were a necessary condition for agency, nobody would ever be an agent.

According to a metaphysically less extraordinary view, agency is compatible with people being subject to all the laws that govern the rest of nature. A feeling of thirst normally causes me to try and quench it. I think I am very lucky to be caused to act in that way and I do not wish it were otherwise. The fact that I am caused to act in a certain way, does not imply that I must act in an insensible or mechanical way. I do not drink just anything; depending on further circumstances I take something hot or cold, sweet or bitter, alcoholic or nonalcoholic. And if I am attending a lecture, I wait until it is over before having my drink, because I think it would be ill-mannered to walk away in the middle of the lecture for such a reason. Normally, what I will actually do and when I will do it, is the outcome of my deliberation. As long as my acts are sensible responses to the requirements of the situation, as long as I am able to respond adequately to all its relevant features, I have all the freedom I can possibly wish. If these relevant features leave me no option but the right (or a right) one, that is no more a serious constraint on my freedom than the analogous constraint on belief formation would be. Our freedom would not be diminished if we were always caused to have only true beliefs.

Best chances

The way Davis describes the women who take recourse to cosmetic surgery, fits this picture very well. These women have a problem—an indisputable kind of suffering—they survey their options, and they pick that option that promises them the best chances to overcome their problem. They respond sensibly to the situation, make an intelligible decision and act accordingly. In particular, they don't expect the operation to work miracles, for instance that it will save a broken marriage. Admittedly, it is a somewhat risky option, but not an outrageously risky one. It seems therefore, that their decisions are based on a prudent cost-benefit analysis. What reasons could there be to call even this particular category of women innocent zombies and their decisions unfree or coerced? They do indeed seem to have all the characteristics of knowledgeable and responsible agents.

But who can tell what the proper amount of attention is to pay to your appearance? Is lipstick OK? Going to the hairdresser? Being choosy about the clothes you wear? Dieting? Fitness? Twice a week? Two hours a day? Everybody can come up with extreme examples of paying either too much or too little attention to appearance, but in between all causes are hard cases. And I think that is how it should be. All lifestyles can give rise to misgivings. Who can ever be sure she is not according too much importance in life to something not really worth it? How can you know that you would not be happier or lead a more satisfying life if you had chosen something completely different? To take up a lifestyle is to forsake other lifestyles that are equally worthy of being chosen. That is one of the reasons Morgan's description of the pursuit of beauty is such an appropriate definition of a lifestyle in general: it is "a deeply significant existential project", with all the meaningfulness and uncertainty that usually go with such projects.

After this, what is left of Morgan's three paradoxes? As to the first, women, except perhaps for a very small category of women, do not conform to a single standard. But even for this category, that fact in itself is no more significant than that a large number of Victorian men had whiskers or that nowadays some men practise body-building. Secondly, that this standard can be traced back to external influences is a property it shares with many, if not all, of our beliefs and desires. Finally, if you actually look at the decision process of these women, you will find that it forms a reasonable and adequate response to their problems and so is an expression of their freedom rather than an obstacle to it.

Alternative explanation

But even if women who have cosmetic surgery have all the characteristics of full-blown agents, the possibility is still left open that they are blameable agents, a possibility I took to be a consequence of Davis's position. That would be so if they knowingly and willingly were involving themselves in a morally reprehensible practice. Is cosmetic surgery reprehensible? According to Davis, the women who have cosmetic surgery do so in order not to be constantly looked at or made the object of offensive remarks, whether well meant or not; and they want to feel at ease in their own bodies. An alternative explanation would be that they want to look more beautiful. Both the ordinary and the beautiful are respectable and it is hardly blameworthy to strive for either.

If you want to become a proficient piano player, you must practise daily; if you write a scientific article, you don't expect the first draft to qualify as the final version; only with effort do we learn to become a good friend, parent, partner. Usually, to actualise values—be it artistic, scientific or moral values—is hard work. Why then should we have to accept our appearances as given?

6. Lingering doubts

Still, I can imagine that not everybody will be persuaded that women have a free choice in these matters. Given that circumstances are as they are, women are free to choose whether they want to have recourse to cosmetic surgery. To be free in a practical sense does not mean to be the uninfluenced originator of all your thoughts and actions; whoever fits that description is doomed to act in a haphazard and unintelligible way. Rather, it means to be able to respond adequately to the circumstances in which you find yourself. We want "a freedom within the world, not a freedom from it", in Susan Wolf's apt phrase.

I suppose that this is what Davis meant when she said she wished circumstances could be different. Plastic surgery should not be an eligible way for women to overcome their problems with their appearance, because in Davis's ideal world, women would not have any problems with their appearance to begin with.

What would the world look like if Davis's wish were realised? It is very hard to imagine a world without such ever-changing beauty norms, but nevertheless, let me end with some speculations. It would be a world in which no woman ever suffered from the way she looked, because no woman, nor anybody else, would care about how she looked. Everybody would have become insensitive to aesthetic properties; nobody would be moved by Vermeer's Girl with the pearl or Schubert's Schöne Müllerin. There would be no poetry, only social-realistic prose. It would be a paradise for pigs, and a boring place for people. In my view, that is too high a price to pay to get rid of cosmetic surgery.

Henri Wijsbek is a Research Fellow on a European Biomed project called Beauty and the Doctor, Department of Medical Ethics, Faculty of Medicine and the Health Sciences, Erasmus University, Rotterdam, the Netherlands.

CRITICAL THINKING QUESTIONS

1. When a passage is long, determining the issue, conclusion, and reasons is particularly important to following the author's logical reasoning. Create a diagram showing the author's reasoning structure for this passage. Review your diagram and determine whether any of your reasons do not support the conclusion. If necessary, create more than one diagram showing multiple arguments present in the article.

2. Notice that Part 4 of this article evaluates the arguments of Morgan and Davis and the reliability of the evidence each argument employs. Do you agree with the evaluation of

the arguments? Using your tools from *Asking the Right Questions,* expand on Wijsbek's evaluation of the authors' arguments.

ESSAY QUESTIONS

1. To what extent is the issue of the role of appearance presented dichotomously in the authors' arguments in this section? Are there two sides to this issue, or many? Provide examples from the articles supporting your position. Which article presented the issue in the least dichotomous manner? Generate different conclusions on the issue of the role of appearances that do not require a simple yes or no answer.

2. Compare and contrast the reliability of the differing forms of evidence presented by the authors. Which articles presented the most persuasive evidence, and why? Which articles had the most flawed evidence? What questions from *Asking the Right Questions* are important to consider when evaluating evidence? How does each article fare when compared with the others?

Final Word

Critical thinking is a tool. It does something for you. In serving this function for you, critical thinking can perform well or not so well. We want to end the book by urging you to get optimal use of the attitudes and skills of critical thinking that you have worked so hard to develop.

How can you give others the sense that your critical thinking is a friendly tool, one that can improve the lives of the listener and the speaker, the reader and the writer? Like other critical thinkers, we are always struggling with this question. But the one strategy we find most useful is to voice your critical questions as if you are curious. Nothing is more deadly to the effective use of critical thinking than an attitude of "Aha, I caught you making an error."

As a parting shot, we want to encourage you to engage with issues. Critical thinking is not a sterile hobby. It provides a basis for a partnership for action among the reasonable. Beliefs are wonderful, but their payoff is in our subsequent behavior. After you have found the best answer to a question, act on that answer. Make your critical thinking the basis for the creation of an identity of which you can be proud. Put it to work for yourself and for the community in which you find yourself.

We look forward to benefiting from what you have learned.

CREDITS

Chapter 3
"Copyright Silliness on Campus," By Fred von Lohmann, Washington Post, Wednesday, June 6, 2007; A23. Reprinted by permission of the author.

Chapter 4
"College Professors Should Be Made to Teach, Not Preach," By David Horowitz, USA Today, March 23rd, 2005.

Chapter 5
"Juvenile Injustice," from The New York Times, Editorial Section, 5/11/2007 Issue, Page(s) 26.

Chapter 6
"Should We Legalize Marijuana?" Published: July 25, 2007, Religion News Blog http://religionnewsblog.blogspot.com/2007/07/should-we-legalize-marijuana.html.

Chapter 7
Gun Control Non Sequiturs by Jacob Sullum. Published February 26, 2008. Hit & Run blog at Reason.com and Reason Magazine. Reprinted by permission.

Chapter 8
"Homeschooling Comes of Age," by Isabel Lyman. Mises Daily, Spetember 10, 2007. © 2007 Ludwig von Mises Institute. Reprinted by permission.

Chapter 9
"Americans Change Faiths at Rising Rate, Report Finds," by Neela Banerjee. The New York Times, February 25, 2008. © 2008 The New York Times Company. Reprinted by permission.

Chapter 10
"The World According to Disney" Published: June 18, 2008, By: Cathy Arnst. Business Week – Working Parents Blog © 2008 by The McGraw-Hill Companies, Inc. http://www.businessweek.com/careers/workingparents/blog/archives/2008/06/the_world_accor.html

Chapter 11
"College Drinking, Drug Use Grows More Extreme" by Buddy T. About.com Guide. Updated December 24, 2007. © 2009 About.com, a part of The New York Times Company. Reprinted by permission.

Chapter 12
"Back to 18?" by Radley Balko. Published: April 12, 2007. Reason Magazine. Reprinted by permission.

Chapter 13
"Should We Stop Eating Meat to Help the Planet?" Published: June 4, 2008 by Maryann Bird. http://www.chinadialogue.net/article/show/single/en/2062-Debate-should-we-stop-eating-meat-to-help-the-planet.

Chapter 15
"Advertising to children: Is it ethical? Some psychologists cry foul as peers help advertisers target young consumers," By Rebecca A. Clay, Published in the Monitor On Psychology, Vol. 31, No. 8 September 2000. http://www.apa.org/monitor/sep00/advertising.html

"Television Advertising Leads to Unhealthy Habits in Children; Says APA Task Force," By Dale Kunkel, PhD and Brian Wilcox, PhD, Published by the American Psychological Association Online, February 23, 2004. http://www.apa.org/releases/childrenads.html) (c) 2004 American Psychological Association. Reproduced with permission.

"Taking Responsibility for Our McActions," by Cam Beck. Published in the blog "Marketing Profs Daily Fix," August 14th, 2007. (http://www.mpdailyfix.com/2007/08/taking_responsibility_for_our.html)

"How to Inoculate Your Children against Advertising," By Lisa Tiffin, Published on the blog "Get Rich Slowly: Personal Finance that Makes Cents, March 5th, 2008. (http://www.getrichslowly.org/blog/2008/03/05/how-to-inoculate-your-children-against-advertising).

"Food Marketing to Children in the Context of a Marketing Maelstrom," By Susan E. Linn, Published in the Journal of Public Health Policy, Volume 25, Numbers 3–4, 2004 , pp. 367–378(12). Edited (Footnotes removed)

Chapter 16

"Taking Marriage Private," from The New York Times, Editorial Section, 11/26/2007 Issue, Page(s) 23.

"Swedish Top Lawyer wants to legalize polygamy . . . "From the New Zonka Blog, posted on December 15, 2007—13:34:25 http://beta.kimcm.dk/index.php/2007/12/15/swedish-top-lawyer-wants-to-legalize-polygamy

"We License Plumbers and Pilots—Why Not Parents?" By Peg Tittle. Published: October 3, 2004, The Seattle Post-Intelligencer.

"Copenhagen Journal: Jens and Vita, but Molli. Danes Favor Common Names" by Lizette Alvarez from The New York Times, Foreign Section, 9/8/2004 Issues, Page(s) 4.

"China's One Child Policy: The Policy that Changed the World" By Malcolm Potts, Published: August 19, 2006, Footnotes Omitted, British Medical Journal.

"The Regulation of the Market in Adoption" Richard Posner, Boston University Law Review, January, 1987, 67 B.U.L. Rev. 59. (Footnotes omitted, Edited for length)

Chapter 17

"Researchers: Choices Spawn Happiness," By Arthur Max and Toby Sterling, Associated Press, Published in the USA Today, August 24th, 2007. http://www.usatoday.com/news/health/2007-08-25-happiness_N.htm.

"Money Won't Buy You Happiness," By Matthew Herper, Published by Forbes.com, September 21,2004. Reprinted by permission of Forbes.com © 2009 Forbes LLC (http://www.forbes.com/2004/09/21/cx_mh_0921happiness_print.html)

"How To Find True Happiness," By Steve Ross and Olivia Rosewood, Posted on the Huffington Post, May 9, 2008. http://www.huffingtonpost.com/steve-ross-and-olivia-rosewood/how-to-find-true-happines_b_100892.html

"Down the Tube: The Sad Stats On Happiness, Money and TV," By Jonathon Clements, Published by the Wall Street Journal, Apr. 2nd, 2008. http://online.wsj.com/article/SB120709012659781613.html

"Does faith promote happiness?" By William R. Mattox, Jr., Published in Policy Review, Sep/Oct 1998.

Pursuing Happiness: Two scholars explore the fragility of contentment, By John Lanchester, Published in the New Yorker Magazine, February 27, 2006.

Chapter 18

24. "The media doesn't influence us . . . except when it does: Why defenders and critics of media violence get it all wrong," By Carrie McLaren, Published in Issue #20 of Stay Free! Magazine. (http://www.stayfreemagazine.org/archives/20/media_influence_intro.html)

"Children's Media Skew Gender: Imbalance Delivers a Damaging Message: Girls Don't Matter," By Geena Davis, USA Today, 05/02/2007.

"Media isn't feeding social ills," By Katie Strickland, Published in the UCLA Daily Bruin, April 23rd, 2008. (http://dailybruin.com/news/2008/apr/23/imedia-isnt-feeding-social-illsi/)

"Snowed: Why is the US news media silent on global warming?" By Ross Gelbspan, Published in Mother Jones Magazine, May/June 2005 Issue. (http://www.motherjones.com/news/feature/2005/05/snowed.html)

"CNN's Global Warming Special Typifies Liberal Bias of Climate Coverage," By Dan Gainor and Amy Menefee, Published by the Business and Media Institute, March 28, 2005. (http://www.businessandmedia.org/news/2005/news20050328.asp)

"Preventing Suicide by Influencing Mass-Media Reporting: The Viennese experience 1980–1996," By Elmar Etzersdorfer and Gernot Sonneck, Published in the Archives of Suicide Research 4:67–74, 1998. Edited (Footnotes Removed)

Chapter 19

MSNBC.COM [ONLINE] [ONLY STAFF-PRODUCED MATERIALS MAY BE USED] by Morrison, Keith. Copyright 2004 by MSNBC Interactive News, LLC. Reproduced with permission of MSNBC Interactive News, LLC in the format Textbook via Copyright Clearance Center.

"Preparing Children For Plastic Surgery," By Susan Kane, Published on the Huffington Post, May 5th, 2008. (http://www.huffingtonpost.com/susan-kane/preparing-children-for-pl_b_100232.html)

Good Looks, Good Pay? By Scott Reeves, Forbes.com ,May 5th, 2005. Reprinted by permission of Forbes.com © 2009 Forbes LLC. (http://www.forbes.com/2005/05/05/cx_sr_0505bizbasics.html)

"The pursuit of beauty: the enforcement of aesthetics or a freely adopted lifestyle? By Henri Wijsbek, Published In the Journal of Medical Ethics 2000; 26:454–458.

INDEX